The Rhetoric of Eugenics in Anglo-American Thought

The University of Georgia Humanities Center
Series on Science and the Humanities

Betty Jean Craige, Series Editor

This series makes available to a broad audience of scholars and
interested lay readers original works of scholarship in such areas as
the history and philosophy of science, the relationship of aesthetic
expression to scientific expression, the ethics of science and
technology, environmental ethics, the social consequences of scientific
research and knowledge, and the study of Western and non-Western
conceptions of nature.

Marouf Arif Hasian, Jr.

The Rhetoric of

Eugenics

in Anglo-American

Thought

The University of Georgia Press

Athens and London

© 1996 by the University of Georgia Press
Athens, Georgia 30602
All rights reserved
Designed by Erin Kirk New
Set in 10 on 13 Ehrhardt by Tseng Information Systems, Inc.
Printed and bound by Maple-Vail Book Manufacturing Group
The paper in this book meets the guidelines for permanence and
durability of the Committee on Production Guidelines for
Book Longevity of the Council on Library Resources.

Printed in the United States of America

00 99 98 97 96 C 5 4 3 2 1

Library of Congress Cataloging in Publication Data

Hasian, Marouf Arif.
   The rhetoric of eugenics in Anglo-American thought / Marouf
Arif Hasian, Jr.
   p. cm. — (University of Georgia Humanities Center series on
science and the humanities)
Includes bibliographical references and index.
ISBN 0-8203-1771-3 (alk. paper)
   1. Eugenics—United States—History—20th century.
   2. Eugenics—Great Britain—History—20th century.   I. Title.
II. Series.
HQ755.5.U5H38   1996
363.9'2—dc20   95-13953

British Library Cataloging in Publication Data available

This book is dedicated
to my wife, **Lisa A. Flores,**
for her infinite patience,
love, and support.

Contents

Acknowledgments

Thanks are due to many people who were generous with their time and counsel. I would like to thank the members of my interdisciplinary dissertation committee at the University of Georgia—Barry Schwartz from Sociology, Peter Hoffer from History, Ed Panetta, Tom Lessl, Cal Logue, and my adviser, Celeste Condit, from Speech Communication. Each of these professors in his or her own way has shown me infinite kindness and willingness to help. I would also like to thank Earl Croasmun, a friend and fellow scholar who shared my interest in the eugenics movement. Several graduate students at the University of Georgia, including Hilary Wilson, demanded that I not forget about the importance of the Human Genome Project. Jeanette Reid, the executive secretary of the Georgia Speech Department, made sure that I took my responsibilities seriously. Cathey Ross, Jean DeHart, Bob Frank, Mike Eaves, John Sloop, Mary Ann Smith, Mike Janas, Bob Kraig, Patrick Wheaton, Diane Miller, and the other graduate students kept me sane.

At DePaul University the entire Department of Communication provided me with encouragement and advice. I would particularly like to thank Lynn Narasimhan and DePaul's Faculty Research and Development Committee for their generous support and encouragement. The committee provided me with a summer stipend that helped me finish writing this book.

Thanks are also due to the communication faculties at the University of Wisconsin-Madison and Arizona State University. Each of these communities provided helpful critiques on my eugenics research.

At the University of Georgia Press, I would like to thank my reviewers and Malcolm Call, Elizabeth Johns, Kelly Caudle, Kristine Blakeslee, and Betty Jean Craige for their help. They were supportive in every stage of the project.

The Rhetoric of Eugenics in Anglo-American Thought

Should the word *eugenics* be consigned to the wastebasket of wrongheaded and pernicious ideas? Perhaps it is so tarred that it should be. But the judicious use of genetic knowledge for the alleviation of human suffering and increase in the well being of future generations is a noble ideal, whatever it is called. **James Crow, 1988**

In a society that came to view its members as just so many cells or molecules to be manufactured or rearranged at will, one wonders how easy it will be to recall what all the shouting about "human rights" was supposed to mean.
Laurence Tribe, 1973

1

The Significance
and Origins
of the Rhetoric
# of Eugenics

Eugenics. For the denizens of our planet, it would be difficult to find a more controversial concept.[1] Some define the word as the "science of improvement of the human germ plasm through better breeding."[2] Others contend that it means any genetic treatments or medical advances that are used for artificially improving human health.[3] While the term itself was supposedly coined by Francis Galton in the second half of the nineteenth century, it gained its pejorative meanings after World War II, when the Anglo-American community associated any study of the "wellborn" or genetic manipulation with the horrors of Nazism.[4] In societies built on notions of equality, justice, and equal opportunity, many eugenical studies were considered to be inextricably tied to racist notions of biological determinism or ethnic cleansing. Living in a developed world of relative abundance and cultural progressivism, many scholars considered "eugenics" to be a term that reflected elitist notions of genetic inheritance that had somehow gained the temporary attention of a small part of the scientific and public communities prior to the Great Depression.[5]

Yet in the 1990s we are seeing a revival of eugenical discourse.[6] With the advent of resource scarcity and shifting epistemic paradigms, we are witnessing a renewed interest in the possibility that human beings may in fact be inherently "unequal," at least as far as their genetic profiles are concerned. The popularity of books like *The Bell Curve* indicates that Americans have not lost their fascination with the relationship between inherited intelligence, class structure, and the problems of "dysgenesis."[7] Journalists, scientists, and biotechnical companies bombard us on a daily basis with information on the relationship between genes and a variety of traits and social behaviors—including homelessness, homosexuality, aggressiveness, shyness, and even religiosity. Our notions of normality and deviance are altered as we are invited to accept new biological explanations for what we once thought were cultural manifestations.[8] The growth of molecular biology and improved diagnostic technologies have brought new claims on the part of researchers that we can detect those "predispositions" that make us who we are. Entire disciplines like sociobiology and genomics have asked us to blur the traditional demarcations in academia, to rethink the respective roles of nurture and nature in the development of human beings. Nations around the world have prioritized genetic research, and programs like the Human Genome Project are ushering in a new age of "geneticization."[9]

Along with the growing power of genetical knowledge has come the specter of eugenics. Scientists, journalists, and medical practitioners who once thought that it was safe to discuss the importance of "preventive" medicine or "gene therapy" have found themselves in the midst of controversy over the nature, scope, and limits of their activities. Claims that human beings have individual rights are balanced against the duty of the state to provide for social necessities. "Necessity" has been a neglected term in scholastic discussions of civic virtue, political participation, and social relationships. While "necessity" has been a key word in our nation's public and legal vocabularies for centuries, its rhetorical influence has waxed and waned. Sometimes the term has been used to discuss exceptional situations when the rule of law can be violated in order to adapt to exigent circumstances. At other times the term is used to indicate some form of compulsion or natural limitation. For example, during times of war or resource scarcity, we are more likely to hear it used to justify restrictions on our freedoms. In no point in our history has the term "necessity" been more routinely a part of the discursive frontier than during the four decades that witnessed the rise of eugenics. The public debates on the use of the coercive force of the state in the name of eugenics provided several important discursive bridges between the laissez-faire approaches of the Gilded Age and the social welfare state created during the New Deal era. My contention is that an understanding of the dynamics of the debate between proponents of hardline eugenics and the opponents of that view gives us some needed insights into the ways social change can be domesticated, contained, or facilitated. I intend to provide a discursive analysis that illustrates the ways in which key terms like necessity were used by both dominant and marginalized collectives in discussing the extent of reproductive rights.

Unfortunately, this growing interest in the inherent association between genetics and eugenical thinking has not always resulted in improved public argumentation or deliberation on issues like genetic discrimination, the need for germ-line therapy, or prenatal screening.[10] Rather than coping with the ubiquitous nature of eugenics and exploring the multiple ways that these types of arguments enter into our popular culture, we have created several polarized views of eugenics that trivialize its importance. In trying to delineate both the promise and perils of some of the applications of genetic research, we have conjured up stories of celebration or lamentation that many times obscure the magnitude of the political, social, and economic problems that we must face. Throughout this book, I will be using terms like "story," "narrative," and "fable" to refer to those discursive units that are used by writers, critics, and even scientists in their persuasive texts.

Traditional Eugenical Tales

In an attempt to gain public acceptance of some of the new diagnostic tools of science, some journalists and researchers have treated eugenics as a pseudoscience that has had little to do with real genetic research. This selective chronicle of events treats eugenics as a temporary aberration, an irrational political appropriation of genetics. It creates distance between the value-free science of genetics and the illegitimate public policies (like coercive sterilization) that were conducted in the name of eugenics.[11] From within this rationalistic perspective, the democratic institutions that supported the advance of molecular biology at the same time contributed to the removal of the taint of eugenics by uncovering the fallacies of racism.[12] In this popular scientific story, eugenics was not a science but rather a movement that had more to do with reactionary politics than with the real laws of biological inheritance. The study of eugenics thus becomes research into the thoughts and activities of people like eugenicists Charles Davenport, David Starr Jordan, Edward East, and Harry Laughlin, who called for the segregation or sterilization of the "unfit."[13] Some of these writers point out that once geneticists were willing to make public some of their private reservations about the extravagant and false claims of the strict hereditarians, a new, more moderate "reform" eugenics came on the horizon to replace the pernicious discourse of the hard-liners.[14] Still others—including some of the eugenicists themselves—espoused the belief that it was primarily the rise of Hitler and his "abuse" of eugenics schemes that discredited an otherwise innocuous movement.[15] For this community of scholars, the eugenics movement's popularity ended in the 1930s, and this disastrous attempt to mix politics and science was relegated to the dustbin of history as a monument to human folly.[16]

These apologetic tales attempt to reconfigure the history of genetics and evolutionary biology as the linear progression of a science away from the politics of eugenics.[17] While these accounts are filled with interesting and frightening stories of how politicians and members of the public have misappropriated genetics, they give the impression that it is only the misunderstanding of technological knowledge that creates social hazards.[18] The rhetorical strategy of distancing molecular biology from eugenics hides the extent to which scientists themselves have often disagreed over both the direction and limits of their research trajectories.[19] At the same time, this progressive tale of the inexorable march of genetics ignores the intimate relationship that has always existed between eugenics and biology. Many of these biologically deterministic arguments were being used by the very researchers who were supposed to be opposed to eugenics.[20] In the words of Müller-Hill, we are left with chronicles that discuss the "rise of genetics" but at the cost of engaging in a "gigantic process of repression of its history."[21]

Yet equally implausible is the other polar narrative of eugenics, a story that sees almost any medical advance or application of genetics as an attempt to make the "perfect baby" or superior race. This second rendition of eugenics and its history asks us to see the quest for improving the quality of our gene pool as just another rationalization for activities like abortion or population control.[22] This equally narrow view of eugenics is promoted by some ethicists, social critics, and scientists who believe that eugenics represents the epitome of science and technology gone awry.

While each of these rationalistic perspectives provides us with some insight into the rise and temporary fall of the eugenics movement, each has had a tendency either to ignore or to mitigate the role of many other Anglo-American communities that grappled with some of the same questions. We are provided with stories of how a few elite researchers felt about eugenics but little understanding of how societies as a whole discussed the issues.[23] One extreme tempts us into uncritically accepting the legitimation tales of empowered researchers who see themselves as the purveyors of a beneficent, pristine science, while the other extreme provides us with a Luddite agenda that seeks to place bans or moratoriums on all medical or genetic advances that conflict with absolute bioethical norms or moral injunctions.[24] While both of these chronicles give us a glimpse of one side of the eugenics equation, they are truncated, and they often bring us superficial public debates that deflect our attention from the power relationships that influence the acceptance or rejection of these tales.

What many scholars who have studied eugenics are reluctant to admit is the extent of the popularity of these types of arguments within democratic communities. The celebration story treats eugenics as a pernicious doctrine invoked by the misguided, while the lamentation tale treats every scientist or practitioner interested in germ therapy as a villain who is duping the public. Both of these orientations run into difficulties when we consider the possibility that a substantial percentage of the Anglo-American public believed (and still believe) in the tenets of eugenics. As sociologist Arthur Fink once wrote,

> Many of the hereditarians, long before the days of the eugenists, were concerned with the quality of the race, and disturbed by the lack of prohibitions, on the part of the state, on the marriage of members of the criminal and other defective classes. It was their strong belief that criminals received their evil proclivities from their parents, that a thief transmitted a secretive, dishonest, sneaking disposition to his offspring, and that such a child came into the world ticketed, as J. H. Kellogg put it, "for the state prison by the nearest route." Jennie M'Cowen, a practicing physician, writing in the *Journal of Heredity* on heredity and its relation to charity work, seized the biblical explanation to describe the transmissibility of crime as the sins of the fathers being visited upon the third and fourth generation![25]

As I will argue in later chapters, many other movements—including the birth control, prohibition, scouting, intelligence testing, conservation, immigration restriction, and war preparation movements—had ties to the eugenics movements.[26] The study of eugenics involved not only scientific rationalizations of class and race prejudices but also explorations of how men and women of the modern era were to accommodate to changing standards of sexual and reproductive behavior.[27] As Duster has explained, eugenics provided a form of understanding for the rapid changes that were taking place in society, and it legitimated particular public policies to correct specific problems.[28] Many of the arguments created and articulated during this period simply reconfigured older claims, and these in turn became a part of our legal, political, and social lexicons.

Searching for an Ideographic Understanding of the Origins of Eugenics

Although a number of possible approaches might be taken in illuminating the complex interrelationship between public argumentation and scientific fields like eugenics, one fruitful method of analysis can be found in rhetorical studies that emphasize the discursive aspects of the problem.[29] This critical perspective—while neither apologetic nor Luddite—asks scholars to take seriously the polysemous nature of any influential lexicon.

Until the early 1970s, the dominant method of assessing the relationship between rhetoric and science assumed that a bright line existed between the two domains.[30] The natural and social sciences were thought to be domains of knowledge that existed independently of the vagaries of politics, power, and human invention. Within this popular paradigm, any persuasive elements that did exist in the production of scientific information were considered to be pernicious influences on a self-contained and self-correcting process of factual investigation. The dichotomous division between facts and opinions meant that few investigators believed that discourse might have constitutive value.[31]

Yet in the last several decades, many academicians have taken the "rhetorical turn" and have looked for ways of articulating their conviction that perhaps symbolic discursive constructs had more than simply heuristic value in understanding the sciences.[32] As Condit and Lucaites recently observed:

> Rhetoric is undergoing a major revival in the closing years of the twentieth century. . . . Whereas in the past scholars frequently treated rhetoric and public discourse as simple or "mere" epiphenomena, the contemporary rhetorical turn coincides with the revision of critical theory and a postmodern shift away from realist epistemologies, including a fairly thorough rejection of rigid objectivism, foundationalism, and essentialism in understanding the human social condition. The result has been a more or less sustained focus on discourse, textuality, and signification as the "material" core of social and political relationships.[33]

In the 1970s, 1980s, and early 1990s, researchers began to take seriously the notion that not only the questions that are asked but also the methods of scientific investigation may be shaped in part by the lexicons used in establishing particular social relationships. Heavily influenced by writers like Foucault, Derrida, Gramsci, and Keller, these writers have looked for productive ways of explicating the close relationship between language, power, and social change.[34]

This rekindling of interest in the power of rhetoric to undermine traditional faiths in foundational knowledges has created a great deal of tension throughout the academy.[35] Novel interpretative perspectives have interrogated the taken-for-granted divisions of labor between the arts and the sciences, and a growing number of critics are beginning to claim that perhaps those who speak in scientific idioms provide us with merely one influential way of gaining knowledge. For those who adopt this rhetorical perspective, citizens who comment on scientific developments are not only spectators watching the progress of any field; they are also participants who legitimate and certify particular performances as science. As Lessl explains, "given the political prominence of science," its "public rhetoric" is often geared toward "maintaining control of the symbolic and material resources that have already been entrusted to it."[36] This legitimation process often involves a discursive struggle for the ideological terrain that will define what various communities will accept as productive inquiry.

Rhetorical discussions of the sciences or pseudosciences have the advantage of allowing critiques of scientism, but taken to an extreme they can at times be pedantic when the claim is made that all reality is discursively constructed.[37] This view of language can be as rigid as its scientific polar opposite, in that it treats all laws and scientific maxims as infinitely malleable.[38] This radical view of rhetoric treats all knowledge constructions as merely power relationships that have over time been formed through the calcification of discursive structures. For these commentators, rhetoric is not only epistemic: it is ontological in its ability to configure and shape all of the arts and sciences.[39]

In seeking a more moderate and productive stance, I adopt a materialist/functionalist view that treats rhetoric as an influential (but not omnipotent) part of the construction of scientific knowledge. Throughout this book, I employ an ideographic analysis that focuses on the persuasive elements of eugenics as a science.[40] Extending the work of McGee, Condit, Lucaites, and other scholars interested in understanding the impact of discourse in facilitating or hindering social change, I trace the ways that both rhetors and their audiences viewed the study of the feebleminded. Historically, the term "feebleminded" was used to describe any individual who was considered to have mental, social, or moral deficiencies. Unlike other investigations of eugenics, I supplement our existing studies of hard-line eugenical discourse with a rhetorical history of the eugenics movement.[41] In my discussion of the rhetoric of eugenics, I suggest that the optimal approach to this debate is to take the middle ground, which acknowledges that some natural boundaries exist independent of discourse yet admits that much of what passes as social knowledge can be viewed as a rhetorical construct. I believe that we need to supplement our existing studies in the rhetoric of the sciences with critical sciences that go beyond the elucidation of the discursive elements within a scientific text, laboratory, or controversy.[42]

An ideographic perspective, which acknowledges the existence of biological and physical limits on symbolic constructions, can nevertheless provide us with an appreciation of the role that rhetoric plays in the creation of power relations in scientific texts and contexts.[43] For example, in the domain of medicine and public health, how communities define a social problem influences the way practitioners think about "normality" or "illness."[44] As Evelyn Fox Keller recently argued, in our new readings of the relations between science and nature, we need to "unravel the insidious power of discourse to generate its own forms of truth, to shape the future of human bodies, not through genetics, but through politics."[45] JoAnne Brown espoused a similar view when she suggested that metaphors could be employed as a way of organizing the principles of scientific theories and ideologies.[46]

An ideographic perspective provides scholars with a useful methodological tool because it attempts to combine the concerns of materialist and symbolic interactionist views of language.[47] While the ideograph may be related to other discursive units of analysis—myths, narratives, and metaphors—it has its own function and form. Unlike vulgar Marxist approaches that see language (especially public discussions) as merely the epiphenomenal superstructure surrounding a core of deterministic economic forces, an ideographic approach sees rhetoric as an influential rather than causal force in facilitating or inhibiting social change.[48] Critics applying ideographic analyses do not try to see through discourse to the "reality" underneath; they assume that discourse is itself a social phenomenon that needs to be investigated. From within this perspective rhetoric is a substantive force, and the symbols of everyday discourse are influential in ways that go beyond mere embellishment.

The importance of an ideographic analysis comes from its empirical approach, which attends to the way that a public actually voiced its concerns over an issue rather than looking fore the ways that the "masses" failed to live up to some rational standard.[49] For example, Locke's discussions on human nature and the contractual obligations of civil society would have ideographic import only if ordinary citizens read and talked about Locke and employed his formulation of key words such as "liberty" in their private or public deliberations to shape laws and practices.[50] Not all humans articulate their concerns in terms of propositional logic, and yet they often are willing to take drastic actions on the basis of their belief in the importance of a few highly evocative words.[51] In order to locate and describe the usages of each of these key words, this perspective encourages a researcher to investigate the diversity of arguments that are supplied in magazines, journals, and newspapers because these are some of the key texts that influence the ways in which ordinary citizens frame controversial issues. For an ideographic researcher, the apparent reality of a situation may be just as important as a physical reality because both often motivate humans to act out their roles in social dramas that may make sense only when we can understand the power of ideographs.

An ideographic approach shifts the role of the critic from that of a specialist engaged in applying an a priori universalizing normative standard to that of an analyst who is trying to decode how those universalizations were created in the first place. This does not mean that universal norms do not exist or are unimportant. It simply asks researchers to take seriously the possibility that those who claim to represent factions of the public are participants in the creation of the social rules that regulate their own lives and channel their opinions.[52] From an ideographic perspective, each generation has a discursive record that chronicles the social changes that have taken place in that society, and investigators can trace this record by reviewing the fragments provided in the popular press. Approaching research from this orientation means that official historical and contemporary documents are not exclusively the repositories of recently discovered "facts," nor are they the "mythologized locus for some prediscursive image of 'reality.' "[53] These historical remnants are parts of the collective consciousness of a society, the fragments that go into the making of what serves as our public vocabulary and cultural memory. In the words of Dominick LaCapra, "documents are texts that supplement or rework 'reality' and not merely sources that divulge facts about 'reality.' "[54] Similarly, Ana Alonso has argued that there are official and popular discourses that work on configuring the imagination of different social communities.[55]

An ideographic perspective assumes that humans are not simply creatures who misunderstand "facts" because of semantic confusion; they also disagree about what it means to be a fact and how to apply facts to our individual and collective experiences. Ideally, rhetorical investigations should try to avoid the reduction of rhetoric to mere flattery, style, or ornamentation. While maintaining a sensitivity to the abuse of language, this stance would recognize that the

existence of multiple interpretations of terms also means that marginalized communities can point out contradictions in traditional tales that allow us to see
examples of oppression in eugenics texts.[56] At the same time, it would also point
out some of the reconstructive possibilities that become evident when we explore the ways in which a part of the eugenics rhetoric was turned against itself.
For example, by tracing the ideographs used by opponents of the mainline eugenics creeds we could look for ways in which the discourse may have been
appropriated for emancipatory purposes.[57]

An ideographic analysis allows scholars interested in a critical science to in-
terrogate the traditional ways of doing science. Tracing the discursive structures
embedded within particular lexicons may allow us to see how some configurations may be inherently reductionist or biased in ways that preclude scientists
from considering plausible alternative perspectives. The goal of an ideographic
approach is not Luddite in nature, nor is it meant to be a nihilistic disparagement
of any form of scientific or technical investigation. Like Foucault, we would sensitize ourselves to the ways in which power, knowledge, and language are inextricably related to each other. A critical scientific perspective recognizes that there
are a number of ways of doing science within each discipline that may at times
provide us with unique and contradictory views of "nature" and understands
that entire lines of scientific inquiry involve a choice of perspectives.

Unlike anarchist views of science that deny the legitimacy of scientific methods, a rhetorical approach would accept the importance of maintaining some of
these myths and narratives in spite of their alleged incoherences and contradictions, but it would look to see how warranted assent was achieved or lacking in
key controversies. As A. G. Gross has recently observed, "from the point of view
of rhetoric as critique, the rationality of science consists in the continuing dia-
lectic among its legitimate reconstructions, each the surrogate for the informed
assent of an interpretative community; analogously, the objectivity of science is
constituted by some configuration of these reconstructions."[58] From a rhetorical
perspective, the "objectivity" of science is not something that is merely assumed
but is achieved. The stance of critics would therefore be located somewhere between the positions both of scientific essentialists who believe in foundational
views of science and of nihilistic commentators who see science as an ad hoc
political enterprise.

Tracing the ideographic components of myths and narratives allows us to
see how a movement like eugenics can appear to provide answers to complex
social questions for a variety of different audiences. We can begin to appreciate
how women, African-Americans, and other marginalized communities lost their

reproductive rights in the name of "liberty," "opportunity," or "necessity."[59] Ideographs like these are evocative terms that are used in technical and public spheres as a means of gaining the assent of multiple constituencies. These ideographs are appropriated by both scientists and laypersons in disputes over theory, funding, and the application of scientific knowledge.

Theoretically, an ideographic analysis assumes that:

1. the acceptance of a particular line of investigation as a part of "normal" science is dependent on both internal and external social relationships;[60]
2. within each scientific field there are multiple ways of conducting scientific investigation, and the belief in a monolithic method is itself a contestable myth;[61]
3. no science is value free, and claims to scientific neutrality are rhetorical topoi that are deployed in public controversies;[62]
4. scientific discourse, no less than art or any other method of signification, legitimates its power by providing truth claims that are self-referential.[63] Scientific criticism thus refuses to allow the self-criticism of science to be the exclusive method of establishing or evaluating normative structures within scientific discourse.

Each of these four arguments helps critics engaged in ideographic research to challenge the scientific ethos that privileges particular knowledge claims in technical and social controversies. The first postulate is based on the position that boundaries between the sciences (and pseudosciences) are rhetorically produced.[64] The second makes an even stronger claim, that multiple epistemologies compete for attention in any scientific inquiry. The third claim assumes that the guise of neutrality in science serves several different functions. It can operate as a means of creating a community that believes that its members are using similar methods or working toward the same objective. At the same time, it can function as an apologetic rhetoric that disguises the human interests involved in particular scientific ventures.[65] The guise of neutrality may at times involve fraud or deception, but more common is a style of doing science that depends on the mask of neutrality in order to insulate scientific investigators from criticism.[66] Claims of neutrality also legitimate certain modes of inquiry while at the same time maintaining ontological boundaries.

In sum, our postmodern world purposefully blurs the line between the "scientific" and the "critical," and rhetoric has had no small part within a variety of disciplines in helping to facilitate paradigm shifts that have altered our previous notions of facticity, objectivity, and logic. Part of the importance of taking an ideographic posture comes from its ability to extend the work of other theorists and critics interested in blurring the orthodox lines between the scientific and the social. Some of the strongest scientific critiques have come from feminist scholars who have argued that the quest for objectivity may itself be a distinct male concern.[67] While these are certainly controversial claims, they open up the possibility of studies of science that go beyond immanent critique. A critical scientific perspective should press facticity to the limit and be self-reflexive enough not to be beguiled by the beauty of elaborate formulas or dense scientific vocabularies. This critical approach to science thus asks us to treat scientific goals, experiments, theories, and even methods as privileged forms of knowledge that should have to compete with equally plausible (and equally scientific or empirical) claims. We need to be especially critical of claims in support of reductionist programs that purport to provide single or exclusive scientific methodologies, and we should consider that interactive alternatives are often hidden in the search for parsimony and simplicity. Rather than being satisfied to analyze the intentions of a master rhetor or to explicate the metaphors or other figurative devices operating within scientific rhetorics, we could take on the responsibility of comparing and contrasting entire mythic constructions and defending alternative reconstructions (countermythologies) that can complement our decoding analyses.[68]

By adopting an ideographic approach to the rhetoric of eugenics, scholars can decode the social interests and linkages that exist within scientific mythic structures. My goal here is not necessarily to test the veracity of particular scientific claimants against some universal measure but rather to illuminate some of the key social constructions that go unnoticed in particular social controversies.[69] While some commentators might be hesitant about making judgments about the worth or value of a project that did not focus on the "correctness" of a belief, I believe that rhetorical standards can be applied to scientific inquiries that allow for either internal or external critique.[70] This is especially important in a postmodern world that sometimes blurs the lines between fact and fiction.[71]

For some critics, the sciences of genetics and eugenics would seem to be the last places where rhetoric resides. For writers composing the traditional history of these fields, the scientific dimensions of genetic studies provide ample illustrations of how natural laws can be discovered that are beyond contention and argument. For example, the immutable rules governing the science of genetics are often said to have been uncovered with the rediscovery of Mendel's work. Genetics is thus portrayed as one of the disciplines that has moved unilinearly out of the dark ages of ignorance and toward the light of scientific progress. Like many other stories, this narrative continues to invite readers to maintain a strict division between the objective world of genetic research and the subjective world of values and rhetoric.[72]

Investigators who are skeptical about these disciplinary boundaries have usually taken one of two different approaches in their studies—they have either provided us with macro studies of the relationship between objectivity, values, and feminism, or they have given us micro studies that have investigated the rhetoric at work in particular scientific documents. At the macro level, feminists like Evelyn Fox Keller, Helen Longino, Sandra Harding, and Donna Haraway have reminded readers of the importance of metacritique, and they emphasize the patriarchal nature of conventional ways of doing science.[73] Unlike more modest types of inquiries, these investigations question the very assumptions of science that have existed since the time of Sir Francis Bacon. Abir-Am Pnina, for example, illustrates how different "genres" have been used in order to legitimate and consolidate new scientific disciplines like molecular biology.[74]

These macro studies provide us with clues on how, across the disciplines, scholars are searching for new ways of breaking away from what Nicole Rafter has called "essentialist" thinking about "truth" in science that seems to have been "created, received, and used."[75] In her own investigation of some of the historical records used in family studies of the feebleminded in America, Rafter found that genealogical studies purporting to be objective were in actuality filled with mythic passages that advanced Progressive preconceptions of social problems.[76] While covering a wide range of issues from alcoholism to the causes of "harlotry," these generic depictions of the feebleminded were said to be "enormously popular, reaching wider audiences" and in the process gave the eugenic movement some of its central "confirmational" images.[77] For Rafter, these family studies were a "rhetorical device" that invited readers to divide the world dichotomously between "us" (the writers and readers of eugenic tracts) and "them" (the cacogenic families of feebleminded).[78]

Yet while these micro and macro analyses have vastly improved our understanding of the rhetoricity and intentions of the authors of these documents, they have provided us with little understanding of how different audiences felt about these constructions.[79] What an ideographic analysis provides is a heuristic tool that allows us to illuminate the ways that rhetoric creates sciences like eugenics without lapsing into essentialist thinking.[80] It furnishes us with a methodology that looks at the performance of rhetoric at several different levels—single words, characterizations, narratives, and myths. Just as importantly, it allows us to see that the rhetorical dimensions of scientific inquiry go beyond studying eloquence, style, and persuasion.

I contend that "eugenics" was an ambiguous term that allowed many respectable Anglo-Americans to voice their concerns on a number of social issues. A variety of reputable communities heard speeches and read articles by presidents, public health officials, social scientists, literary critics, and laypersons.[81] What was known as the "eugenic creed" was not just applied genetics: it was also a form of discourse that influenced the way ordinary citizens gave meaning to their lives. Although eugenicists could frequently be heard arguing that their science was "new," often their arguments were merely new configurations of some old commonplaces.[82] In order to substantiate this claim, in the rest of this chapter I will provide a brief overview of some of the historical origins of eugenics prior to 1900.

The Ideographic Roots of Eugenics

Throughout much of the history of Western civilization, societies have debated the relative importance of nature and nurture in the creation of human characteristics, and eugenical arguments have been a significant part of this ancient quarrel. One of the earliest discussions of how communities needed to make social reforms on the basis of the genetic makeup of their citizenry came from Plato, who in the tenth chapter of *The Republic* described for us his allegory of the metals:

> [W]e shall tell our people in this fable, that all of you in this land are brothers; but the god who fashioned you mixed gold in the composition of those among you who are fit to rule, so that they are of the most precious quality; and he put silver in the Auxiliaries, and iron and brass in the farmers and craftsmen. . . . If a child of their own is born with an alloy of iron or brass, they must, without the smallest pity, assign him the station proper to his nature. . . . Such is the story; can you think of any device to make them believe it? Not in the first generation; but their sons and descendants might believe it, and finally the rest of mankind.[83]

Within this antiquated mythic tale, the best civilizations were made up of tough citizens who were willing to make noble sacrifices, and even lie if necessary, in order to ensure that city-states were organized in ways that reflected human nature. In this early utopian vision, families were supposed to admit that people were not equal and acquiesce in the belief some privileged few were destined by nature to have superior powers.

Plato's allegory was one of the favorite stories circulated in Anglo-American communities in the late nineteenth and early twentieth century, but it was by no means the only historical precedent for modern renditions of eugenical arguments.[84] While some critics and theorists believed that the environment was responsible for differences between the races, others thought that the best way to improve the human race would be by imitating the techniques of plant and animal breeders, who seemed consistently to be able to eliminate the so-called undesirables, and then multiplying so-called desirables in different populations.[85] Xenophobic societies looked for ways of scientifically categorizing the "races" on the basis of physical and mental characteristics.

Centuries after Plato, on the European continent, nations and races were divided on the basis of their ability to contribute to the "political economy" of a state, and writers like Mandeville began to classify humans on their resemblance to "drones" or "bees."[86] Independent workers were depicted as the bees or contributors to society, while the "necessitous" poor were said to be society's drones. Many of these characterizations were based on perceived biological or physiological differences.

The Enlightenment brought with it an intensification of the debates between defenders of nature and nurture, and many Europeans watched with horror as participants in the French Revolution began to take seriously the sentimental notion that men and women were inherently "equal." When William Godwin, a nonconformist British minister, attempted to follow French writers like Rousseau and Helvetius in arguing that all human beings were perfectible, he found himself vilified by Sir Thomas Malthus and others for preaching nonsense.[87] Godwin believed that the human species was capable of gradual improvement both morally and intellectually, and he asked his readers to think of ways of educating English workers to prevent their becoming deferential, dependent, lethargic, and contemptible. When Malthus read Godwin's discussion of perfectionism, he immediately responded by writing his famous *Essays on Population*.[88]

In the *Essays on Population*, Malthus was able to weave together a tapestry of arguments that summarized many criticisms that had developed over time having to do with the limits of cultural and environmental change. Malthus, unlike Godwin, believed that material benefits without "moral restraint" brought about an increase in the quantity but not in the quality of a population. From within this perspective, a person did not have any inherent "right" to food or a "liberty" to procreate if natural "necessities" imposed limits on the ability of a nation to take care of its citizens.[89] In one of his revisions, Malthus observed that "In the moral government of the world, it seems evidently necessary, that the sins of the fathers should be visited upon the children; and if in our overweening vanity we imagine that we can govern a private society better by endeavoring systematically to counteract this law, I am inclined to believe that we shall find ourselves very greatly mistaken."[90] For Malthus, humans who violated nature's laws simply perpetuated necessitous conditions. Morality demanded the control of one's pride and the acceptance of the physical limits that controlled the demands of nature. Individual morality was one of the keys to understanding the problems of poverty and population. As the famous parson explained to his readers, "Through the animal and vegetable kingdoms, nature has scattered the seeds of life abroad with the most profuse and liberal hand. She has been comparatively sparing in the room, and the nourishment necessary to rear them. The germs of existence contained in this spot of earth, with ample food, and ample room to expand in, would fill millions of worlds in the course of a few thousand years. Necessity, that imperious all pervading law of nature, restrains them within prescribed bounds. The race of plants, and the race of animals, shrink under this great restrictive law."[91] Malthus went on to argue that "Nature" would ensure one way or the other that humans learned of the "absolute necessity" of the "preventive" and "positive checks."[92] Preventive checks were those that came from societal efforts to "indispose greater numbers of persons" from marrying early, while the positive checks were those natural causes of mortality that included famines and other population disasters.[93]

The Godwin-Malthus debate was just one part of a rich, discursive template that would provide antecedent genres and fragments that would go into the construction of what scholars today come to think of as eugenics arguments. For Malthus, allowing the poor to believe in false necessities spelled moral, political, economic, and social disaster. Their chances for upward mobility depended on their success in emulating the best classes. Like Plato before him, Malthus could not resist commenting on which classes he thought were contributing the most to society: "It has been generally found that the middle parts of society are most favourable to virtuous and industrious habits and to the growth of all kinds of talents. . . . Superior and inferior parts are in the nature of things absolutely necessary, and not only necessary but strikingly beneficial. If no man could hope to rise or fear to fall in society, if industry did not bring with it its rewards and indolence its punishment, we could not expect to see that animated activity in bettering our condition which now forms the master-spring of public prosperity."[94] Malthus hoped that as the lower classes followed the lead of the middle classes, they would use their moral restraint and improve their station in life so that human society would appear to consist of "fewer blanks and more prizes."[95]

Yet not all Anglo-Americans shared in this middle- and upper-class mythology. Malthus gained a reputation as a prophet of gloom, and detractors pounced on some of his metaphors to describe nature's necessity. For example, Thomas Jarrold, in his *Dissertations on Man,* noted that some guests might be excluded from diocesan dinners but not from nature's feast, where "none are bishops but all are men . . . and the life of a guest is sacred . . . nor is it the prerogative of one guest to dismiss another from the hall."[96] Some social reformers argued that it was the elites in society that had not learned the lessons of nature. For example, Mary Wollstonecraft, in her *Vindication of the Rights of Woman,* criticized a degenerate upper class that was composed of "men of rank and fortune" who have all of their wants instantly supplied and where "invention is never sharpened by necessity."[97] William Cobbett made a similar claim when he lamented the fact that the "check-population philosophy" was being used as a cloak for injustice and a bar to higher wages and political reform.[98] One critic claimed that the Malthusian passage on "nature's feast" was repulsive because it accepted the rich "as a sort of Gods upon earth," and "allotted to the poor all of the misery."[99] Not everyone was willing to accept squalor and poverty as inexorable scientific laws.

Several decades following these disputes over the limits of nations' "political economies," a new science was developing on the European continent that helped to perpetuate the notion that heredity explained social distinctions within Anglo-American communities. Known as phrenology, this new science provided a lexicon that was used by intellectuals and laypersons alike in their discussions of the fit and unfit in America.[100] Influential writers including Benjamin Rush, Daniel Webster, Samuel Gridley Howe, and Walt Whitman accepted phrenology in whole or in part.[101]

Phrenologists thought that too many natural resources were going into educational programs that ignored the links between physical features and mental abilities. For writers like Franz Joseph Gall, humans were not born with a mental tabula rasa, and inheritance was the key to understanding the organization of the human brain.[102] In the early 1830s, he opined that "From the time of Horace, men have never ceased to observe, that certain moral qualities are often propagated for ages in the same family . . . I shall hereafter cite several instances in which a propensity for theft, to drunkenness, and even the unhappy propensity to suicide, were hereditary."[103] Like many generations before them, phrenologists were fascinated with the ways that "like produced like," and they constantly argued that external factors could not be the sole determinants of human behavior.

These phrenologists found themselves arguing before scientific and public audiences that researchers like Lamarck erred in believing that environmental changes were primarily responsible for organic changes.[104] Gall, for example, argued that Lamarck's contention that new organs could be produced in an individual "by necessity and exercise" was a "strange opinion."[105] Before the emergence of social Darwinism and modern eugenics, it would be the phrenologists who would be responsible for helping to keep alive necessitarian notions of heredity.

Today phrenology is considered to be a classic example of pseudoscience, but during the first decades of the nineteenth century, this type of movement helped to circulate many of the rhetorical commonplaces, metaphors, and clichés that would become standard arguments in eugenical tales. One of Gall's followers, Johann Spurzheim, once wrote that "three successive generations appear to be necessary to impregnate a race to a certain effect."[106] Years before Galton put pen to paper, Spurzheim noted that "It is a pity that the laws of propagation are not more attended to. I am convinced that, by attention to them, not only the condition of single families, but whole nations, might be improved beyond imagination, in figure, stature, complexion, health, talents, and moral feelings. . . . He who can convince the world of the importance of the laws of propagation, and induce mankind to conduct themselves accordingly, will do more good to them, and contribute more to their improvement, than all institutions, and all systems of education."[107]

These sentiments would be echoed over and over again by scholars, researchers, and laypersons who were convinced that their own scientific investigations had empirically illustrated the genetic component of a variety of social behaviors or mental characteristics. Inevitably, these rhetorical fragments were employed by articulate commentators who were willing to give advice on how to improve heredity. Spurzheim, for example, claimed that he understood the "laws of degeneration" and applied them to the social issues of hygiene, marriage, and race relationships. He argued that "Nature, morality and Christianity" commanded nations to "live in peace" by "crossing their blood," and he hoped that both mind and body would be strengthened and improved if humans paid attention to the laws of breeding.[108] In 1821, Spurzheim wrote a fellow phrenologist that "I have no objection to our confining all our doing to moral influence, but it is my opinion of the utmost necessity to regulate marriage in order to improve mankind. On the other hand, in general man must be ordered, few can be left to themselves. The ancient philosophers have felt the same necessity. . . . Unhappily they have proposed errors and truths together, but speaking of their proceedings—the great object to ascertain is whether private or public happiness is the aim of society. . . . In Austria no man can marry without proving that he has the means of maintaining a family. It is to prevent begging."[109]

Long before the eugenicists worried about race crossings and the discovery of the "feebleminded," other phrenologists like Combe (1825) were telling their readers that "It is a law of Nature, that the physical qualities of parents descend to their offspring. . . . Suppose a person, ignorant of this law, or disbelieving it, marries a partner beautiful to the eye, and fascinating to sense, but deficient in Conscientiousness and other moral organs; the offspring will probably inherit this development."[110] The phrenologists thus provided many Anglo-Americans a means by which they could make sense of their material and spiritual world. Like the modern eugenicists that followed them, they debated critics who were still caught up in the romance of believing in the power of nurture over nature.

After the Industrial Revolution, social reformers like Herbert Spencer, Charles Darwin, and Francis Galton took many of these ideas, modified them, and circulated them in the public sphere. The comparative quantity and quality of the human race was a continual concern. In 1874, for example, Spencer argued that to "aid the bad in multiplying is, in effect, the same as maliciously providing for our descendants a multitude of enemies." He went on to note that some organizations were undertaking "in a wholesale way to foster good-for-nothings" and in so doing committed an "unquestionable injury," for they "put a stop to that natural process of elimination by which society continually purifies itself."[111] As one of his contemporaries observed, "According to Herbert Spencer, no teaching or policy can advance the work of social development beyond a certain normal rate, while it is quite possible to perturb, to retard, or to disorder the process."[112] For Spencer, the best societies were those that followed biological laws that were just as immutable as the laws of gravity.

Darwin's discussion of natural selection provided another thread in the fabric of biological determinism that was being constructed during the nineteenth century. The author of the *Origin of Species* was more ambivalent than some of his contemporaries when it came to the issue of environmental influences, but he also worried about the effects of massive population growth on human heredity. Darwin wrote in 1871 that "It is impossible not to regret bitterly, but whether wisely is another question, the rate at which man tends to increase; for this leads in barbarous tribes to infanticide and many other evils, and in civilised nations to abject poverty, celibacy, and to the late marriages of the prudent. But as man suffers from the same physical evils as the lower animals, he has no right to expect an immunity from the evils consequent on the struggle for existence. Had he not been subjected during primeval times to natural selection, assuredly he would never have attained his present rank."[113] Darwin thought that humans could and should live with some interference with nature. Yet he also objected to Lamarck's interpretation of evolution and the assumption that the behavioral patterns of the parents could be inherited by the offspring.[114]

Ideographically, these biological discussions of "necessity" allowed rhetors to claim that nature, rather than free will, dictated just how society was to be ordered and what needs would be supplied. These debates over Lamarckian and Darwinian theories of evolution were not simply scientific disagreements over the truth of the origins of humanity — they were also social disputes over how much aid and charity would go to certain members of the chain of being. Amos Warner recognized the importance of some of these issues when he argued that "If acquired characteristics be inherited, then we have a chance permanently to improve the race independently of selection, by seeing to it that individuals acquire characteristics that it is desirable for them to transmit."[115] These were not just abstract issues of scientific or philosophical importance. Le Conte knew the importance of this debate for public policies. He went on to argue that if it were true that "selection of the fittest is the only method available," then it seemed to follow that "if we are to have race-improvement at all, the dreadful law of destruction of the weak and helpless must with Spartan firmness be carried out voluntarily and deliberately. Against such a course all that is best in us revolts." He noted that "the use of the Lamarckian factors, on the contrary, is not attended with such revolting consequences." Le Conte and other Lamarckians hoped that changes in individuals could have a cumulative positive impact on the human race.[116]

By the early 1860s, scientific and public debates over the role of inheritance provided audiences with a mélange of arguments that mixed hard-line genetic determinism with neo-Lamarckian claims about the impact that culture and the environment played in the formation of individuals and civilizations. After World War II, when the scientific community heralded a new age of genetics with the discovery of the DNA structure by Watson and Crick, many historians began to write about a genetic past or the progress of a science that did not include Lamarckism or neo-Lamarckism, but this was wishful thinking.[117] Even with the rediscovery of Mendel's work and the growing appreciation of the contributions of researchers like Weismann, many scholars and citizens continued to believe in the importance of the inheritance of "acquired" characteristics. Geneticists and other scholars searched the historical records for any indication of work that repudiated Lamarckism, and they then wrote their accounts of the past based on presentist views of molecular biology.

While future historians of science and other writers would recognize some of the contributions of writers like Malthus, Gall, Darwin, and Spencer, it would be Francis Galton who was given credit by eugenicists and geneticists for founding the modern eugenical movements.[118] Galton, with his studies of hereditary "genius," seemed to be one scientific figure who was not caught up in neo-Lamarckism.[119] Through eugenics, Galton intended to improve human stock by giving "the more suitable races or strains of blood a better chance of prevailing speedily over the less suitable."[120] Building on his work as an English statistician and lifelong student of biology and heredity, he argued that this could be done either through positive eugenics, the encouragement of the "fit" members of the society to reproduce themselves, or through negative eugenics, discouraging or preventing the "unfit" from procreating.[121]

Although most of Galton's work was primarily concerned with what would later be called "positive" eugenics, his ideas were appropriated and reconfigured in the following decades and used to justify a variety of social and political projects—including the sterilization and the segregation of the unfit, restriction on immigration, regulation of marriages, the introduction of mental and physical tests, and the establishment of health care programs that sought to improve "hygiene." Galton's ideas of artificially regulating human heredity gained popular acceptance after the turn of the century, finding large followings in the United States, Britain, Germany, and other countries.[122] In the first quarter of the twentieth century, American and English researchers, social workers, civic leaders, judges, and others began to suggest that society needed continually to improve its genetic makeup and weed out the unfit.[123] The movement found particularly fertile ground in the United States in the period just prior to and following World War I.[124]

What made many of these "hard-line" eugenical arguments so persuasive was the realism and boldness of some of the claims that were being espoused by these modern eugenicists. Writers like Charles Davenport and Harry Laughlin told their readers that environmentalists had had their day; now it was time to admit that societies needed to be based on the natural inequities that came from good and bad "germplasm."[125] Many of the earliest eugenical discussions were written at a time when Anglo-Americans were worried that the "better" classes were beginning to "degenerate." From within this worldview, any attempt at amelioration of social conditions seemed merely to perpetuate the problem of distinguishing between the fit and the unfit.

Yet an ideographic analysis of the times reveals that alongside of this hard-line eugenical stance, which saw nature as supreme in its struggle with nurture, there always existed other forms of hereditarian arguments that called for medical and environmental advances in societies that were trying to improve their health. In a juxtaposition of scientific and moral claims, couples were warned that their behavior or actions as parents could affect their children biologically.[126] Unlike the hard-line eugenicists who ridiculed the notion that education could improve the health of the nation, social reformers (who often called themselves eugenicists as well) sought to perfect the external influences that affected human heredity.[127] They eagerly appropriated evolutionary discussions of "adaptation" in their efforts to purify America.[128] Optimists could point to a Lamarckian view of the world that emphasized the plasticity and perfectibility of human nature, where volition and discipline on the part of parents might bring drastic improvements in the condition of the children. American mothers and fathers were lectured on the necessity of avoiding alcohol and other impurities that could alter the physical and psychic makeup of the offspring. In the neo-Lamarckian world, evolutionary improvements in the species depended on education and the building of character in one's lifetime.

Eugenical arguments gained in complexity over time. Granted, many of these writers were conservative, racist, or xenophobic, but these were not the only factors that contributed to the popularity of eugenics. These perspectives were not grafted onto a pristine genetics; they were inextricably related to its rise as a science. As both a science, movement, and ideology, eugenics was popularized in part because of its very ambiguity. To the chagrin of hard-liners, millions of Anglo-Americans believed that the term was simply another name for heredity. At the same time, hard-liners did gain the support of others who believed that the existence of socially stratified communities seemed to provide natural evidence of the immutable physical, biological, and social differences between "races" and "classes." Ordinary citizens who believed themselves to be living "eugenically" disagreed on the degree to which the cold and harsh "necessities" of life demanded that there be an abandonment of the right to reproduce or the liberty of avoiding sterilization.

In sum, eugenical arguments were not simply the creation of a coterie of pseudoscientists, nor were they the products of politicians who misunderstood or misapplied genetical analysis. They were also *rhetorical* fragments, representing the ideologies of multitudes of social actors who at different historical junctures have reconfigured these ideographs to legitimate a plethora of political, social, and economic agendas. Yet in spite of these diverse and often contradictory meanings of eugenics, recurring argumentative patterns are discernible, and they are important for us to consider in trying to understand this intersection of science, politics, and social policy. It is these patterns and not Whig histories that need to be explored.

In the 1990s, we are witnessing a revival of eugenics, and many of the problems we face are similar to the ones that other generations have had to deal with. Just as Americans in the 1990s are confronted with the specter of armies of the homeless, dependent AIDS patients, and violent inner-city gangs, in the 1910s and 1920s the nation was concerned with what it termed problems of the feebleminded, the congenital defectives, and other degenerates. Genetic explanations are once again gaining in prominence. Treating eugenics as the product of exclusively tyrannical governments hinders our ability to understand the social complexities of issues like gene therapy and "homemade eugenics." If our society is going to engage in a profitable public debate on the issue of eugenics, we need rhetorical histories that look at the ways in which eugenical arguments have been deployed and reconfigured. As long as we concentrate on the eugenic experts themselves, we will have an incomplete picture of the range of possibilities and the actual choices that were being made about the role of government in facilitating social change in the first quarter of the twentieth century.[129] When we stop at an analysis of the arguments of the eugenicists themselves, we accomplish discursively what they tried biologically, by denying a voice to the members of the underclass—the "residuum" in England and the "mongrels" in America.

What we need are investigations of the public debates that have taken place over the meanings of eugenics. Nancy Stepan, who herself provided us with an exhaustive study of the Latin American eugenics movement, commented, "I am especially sorry to have to leave for another book, or another historian, the study of the reactions of the people, most of them poor and many of them illiterate, who were the targets of the eugenists' ill-considered plans and policies."[130] In this book, I take up Stepan's challenge and use rhetorical histories to look at some of the dynamics of the eugenics debate. I will argue that the rise (and temporary fall) in the popularity of eugenical explanations of individual and social behavior reflects the changes that were taking place in the public vocabulary that instantiated particular views of the relationship between citizens and the government. By illuminating the ways in which eugenics was defined and redefined, I would like to contribute to the growing community that wishes to take seriously the notion that the "people" may be treated as involved social actors who have the responsibility and ability to discuss significant social issues.[131]

> The improvement of the race, for that is what "Eugenics"
> broadly means, has been looked upon with suspicion; but in
> a few years this scheme will be proclaimed a working fact
> and an unalterable necessity. **Ethel Alec-Tweedie, 1912**

> Race-betterment has become the dominant—well, I will
> not say fad, because the subject is too sacred—but let me
> say the dominant trend of our age, and many of us are
> willing and ready to sacrifice even our liberty upon the
> altar of race-betterment, entirely forgetful that the very
> basis and foundation of all human betterment thus far
> achieved has been precisely that liberty which we are so
> blindly ready to sacrifice. **Percy Andreae, 1915**

2

From Cradle to Grave: The Popularization of Eugenics within the Rhetorical Sphere, 1900–1940

Interest in eugenical arguments may have waxed and waned throughout the centuries, but in the first few decades of the twentieth century, the study of degeneration and the preservation of the "germplasm" became an Anglo-American obsession.[1] Commentators on both sides of the Atlantic reminded readers of the political liberties that they enjoyed, but other writers emphasized the limitations inherent in nature. Edward Ross typified this fin de siècle outlook when he observed during a visit to Europe that, "The doctrines of transmission and inheritance have attacked the independence of the individual. Science finds no ego, self or will that can maintain itself against the past. Heredity rules our lives like that supreme primeval *necessity* that stood above the Olympian gods. 'It is the last of the fates,' says Wilde, 'and the most terrible. It is the only one of the gods whose real name we know.' It is the 'divinity that shapes our ends' and hurls down the deities of freedom and choice" (my emphasis).[2] Ross was not alone. Another writer noted that arguments for "biological necessity" were frequently presented along with discussions of "nature" and "the law of struggle."[3] Calls for the amelioration of the human condition—through education, improved sanitation, and access to health care—were answered with reminders that social improvements began from within, not from without.

Within this cultural milieu, the rhetoric of eugenics flourished, especially in the years immediately prior to World War I. American and English audiences were exposed to thousands of sermons, speeches, and journal articles discussing how societies had evolved to the point that social needs were now considered to have priority over individual rights. In 1911, one observer opined that the future of civilization made it an "absolute necessity" that society study the laws of heredity and the elimination of the unfit.[4] William Fielding, writing in *Birth Control Review,* voiced his belief in the great "law of biological evolution" that was "natural," "socially desirable," "even necessary" and thereby "moral."[5] Another critic exhorted his readers to accept the "necessity of radical reform" and claimed that public opinion needed to supplement "natural selection" with "reproductive selection."[6]

Today we are accustomed to thinking that words like "liberty" and "freedom" symbolize emancipation, but at the turn of the century they were considered to represent outmoded and unscientific ways of thinking. "Progressive" realists of various political persuasions claimed that they were no longer misled by the abuses that had taken place in earlier decades in the name of "liberty."[7] As one observer wrote in 1914, " 'Personal Liberty' is at last an uncrowned, dethroned king, with no one to do him reverence. The social consciousness is so far developed, and is becoming so autocratic, that institutions and governments must give heed to its mandate and shape their life accordingly. We are no longer frightened by that ancient bogey—'paternalism in government.' We affirm boldly, it is the business of government to be just that—paternal."[8] To the modern ear, this willingness to accept such limitations may have a hollow ring, but for many Anglo-Americans living at the turn of the century, denying the "necessities" of nature meant a return to those metaphysical speculations of a bygone era.

As many scholars and critics have argued, the eugenics movement was an important part of this transitional period that witnessed the rising power of the "social" world.[9] The "individualist" beliefs of nineteenth-century writers were seen as relics of a time that did not have to deal with the harsh trials brought by modernity. Earlier generations did not have to cope with the complexities of urbanization, capitalism, and imperialism. Members of the public, as well as the most enlightened of the Progressives, were trying to find ways of adjusting to rapid social change. Social reformers of the period, peddling everything from war preparation to prohibition, articulated a public vocabulary laden with notions of "social control" and the importance of directing rather than trying to combat the inexorable march of "nature." This was the era of social movements, and each of the reforming groups vied for the right to define the "necessities" of the times.

For several decades eugenic writers and orators exhorted their audiences to leave behind their antiquated notions of human volition and choice and learn to model their behavior on the immutable laws of nature. Included in this discourse were calls for social control over the reproductive rights of millions of Anglo-Americans.[10] Martin Barr, one of the early advocates of the sterilization of the unfit, explained that, "What in the beginning was a philanthropic purpose pure and simple, having as its object the most needy and therefore naturally directed toward paupers and idiots now assumes the proportions of a socialistic reform as a matter of self-preservation, a *necessity* to preserve the nation from the encroachments of imbecility, of crime, and of all the fateful heredities of a highly nervous age" (emphasis mine).[11]

Other eugenicists were insistent that focusing on the environment had brought chaos in the nineteenth century and that society needed to accept the primacy of nature over nurture. Joseph DeJarnette, for example, in a report to the Western State Hospital of Virginia would write, "In the case of the farmer in breeding his hogs, horses, cows, sheep, etc, he selects a thoroughbred, and even in farm and garden products he selects the best seed to produce from, but when it comes to our own race any sort of seed seems to be good enough, and the rights of the syphilitic, epileptic, imbecile, drunkard and unfit generally to reproduce must be allowed, for otherwise we are encroaching upon the so-called inalienable rights of man."[12] DeJarnette, like millions of other Anglo-Americans, began to suspect that giving everyone equal rights might interfere with the selection of the fit— socially, politically, and economically. "The bearing of children is, of course," one Oberlin professor told his readers, "not an individual right, but a social privilege, and in time it must come to be so recognized."[13] In some intellectual circles, this was considered to be a biological fact beyond dispute.

Yet like all ideographs, the terms "necessity" and "eugenics" were ambiguous. The pervasive concerns of the eugenicists for regulating society according to the laws of heredity could often be interpreted in multiple and sometimes conflicting ways.[14] An analysis of the eugenical literature in both scientific and public discussions reveals that "eugenics" could take on one or several of the following categorical meanings.

1. It might refer to the physical or mental improvement of a "fit" human being by preserving the "germplasm" that a person inherited. This was the most restrictive definition of eugenics, which focused on the genetic makeup and not the external environmental conditions of human beings.[15] For some eugenicists, the people who wanted to improve the environment should adopt the term "euthenics," not "eugenics." An emphasis would be placed on "natural selection" rather than the "inheritance of acquired characteristics" as an explanation for human progress. From within this definition of eugenics, "judicious breeding" was paramount.[16]

2. Eugenics could also mean the improvement of national "races." For example, Karl Pearson thought that a national eugenics initiative was needed to help England maintain her imperial holdings against competitor nations.[17] Many Anglo-American eugenicists insisted that you could predict a person's character by the place of his or her birth.

3. Sometimes eugenics was defined in ways that focused on the perpetuation of the white race.[18] These interpretations were used to justify marriage restrictions between "normal" whites and atavistic immigrants or African-Americans. This strain in the eugenic discourse was especially strong in the first two decades of the twentieth century.

4. Some rhetors treated eugenics as another name for "scientific *philanthropy.*"[19] This expansive category could include the provision of housing and maternal care for the "fit" as well as the elimination of aid for the "unfit." Charity would no longer help the weak but the strong.

5. To some the term meant the improvement of both genetics and the environment. The aim here would be to improve the condition of the "wellborn" in ways that sometimes contradicted definition one above. For example, Caleb Saleeby believed that strict hereditarians were ignoring the elements of Galtonian eugenics that involved both "positive" and "negative" eugenics and the removal of "race poisons" (smoking, alcohol).[20]

6. Some of the vaguest definitions of eugenics claimed the right to be "left alone," which was simply a means of insuring that society would not interfere with nature.[21] This description perpetuated the notions associated with laissez-faire economics.

7. One definition of eugenics seemed to include anything that tended to increase the social control of the unfit by a meritocracy composed of the fit.[22] One

of the most popular definitions of eugenics claimed that it was "the study of agencies under social control that may improve or impair the racial qualities of future generations either physically or mentally."[23]

8. Galton supplied one of the most ambiguous definitions of eugenics when he claimed that the word referred to the practice of making people "*noble* in heredity" or "good in birth."[24] This mixed moral evaluations with scientific descriptions and allowed writers to talk about anything that would improve a person's "character." Many eugenicists for decades could thus include "moral delinquency" as a reason for people to be segregated or even sterilized.

In sum, "eugenics" was an evocative term that could be employed in a myriad of ways. Most researchers who have explored the arguments employed by eugenicists often cope with this ambiguity by accepting one or two definitions of eugenics as representing the thinking of most eugenicists for a period of years. By spotlighting the writings of the major eugenical leaders—Galton, Pearson, Davenport, and Laughlin—scholars have attempted to uncover the most semantically pure expression of eugenical ideas and then treated applications of those ideas in the political or public sphere as deviations from the pristine ideals of these eugenicists.[25] For example, some of these critics claim that the abuses of genetics came when propagandists supported legislation based on an inadequate understanding of the basic laws of Mendelian biology.[26] Within this scenario, there were good eugenicists, who were cautious and more moderate in their claims, and bad eugenicists, who misunderstood the limitations of genetical explanations. At other times, historians and philosophers of science have divided eugenics into two dominant periods, where the first eugenicists were hard-line conservative hereditarians and the second group were "reformers" who had a better grasp of the relationship between genetics and the environment.[27] In these and other variants of the traditional eugenics tale, it was the premature application of the hard-line perspective that gave eugenics its bad name. Within these orthodox stories, any application of the term "eugenics" to include environmental concerns or social programs that did not conform with the ideas of the leaders of the movement is treated as either non- or anti-eugenical.[28]

In critiquing this dominant interpretation of eugenics, I use an ideographic analysis of the eugenics movement and contend that neo-Lamarckian interpretations of eugenics were just as powerful in Anglo-American communities as they were in other countries.[29] At the same time, I argue that the reformers who attacked the hard-line eugenical stance were merely using arguments that had existed for decades in the popular discourse on the subject. Part of the reason for the rising influence of the eugenics movement was that it had mass appeal, and its very lack of univocality meant that its goals could be construed in many ways. While many scholars have mentioned the racist appeals of the science of the "wellborn," other concerns were inextricably intertwined with the eugenics movement. Eugenics was a part of dozens of local projects, including better-baby contests, improved parenthood programs, control of race poisons, conservation of resources, women's temperance movements, and even military preparation for war.[30] In the vernacular of the times, it affected everything about a person's lifestyle from the cradle to the grave.[31]

Taking Care of "the Cradle": Infancy, Alcoholism, and Popular Eugenics

In the first several decades of the twentieth century, "eugenics" was a term that Anglo-Americans heard about from the time of their infancy. As the word entered the public vocabulary, it colored the way people perceived themselves and those around them. Although most eugenicists dated the revitalization of their movement from the mid-1880s, it took several decades before the new science captured the imagination of the average citizen. Yet as the term "eugenics" simultaneously gained in popularity as well as ambiguity, its adherents found themselves embarrassed at the way the events were unfolding. "You would be amused to hear how general is now the use of your Eugenics!" exclaimed Karl Pearson in correspondence with Francis Galton in 1907. "I hear most respectable middle-class matrons saying if children are weakly, 'Ah, that was not a eugenical marriage!' "[32] In America a few years later, one speaker told his New Jersey Chamber of Commerce audience that "In these days of sanitation, and eugenics and hygiene, and the race for perfect efficiency of muscle and brain . . . where ever we turn, we meet an anti-this society or anti-that league."[33] Not all hardline eugenicists were sure what to make of some of the public usages of their term, and they anxiously watched the spread of the eugenical creed.

Part of this interest in eugenics came from its apparent practical application in the daily lives of many Anglo-American citizens. Among the many diverse issues that touched on the subject of eugenics, no question was more prominent in the minds of many English and American audiences than what to do about protecting the future members of the race. Debates over the raising of children had always been controversial, but now the "rights of the wellborn" became the preoccupation of millions. The wealthy used the term "eugenics" to invoke earlier times when heredity and success went hand in hand. For many scions, philanthropy was a way to contribute to a science that recognized that their inherited wealth would go to the preservation of their "germplasm." Wealthy rural land-owners thought that the back-to-the-farm or -country movements supported by eugenicists were signs that at last the health of the nation would be restored in spite of the political corruption brought on by the "masses" who huddled in the confines of the slums, dreaming of competing with their betters. For the middle classes, the eugenic concentration on the intellectual, emotional, and genetic character of the young meant that someone was finally recognizing that merit, hard work, and clean living were more important than primogeniture. For the working classes, eugenics seemed to hint that the triumph of socialism might be here at last.

Many Americans not only listened to speeches and read articles on eugen-ics: they also acted out their roles as "fit" members of a civilization that was recognizing the importance of parenthood. Following the establishment of the privately funded Eugenics Record Office in the first decade of the twentieth cen-tury, thousands of families eagerly filled out their "Record of Family Traits" and rushed to mail them to eugenicists for analysis by Davenport or other experts stationed at the Cold Spring Harbor Research Laboratory on Long Island.[34] In the 1910s and 1920s, members of the clergy took care of your afterlife and doc-tors made sure that you stayed healthy in this world, but it was the eugenicists who claimed to be experts when it came to making sure of the quality both of your ancestors behind you and your children ahead of you. While the sci-ence was new and mysterious and controversial, its mystery only added to its attractiveness.

While certainly many eugenical appeals were written with the intent of play-ing on racial and class prejudices, many audiences took fragments of these stories and reinterpreted them selectively to fit their own personal, social, or economic agendas. Many of the articles on eugenics that appeared in the popular press in the first quarter of the twentieth century contained discussions of both heredity and the environment and often talked about much more than purely Mendelian principles of heredity. Eugenical articles in newspapers, journals, and books con-tained advice on marriage, divorce, and most importantly, how to deal with race poisons.[35]

Anglo-American exposure to eugenical arguments began with infant care. The parents of children born in the first several decades of the twentieth century were often assailed with messages about the necessity of eugenic parenthood. Many Anglo-Saxon mothers and fathers continued to hear speeches about the influence of nurture as well as nature. For example, one of the most influential means of protecting the "wellborn" in this period had to do with the relation-ship between alcohol and birth defects.[36] Building on arguments developed in the temperance movements of the nineteenth century, many hard-line and re-form eugenicists believed that there was an intimate relationship between this particular race poison and the future of the Anglo-Saxon race. Some of the eu-genicists who frequently wrote and spoke on the effects of alcoholism included Karl Pearson, Irving Fisher, and Raymond Pearl.[37] These discussions went be-yond laboratory discussions of genetical experimentations to include commen-taries on social legislation. For example, Albert Wiggam, one of the most famous popularizers of eugenics, noted in 1924 that:

> the Eighteenth Amendment, if it really prohibits, is the most tremendous "eugenic law" ever passed in the world's history, because it will profoundly influence the health, sanity, and stamina of generations yet unborn. Some biologists believe it will weaken the race, because they believe alcohol has for ages killed off the weaklings and those lacking self-control; and that if such persons are permitted to live and reproduce and spread their inborn weakness, in time the whole race will become potential drunkards. Other biologists believe that counteracting factors will prevent this disaster. I shall not enter the controversy here. But I cite it as a tremendous eugenical problem, which is also a political problem.[38]

Eugenicists could thus gain adherents within the social sciences by pointing to some of the practical applications of eugenics and linking the protection of germplasm to other popular movements like the temperance movement.

In England, eugenics became associated with the problem of alcoholism through the efforts of popularizers like Caleb Saleeby, and by 1914 there were branches in Belfast, Birmingham, Liverpool, and Oxford.[39] Saleeby's concern with both nurture and nature provided an interpretation of eugenics that had a broader base of support than the more hard-line eugenical perspectives. Many of these groups provided the opportunity for discussions on issues like the prob-lem of inebriate women.[40] Oftentimes these eugenical societies would combine discussions of alcoholism with the dangers of "race crossing" or "class degen-eration." Many anxiously worried that the new race poisons only exacerbated the social problems that had already come to the attention of the public through the work of some of the voluntary and royal commissions. Influential eugenicists joined the Royal Commission on Divorce and gave evidence to the Home Office Inebriates Enquiry. The Eugenics Society in England was also partially respon-sible for the creation of the Royal Commission on the Care and Control of the Feebleminded and a special education conference in 1913. At these meetings, hundreds of speeches and addresses were presented to teachers, headmasters, and anyone else who would listen.[41]

In America many opponents of prohibition also turned to eugenicists for arguments.[42] In 1926, commenting on a seeming tendency of certain people to engage in excessive drinking, Irving Fisher noted that, "This fact has been used as a eugenic argument against Prohibition. The work of Karl Pearson, Dr. Stockard, and Dr. Pearl indicates that alcohol is a selective agent for killing off the unfit, while leaving the fit relatively unharmed. The idea is especially applied to alcoholized parents affecting the germplasm. This is the old argument, in a new and improved form, that alcohol is a good fool-killer."[43] Many "wets" used the argument that natural selection had created within the human race a biological division between those who became moderate drinkers and the inferior specimens who could not handle their liquor. When Raymond Pearl came out with research indicating that some moderate drinkers lived longer than teetotalers, members of "personal liberty" and moderation leagues, brewers and distillers, and campaign orators in national and state political organizations all began quoting Pearl triumphantly.[44] In 1926, eugenicists were among those who gave testimony at hearings of the Senate subcommittee of Judiciary on the issue of prohibition. Irving Fisher once claimed that the great objective of prohibition was to break the chain by which the custom of drinking was "passed on from generation to generation."[45]

As Joseph Gusfield and other scholars have recently observed, these discussions of alcoholism and its effects were much more than utopian hopes that laws and society could be shaped by temperance movements filled with the righteousness of moral perfectionism.[46] Many of the arguments used in the alcohol debates changed the ways in which social agents were asked to maintain or alter particular social relationships. Eugenicists who joined the ranks of those in favor of prohibition often built on a sound rhetorical foundation of arguments that had traditionally tried to assert the superior needs of society against the licentiousness of the individual. As early as 1831, James Appleton, who would later be called the "Father of Prohibition," petitioned the Massachusetts state senate and voiced his concern that the "laws assume that the sale of Ardent Spirits, to a certain extent at least, is of public benefit and necessity and promotive of individual advantage and happiness. This assumption, your petitioner humbly apprehends, has been ascertained to be utterly unsupported."[47] Decades later, Frances Willard's Women's Christian Temperance Union had departments of "Health and Hygiene," of "Heredity," and of "Physical Culture" that condemned patent medicines containing alcohol. Often considered under the rubric of "race hygiene" were such disparate subjects as vivisection and intercollegiate athletics.[48] Carrie Nation would tell her audiences that "the deterioration of the race is upon us," and she claimed that some race poisons were responsible for transmitting nervous diseases, epilepsy, weakened constitutions, depraved appetites, and deformities of all kinds.[49] Often these temperance debates became a reflection of the tensions between groups within the wider American culture — agrarian against industrial, native Yankee against the immigrants, Protestants against Catholics and Jews.[50]

The propaganda on both sides of the issue of prohibition served as an effective vehicle for the dissemination of information on eugenics. Writers like Wiggam used these discursive battles between the "wets" and the "drys" as a means of explaining why eugenics was a necessity in stopping hereditary alcoholism and other problems of civilization that were contributing to the "Rising Tide of Degeneracy."[51] The saloon leagues published newspapers like *The National Daily* and monthlies like the *American Patriot*. Some scholars estimate that the combined circulation of these publications exceeded fifteen million.[52] One league's general manager of publication, Ernest Cherrington, helped to distribute millions of books, pamphlets, leaflets, charts, window cards, and even marching songs to bring out the faithful.[53] Many of these publications invited their readers to learn about the links between the hereditarian effects of alcohol and crime, truancy, divorce, insanity, gonorrhea, syphilis, and even tuberculosis. These and other evils were ascribed in large part to the availability of liquor.

Eugenical arguments became a key part of congressional and public debates on alcoholism. Congressman Richmond Hobson, a Democrat from Alabama, would claim that alcohol was the main cause of "feeblemindedness" and sexual perversion in women.[54] In the early 1913–14 session, some legislators argued that scientific research had demonstrated that alcohol was a narcotic poison that was "destructive and degenerating to the human organism . . . produces widespread crime, pauperism, and insanity, inflicts disease and untimely death upon hundreds of thousands of citizens, and blights with degeneracy their children unborn, threatening the future integrity and the very life of the nation."[55] As usual in many of these debates, the unborn child or the infant took center stage. One senator opined before Congress that, "The laboring millions cannot afford to waste over two billions a year on a beverage that impairs strength, undermines health, corrupts morals, and sends an everwidening stream of defectives and incompetents to the asylum, the penitentiary, the hospital, and the grave. Add to this the fact that even the moderate drinker transmits the alcoholic taint to the unborn child, predisposing the helpless little being to disease, to shame, and to sin, and the horror of it all will begin to appear."[56]

At the same time that people were debating the effects of alcohol in Congress, twenty thousand people volunteered to be speakers for the cause, and carloads of prohibition propaganda were being produced daily.[57] With the outbreak of the First World War, food control bills became controversial, and eugenicists like Major General Leonard Wood encouraged Americans to follow the lead of Kansas, a dry state since 1881, by claiming that this state bred "the finest, the cleanest, the healthiest and the most vigorous soldiers . . . Kansas boys were brought up in a clean atmosphere. They started right."[58] In dealing with the liquor question, Progressives rejected the doctrine of laissez-faire and insisted that since alcohol was retarding the progress of civilization, the state had a duty to intervene and control it.[59]

For many children born in the first decades of the twentieth century, there was no escaping the rhetoric of eugenics. Even before they were born, they themselves had been the objects of controversy and attention.

Growing Up in a Eugenical World

For many Anglo-American children, learning about eugenics was more than learning the immutable laws of nature—it was a way of life, a perspective that informed a person's everyday social interactions. As one commentator would write in the *Nation* in July 1912, the study of eugenics was about "happiness," and this involved moving beyond "social control that may improve or impair the racial qualities of future generations" to a "broadened" endeavor that heightened the "dignity" of parenthood and "civil responsibility in general."[60] Alec Tweedie, writing in the *Fortnightly Review,* thought that British schemes for stamping out degeneracy were "all very well, but a little of the hygiene of domestic life, and some knowledge of the newest of all sciences, eugenics, could advisedly be laid before the children in simple, careful, and well-thought-out way. It is so easy to interest little people in the mysteries of botany and with that foundation everything can be kept pretty, poetic, and charming, yet true to nature, while the children's minds are led along the lines that will finally result in their acceptance of the great truths of heredity and eugenics."[61] While many eugenicists frequently claimed that little could be done for those with poor germplasm, at the same time they were firmly convinced that educating the young would be the best way to insure that these problems were not passed down to the next generation.

Michael McGee has argued that some of the most persuasive ideologies are those we adopt when we are young, and the classrooms of many English and American secondary schools were filled with the tales of eugenics.[62] In England,

Manchester and other cities voted funds for the study of eugenics in the municipal schools.[63] Not only the topics that were discussed but the fields that were created within the pedagogical communities reflected the role of eugenics in the education of youngsters. Stories of biological determinism became part of curriculums of many normal schools, and people like Helen Putnam worked within organizations like the National Education Association to make sure that Americans understood the importance of racial well-being.[64] Many educators of the time not only knew a little about eugenics but actually supported it as well and told some students about the "worm-eaten stock" and the importance of "eugenic marriages."[65] School textbooks warned their readers of the differences between immigrants and natives, whites and blacks, "fallen women" and the chaste. At one 1916 conference, one teacher claimed that "if humanity is to survive, individualism and nationalism must conform to the laws of racial well-being."[66] Dean Freeman, in his article entitled "Criteria of Judging a Science of Education," wrote in the 1920s that "When race or national competition becomes sufficiently keen, conscious and well ordered adjustment by eugenical principles will become a powerful and education [sic] and sociological weapon which may determine the dominant races of the future. [Today the] . . . segregation of classes on ability basis and personal studies are just a few reflections of inheritance differences. . . . Heredity has also to do with vocational guidance."[67]

In order to provide their students with the latest in progressive scientific information, members of the National Education Association kept in touch with eugenical experts like Charles Davenport. One dedicated teacher thought that it was the "duty of educators to assure through educational procedures that individuals shall be well born as they shall be well reared."[68] In Wisconsin and Wyoming normal schools, awards were given out to members of civics classes, and the germplasmic "unit characteristics" became a part of the subject matter in geography, biology, psychology, and related topics.[69] The vast majority of biology textbooks of the period were filled with eugenical tales of the superiority of the Bach, Darwin, and Edward family over the degenerate Kallikaks, Pineys, and Jukeses.[70]

These types of texts served to legitimate a hierarchical social order and served as warrants for the study of both positive and negative eugenics. One textbook written in 1914, entitled *Civic Biology: Presented in Problems*, noted that "Hundreds of families such as those described above [Kallikak and Jukes] exist today, spreading disease, immorality, and crime to all parts of this country . . . they not only do harm to others by corrupting, stealing, or spreading disease, but they are actually protected and cared for by the state out of public money. Largely for them the poorhouse and the asylum exist. They take from society but they give nothing. They are true parasites."[71] Sometimes this type of rhetoric was addressed specifically at the young man or woman. A passage in one of these texts warned that "Even though you are in high school, it's only fair to yourselves that you should remember the responsibility that marriage brings. You should be parents. Will you choose to have children well-born? Or will you send them into the world with an inheritance that will handicap them for life?"[72] For the audiences reading this and similar passages, the messages were fairly clear: in order to be a normal adult, one needed to live eugenically. Many of these texts went through several editions and were used for decades.[73]

Yet a youngster's education was not confined within the walls of the secondary school classroom, and the eugenics principles did not remain contained either. In England, one of the popular means of disseminating information to various classes of people was through the use of the pedigree charts, which one writer constructed in order to codify statistical information and show the transmission of the "idiosyncrasies."[74] In college, English youth could learn about eugenics by joining the Fabian Society and other groups that allied themselves with eugenics.[75] In America, they could sing along with undergraduate F. Scott Fitzgerald, who in 1914 wrote the song "Love or Eugenics" for the Princeton Triangle Show. Fitzgerald put to music what others were putting on paper:

> Men, which would you like to come and pour your tea,
> Kisses that set your heart aflame,
> Or Love from a prophylactic dame.[76]

Growing up in the Anglo-American world in the first few decades of the twentieth century meant being constantly bombarded with lectures on eugenics from ethical, debating, and philosophical societies; health, women's, and medical associations—sometimes even the YMCA.[77] Hardly a year passed without new books coming to print written by both scientists and laypersons imbued with the zeal of the new faith. Much of this rhetoric followed a familiar format, beginning with the birth of the movement founded by Galton and ending with a call that the world take up the eugenics creed.[78]

Outside of academia, young adults could listen to lecturers espouse the latest in eugenical developments. On the Chautauqua circuit, people like Albert Wiggam brought the infant science to the attention of the masses. Wiggam, a journalist and author as well as a speaker, had educated himself before the war by visiting the Eugenics Record Office on Long Island. Wiggam's audiences were given blank family-record forms to fill out and mail to the American Eugenics Society.[79] For youngsters growing up in the 1910s and 1920s, the air was filled with the voices of eugenicists beckoning them to remember the eugenics creed, which seemed to be what Kevles has called a combination of "science with statesmanship, morality, and religion." [80] More conservative writers and speakers usually argued that eugenics was the new "Golden Rule," and adolescents in England and in America were expected to learn nature's laws. Sometimes eugenical films were shown in small-town theaters in Scotland, England, and Wales.[81] In 1926, the American society published "A Eugenics Catechism," which taught that the science of the wellborn was much more than a plan for breeding super-beings or treating people like cattle.[82] In one part of the catechism, eugenical answers were given to complex questions:

> Q. Does eugenics contradict the Bible?
> A. The Bible has much to say for eugenics. It tells us that men do not gather grapes from thorns and figs from thistles. . . .
> Q. Does eugenics mean less sympathy for the unfortunate?
> A. It means a much better understanding of them, and a more concerted attempt to alleviate their suffering, by seeing to it that everything possible is done to have fewer hereditary defectives. . . .
> Q. What is the most precious thing in the world?
> A. The human germ plasm.[83]

In 1926, the American Eugenics Society launched a eugenics-sermon contest in New Haven, Connecticut, and famous scientists like Charles Davenport and Yale literary critic William Lyon Phelps served as the judges.[84]

By the time Anglo-American children reached adolescence, if they hadn't learned about eugenics in school or on the streets, they might have heard about it in their scout troop.[85] Because it is one of the most popular movements of the twentieth century, many people forget that scouting arose from a set of specific historical and social circumstances.[86] One of the primary interests that influenced the creation of the scouting movement was eugenics. In the early scout literature of Baden-Powell, the charts and textual arguments presented to hundreds of thousands of young scouts concern the ways that scouting could remedy a nation's ills.[87] Whether the concern was poverty, drink, labor unrest, faulty education, unemployment, or even weak "character," scouting confronted the issues and provided some answers. Scouting was portrayed as the safest and surest antidote to some of the "poisons" of society.[88]

While the scouting movement liked to portray itself as a universal and apolitical community, at its inception it was used to inculcate in the lower classes the values and ideals of the more privileged members of society.[89] Putting on the right uniform and learning the ways of the scouts helped to create an ideology that was intent on taking morally inadequate, lower-class youth and turning them into solid citizens. Baden-Powell, writing in the *Headquarters Gazette* in November 1911, proudly proclaimed, "Our business is not merely to keep up smart 'show' troops, but to pass as many boys through our character factory as we possibly can: at the same time, the longer the grind that we can give them the better men they will be in the end."[90] Many youngsters would find that the eugenical lessons of scouting promoted "fitness" through unquestioned obedience to properly structured authority, the deferential acceptance of one's social and economic position in life, and an unwavering patriotism for which one should be prepared, if necessary, to die.[91] As Arnold Freeman indicated in *Boy Life and Labour* in 1914, "The working class must be taught to accommodate themselves happily to those straitened circumstances of manual labour for which Nature seems to have fitted them."[92] At a time when many feared the effects of national or race degeneration, scouting seemed to offer a way of making sure that Anglo-Saxon youths learned the habits that would save their society— loyalty, obedience, and cleanliness. Baden-Powell typified the feelings of many of the early scout leaders when he wrote, "A dull lad who can obey orders is better than a sharp one who cannot."[93]

In England, British youngsters were admonished to build up savings so that in times of unemployment they would not be "a burden on others."[94] For many of the English scout leaders, it was the gambling, drinking, and other expensive indulgences—and not any institutional barrier—that accounted for the squalor and poverty of the working classes.[95] Some Scout leaders like Baden-Powell repeatedly claimed that 60 percent of British youngsters were unfit for military duty.[96] Readers of scout articles implored their readers to think of the benefits of universal military training. In one edition of *Scouting for Boys*, audiences could learn that the "cost of living and the growth of luxury, overpopulation, and want of thrift produced masses of unemployed in Rome before its fall, as they are doing today."[97]

It was no coincidence that some of the most vocal supporters of the scouting movement were also among the founders of the British eugenics movement. People like Karl Pearson would commend the work of the scouts in general and Baden-Powell in particular for providing the cause with an "excellent little book" that was a "capital introduction to the true scientific method."[98] Caleb Saleeby, in his *The Progress of Eugenics*, called Baden-Powell the "greatest educator of our time."[99] Effusive praise was heaped on the scout movement for providing what Saleeby considered the "greatest step towards the progress of eugenics since 1909."[100] In one of his books, Saleeby asserted that "If national eugenics is ever to be achieved in Great Britain it will come through the Boy Scouts and the Girl Guides, who almost alone, of all our young people, are being made ready, by 'training in citizenship, character discipline, and patriotism,' for education for parenthood, which must be the beginning of national eugenics. This movement is what national education in Great Britain has tried and failed to do for forty years."[101]

Saleeby's feelings on the links between eugenics and English patriotism were typical of the rhetoric of the period. In 1912, Horton would argue in his *National Ideas and Race Regeneration* that "Eugenics becomes a method of patriotism. The worker in this science is now a greater national benefactor than the soldier or the captain of industry."[102] Arnold White, a leading apostle of national efficiency and an ardent eugenicist, argued in 1909 that England needed to train a body of citizens that would be "fit to reproduce their kind," through a process that would avoid "maudlin philanthropic sentiment."[103] Early scout manuals were filled with stories and accompanying pictures that graphically illustrated how scouts needed to follow the model of the English soldier in India, who "never brooks an insult even from an equal, much less from a native of this land."[104] In 1909 one critic writing in the *Spectator* magazine lamented that "The boys are instructed in the story of Empire and the duties and privileges which its possession entails. They are made to feel the responsibilities of citizenship and the bond of a common race; and if any party politician objects to this teaching, so much the worse for that party politician. They are taught the fundamental truth that unemployment and kindred evils are not the outcome of private ownership of capital, but of unfitness and deterioration in one class of citizens. Boy Scouts when they grow up will not be sentimentalists and doctrinaires."[105] By 1916, over one hundred thousand scouts would serve in Britain's armed forces.[106]

In the United States, much of the popularity of the scouting movement was due to the efforts of Ernest Seton, David Starr Jordan, and others. Among the luminaries who supported the movement in America were Presidents Taft and Theodore Roosevelt, who was elected to be honorary "chief Scout citizen."[107] When it came to standardizing the scout oath and the law, that was written by Jeremiah Jenks of Cornell University, a known proponent of hereditarian ideals.[108] The credo of the Boy Scouts, written by E. B. De Groot, observed that scouting "embodies a code of self-discipline that commands boys to talk clean, live clean, and fight clean — even as the immortal Roosevelt played the game."[109] Many of these dignitaries shared with their neighbors the wish to see a scout movement that would help the nation improve the quality of the next generation of youngsters. America at the turn of the century was preoccupied with ways of fulfilling its manifest destiny, and a part of that destiny involved the desire for biological fitness and race betterment. In the *Handbook for Scoutmasters*, scout leaders were advised that the "*heredity* of the boy is a heritage which accompanies him into life. It is a fixed influence limiting the boy's possibilities. The Scoutmaster cannot change it" (emphasis in the original).[110] Much of the early scout literature reinforced existing beliefs that the world was divided into inferior and superior classes and that certain nations were naturally superior in the great chain of being.[111] Combining humanitarian concerns with the need for social control, the scouting movement legitimated the notion that some in society were born to rule and that others were supposed to obey. Many of the founders of the scouting movement were eugenicists, who were caught in a unique rhetorical situation. They abhorred much of modernity and the habits of the "masses," and yet they needed to spread the gospel of the movement if they were going to engage in any meaningful social reforms.[112]

By the early 1920s, it was estimated that there were almost a million scouts in the United States alone.[113] At first many American scouts learned their scouting principles from British manuals, but in later years the American scout movement created its own texts and variants of the eugenics tale. Many times the advice given to young scouts on eugenics mirrored the ambiguity within the larger movement. The same ideographic tensions that existed between nature and nurture reappeared in the eugenical arguments within scout texts. For example, in the same *Handbook* that discussed the immutability of heredity, a scout living in the early twenties would read that "Some writers lay great emphasis on the theory that the boy relives the life of the race; that he and his interests and play pass through barbaric and savage and other stages. While it is true that prior to his birth the embryological changes of the boy's body roughly summarize the anatomical history of the race; and while it is seemingly true that the maturing of certain social trends in the boy's life touches the peaks of racial progress in these matters . . . it seems sane counsel to the Scoutmaster not to construct his program along post glacial or savage lines."[114]

Such texts thus provided ambiguous advice based on often contradictory eugenic associations. A scout manual could claim that the ultimate "character" and quality of any person was the result of both internal and external forces.[115] In another passage, one handbook opined that "Misfits are among life's most common tragedies . . . the annual loss to society amounts into billions but greater still is the loss to the individual—the undermining of his confidence and hope and courage which robs him of his power."[116] Many American scouts were tested for intelligence, and some were told about how "The Army Draft revealed clearly the results of neglect of physical welfare by the country at large. Nearly one third of those called by the draft were found to be physically unfit for the exacting physical demands of full Army Service."[117]

Stories constantly circulated in this scout handbook that painted an idyllic picture of life before the advent of modernity, and such leaders complained about the way that America seemed to be losing the type of citizen that had been developed on the farm and in the country schools.[118] Supporters of the Boy Scout movement would claim that the nervous disorders and mental irritation that seemed to be spreading were not known in the colonial or frontier days.[119] Richardson and Loomis, in a 1915 book on the scouts entitled *The Boy Scout Movement,* invited their readers to believe that scouting could help with the "mental vacuity" that seemed to exist in modern societies.[120] Many scouting works quoted liberally from eugenicists like Saleeby and McDougall.[121] For example, one book warned that without the "necessary human experiences," some young people might suffer different forms of "neurasthenia or even insanity."[122] Some scouting enthusiasts went so far as to claim that the movement would help those who had "not degenerated to the level of the criminal or of the mentally defective."[123] Young readers were warned not to become part of the "submerged tenth" or the "parasites" that infected society.[124]

Adult Entertainment and the Popularization of Eugenics

While many Anglo-Americans learned about eugenics in the media of the written word, some communities were exposed to the eugenic creed through social or political events. David Procter has recently claimed that some events are "dynamic spectacles," serving as catalysts for social change.[125] Such events are rhetorical in nature because they invite participants to reenact particular performances, which in turn suggest ways for communities to rethink their views and attitudes toward controversial social issues. As Murray Edelman explains, some unique events have the power to orient an audience in such a way that a "spectacle" is created that "serves as a meaning machine: a generator of points of view and therefore of perceptions, anxieties, aspirations, and strategies."[126] Thomas Farrell contends that part of the power of any such spectacle comes from its ability not only to blur the lines between reality and imagery but to allow audiences the aesthetic pleasure of witnessing certain experiences.[127] While not all social dramas that are constructed by the media, politicians, or other opinion leaders are dynamic spectacles, on occasion events allow communities to define themselves as collectives by sharing certain configurations of beliefs.

In the first quarter of the twentieth century, leaders of the eugenics movement tried valiantly to popularize their principles, and in the process they attempted to create some of these dynamic spectacles. Some eugenicists were sensitive to the fact that the movement had an image problem—many Anglo-Americans regarded the study of the wellborn as more of a cult than a science—and they searched for ways of improving popular perceptions. Realizing that the average English or American citizen might not read the *Eugenical News* or the *Eugenics Review,* they looked for persuasive devices that would graphically convey to the masses the perils of the unfit and the promises of eugenics.

One of the most popular ways of disseminating eugenical messages to the public was by combining entertainment with art and education with recreation.[128] In England and the United States, contests were set up in which people competed to be named parents of "fit" babies. Often such forms of entertainment were dreamed up by people like Elizabeth Tyler, who started her public career working as a hygienist in tenement communities. In the early 1910s, Tyler helped start some of the American "better babies" movements.[129]

In the early 1920s, eugenicists began to create spectacular shows that would be displayed all over the country and demonstrate to the farmer and urban dweller alike the dangers of the feebleminded and the degenerates in America. Leaders of the eugenics movements began to construct elaborate displays to show how tainted families threatened the germplasm of civilization. Perhaps the most famous of these displays stood in the halls of Congress for months prior to the passage of the Immigration Restriction Bill in 1924, but I would argue that just as effective were the local displays that were presented by eugenicists at many state fairs and carnivals in the 1920s.[130] During that second decade of the century, "fitter family contests" were added to the repertoire of techniques employed by eugenicists. The American Eugenics Society was able to convince officials in Topeka, Kansas, to add exhibits and contests at their Kansas Free Fair.[131] In the following years, eugenics propaganda was disseminated at seven to ten fairs every year, and local papers often gave front-page attention both to the competitions and to their winners.[132] One contest brochure advertised that the time had come to accept the fact that the "science of human husbandry must be developed."[133]

These fairs were powerful tools of persuasion because they allowed anyone to participate who could show that they had taken the trouble to discover their family eugenic history. Individuals who submitted themselves to the examiners had to suffer the ordeal of a medical examination, a Wasserman test, psychiatric scrutiny, and various intelligence tests, but this seemed a small price for being certified as eugenically fit.[134] Governor Jonathan Davis appeared at the 1924 Kansas Free Fair to hand out the "Governor's Fitter Family Trophy." As one fair brochure proclaimed, "This trophy and medal are worth more than livestock sweepstakes or a Kansas Oil Well. For health is wealth and a sound mind in a sound body is the most priceless of human possessions."[135] Medals were given to the winners of these fitness contests, and these medallions portrayed two "diaphanously garbed parents, their arms outstretched toward their eugenically meritorious infant."[136] By staging these events, eugenicists were bringing together both the material realities of the participants and the symbolic world of eugenics. Regardless of whether one was found "fit," many people acted out the process of trying to prove their fitness, thereby helping to legitimate the process itself. By submitting to the rules of the contest, families articulated their belief that there was such a construct as "parenthood" and that this involved some issue of eugenical "fitness."

At British and American fairs these exhibits served the same function as when they appeared in the halls of Congress during debates over immigration restrictions—they allowed their audiences to visualize the importance of "positive" and "negative" eugenics and to observe firsthand the havoc that came from the reproduction of the unfit. The exhibits presented at these fairs and expositions reinforced the lessons of the eugenicists' lectures and books, and they also made it easier for the public to understand the rudiments of the laws of Mendelian inheritance.[137] At the same time, the charts could show some of the differences between "normal" and "abnormal" crossings, and children could follow out their ancestral lines to watch the hereditary power of the germplasm within their own families. One of these charts admonished its readers to remember that, "Unfit human threats such as feeblemindedness, epilepsy, criminality, insanity, alcoholism, pauperism, and many others run in families and are inherited in exactly the same way as color in guinea pigs."[138] Farmers and other audiences had seen with their own eyes how color worked in animals, and they had seen families that they considered unfit, so some of these eugenical arguments must have seemed reasonable. A placard at one of these fairs asked: "How long are we Americans to be so careful for the pedigree of our pigs and chickens and cattle, and then leave the ancestry of our children to chance, or to 'blind' sentiment?"[139]

By the turn of the century, some of these exhibits were altered to reflect the progress of eugenics. In the early thirties, as advocates of the new science moved away from hard-line stories and toward more reform-oriented interpretations, the exhibits also changed. One eugenicist, writing in the *Eugenics Review* in 1932, claimed that road tours were being used to help with the "democratization of eugenics."[140] In one small town in the Midlands of England, exhibits were presented to the factory workers, wives and children who "realized, for the first time, that heredity meant something. The next week it would be in a southern market town, taking a decorous part in a municipal demonstrating of mutual admiration, and being intelligently, critically, and sympathetically investigated by farmers and rural labourers. It was (and is) always accompanied by a lecturer, whose frequent five-minute talks to groups, ranging from three or four to twenty or thirty, form half the value of the show."[141]

Sometimes these exhibits were provided to keep up the morale of some of the upper classes. For example, one eugenicist wrote that it was a real "scoop" when the Royal Agricultural Society was persuaded to allow the Eugenics Society to have exhibits in its annual shows. This commentator believed that this meant that eugenicists had touched a "ready-made public, and for ten hours a day, five days in the year, 'put eugenics across' to people who had never heard the word, but thoroughly believed in the principle."[142] Yet by the 1930s, it was obvious that the more difficult task of these exhibitors was to persuade the members of all classes of the need for eugenics. Commenting on Hobson's work, one writer noted that "While she also secured a great deal of support from the Press, from medical men, psychiatrists, and other intellectual quarters, undoubtedly the greatest achievement was the enlisting of a large number of working-class organizations. In other words, she has been largely instrumental in providing that the demand for sterilization should be a spontaneous movement from below, from the general population, instead of an attempted imposition—as it would surely have been called—by a minority of the 'privileged' classes."[143] In both England and the United States, eugenicists obviously put a great deal of stock in the ability of these shows to influence the growth of the movement at all levels.

Dying a Eugenic Death: The Temporality of War and the Eternal Germplasm

In the years prior to World War I, eugenics became so popular that many thought of it as a cult rather than a science, yet the quest for "national efficiency" was soon to turn deadly. In England the study of the wellborn came to involve more than the provision of facilities for the "mentally deficient": it became a way of thinking for many who anxiously watched the approach of war in Europe. The college educated joined Fabian societies in their youth and found themselves having to prove their fitness on the fields of Flanders. Eugenical ideas offered a way of discussing whether Britain should go to war.

By 1917, the staggering losses during the war intensified the fears of neo-Malthusians and eugenicists alike, who now began to wonder if in the long run the "thousands of empty, silent cradles" were proof of Britain's declining imperial fortunes.[144] Reports from the front of staggering losses seemed to give credibility to the eugenicists who lamented the "dysgenic" effects of the war. In 1916, the National Birth-Rate Commission finally presented its delayed report, and many members concluded that the war had exacerbated the problems associated with declining fertility rates among native Englanders.[145] Some estimated that with the loss of 700,000 men of child-producing age and more than 1.6 million wounded and maimed, it would be difficult to replace the cream of the British empire. Now eugenicists found themselves allied with various other communities intent on improving both the numbers and qualities of the next generation of Britishers who would fill the ranks of the dead. When it came time to reappoint a chair for the National Birth-Rate Commission, the moderate eugenicist Caleb Saleeby was chosen.

Although he had been sympathetic to some of the neo-Malthusian arguments before the war, Saleeby now believed that the casualties of war demanded that the nation be concerned with more than the quality of its citizens. The head of the National Birth-Rate Commission began to warn his audiences that England was surrounded by nations like Germany, which had the ability (with a population of seventy million) to place twice as many troops on the battlefield as England could.[146] In order to counterbalance this demographic imbalance, eugenicists, public health officials, and other concerned citizens began to support measures like the encouragement of early marriages, the birth of more children, tax inducements, educational bonuses, better housing, expanded medical facilities, and improved prenatal care.[147] Within this cultural milieu, eugenical arguments became a way of thinking about the world that went well beyond simply discussing the laws of genetics. Now British audiences found themselves being lectured about the selfishness of the "better" classes.

Eugenics became popular as a means of explaining how British men and women should respond to the exigencies of war, yet not all protectors of the germplasm were sure that a nation of forty million people even ought to be fighting—especially fighting other members of the white race. The war divided the eugenicists as it did other communities. Some like Inge, Hobson, and Crichton-Brown did not believe there was any need for an enlarged birth rate, and they refused to sign some of the proclamations of the Birth-Rate Commission.[148] Other eugenicists, such as Marchant, began to assert that contraception was causing sterility and "life destroying tragedies" like miscarriage and infant mortality.[149] Stories that had been manufactured at the turn of the century regarding artificial means of birth control became a part of new narratives that attacked famous freethinkers and liberals as villains who were contributing to the race suicide of the nation.[150]

Many eugenicists took the podium to complain that the war was being fought by the best that England had to offer while the shirkers and defectives stayed home to pollute the germplasm of the nation. The roll of honor that was called in every school and college reminded the living that British officers were paying a disproportionate price on the battlefield. Even before hearing of the casualty reports, one writer in the *Eugenics Review* claimed that "eugenics and [the] dysgenic effects of war are about to be put to the supreme test."[151] In the early years of the war, Britain relied on volunteers, causing eugenicists to warn that the nation's "battle death-rate must strike unevenly and reduce the number of her males amongst the class from which it is most desirable that she should produce the stock of the future" and that the "cream of the race will be taken and the skimmed milk will be left."[152] Eugenical arguments thus became a way of rationalizing to family members the sacrifices that were being made by the virile, chivalrous, and patriotic members of the empire. Some eugenicists, like Eugenics Education Society president Leonard Darwin, hoped that conscription would mean that the casualty lists would begin to represent a random sample of the population rather than simply "the best."[153] Caleb Saleeby went so far as to admit that the National Birth-Rate Commission was "trying to persuade the men as far as possible to marry before they go."[154] "Baby Weeks" were established in order to help encourage the population to think about baby bonuses, maternal allotments, milk funds, and other pronatalist schemes.

While England fought the Kaiser's troops, Americans joined the "preparedness" movements that sprang up across the country in case America should enter the European conflict.[155] Some citizens thought that preparation for war would bring the nation together by making foreigners and misfits part of the readiness effort. Disregarding the rhetoric of some of the strict hereditarians, many who wrote on the need for the United States to have its own fit military selectively incorporated eugenical fragments in their efforts to persuade both Congress and the American public that preparedness was the antidote for the poisons that plagued the masses. Groups like the Military Training Camps Association began lobbying Congress for universal military training.[156] Many who joined in the preparedness movement were successful business and professional men from old

East Coast families who wanted to stem the disunity that challenged their social principles and position by reestablishing a moral code reminiscent of the puritan tradition.[157] A plethora of speeches, pamphlets, and journal articles were written encouraging Americans to remember that "class hatred" was unnecessarily dividing the nation into hostile camps of plutocrats and proletarians, where the "selfish rich" were pitted against the "lunatic fringe."[158]

Many Americans learned their lessons about "race suicide" and eugenics not from Madison Grant or Charles Davenport but from one of the greatest of American heroes, Theodore Roosevelt. During the years before the First World War, Roosevelt and his Rough Rider regiment were turned by the American press into living legends who continually invited their audiences to believe that a divided country could be united and uplifted through military training and preparation for war. Like other eugenicists, Roosevelt felt that it was "character" and not economic programs that could resolve some of the social problems of the civilized world. Writing on "Twisted Eugenics" in January of 1914, Roosevelt told his readers that

> a trained "Professor of Eugenics" forgets that a great war may do for the whole nation a service that incalculably outweighs all possible evil effects. The type [*sic*] example of this is our own Civil War. That war cost half a million lives. It is certainly a sad and evil thing that timid and weak people, the peace-at-any-price and anti-militaristic people who stayed at home, should have left descendants to admire well-meaning, feeble articles against militarism, while their valiant comrades went to the front and perished. Yet the price paid, great though it was, was not too great to pay for the union of the Nation and the freedom of the slave. Worthy writers on eugenics must not forget that heroes serve as examples. . . . if war is so demanded, then the timid prig who shrinks from it, whether or not he covers his shrinking under the name of "eugenics," stands beside the man who will not risk his life to save women and children from a burning building, or the man who declines to work for his wife and children because there is danger in that work.[159]

For Roosevelt and many members of the preparedness movement, the true application of eugenics came from living a life of personal and civic well-being and not from sitting behind a desk.

The persona that Roosevelt created allowed both conservative and liberal, cowboy and Eastern banker, to share in the experience of building up one's mind and body and at the same time serving one's country. During the Spanish-American War, a variety of factions had come together in the Rough Riders—the "sons of New York Bankers, East Coast industrialists, and agrarian debtors"—and now with the development of war preparedness some thought it was time to relive those times and bring back the American virtues of the hardy frontier days.[160] From 1898 until 1927, speakers like Leonard Wood claimed that military training would promote the work ethic, lower the crime rate, Americanize the immigrant, and bind together all of the classes of society.[161] A professor of "mental diseases" at the University of Pennsylvania testified before the Senate in 1917 that "Universal military training will do much to stiffen up" and "make firm-fibered and manly" America's youth.[162] The editor of the *Boston Medical and Surgical Journal* claimed in 1913 that certain patients would stand a better chance of recovery if "they were sent to the battlefield instead of the sanitarium."[163]

In sum, the vague ideograph "eugenics" provided both hard-line hereditarians and more environmentally oriented social reformers with plenty of verbal ammunition in British debates over the eugenic or dysgenic effects of war. Those militarists or pacifists who discussed fitness and the positive influence of a healthy environment were not anti-eugenic but rather the exponents of a more expansive concept of what it meant to be healthy or wellborn. Rhetorically this allowed advocates of eugenics to appeal both to the officer classes and to the soldiers who served under them. For many who fought or prepared to fight, World War I could yet redeem the immigrants and make for lasting social reforms.[164]

There were also divisions within the eugenics movement over the issue of the assimilation of immigrants and non-Anglo-Saxon "races." Long before the passage of the Immigration Restrictions Acts of 1924, foreign men and women who came to America found themselves being depicted as parasitic carriers of tainted germplasm that threatened the purity of native Americans.[165] With the popularization of eugenics in the decades before the Great War, many Americans found themselves ambivalent about what to do with their new neighbors. Members of the preparedness movement appealed at various times to immigrants who seemed to have the potential to become United States citizens. Yet many movement leaders reassured their audiences that it took time to become an American. Henry Stimson, for example, believed that training would inspire "the great stream of immigration composed largely of men who never had the lesson of loyalty which was instilled in our fathers by the wars, the privations and the common experiences of our national growth."[166] Nicholas Ray Butler saw war as a "unifying force of national necessity and conscious national purpose."[167] Many felt that while inequality within society would still persist, at least the idea of universal military training would allow a certain amount of respect to be instilled, and some of the misunderstandings that contributed to class struggle would be reduced. For Wood, the presence of millions of immigrants from southern and eastern Europe, combined with industrial growth that brought a corrupting marketplace morality, threatened to lower the fitness of the average American.[168] One method that was suggested for combatting some of the nation's ills was to have military action that would be "a Crucible burning out selfishness." [169]

While universal military training was supposed to remove some of the objectionable qualities of the alien, it was also supposed to be a means of creating eugenically fit native Americans. The U.S. Army chief of staff wanted a system of universal military training for "character building" that would provide the means of developing "a new and better [form of] American manhood." The last thing Americans needed were pacifists, who were a form of "moral syphilis" and the "typhoid carriers [who] poison the very life of the people." [170] The universal military training program had wide public support, evidenced by the fact that in 1916, seventy-nine presidents of state medical associations, nineteen presidents of national medical societies, and representatives of ninety-five medical schools went on record favoring universal military training.[171] In many ways, those Americans who prepared themselves for war believed themselves to be eugenically fit and ready for combat.[172]

America would eventually enter World War I, and on the fields of Europe millions of soldiers would provide the ultimate sacrifice for some of their eugenical beliefs. While the eugenical frame of mind was obviously not the only rhetorical influence in the constellation of forces that helped make war a reality, it was in its own right a very powerful rationalization for engaging in global warfare. At least one generation would make the full circle from the cradle to the grave. By 1927, Raymond Pearl could claim that eugenics had "largely become a mingled mess of ill-grounded and uncritical sociology, economics, anthropology, and politics, full of emotional appeals to class and race prejudices, solemnly put forth as science, and unfortunately accepted as such by the general public." [173] Over time, many scholars would ask critics of the movement to celebrate our escape from a dark and haunting past. Yet the graves of millions on the European continent serve as eloquent reminders of the risks we take in ignoring the power of eugenical discourse.

No bill considered by the General Assembly in recent years has had a national significance so great as that providing for racial integrity. It is the first step toward guaranteeing to future generations a white America. It is of interest, not only to Virginia, but to the rest of the United States. . . . Unfortunately, the solution of it has not yet commended itself to the less thoughtful persons as a vital necessity.

Richmond Times Dispatch editorial, 1924

[R]ace amalgamation proceeds much, more rapidly where the races are socially and economically unequal. . . . Education opportunity to develop economic independence and the guarantee of basic independence and the guarantee of basic justice and common citizenship rights are the three factors which I regard not only as the most promising but as the fundamentally necessary conditions for the amelioration of race relations in America.

Alain L. Locke, 1925

3

Race and African-American Interpretations of Eugenics

From writers like Haller, Pickens, Ludmerer, and Kevles we have a wealth of information on the views of hard-line eugenicists on subjects like "race crossing" and "amalgamation," but in many of the discussions of race and eugenics in the United States there is a conspicuous absence of the views of African-American writers.[1] At first one might think that American blacks would have been univocally opposed to any form of racism or biologically deterministic arguments, but an ideographic analysis of the first several decades of the twentieth century reveals a far more complex picture. As I illustrate below, the upper- and middle-class blacks who made up the "talented tenth" of the African-American population found themselves in a precarious position. Black intellectuals had to address the claims of nativist whites while at the same time exhorting their economically impoverished brothers and sisters to rise out of their lower-class positions. African-American rhetors soon found that the new science of eugenics was a sword that cut two ways.

Racism and the Hard-line Eugenics Challenge

Long before Galton mentioned the word "eugenics," many African-Americans had experienced what it meant to live in a system that counted both the quantity and "quality" of a race. During the years of slavery, black men and women were dehumanized by a system that profited from the breeding of slaves. Historian Frederick Bancroft once wrote that next "to the great and quick profit from bringing virgin soil under cultivation, slave-rearing was the surest, most remunerative and most approved means of increasing agricultural capital." [2] Frederick Douglass, the black abolitionist who himself was once a slave, remembered when poor whites purchased black women as "breeders." [3] By slave law, the progeny of slave unions were the property of the slave owners, thus creating incentives for the breeding of slaves.[4] Although historians have debated the exact extent and the nature of slave breeding, we have eyewitness accounts and narratives by slaves themselves who have reported on their own mistreatment.[5]

In order to legitimate the existence of slavery in the land of "liberty," slave owners and anxious Northerners had to craft a rhetoric that differentiated between those humans who could stand the mental strains of freedom—the whites higher up on the evolutionary scale—and those races that had to remain bound by positive laws that placed restrictions on this liberty—usually people of color within the symbolic world of slave communities.[6] African-Americans living in the first half of the nineteenth century thus faced a symbolic world in which they were designated at birth as members of an immature species that could not enjoy either "perfect liberty" or "perfect independence." They were destined to live under the humanely constructed laws that were written in order to protect them in this state of "infantile helplessness."

Some of these ancient interpretations of the relationship between liberty and necessity have discursive roots that go back thousands of years, and many slave owners turned to some of these classical writings in their effort to legitimate the institution of slavery. George Fitzhugh, for example, argued in 1856 that the word "government" was itself nothing but the term "slavery" modified, and he asked his readers to accept the fact that "slavery in the abstract, slavery in the general, [and] slavery in principle, is right, natural, and necessary." [7] Defenders of slave practices used fragmentary arguments taken from politics, economics, and even human biology in order to rationalize their activities. As Thomas Szasz pointed out, slaves who fought their "enslavement" as a "necessity" found themselves labeled as insane, suffering from diseases like "drapetomania" (ideographically "runaway" + "madness") or "dysaesthesia Aethiopis" (neglect or refusal to work).[8]

African-Americans who managed to endure under this system could at least hope that the evolution of their species or of society itself would allow for more freedom and liberty, if not for themselves then for their children and grandchildren. Decades later, however, the introduction of hard-line eugenical discourse into an already volatile racial situation removed even this slim hope. In the nineteenth century, the influence of neo-Lamarckism in scientific and public discourse had made it possible to argue that the habits of the African-Americans might be changed and that education and moralization might indeed redeem the "inferior" race.[9] Thanks to the discovery of the immortal germplasm nativist Americans could now perpetuate inequitable social, economic, and political conditions on the basis of biological necessity. By refracting social relationships in the United States through the lens of hard-line eugenics ideology, racists could exhort Americans to cleanse the blood of the nation in a seemingly unprejudicial manner.

At first, some eugenicists argued that laissez-faire policies that allowed for "natural selection" would in time spell the end of the "Negro problem."[10] For decades, the media on both sides of the Atlantic had disseminated the work of Darwin and Spencer and appropriated some of their arguments in social Darwinistic accounts of human nature.[11] Many hard-line eugenicists believed that doctors, philanthropists, and social scientists were wasting their efforts in coddling a race that was rapidly becoming extinct.[12] As Carol Taylor has observed, the power of this form of racism lay in its ability to define blacks as inferior beings who could not compete with their superiors and "naturally" occupied the lowest place in the Anglo-Saxon hierarchy.[13] Francis Galton, for example, claimed in 1869 in his *Hereditary Genius* that "the average intellectual standard of the negro race is some two grades below our own."[14] The laws of nature seemed to have predestined the Native American for extinction, and blacks were considered to be the next race targeted by fate.

There were several variants of this extinction theme in the early rhetoric of the nativist eugenicists. Some neo-Lamarckians argued that the environmental conditions accompanying slavery or life outside of the tropics would bring about the end of the black race, while hard-line eugenicists believed that some essential strains of germplasm would die out if no "race crossing" with the superior whites took place. Either way, African-Americans came out the losers when they clashed with superior races in a world governed by the "survival of the fittest." Within these racial narratives, social problems like poverty, tuberculosis, venereal disease, and other ailments would eventually bring their destruction. Frederick Hoffman, author of *Race Traits and Tendencies of the American Negro*, wrote in 1896 that blacks suffered these ills because of their inherent immorality, and this would eventually destroy them as a race.[15] Any social reformers who tried to change this order could be "dismissed as romantic dreamers who had neither knowledge nor appreciation of hard scientific fact."[16]

Decades later, as it became evident that the African-American community was not going to disappear, hard-line eugenicists scrambled to find new ways of explaining the population growth of the black race that would fit their preconceived notions of hereditary unfitness. New narratives were crafted in order to explain why legislation and government intervention were needed to redress the failure of "natural selection." Hard-line eugenicists became some of the most vehement advocates of racial inequality, and their analyses provided some of the most ossifying of perspectives. Rhetors in both England and America began to claim that not only classes but *nations* needed to get involved in efforts to save the Anglo-Saxon race. Karl Pearson espoused the belief that the "superior race must reject the inferior or, mixing with it, or even living alongside of it, degenerate itself."[17] Other eugenicists thought that drastic changes were needed in the laws that seemed to treat the races as equal in ability. Edward East perhaps spoke for many when he claimed that "the Negro is a happy-go-lucky child, naturally expansive under simple conditions, oppressed by the restrictions of civilization, and unable to assume the white man's burden. He accepts his limitations; indeed, he is rather glad to have them. Only when there is white blood in his veins does he cry out against the supposed injustice of his position."[18]

Eugenicists told stories of how most blacks were content with gradual evolutionary change and that it was only the "mulattoes" or the exceptional African-American who ever tried to fight the biological necessities of life. Hard-liners assumed that many people of color simply did not have the mental equipment to do more than survive and reproduce. For one researcher, groups of blacks, Indians, and Mexicans "cannot master abstractions, but they can often be made efficient workers, able to look out for themselves. There is no possibility at present of convincing society that they should not be allowed to produce, although from a eugenic point of view they constitute a grave problem because of their unusually prolific breeding."[19] Madison Grant, a lawyer and popularizer of racist eugenics, announced in 1918 that "races vary intellectually and morally just as they do physically," and he attacked the sentimentalists who were unwilling to face life's harsh realities:

> There exists today a widespread and fatuous belief in the power of environment . . . to alter heredity. . . . Such beliefs have done much damage in the past and if allowed to go uncontradicted may do even more serious damage in the future. Thus the view that the Negro Slave was an unfortunate cousin of the white man, deeply tanned by the tropic sun and denied the blessings of Christianity and civilization, played no small part with the sentimentalists of the Civil War period and it has taken us fifty years to learn that speaking English, wearing good clothes and going to school and church does not transform a Negro into a white man.[20]

Hard-liners like Grant were convinced that the Mendelian laws of biology had disproved the neo-Lamarckian claims that blacks could pass on "acquired characteristics" gained through education, and they vilified those naive social reformers who ignored the differences between nature and nurture. Hard-liners argued that if any new legislation was to be passed, it needed to conform to the laws of biological necessity and inherent inequality. What Grant wanted was a "rigid system of selection" that would involve the sterilization of the unfit. He hoped that such state intervention would begin with the criminal and the insane but would extend eventually to include all of the "worthless race types."[21]

Grant's vocabulary and stance were neither unusual nor novel: they represented part of a much larger hard-line eugenic strategy that called for "racial purity." This ambiguous term often involved plans for legislation that would bar miscegenation, the immigration of the southern European races, and any government extension of aid to the prolific lower classes.[22] Racial cleansing would take place both within and outside of the United States. Many whites were sure that both science and politics demanded that the nation face up to the biological facts of nature. Lothrop Stoddard during a public debate with W. E. B. Du Bois claimed that "modern science" was telling America that, "Today, as never before, we possess a clear appreciation of racial realities. . . . We know that our America is a White America. . . . And the overwhelming weight of both historical and scientific evidence shows that only so long as the American people remain white will its institutions, ideals and culture continue to fit the temperament of its inhabitants—and hence continue to endure."[23]

Tragically, these views were shared by a significant portion of the white American public. Senator Walter F. George of Georgia claimed in 1928 that there was "no statutory law, no organic law, no military law" that "supersedes the law of racial necessity and social identity. Why apologize or evade?"[24] David C. Jones

perhaps typified the feelings of many of his neighbors during the first two decades of the century when he argued that "intermarriage produces halfbreeds,
and halfbreeds are not conducive to the higher type of society. We in the South
are a proud and progressive people. Halfbreeds cannot be proud. In the South
we have pure blood lines and we intend to keep it that way." [25] As America would
learn the hard way, these beliefs were not easily dislodged.

Deconstructing Biological "Necessity," 1900–1920

Opponents of hard-line eugenics thus had formidable foes. People like Stoddard,
Grant, and Davenport were not publicly stigmatized like members of the Ku
Klux Klan. Their credentials were impeccable and their scientific ethos was beyond question. American presidents kept in constant touch with many of these
writers. Yet some African-Americans did speak out against this form of eugenics.

To be sure, some African-Americans had always opposed such racism, and
they debunked these notions of inherent inferiority. Benjamin Banneker, for example, wrote as a free man to Thomas Jefferson defending the mental capabilities
of blacks, and Dr. James Smith responded to some of the racist remarks of people
like John C. Calhoun.[26] Yet the particular constellation of arguments within the
hard-line eugenics rhetoric offered African-Americans a difficult new challenge.
The abolitionist rhetoric of "equality" and "freedom" had some credibility as a
moral stance against slavery, and many thousands of Americans during the Civil
War had given their lives in the name of human justice. Yet other members of
the same Anglo-Saxon communities a half century later were espousing a creed
based on the iron laws of "biological" necessities.

In the rest of this chapter, I argue that African-Americans challenged the eugenicists in two primary ways. First, they tried to deconstruct the arguments of
the hard-line eugenicists by pointing out contradictions in the racist literature.
In time they developed their own researchers and conducted their own studies,
focusing on the environmental causes of any alleged inferiority. During this time
blacks tried to substitute the concept of "social" necessity for that of "biological"
necessity.

In their efforts to deconstruct the hard-line eugenical beliefs, African-
American writers had to contend with three major arguments. First, they had
to combat the notion that race antagonism was natural. Second, blacks had to
rebut the arguments of hard-line eugenicists that the black race was genetically
inferior. Finally, African-Americans had to disprove claims that the "unfit races"
were dying out.

Some of the fragments making up the myth of race warfare go back at least to the time of the ancient Greeks and their fear of foreigners. In the nineteenth century, writers like Arthur de Gobineau combined some of these discursive units in new rhetorical forms to show the inevitable tensions that existed between the races.[27] In America, the Reverend Josiah Strong sold hundreds of thousands of copies of *Our Country* (1885), which reminded rural Protestants that their country was about to enter a new stage of history where there would be the "final competition of the races."[28] This discourse so permeated Anglo-Saxon society that the apostle of "degeneration" theories, Max Nordau, would complain in the *North American* in 1889 that since "the theory of evolution has been promulgated, they [advocates of war] can cover their natural barbarism with the name of Darwin and proclaim the sanguinary instincts of their inmost hearts as the last word of science."[29] These laws of the survival of the fittest became an integral part of American foreign and domestic policies, but they especially impacted black men and women, who lived in a society that characterized them as a foreign, threatening race.[30]

In order to counter some of this racism and focus on the war between social communities in America, some blacks turned to their belief in the power of Christianity, humanitarianism, and the democratic elements in American constitutional language. Some claimed that the way to prevent riots and wars was simply to apply the lessons of the "gospel of wealth" to the problems of modernity.[31] Many African-Americans followed the teachings of Booker T. Washington and insisted that the creation of an independent farming and business class would eliminate the need for warfare. Others saw racial solidarity as a means of dealing with an impersonal economic and social Darwinism, and they hoped that eventually an advanced and progressive race could come out of the backward race. Many African-Americans tried to argue that racial conflict was simply a symptom of economic inequality and that over time cooperation would replace racial disharmony.

Even more difficult to combat in the eugenics narratives were the stories told about the biological inferiority of blacks. Eugenicists often argued that African-Americans had been given the chance to prove their worth and claims about social inequities following the Civil War and that blacks had failed miserably in the race of life. Many racists would have agreed with Gobineau, who lamented the fact that some people just "refuse, quite wrongly, to admit that certain qualities are by a fatal necessity the exclusive inheritance of such and such a stock."[32]

One group of individuals who refused to believe in their own inferiority were the members of the "talented tenth"—those African-Americans who had proven themselves to be the intellectual equal of most if not all whites. From the pulpit and podium these elite members of the black community attacked the assumptions of hard-line eugenicists who promoted the notion of the superiority of the "Nordic" race. Many of these writers familiarized themselves with the works of people like Grant, Stoddard, and Cox, and they attempted to eliminate the social distances between middle-class whites and the "talented tenth." Herbert Miller, for example, in an article entitled "The Myth of Superiority," lambasted those eugenicists who pretended to wield hereditary knowledge in the name of science: "When chiefs ruled by hereditary power, there was no criterion except the possession of power; but when kingship became hereditary and the birthright was not so obvious, it was necessary to call in the divine right of kings. This particular myth has been exploded . . . now the divine or cosmic power is inherent in the process itself . . . it has made easy, however, the rationalization of group egotism, through religion, the press, the law, neighborhood gossip, and now by science." [33]

Just as English writers for centuries before them had attacked the hereditary claims of the king, now blacks refused to admit that science dictated inherent Nordic superiority. One writer claimed that the Nordic superiority myth and the notion of "hundred-percent Americanism" were the two most dangerous ideas in the world.[34] Hard-line eugenicists who used intelligence tests to classify people as unfit were characterized as "pseudo-" and "half-baked" scientists who "in a few hours or weeks learned to give Binet tests" and then claimed to have so much "confidence" in their work that they treated their results as if they had "a patent medicine panacea." [35] Howard Long, writing on the relationship between eugenics, mental tests, and race psychology in the Urban League's *Opportunity,* would claim that "One who reads the work of Stoddard and Grant cannot fail to be amazed at their apparent ignorance. . . . If mental heredity is fixed, specific and unchanged by environment, why was it that the Caucasians in Western Europe awoke from their mental slumbers only recently?" [36]

Some African-Americans pointed out that hard-line eugenicists were basing many of their claims of black racial inferiority on innuendo and hearsay evidence. One commentator illustrated how white nativists were able to reconcile the contradictions that existed within eugenic ideology: "There is always a whisper for your private ear—confidential information relating to certain innate characteristics, by which this man, though personally clean, sprang from dirty seed and to dirty seed must inevitably return; by which this man, though a gentleman of ability, must be treated like a dog on account of a temporarily hidden (but absolutely certain) dog nature." [37] Hard-liners who prided themselves on their collections of family pedigrees found themselves ridiculed for assuming that "seeds" determined character.

African-American leaders hoped that over time the American public would learn that mainline eugenical prejudices depended on a false scientific paradigm that was being promoted by people who knew little if anything about the real problems of blacks. A favorite subject discussed in the leading African-American newspapers and magazines was the topic of the intelligence tests. At the same time that white social scientists were questioning the results of some of the early psychological testing methods, blacks were taking the lead in pointing out inconsistencies in some of the aims of the hard-line eugenicists. Many writers would focus their readers' attention on studies that were overlooked.[38] Like Walter Lippmann and other critics of the Army intelligence tests, these rhetors and authors found it hard to believe that educated Americans could believe in the "Nordic nonsense."

Yet many African-American writers in the years before World War I found that their attempts at deconstructing the hard-line eugenics stories were only partially successful. When blacks tried to disprove any necessary relationship between the color of their skin and their physical, mental, and moral fitness, they found that hard-line eugenicists simply responded that any intelligent or "superior" members of the "talented tenth" were exceptional blacks who merely proved the rule of racial inferiority. Within these eugenic stories, any sign of intelligence or education by African-Americans was taken as evidence that those particular persons had *white* blood somewhere in their past.[39] Black leaders like W. E. B. Du Bois were beginning to learn that as long as this hard-line eugenical sanction for racism existed, it would be nearly impossible to argue for any significant improvement because the standards were being created by an Anglo-Saxon universe of discourse. Deconstructing white rhetoric would not suffice. Du Bois perhaps summed up the problem when he wrote in *The Crisis* in 1914:

> For now nearly twenty years we have made of ourselves mudsills for the feet of this Western world. We have echoed and applauded every shameful accusation made against 10,000,000 victims of slavery. Did they call us inferior half-beasts? We nodded our simple heads and whispered: "We is." Did they call our women prostitutes and our children bastards? We smiled and cast a stone at the bruised breasts of our wives and daughters. Did they accuse of laziness 4,000,000 sweating, struggling laborers, half paid and cheated out of much of that? We shrieked: "Ain't it so?" We laughed with them at our color, we joked at our sad past, and we told chicken stories to get alms.[40]

Du Bois thus highlighted some of the problems that were created when African-Americans accepted the white portrayals of blacks in the popular press. He was inviting the liberal black intellectuals who made up the "talented tenth" to take up the challenge of creating new standards as well as deconstructing white mythologies.

In the first several decades of the twentieth century, because few black intellectuals felt qualified to attack some of the eugenical claims, they depended on the authority of liberal white scholars. African-Americans invited speakers like Franz Boas to lecture on the problems of unilinear, hereditarian views of race. In 1909 John Dewey addressed the National Negro Congress and warned his audience that "a society that does not furnish the environment and education and the opportunity of all kinds which will bring out and make effective the superior ability where ever it is born" was depriving itself of social capital.[41] At the same conference, Livingston Farrand of Columbia University remarked that "Blood will tell, but we do not know just what it tells, nor which blood it is which speaks." [42]

Many of the speeches and articles written by white intellectuals were disseminated into the African-American press in newspapers like the Chicago *Defender* and periodicals like the *Crisis* and *Opportunity*.[43] Within these and other newspapers and journals, eugenical arguments were attacked for their prejudice, reductionism, and pseudoscientific foundations. Intellectuals like Herbert Miller would lampoon concepts like the "Nordic myth" by pointing out that the hard-line eugenicists had merely taken "the vocabulary of science" and "appropriated its methods" in order to "prove what men want to prove, namely their moral right to keep what they want." [44]

The third element of the hard-line racial narrative that had to be deconstructed was the notion that the black race was eventually going to become extinct. As census reports and other surveys began to show that African-Americans were growing in numbers, blacks triumphantly used this information to illustrate the fitness of their race. If survival or ability to reproduce was going to be a eugenical criterion for race potential, then African-Americans were going to make the most of biological discussions. As one black would triumphantly observe, "Unlike the Indian, the Negro is destined to remain a big factor in our civilization. He is here to stay." [45]

On the surface eugenical claims that called attention to the extinction of the black race seem to have been based on ignorance of the laws of genetics or simply blatant racism, but they served an important ideological function for the hardliners. By claiming that the black race would die out if left alone, natives could claim that "amalgamation" meant that African-Americans were interrupting a natural process. This type of argument served two rhetorical functions. First, it framed racial issues in social Darwinian terms that involved notions of the "survival of the fittest." Second, it answered the claims of blacks who continually mentioned the effect of slavery on race relations. Hard-line eugenicists could thus claim that it was blacks and not whites who wanted racial amalgamation. When native whites talked about the "necessity" of "racial purity," blacks used these discussions for their own political and social agendas. Eugenical arguments were reconfigured into stories of white oppression and racial injustice. Many African-American articles on miscegenation refuted white notions that blacks favored the mixing of the races in order to survive. Pickens, for example, argued that the effects of a law forbidding intermarriage between the races was to lower the status of colored women without raising the status of white women or preventing racial intermixture.[46] In the black narratives, it was not the white race that was being threatened with racial impurity but rather the "minority" race that was being hurt by giving "immunity to the men of the stronger race."[47] African-Americans warned that antimiscegenation laws would do nothing to stop the lust of some whites but would simply produce a race of bastards. For many blacks, the issue was not pollution of the blood but the power relationships that existed in a purportedly democratic society. One angry writer claimed in 1915 that

> not since the foundation of human society has any serious problem existed between the men of a weaker and the women of a stronger group. The weak are never tempted to impose upon the strong, and a prohibition of marriage simply further protects the strong in its imposition upon the weak, by nullifying the traditional rule of objective morality which compels the man to accept his mate and acknowledge his offspring. The intermarriage law is in effect a discrimination against the women and the weak. And wherever any race is ninety millions and rich and powerful, while another race is ten millions and poor and disadvantaged, the case will be the same.[48]

Blacks thus redeployed some of the language of social Darwinism and patriarchy in order to force white racists to cover up the contradictions in their own stories.

At first, many leaders believed that the way to combat the miscegenation rumors would be for the legal system to tackle the problem of racial prejudice and segregation. In the first few decades of the twentieth century, some African-Americans interested in continual opposition to Jim Crow laws and eugenics legislation believed that any lasting social change needed to come from the highest court responsible for dispensing justice—the United States Supreme Court. In spite of occasional setbacks like the 1896 *Plessy v. Ferguson* "separate but equal" decision, and the existence of Jim Crow laws, many blacks felt that the most efficacious method of consciousness raising was still through the federal courts. Kelly Miller, who wrote profusely on the eugenics issue, argued in the late 1920s that even though states like Virginia were passing miscegenation statutes, hope still remained because the Supreme Court had only dealt with the issue of "race identity superficially." The nation's highest appellate court has passed upon many cases involving the question of race distinction and race discrimination, but it had always dealt with race identity superficially.[49]

While hopeful that Americans would recognize the contradictions that existed within their nation, blacks living during the first quarter of the century were also pragmatic. They understood that simply pointing out contradictions in the land of liberty and appealing to the judiciary for fair treatment would not be enough. If racists were going to employ the weapons of science, then they had to be countered with scientific as well as moral arguments. Without scientific proof of the inherent equality of human beings, claims that blacks were entitled to "equal opportunity" could be countered by racist claims that no advancement had been made by blacks since Emancipation and that "freedom" had therefore failed to make African-Americans equal to whites.[50] Eugenicists argued that attempts at amelioration had if anything worsened the condition of blacks and attempts at forcing equality had meant retrogression for both races.

Reform Eugenics and the "New Negro": Redefining African-American Necessities, 1921–1935

By the early 1920s many blacks in America were disheartened. Leaders like W. E. B. Du Bois had encouraged minorities to join the ranks of Americans fighting in World War I in the hope that this would prove black fitness, but in many cases exposure to less discriminatory cultures abroad merely exacerbated tensions when the troops returned. Adult blacks found that they were coping with a racist ideology that was planted deeply in the hearts and minds of even the young. One African-American, traveling in the South after Virginia passed its "Pure Race Law," complained that the "same white boy that plays in the streets with the colored boy by day may be taken on his mother's lap by night, and told that all Negroes carry razors, that they rape white women, that they steal chickens and watermelons, that they shoot craps, that they are ignorant and lazy, that they are not to be trusted, and that they are to be kept in their places. This propaganda is drilled into the boy; it is illustrated by newspapers and magazines; the Sunday School literature which he studies emphasizes the truth of it; the pulpit from which he hears the gospel preached sanctions it."[51]

For Joseph Carroll, what made things worse was the fact that people were listening to the rhetoric of the "Anglo-Saxon clubs of America" in Virginia and believing their claims that "industrial education" had failed to solve the "Negro problem." [52] Carroll asked each of his readers in the 1920s to remember that "His blood runs like a scarlet thread, all the way from Boston Commons, across three thousand leagues of blue deep to Flanders Fields and the remotest shores of France. Our fathers helped to plant the tree of liberty, and we their sons in every generation have been ready and willing to water it with our own blood and tears. We claim allegiance to no other flag save that of the stars and stripes; we are not hyphenated Americans." [53] Many young African-Americans were confused by a system that seemed to welcome with open arms millions of foreign immigrants and yet paid little attention to what happened to blacks unless it "be a Rhinelander or a Sweet case." [54]

In their efforts to counter the influence of the eugenical racism many African-American scientists, writers, and journalists went beyond repudiations of hardline racism. These blacks emphasized the equality or even superiority of black germplasm. While still inviting and using research conducted by white liberals, now blacks drew on the efforts of members of their own race. As one writer lamented in the *Crisis* of 1924: "The trouble with most white scientists who study the problem of the Negro is that they lack sympathetic understanding. Hence the number of quasi-scientific studies of the Negro. . . . The army tests only furnish a glaring example. There are others equally as absurd. . . . The social attitude and sympathetic insight, as well as scientific accuracy are essential in the study of group and racial problems. Eugenics will improve the Negro of the future." [55] Many liberal blacks believed that white America needed to see a new image of the typical African-American that would counter the caricatures being circulated in the popular press by eugenicists and other racists. People like Joseph Carroll began arguing that if any "necessity" existed, it was to challenge the ignorance of the white people by showing them the power of the "New Negro." [56] In order to persuade white America that eugenics was a false scientific creed, many black intellectuals began to launch a counteroffensive in an all-out war against hereditarianism. Horace Bond, writing in 1924, would contend that through "ignorance of the facts, we have chosen to be silent rather than to expose our naivete. That time has passed. No longer is there justification for the silence of the educated Negro." [57]

To go along with the new image of the African-American there had to be change in the traditions and stories that were created to support the beliefs that were circulating in the African-American press about the need for "social" necessities. Blacks refused to accept the hard-liners' attacks on equality and opportunity, and they rarely failed to mention the environmental conditions that created necessitous circumstances. Much like other groups who opposed hereditarian eugenics, intellectual blacks did not abandon all interpretations of eugenics but rather attempted to create a "reform" perspective that took into account the effects of environment and culture in the progress of the races. Editorials began to appear in the 1920s African-American press that, on the basis of research conducted by blacks, directly challenged some of the assumptions at the core of the eugenics creed. For example, in the *Opportunity* of June 1923, one critic claimed that the amount of "white blood" in southern Negroes was as general as it was in Northern Negroes and that this blood had nothing to do with the state of mind of blacks or their mental abilities.[58] Social scientists like Horace Bond would have the audacity to question the results of the Army intelligence tests by pointing out that according to the test scores, there seemed to be a marked difference between the intelligence of northern and southern *whites*.[59] As one scholar has recently observed, the discourse that was produced within the first African-American scientific communities did not attack the testing measures themselves but rather focused attention on the lack of "opportunities" evidenced by such tests.[60]

New stories began to be created that looked at the way in which both "positive" and "negative" eugenics could be used in helping blacks improve their economic and social well-being. A typical example of the constructive arguments that appeared in African-American newspapers can be found in the work of Albert Beckham, who wrote an article entitled "Applied Eugenics," which appeared in the *Crisis* in 1924.[61] Beckham, unlike many hard-line eugenicists, saw eugenics as a science that could improve *any* race. Beckham commented how strange it was that "scientists, sentimentalists, and even philanthropists have almost entirely overlooked eugenics in the universal consideration of the Negro and his problems." In Beckham's reconstruction of the goals of eugenics, blacks would profit from a study of the mental, moral, and physical aspects of a race. Beckham claimed that "Eugenics is interested in breeding for tomorrow a better negro. One more anxious, more capable, and more courageous to assume a larger share of our economic, political and social responsibilities. No one nowadays doubts unusual abilities in the individual Negro. . . . What the Negro needs and needs now is more attention given to the group."[62]

In the 1920s, some of this discourse began to resemble the eugenical narratives that were being constructed by other groups — women, liberals, and laborers — that used a combination of nature and nurture to legitimate radical social reforms. Beckham's reconstruction claimed that "Eugenics is not a panacea for all racial ills, but it is a pathway that leads to the solving of a number of racial problems with which we have to contend."[63] Beckham's discourse was unlike mainline white eugenical stories in several ways. First, he did not emphasize the need for legal measures to redress the evolutionary balance. For this African-American writer, "eugenics in the religion of the Negro" would mean a "rise of a better and educated ministry."[64] At the same time, Beckham did not differentiate between the races—eugenics was "necessary" for all the races. Third, Beckham was willing to concede that eugenics was not a panacea for all racial ills, something that hard-liners were rarely willing to admit. Yet Beckham was convinced that eugenics might offer a way for his race to prove its fitness, and he argued that "The future problems of the Negro will be the elimination of the unfit and the perpetuation of the fit. Eugenics applied to the Negro will be a successful experiment. If the Negro is to come into his full capacities he must not be afraid to experiment. He must see how the facts of modern science can contribute to his progress."[65] This reform variant of eugenics would have been attractive to those blacks who wanted to advance social reforms in the name of a new applied science.

In the abstract, many African-Americans could agree on the importance of eugenics and race betterment. But in the latter part of the 1920s, they were faced with concrete manifestations of the applied science that were clearly objectionable. When Virginia began passing miscegenation regulations that aimed at improving the health and "racial integrity" of the Commonwealth, the black press went on the offensive.[66] African-Americans had been successful in previous decades in preventing the passage of such laws in other states (for example, New York), but Virginia seemed to be a losing case.[67] But blacks used even this setback to voice their concerns over the precedent that had been set. One critic commented that: "Science has established no racial discriminant. The microscope reveals no distinction in human bloods based on race. Besides, who can declare the Negro generation? Frederick Douglass used to say that genealogical trees did not flourish among slaves. The recent eugenic law of Virginia forbids the intermarriage of a white person with any other person with a traceable degree of non-white blood."[68]

Passing a "necessary" law was one thing and enforcing it another, and whites in Virginia found that it was sometimes extremely difficult to tell who was white under the new miscegenation statute. The African-American press began a campaign across the country aimed at pointing out some of the contradictions in the racists' stories. One commentator in the *Chicago Defender* described (in an article entitled "Racial Integrity Bill Hits Snag in State of Virginia") "the consternation in the Virginia Legislature when the law-makers found that the proposed law prohibiting the marriage of any colored person to any white person threatened to expose many family skeletons."[69] When blacks pointed out that the legislators themselves might have "mongrel blood," embarrassed white Virginians began to claim that their descendants had Indian rather than African-American germplasm.[70]

Yet what seemed to be a temporary embarrassment for whites was deadly serious for blacks, who expended a great deal of energy turning talk of necessity away from issues of nature and toward those of nurture.[71] African-Americans had good reason to fear miscegenation statutes and the stories told by racists, not because they were in a rush to marry whites but because of the loss of racial pride and cultural identity they threatened. Miller, commenting on the Virginia law, observed that "no subordinate group, shut off socially from the dominant majority, can hope for equality of rights or privileges without identity."[72] Many African-Americans believed that the miscegenation laws were written to imply that blacks were members of an impure race trying to hide its inferiority by "mixing" with pure Anglo-Saxons.

Many of these new African-American reconstructions of eugenics were meant to sever the links between the power of the new science and miscegenation legislation. Black narratives in the 1920s claimed that miscegenation laws represented the latest threat to the economic and political power of future generations of African-Americans. Many realized that if the nation followed Virginia in its passage of "racial purity" laws, there would be little chance that whites would take seriously the notion that education and equal opportunity were the ways to bring about racial assimilation. Arguments about the "mongrelization" of the races were in part based on theories of how one generation of blacks might appear to be intelligent or equal but that impure germplasm could show up at any time in a person's descendants. The *Searchlight,* a weekly publication of the Ku Klux Klan in Atlanta, on April 1, 1922, quoted a minister in Texas as saying, "Imagine the next generation of a mulatto generation. Two thousand years of Anglo-Saxon civilization, purchased on a hundred fields of blood, calmly sacrificed on the altar of social equality."[73] Thus even blacks who prided themselves on being members of the "talented tenth" were treated as "mulattoes" who stood in the way of racial progress. Any scheme to improve the health, housing, medical care, or education of African-Americans in the hard-line eugenics worldview was simply money wasted on the selfishness of a single generation.

African-Americans who were part of the "talented tenth" countered claims of biological necessity with stories about the impact of environment and the need for America to respond to "social" necessity.[74] The "New Negro" joined organizations like the National Association for the Advancement of Colored People (NAACP) and the National Urban League and used their publications as forums to discredit nativist eugenical accounts. While nativists tried to paint blacks as some of the primary carriers of inferior germplasm, African-American rhetors reminded audiences that health-related issues crossed social boundaries. One writer of the period observed that "germs of disease have no race prejudice. They do not even draw the line at social equality, but gnaw with equal avidity at the vitals of white and black alike, and pass with the greatest freedom of intercourse from one to the other."[75] While some African-American newspapers occasionally accepted hereditarian eugenics, most constantly voiced their opinions about the need for the improvement of the environment.[76]

Ironically, the passage of some of these miscegenation laws served to reinvigorate rather than discourage blacks in their quest for racial equality. Many writers of the period believed that the Anglo-Saxon clubs represented the rear-guard actions of racists who were trying to bring back their own version of the lost cause.[77] The "talented tenth" in the 1920s began to write stories of how if anything was inevitable it was not the extinction of the black race but the future amalgamation of the races. W. E. B. Du Bois wrote that "In the future, miscegenation is going to be widely practiced in the world and that despite the likes and dislikes of present living beings. We today can at least determine whether such race mixture shall be between intelligent, self-respecting and self-determining people, or between masters and slaves. Any attempt to stop miscegenation today by forcing millions of men into pauperism and ignorance and by making their women prostitutes and concubines is too nasty and barbaric to be faced even by hypocritical America."[78] For many African-Americans, racist eugenical debates simply provided new ways of pointing out the power relationships that contributed to pauperism and ignorance.

Oftentimes the "New Negro" crafted stories out of these racist fragments in order to provide social commentary on activities like lynching, rape, and marriage restrictions. When nativists talked about natural "repugnance" and the need for lynchings, blacks articulated their concerns that miscegenation laws shielded whites who were trying to keep African-Americans in a servile state. James Weldon Johnson and Herbert Seligmann claimed in 1928 that the NAACP was working toward opposition to laws proposed in northern states which would prohibit marriage between persons of white and Negro ancestry, on the grounds that such laws deprived "colored women of the legal protection and in effect constitute a Magna Charta of concubinage and bastardy." [79] When nativists told chivalrous tales that allowed eugenicists to play the role of knights defending the honor of white women, blacks responded that these same laws deprived colored women of that same protection.

For white nativists, miscegenation laws represented simply one part of a much larger hard-line eugenic program, but for blacks these debates illustrated the depth of their dilemmas. Many blacks wanted to maintain their ethnic integrity while at the same time receiving the same social opportunities as whites. Accepting the concept race purity might help maintain racial ethnicity but at a cost of acquiescing in a separateness that might preclude social mobility. If blacks contested miscegenation statutes, they were labeled as "mulattoes" attempting to imitate whites. African-Americans compromised by attacking eugenical laws but providing their own stories and rationales for these attacks. [80]

In Virginia, the African-American press used some of the arguments of their "talented tenth" in an effort to stop the passage of the "racial integrity" bill. [81] For example, the Norfolk *Journal and Guide* was quick to point out that the bill made provisions for the white race but neglected the racial integrity of blacks entirely. The *Journal and Guide* seemed to indicate that blacks on the whole did not oppose all antimiscegenation legislation but bitterly contested any laws that focused attention exclusively on *white* "racial integrity." One editor of the Norfolk paper classed Lothrop Stoddard's book, *The Rising Tide of Color*, and Earnest Sevier Cox's *White America* as unscientific and "alarmist" in nature. James Weldon Johnson's famous remark that Grant and Stoddard were "kindergarten writers" was repeated as the local papers joined in attacking Virginians who reprinted this racist rhetoric. [82] One commentator claimed that the "mulatto" should not be characterized as a culprit for this was a "victimized man." [83]

Yet African-American scholars who studied and commented on eugenics did not speak in one voice. Although many blacks were united in their opposition to white institutional racism, they were divided on what to do about the "masses" of their neighbors who did not belong to the "talented tenth." [84] There were disagreements concerning racism that involved both class and generational lines of argument. In the latter part of the 1920s and the early 1930s, some African-American researchers shared the white middle-class fear of the reproductive rates of the "submerged group." One worried observer lamented that "The probabilities are that the race problem in America is infinitely aggravated by the presence of too many unhappily born, sub-normals, morons, and imbeciles of both races. It will be a tremendous misfortune if those who are fighting the battle for birth control should remain unmindful or indifferent to the plight of the Negro. For at present the practice is confined to those whose offspring would be best fitted to carry the lance of racial progress." [85]

Many writers thought that all blacks needed to acknowledge the realities of their social and economic conditions, and sometimes this was described as a painful experience. Albert Beckham contended that:

> No intelligent and farsighted Negro will deny that the intelligence quotient or mental level of his group ought to be raised. The need for a higher moral tone of the urban Negro especially, is seen by the social worker, the educator, and philanthropist. It is obvious that a campaign of education would be in order that impressed upon the Negro the immediate necessity of physical fitness. It must be borne in mind that the average percent of Negroes that die from pulmonary and other forms of tuberculosis is much greater than that of whites. Science says this is partly due to a weaker resistance. This physical condition has nothing to do with the Negro's environment.[86]

Other groups were not as confident as Beckham was concerning the role of biology in guiding social reformers, but many members of the growing black middle class were sure that "fitness" had something to do with the progress of their race. W. E. B. Du Bois commented in the *Birth Control Review* in 1932 that "the mass of ignorant Negroes still breed carelessly and disastrously, so that the increase among Negroes, even more than the increase among whites, is from that part of the population least intelligent and fit, and least able to rear their children properly." [87] Charles Johnson, in the same issue, would claim that "the more competent economic elements already use some measure of birth control." [88] Du Bois worried that even intelligent blacks were "led away by the fallacy of numbers. They want the black race to survive. They are cheered by a census return of increasing numbers and a high rate of increase. They must learn that among human races and groups, as among vegetables, quality and not mere quantity really counts." [89]

These accounts by black intellectuals were filled with vocabularies that clearly defined which classes were most in need of fitness education. Elmer Carter, in an article entitled "Eugenics for the Negro," voiced his concern that

> Birth control as practiced today among Negroes is distinctly dysgenic. On the higher economic levels, Negroes have long since limited the number of their offspring, following in the footsteps of the higher classes of white America. . . . Negroes who by virtue of their education and capacity are best able to rear children shrink from the responsibility and the Negro who, in addition to the handicaps of race and color, is shackled by mental and social incompetence serenely goes on his way bringing into

the world children whose chances of mere existence are apparently becoming more and more hazardous.[90]

Black intellectuals began to tinker with the complexities of eugenics rather than totally rejecting this science of the newborn. Writers like Carter were willing to admit that there might be a hereditarian element that helped explain some of the "mental and social incompetence" that hindered the evolution of a race. Yet one of the arguments that African-Americans could use from the eugenical fragments was the possibility that *racial selection* might be one method of social mobility. Thomas Garth, for example, noted that "The differences [in intelligence] would not need to be permanent differences. By means of eugenical practice a racial group may raise its level of worth. By selecting the best for purposes of racial propagation the progeny will on the average be better than its progenitors. No race should take pride in its inferior members. It should seek to eliminate them—weed them out—and thereby obtain by means of selection a better stock."[91] Dichotomies along *class* lines were those discursively created between blacks who had learned to follow white members of the "higher classes" and others of the same race who had "handicaps" that made them even more dependent on others.

Eugenical discussions thus provided another occasion for members of the middle class to remind their unfortunate neighbors of the relationship between economics and reproductive rates. One member of the "talented tenth" claimed that "Eugenics can only help the Negro in respect to the degree in which he controls his mating. Is the Negro mating properly? Is he breeding for brains, beauty, physical prowess or just breeding? Is he transmitting to his progeny a better mental, moral and physical equipment? He should remember that undesirable tendencies are transmitted."[92] Professional blacks thus shared with their white counterparts a healthy respect for those who engaged in mental and moral self-control, improved mental, moral, and physical prowess. The progress of the race seemed to be linked in part to the spread of birth control and other eugenical applications of science.

Not all blacks were thrilled with the narratives that were being constructed by urban intellectual elites who seemed to emphasize the importance of material goods and lower birth rates. Some African-Americans were concerned that when the "talented tenth" used the term "all" in describing those who deserved rights in American society, they meant all *intelligent* blacks. The adoption by some blacks of IQ tests and other such instruments worried those who realized that now African-American students were going to have to cope with discrimination from members of their own race. One educator, William Robinson, a principal in the Atlanta University Laboratory School, remarked on some of the tensions that existed during the period:

> These men, who are consciously or unconsciously establishing their ideas in the thinking of boys and girls, have very little faith in the possibilities of Negroes in industry or business or professions. They believe far more in the inherent inferiority and perversity of Negro people than in the fact that, as human beings, they normally act like all other people and are worthy of equal consideration with other human beings. In other words, too many of us in Negro schools are accepting without much inner protest a deterministic and defeatist philosophy about a group with which they are connected and willy-nilly, we are indoctrinating our charges with our professional belief.[93]

Blacks like Robinson were saddened to find that the same "deterministic" arguments that supposedly separated whites and blacks could also be used to create divisions within a race as well.

Yet in spite of their differences and sometimes contradictory positions on eugenics, African-Americans had made a significant contribution to the American opposition movements that no longer were willing to tolerate hard-line eugenics. Near the end of the third decade of the twentieth century, Du Bois could proudly claim that scientific racism was on the decline and that it was "becoming more difficult for them to state frankly the case against the negro."[94]

Today Eugenics is suggested by the most diverse minds as the most adequate and thorough avenue to the solution of racial, political and social problems. The most intransigeant [*sic*] and daring teachers and scientists have lent their support to this great biological interpretation of the human race. The war has emphasized its *necessity* [emphasis mine].

Margaret Sanger, 1921

4

Women

and the

Eugenics

Movement

In orthodox tales about the relationship between women and eugenics, it is usually the opinions of white males like Galton, Pearson, and Laughlin that take center stage, while women's voices are muted or marginalized. Occasionally we might read about the work of a Gertrude Davenport (usually identified as the wife of Charles Davenport) or hear of the abuse of a Dorothy Kallikak or a Carrie Buck, but we rarely get a sense of the feminist dimensions of the eugenics movement.[1] What I argue in this chapter is that women were among the primary social actors in the eugenics controversies and they were also important characters in stories told by the hard-line eugenicists themselves. I spotlight the work of feminist writers to illustrate once again the elasticity of the words "necessity" and "eugenics," and I continue to show the ways in which the popularization of eugenics involved neo-Lamarckian as well as Mendelian explanations of heredity. I will argue that women were among the prime social actors assuring that eugenics was more than a name for racist or statist hereditarian beliefs.

In the first quarter of the twentieth century, women were divided in their attitudes toward the "necessity" of eugenics. On the one hand, discussions by eugenicists of the importance of "social purity" seemed to be a direct continuation of arguments that women had themselves crafted in the latter half of the nineteenth century in their discussions of "voluntary motherhood."[2] Women had constantly agitated for more control over their reproductive lives, and the new eugenics movement seemed to recognize the importance of reproduction in the creation of social, economic, and political relationships. Many women sympathized with a movement that seemed to be concerned with both the quantity and the quality of the race, and they were drawn to the new science that favored selective limitation of the population as a way to prevent the deterioration of the race. On the other hand were feminists who appropriated only parts of the eugenics narrative, at times agreeing on some of the goals of the movement but differing with eugenicists over what social reforms were needed. For example, women could claim that they acknowledged the primary importance of the quality of offspring and the racial health of the nation, but they asserted that more studies were needed to establish that educated women were healthier and not weaker members of the race.[3] Other women, especially suffragists, argued that increased rights and opportunities would improve "motherhood" rather than threaten the family.[4] As Linda Gordon recently observed: "This concern with eugenics was characteristic of nearly all feminists of the late nineteenth century. At the time eugenics was mainly seen as an implication of evolutionary theory, which was picked up by many social reformers to buttress their arguments that improvement of the human condition was possible. Eugenics had not yet become a movement in itself. Feminists used eugenic arguments as if they instinctively felt that arguments based solely on women's rights had not enough power to conquer conservative and religious scruples."[5] Still others, like Margaret Sanger, would come to accept the "necessity" of eugenics for reduction of the numbers of the "unfit." Eugenics was thus an exceedingly interesting but complicated subject for women involved in a variety of social movements.

British Women and the Early Eugenics Movement

Hard-line eugenicists believed in primarily biological interpretations of human nature. A person's germplasm was said to contain that person's "character," including his or her mental, physical, and moral potential as a human being.

Within hard-line narratives, once someone was diagnosed as "feebleminded" or "criminal," there was no cure for that person and society needed either to make sure that the unfit were segregated from normal people, or sterilized and let back into the community (usually as domestic servants).[6] Those who went to eugenical meetings, giving speeches and circulating stories about the mysterious germplasm, often argued that women were primarily responsible for spreading feeblemindedness and similar social problems. In the biological narratives constructed by hard-line eugenicists, a woman's germplasm determined her destiny and the survival of Anglo-Saxon civilization was often said to depend on women's reproductive behavior.

Since the time of Malthus, several kinds of population stories had been created in English rhetorical cultural memory, and over time these layers of stories about the "necessitous" were adapted to fit changing social situations.[7] In Victorian and Edwardian cultures, several discursive formulaic structures were invented by social actors who asserted that men enjoyed liberty within a social hierarchy because of their superior cultural and biological evolution, while women were considered to have necessities that precluded them from sharing equal rights. For example, Herbert Spencer claimed that the differences between the sexes came from "a somewhat earlier arrest of individual evolution in women than in men; necessitated by the reservation of vital power to meet the cost of reproduction."[8] Building on multiple discussions of how individuals and societies needed to be concerned with the conservation of energy, many speakers and writers in nineteenth-century England claimed that female energy was naturally expended in reproduction, and theoretically there was precious little left over for psychic and intellectual growth. Within this symbolic universe, males contributed to reproduction solely through fertilization and therefore did not have to worry about the strict constraints that confronted the future mothers of the empire. Men, who were freed from the necessities of motherhood, were thought to have unique capacities for abstract reasoning, and this provided one more indication that males must be a more highly evolved life form.[9]

These earlier Spencerian and social Darwinian discussions of the "necessities" of women in both the scientific and popular literature provided hard-line eugenicists with discursive fragments that could be reconfigured to justify a variety of social reforms in the name of biological necessity. Regardless of their political proclivities, women in England found that they were having to cope with interpretations of Darwinian biology that inscribed social codes that separated men from women on the basis of supposedly immutable physical laws. While women were constantly called necessitous in England for quite some time, the English eugenics movement made explicit what had at times been only reluctantly acknowledged. Hard-line hereditarians at the turn of the century began to claim that both the British nation and the "race" demanded that women who were trying to emancipate themselves submit to the iron dictates of human nature. British eugenicists along with some Fabians, socialists, and nationalists talked about the relationship between imperialist necessity and English motherhood.[10] Ever mindful of the growing power of Germany and other trade competitors, these writers began lecturing English women on the need for "national efficiency." For some of these rhetors and writers, no amount of moralizing, enfranchisement, or economic redistribution of income could alter the inherent differences between men and women.

An important aspect of this quest for maintaining respect for English motherhood required that hard-line eugenicists encourage the women of the nation to change their sexual habits. As I indicated in chapter 2, some anxious members of the British empire were concerned that the birthrate of the higher classes was dwindling at the same time that the paupers and other unfit classes sprang up like "weeds." Within a fifty-year period of time, the fertility of women in England declined by more than half and the average size of a British family fell to one-third of what it had been.[11] In contrast to the earlier population questions posed by Sir Thomas Malthus, now English men and women worried that their nation might not produce enough civilized human beings. Hard-line eugenicists and English nativists believed that the decline in the birthrate was a sign that the empire might be crumbling. Children were said to belong "not merely to the parents but to the community as a whole"; they were described as a "national asset," the "capital of a country"; on them depended the "future of country and Empire."[12] The British Eugenics Education Society, founded in 1908, was part of a vast ensemble of groups worried about the reproductive habits of women — among them the Institute of Hygiene, the Infants' Health Society, the National League for Physical Education and Improvement, and the National League for Health, Maternity and Child Welfare. At the head of these organizations were usually prominent ladies and gentlemen, but at the local branches were doctors, members of the clergy, social workers, teachers, nurses, and other concerned citizens who spread the gospel of national "efficiency" throughout the English nation. The debates generated within these organizations were reported in the national press, the medical press, and the journals of these societies, and they often dramatized some of the fears of a small island struggling to protect itself from other predatory imperialists.[13]

In order to cope with these imperial "necessities," many eugenicists helped create an ideology of motherhood that invited fit British citizens to become conscious of their social and civic duties. As Davin has recently observed, the middle-class conventions that existed at the end of the nineteenth century placed the responsibility for class birth differentials on the families of England—particularly mothers.[14] Child rearing became a national as well as a moral duty, and the ideology of biology as destiny became part of the discursive fabric of a nation intent on maintaining its power in the early part of the twentieth century. Before this period social reforms had often been based on the individual shortcomings of the necessitous, but the myths of national degeneration asked audiences to see that this was a social problem.

Hard-line eugenicists combined the ideographs "necessity" and "motherhood" to create an ideology that attempted to convince the enlightened women of Britain to accept their role as primary caretaker. Eugenicists could be found giving speeches on the importance of the authority of the state over the individual, the professional over the amateur, of science over superstition, of male over female, and of the ruling class over the working class. Motherhood was redefined in such a way that the mothers of the English "race" had to be carefully guided and steered away from social schemes that were dysgenic in nature.[15] "Positive" eugenical themes that had been developed in the early work of Galton harped on the ability of the mothers of this class to provide the "geniuses" who would spread English civilization across the globe. At the same time, other eugenicists were focusing on "negative eugenics," and British working class women were told of the dangers of both race poisons and inadequate germplasm operating within the symbolic national body.[16]

Ideographically, the necessities of the state were used against feminist interpretations of voluntary motherhood to legitimate the use of social controls in the area of sexual reproduction. Instead of agitating for the vote or some metaphysical equal rights, women were supposed to understand that this was a time when individual liberties had to give way to national necessities. Many eugenical speeches and articles written at the turn of the century contained lurid stories of how feminists were filling the heads of women with nonsense about freedom and equality. Stories of racial degeneration often depicted working class women as "shirkers" who ignored the importance of maternal health or acted irresponsibly in the face of national emergencies. Halford, for example, claimed that women existed primarily for "sexual ends" and those women who were "sexless" were threatening the "inevitable need" of men to think beyond the "sentimental grievances of women."[17] In the hard-line eugenical hierarchy of needs, women's rights were important only to the extent that they furthered the preservation of the British empire or the fittest of social classes.

The cumulative impact of this kind of rhetoric was to put an inordinate amount of pressure on British women to fulfill their personal, family, and national duties. At the very time that English feminists seemed to be gaining in strength and power they had to confront a hard-line eugenic ideology that accused them of trying to turn England into a land of "spinsters" and slackers. Much of this eugenics discourse worked under the assumption that biological justifications were progressive and that those who resisted some of the new creeds were themselves obstructionists standing in the way of social reform.[18] The rhetorical power of the Galtonian/Pearsonian interpretation of eugenics was that it could combine several strands of earlier concerns of English intellectuals. Its discussions of the importance of free speech and expression in telling society of some of the harsh realities of the existence of the unfit and the need for a new "religion" resonated with some of Britain's freethinkers and socialists, who had also demanded changes in orthodox church structures. The recognition of the existence of a pauper class in London and the biological explanations offered for their resilience helped to ease the conscience of an upper class that needed to rationalize the existence of poverty in the midst of plenty. By combining statistical studies of national decline with more constructive proposals for improved parenthood techniques, the eugenics tales could thus be presented to British women as more than simply lectures about the hordes of degenerates. At the same time, this narrative allowed the members of the Eugenics Education Society to appear radical while defending the traditional English values of nation, family, and personal character. The advocacy of sterilization, segregation, and marriage restriction of the unfit, and the provision of family allowances for the fit, deflected an audience's attention away from the radical changes that were being advocated by socialists, feminists, and other communities that wanted direct help for the "necessitous." It is not surprising that most English eugenicists were anti-feminists who argued that the best women in society ought to be home fulfilling their maternal duties—for queen, empire, and race. These writers had faith that the British "Mrs. Grundy" could have an enormous influence in checking the marriages that "she considers indiscreet."[19] In sum, hard-liners were convinced that England's right-thinking women would voluntarily change their reproductive habits on the basis of accepting the "necessities" of the state.

British Feminists Reconstruct the Eugenics Stories

Not all women were willing to believe that state "necessities" demanded the relinquishment of equal rights or individual autonomy. What I will argue in this section is that British women appropriated neo-Lamarckian and Darwinian interpretations of eugenics in order to craft *feminist* eugenical creeds. Building on the work of men and women who had been writing for decades on the need for "voluntary motherhood," these British feminists deconstructed the myths of hard-line eugenics while offering their own constructive visions of the way that English society needed to be reformed.[20]

In their attempt to craft a feminist interpretation of eugenics, British women used three different (and sometimes contradictory) rhetorical strategies. First, they continued to provide vocal support for many programs that hard-line eugenicists considered to be "dysgenic." Second, they attacked antifeminist claims as an interference with "voluntary motherhood." Finally, they attempted to co-opt the hard-line eugenics terms in order to justify their own social reform agendas. This third strategy at times meant accepting some of the racial or class-oriented arguments of eugenicists in order to obtain a hearing for controversial issues like birth control.

Some feminists attacked the hard-line eugenics creed by continually demanding that the British government provide financial support for programs that some hard-liners thought "dysgenic" in nature. While hard-line eugenicists wanted health or maternal benefits provided exclusively for the "fit" classes, feminists argued for broader benefits that would be provided for all British citizens as a matter of right. Many women continued to urge their municipal and national leaders to extend the coverage of factory laws, sanitation measures, and maternity benefits that would help reduce death rates among British children.[21] For example, in an article entitled "An Ethical Birth Rate," published in the *Westminster Review,* Frances Swiney chastised those individuals who bewailed the decline of the birth rate while ignoring the problem of infant and maternal mortality rates.[22]

A second strategy for feminists involved use of the ideograph "voluntary motherhood" to combat hard-line interpretations of eugenics. Some British women believed that individual "choice" or "liberty" was just as important as state "necessities." Many of these feminists — liberals and radicals — voiced their concerns in numerous speeches, pamphlets, and journal articles that what was needed in England was "voluntary motherhood" and that unlimited, unwanted pregnancies could no longer be accepted. Where hard-line eugenicists talked about the need of society to be protected from hordes of the feebleminded, feminists moved the focus away from the rights of the state to the rights of women that were being violated. This focus on individual autonomy allowed feminists to provide social commentary on the coercive behavior of men who violated the rights of women. As antifeminist James Merchant would note in 1917, it had been people like Josephine Butler who had "found it necessary to insist upon the right of every woman to the control of her person. . . . Now in the new Charter of Woman's Liberty that inviolable principle will be reasserted with this enormous extension in its application. Woman will claim full control over her person within the married state." [23] Thus feminists were able to counterpose "woman's liberty" to eugenical claims of state "necessity."

Their second strategy of focusing on "voluntary motherhood" allowed feminists to argue for the inclusion of the "New Woman" in the evolutionary equation.[24] Some eugenicists, like Alice Vickery, agreed that racial progress was important, but she questioned Galton's neglect of the relationship between family size and the need for female emancipation.[25] Eschewing visions of human nature that reduced women to the subordinate status of keepers of the home, many of these writers claimed that a progressive nation needed the physical, spiritual, and political contributions of all its citizens. Feminists attacked the British Eugenics Society for proposing schemes that tried to pressure women into breeding for the state.[26] Alice Stockham wrote in 1896 that it is "especially necessary for the wife to be freed from the mental dread of excessive and undesired childbearing." [27]

While the traditional eugenic narratives constructed by men like Pearson and Galton designated the state to stop the reproduction of the unfit, feminist eugenical tales redefined the issue as one that could only be worked out by mothers. Jane Clapperton, for example, claimed that "These are delicate matters for mothers alone. They must limit their families. They must learn what their duty is to their own health, the health of their children, and the health of the nation. We women will instruct them in self-respect, and show them how to support one another in cases where men are brutal and ought to be resisted." [28] As a rhetorical construct, this alternative version of eugenics invited women to engage in a form of sisterhood that benefited individual and nation, regardless of social class and without the need for male or state intervention. Attacks on false claims of "necessity" on the part of males became part of the rallying cry of feminists interested in the rights of women in the area of reproductive choice. While hard-line eugenicists interpreted the falling birth rate among the fit middle and working classes as a sign of selfishness, these women viewed the voluntary restrictions as a relief from necessitous conditions.

The final strategy used by British feminists in their effort to develop a feminist vision of reform involved the co-optation of hard-line eugenic arguments. Rather than directly attacking the merit of nationalist, racial, or class-oriented arguments, some feminists constructed their own eugenics stories that forced hard-liners to face some of the contradictions in traditional eugenical tales. In order to cope with the arguments of hard-line eugenicists, many women helped to legitimate the demands of nineteenth-century feminists by turning to Victorian middle-class myths that valorized efficiency, purity, and self-control. If hard-line eugenicists were going to insist on government interference in biological affairs, then feminists wanted to use these arguments for their own social agendas. For example, whereas the eugenicists used the concept of bacterial infection in order to control prostitution, feminists used that same concept to call for the control of male vices. In place of hard-line stories of how immoral, feeble-minded women spread tainted germplasm, feminist narratives told of innocent housewives who were being physically and morally infected by spouses who had been visiting an underworld of prostitution, drink, and smoke. While hard-line eugenics stories usually glossed over the inequities in institutional and familial relationships, many feminist tales highlighted the exploitation of women in British society.

Feminists thus constructed eugenics narratives that built on the neo-Lamarckian stories that had circulated throughout the nineteenth century. Instead of accepting at face value the hard-line eugenical claims that neither education nor "moralising" could work changes on the character of men and women with bad germplasm, these writers emphasized the need to alter the habits of men who were oppressing women. Feminists like Christabel Pankhurst wrote that about three-quarters of all men were infected before marriage and that they often engaged in a conspiracy of silence.[29] When hard-line eugenicists tried to claim that women were the inferior sex biologically, feminists could choose to accept this characterization but use it to their advantage. For example, Pankhurst argued that if women were being denied the vote because they were weaker than men, then Englishmen needed to concede that this weakness was caused by the physical degeneration of men themselves. Within this tale, the only way that society could gain any form of social purity was to provide women with the full equality that would allow feminists to reeducate men.

American Women and the Stories of the Eugenics Movement

In America, the influence of Mendelian genetics and the search for "unit" traits meant that eugenic researchers and advocates focused the nation's attention on the reproductive habits of the women who seemed to be bringing an increasing number of degenerates into the world. Unlike English Pearsonian eugenics, the American variant of the study of the wellborn looked not at large aggregate numbers of people in order to find "normality" but rather looked to see how particular *families* contained generations of feeblemindedness, pauperism, and hundreds of other traits.[30]

In the late nineteenth and early twentieth centuries, eugenicists circulated stories that demonstrated that family members possessed the same inferior heredity that had led their relatives to alcoholism, crime, laziness, and poverty. Often poor women were characterized as the carriers of "germplasm," and those afflicted with this disease became the targets of massive publicity campaigns to cleanse America of the dysgenic.[31] Gertrude Davenport and others claimed that "negative" eugenics was a necessity, and she worried that the feebleminded were hiding their hereditary traits and not marrying "judiciously," which in turn meant trouble for "this class" of "paupers, prostitutes, rapists, and criminals."[32] Under the guise of objective scientific investigation, many of the family charts told America the story of the Jukes, the Nams, the Zeros, and the Kallikaks. These narratives attracted an enthusiastic audience among welfare workers, criminologists, and members of the reading public, who saw in them proof of the claims of the hard-line eugenicists.[33] American eugenicists were even more firmly convinced than their British counterparts that no amount of education or improvement of the environment would enable women to remove the ill effects of tainted germplasm.[34]

The characterizations of American women in hard-line eugenics stories often involved a rhetorical division between those moral women who had good habits and healthy germplasm and the unhealthy, "shiftless" women who polluted America's genetic pool. Normal women married, had the requisite number of children to perpetuate the race, and raised their children eugenically. Unhealthy or abnormal women were biologically "feebleminded" or otherwise inferior. In these hard-line eugenics morality plays, the United States needed the courage to weed out those unfit mothers who either had children out of wedlock, married non-nativists, had too many children, or refused to behave as normal citizens were expected to.[35] Women who became prostitutes or had illegitimate children were often claimed to be "dysgenic" and the "potential carriers" of diseases and mental afflictions.[36] One article in the *American Magazine* of October 1913 warned readers that the "village girls who had illegitimate children" might be medically, pedagogically, psychologically, or sociologically "feebleminded."[37] Convinced that there was an intimate relationship between a person's bloodline and their social behavior, hard-liners looked for ways of more accurately detecting the deficiencies that affected a person's character. Eugenical doctors like Harvey Wiley wrote that "The welfare of the state does not depend alone upon the number of its inhabitants, but upon their character. Imbeciles, epileptics, syphilitics, and tuberculines are undesirable. Therefore, the state has a right to limit their number as far as possible."[38] Years later, when sterilization became the focal point of the eugenics debate, women like Carrie Buck would find that society had the legal right to enforce compulsory sterilization because of the "necessities" of the state.[39]

Many of the stories crafted by hard-line eugenicists were based on fragments of information collected by thousands of women who worked under the guidance of men like Charles Davenport and Henry Goddard.[40] Because of their supposed emotional and intuitive powers, eugenicists believed that women were more adept than men at quantifying the numbers of the feebleminded.[41] After a few weeks' training, field workers were thought to be able to tell at a glance whether someone had pure or tainted germplasm.[42] Many of these accounts talk about the dangers of leaving at liberty feebleminded people who were trying to provide the "bare necessities of life."[43] Hard-line eugenicists often claimed that a woman might appear to be normal or even physically attractive (the usual example was a person named Dorothy Kallikak) but that a trained eugenicist could use pedigree charts and neighbors' information to prove that underneath her normal exterior she had bad germplasm.[44] Hard-line eugenicists like Elizabeth Kite could contend in 1913 that her study of the pseudonymous Piney family revealed some "human degenerates" that demanded the "careful attention of those interested in the preservation of the high standards of our commonwealth."[45]

Many American women were interested in parts of the hard-line eugenics narratives who were not necessarily workers for eugenic researchers. In the South, influential women's clubs used hard-line eugenical arguments in their lobbying efforts to get states to provide for the "feebleminded."[46] At other times, eugenics literature was disseminated through popular organizations like the Ku Klux Klan.[47] Some women, like Elizabeth Tyler, started their public careers working as hygienists in tenement communities.[48] Many members of the Ku Klux Klan were in favor of the congressional emergency acts that were passed to restrict immigration and the openly racist systems of national quotas that were established in 1924. Like the hard-line eugenicists, many members of the Klan used some of the language of science to mask their nativism and oppose activities like miscegenation.[49] By the mid-1920s, some five to six million men and women were said to be members of the Klan in America.

Granted, some women either participated in the creation of hard-line eugenics discourse or had heard the hard-line addresses. Yet there were also millions of American women who were exposed to other discussions of eugenics and "necessity" who were not strict biological determinists.

American Women and "Reform" Eugenics Discourse

Like their neighbors across the Atlantic, American women were exposed to both neo-Lemarckian and Darwinian forms of eugenical arguments.[50] Many attended lectures and read articles by doctors, social workers, and other intellectuals who broadened the scope of eugenics to cover many forms of motherhood or parenthood. American women who might not have heard of Davenport or East were able to read about them in popular articles like Stoddard Goodhue's "Do You Choose Your Children?" published in the July 1913 issue of *Cosmopolitan*.[51] Goodhue's work was an example of a genre of eugenical writing addressed to the average man or woman curious about the mysteries of genetics or perhaps interested in applying some of the principles of eugenics in their everyday lives. By addressing citizens directly, these writers hoped that women would be persuaded to uphold the traditional values of purity and cleanliness that had built the nation and that readers would exercise discretion in their selection of marriage partners. For example, Goodhue warned his *Cosmopolitan* readers:

> In a word, then, each of you is the bearer of a message from your ancestry to your posterity. You stand at the meeting point between galaxies of ancestors and other galaxies of prospective progeny. In your system lies the bit of germ-plasm that— miracle of miracles!—conveys the potentialities of good and evil of the past—the epitome of the racial history of all your myriads of ancestors. Nothing that you can do will change the character of that germ-plasm. Its potentialities are fixed irrevocably. In a sense it is not a part of you; it is a heritage placed temporarily in your stewardship. But it is open to you to decide whether you will be a true or a false steward.[52]

Through the rhetorical process of identification, the average reader is invited to become an integral part of the eugenics movement by acting eugenically and making sure that no impure germplasm enters the bloodstream of his or her children.

Many of the eugenical stories that appeared in women's journals contained elaborate narratives, complete with plots, heroes, and villains. Women were told that they had to make a choice between having children that were "bright," "healthy" and "robust" or "sickly," "depraved," or "unintelligent." [53] These tales conveyed not only scientific information but advice on how readers could take control of their own lives. One eugenicist would write in *Good Housekeeping* that "If we could introduce in the breeding of human beings those dynamic facts and principles illustrated by the descendants of Max and Jonathan Edwards, and carried into practice in the breeding of domesticated animals, we would lay the foundation of a future State whose splendor, efficiency, and fame would be the outstanding glory of history." [54] American women who engaged in eugenical practices were thus invited to believe that they held their own destiny and that of their nation in their hands.

Yet eugenical arguments had a way of going beyond discussions of the benefits of Mendel and hard-line eugenics, and the stories told in women's journals often integrated a variety of eugenical interpretations. What one author considered to be "good breeding" might simply refer to the way that a woman selected her husband, but it could also refer to neo-Lamarckian concerns that were often denied relevance by hard-liners—child mortality, education, natal care, and other environmental issues. At the same time that readers were assured that professors like Davenport and East had "settled" the controversy between heredity and the environment for all time, they were admonished to change their behavior in ways that seemed to reopen the controversy. On the one hand women were warned that if "two neurotic taints" were brought together, this would be like "fire and tinder" in that "your offspring will be neuropathic—feeble-minded or epileptic or sexually perverted or destined to become insane." [55] Yet at the same time they were asked to educate themselves and their children on the ways that even those without training could follow the rules of heredity. The really good parent was supposed to be a cautious person who checked his or her prospective mate's ancestry and background. One writer urged his readers to

> consider the families of your neighbors. More than likely some of them include children that are congenitally crippled or scrofulous or "backward" or vicious and depraved. You have supposed that this was an unavoidable misfortune; an inexplicable "interposition of Providence." You are wrong. The seeming misfortune that is bringing the head of your neighbor in sorrow to the grave is really of his own choosing. He predetermined that his child should be neuropathic or epileptic or deformed or congenitally blind or deaf or morally depraved when he selected the mother of that child. . . . You will invite the same disaster if you act with like lack of foresight. [56]

In typical hard-line discussions of foreigners with bad germplasm there is usually little discussion of "choice" (beyond not coming to America), but here it is the father of the native child who can stop future "misfortune."

Many of the popular journals continued to carry stories that involved neo-Lamarckian themes. Before World War I, writers warned American women of the "necessity" of preventing marriages between epileptics or persons who carried the taint of the "white plague" (tuberculosis). These morality plays often pointed out that good mothers and fathers were the ones who wanted to learn about proper parenthood. Sometimes even eugenical poems were published to reinforce the message that fit parents had a responsibility to act maturely rather than sentimentally. In July of 1912, Ella Wilcox published a poem ("The Forecast") in *Good Housekeeping* that read in part:

I seemed to dwell in this same world, and in this is modern time;
Yet nowhere was there sight or sound or poverty or crime . . .
There were no beggars in the streets; there were no unemployed.
For each man owned a plot of ground, and labored and enjoyed . . .
All Motherhood is now an art; the greatest art on earth;
And nowhere is there known the crime of one unwelcome birth.
From rights of parentage, the sick and sinful are debarred;
For Matron Science keeps our house, and at the door stands Guard.[57]

For Wilcox and other American women, eugenics meant just about anything that would contribute to the art and science of correct parenting.

Part of this expanding literature on eugenics focused on the child.[58] Many of the articles that appeared in the women's press reflected the changes that were taking place within the eugenics movement itself, as more and more publications began to discuss the "rights of the unborn" in terms of both heredity and the environment. In 1922 one contributor to *Good Housekeeping* wrote:

If all the readers of *Good Housekeeping* could have read the many letters which I have received from anxious mothers whose daughters were about to be married, they would as eagerly join in promoting a sufficient protection. No one but a mother can realize what it means to have her daughter to get married. No one but a mother can so longingly and eagerly anticipate happy results of the union, and no one but a mother can be so filled with fear and horror of a marriage resulting in deformed, deficient, or physically and morally tainted children. I appeal, therefore, to the women of this country to aid in promoting this most important factor in safeguarding the future of our citizens. It is not in my place to suggest particular amendments to the marriage code, but only to preach the gospel of a sound, sanitary, and hopeful parenthood.[59]

Invoking the horror of the "morally tainted" child was a eugenic tactic to show women the urgency of marriage regulations. While denying any particular expertise in health or the law, these writers were willing to give very general information of how couples and potential parents should live their life in order to stay "sanitary."

A second major factor in the spread of non-hard-line or "reform" eugenics involved the use by American feminists of eugenical fragments in the construction of their own agendas for rights and social welfare reform. Many women were very ill at ease with the way that eugenicists talked about the concept of motherhood.[60] American feminists often argued that eugenicists who wanted the state to regulate marriages and the birth rate had ulterior motives for spreading their creed. Some Americans, like Kate O'Hare, believed that imperialistic men were using breeding regulations in ways that were criminal. In the summer of 1917, O'Hare charged that "When the governments of Europe, and the clergy of Europe, demanded of the women that they give themselves in marriage, or out, in order that men might 'breed before they die,' that was not a crime of maddened passion, it was the cold-blooded crime of brutal selfishness, and by that crime the women of Europe were reduced to the status of breeding animals on a stockfarm."[61]

Not all American women were as radical as O'Hare, but her words expressed the uneasiness of many when eugenicists talked about birth selection.[62] Some reformers sensed that focusing on the nation or the race detracted from the personal autonomy of the individual women. Some reformers refused to accept the hard-line eugenics line, and they advocated birth control for all women as a matter of right. These social commentators often found that their ideas were in conflict with those of eugenicists who wanted higher birth rates for some Americans.[63] In their efforts to obtain voting rights, equal education, and access to the labor market, many women had emphasized the social and cultural aspects of parentage and deemphasized the biological ones.[64] Margaret Sanger, one of the leading feminists of the period, commented that "The eugenist also believes that a woman should bear as many healthy children as possible as a duty to the state. We hold that the world is already over-populated. Eugenists imply or insist that a woman's first duty is to the state; we contend that her duty to herself is her first duty to the state."[65] Thus even women who were generally willing to accept some of the hard-line eugenics claims concerning degeneration also understood that strict hereditarian arguments had a tendency to circumscribe drastically the range of social reforms. The eugenics creed seemed to be an invitation to accept a view of the world where women would be important "breeders" in the natural order of things but insignificant in other spheres of human endeavor.[66] Hard-line eugenicists had asked women to keep some notion of motherhood but at the cost of altering women's conceptions of voluntarism.[67]

Those writers who claimed to represent the poorer classes were generally more antagonistic toward strict hereditarian interpretations of eugenics, but they were not adverse to using eugenical arguments in their efforts to legitimate feminist programs like the extension of birth control. While some women turned discussions of positive eugenics away from the study of genius and toward the elimination of race poisons, other writers used discussions of negative eugenics to justify the encouragement of voluntary birth control as a means of reducing the poverty of the period. These narratives often focused attention on the plight of the poor rather than the declining birth rates of the "fit." For example, Emma Goldman, writing on the "Social Aspects of Birth Control" in 1916, noted that: "Wretched as the earnings of a man with a large family are, he cannot risk even that little, so he continues in the rut, compromises and cringes before his master, just to earn barely enough to feed the many little mouths. . . . Masses of workers have awakened to the necessity of Birth Control as a means of freeing themselves from the terrible yoke."[68] Unlike mainstream eugenicists who focused on the biological necessities of the human condition, these radicals wrote about the need to redress economic inequalities as well. While mainstream eugenicists worried that birth control threatened "race suicide," radicals like Goldman were willing to smuggle contraceptives into the country in the early 1900s.[69]

Perhaps one of the most effective strategies used by feminists in appropriating eugenical discourse involved reminding audiences of the historical roots of the eugenics movement. Hard-liners were adamant in their claims that only geniuses (predominantly male) could effect massive social change, but American feminists constantly reminded the traditionalists of the deeper roots of their own movement. Unlike writers who claimed that the eugenics movement began with the work of Francis Galton, Margaret Sanger espoused the belief that the "new" eugenics program was simply one aspect of a larger concern with reproductive rights. Sanger noted in her autobiography that "Eugenics, which had started long before my time, had once been defined as including free love and prevention of contraception. . . . Recently it had cropped up again in the form of selective breeding."[70] This attempt to subsume eugenics under the general rubric of "birth control" or "contraception" often enraged the hard-liners who wanted women to obey the edicts of nature and accept their biological destiny. Yet feminists like Sanger used the growing power of eugenics and, like other rhetors of the period, presented birth control "as a necessity for the Establishment to maintain power."[71]

In later years, when Hitler came to power, some forms of eugenics would lose their rhetorical force, while birth control would one day be associated with the very antithesis of state power—the right of privacy. Both English and American feminists sought to associate necessity with equality of opportunity in the political, social, and economic spheres. They would find in hard-line eugenics a

worthy ideological opponent—one that insisted on reducing necessity to its biological components. Feminists crafted a variety of responses to the science of the
wellborn, but they were united in their belief that voluntary motherhood could
not be relinquished in the name of state necessities. Many women were in favor
of eugenics as long as it meant "free, self-determined motherhood." [72] While
some middle-class American women (like Gertrude Davenport) were willing to
accept coercive forms of eugenics, other rejected anything that threatened voluntary motherhood. [73] By crafting their own interpretations of neo-Lamarckian and
hard-line eugenics stories, they contributed to the move toward reform eugenics.

The richer classes have many ways of shielding
themselves. . . . it is for this reason that wage-earners, who
are undoubtedly among the weak and necessitous, should
be specially cared for and protected by the government.

Pope Leo XIII

5

Catholic
Interpretations
of Eugenics
Rhetoric

When historians of science and other researchers
talk about the relationship between religion and genetics, they usually begin
with one of two well-known story lines. The first treats science and religion as
incommensurable worldviews, and religious figures are viewed as potential allies
of activists like Jeremy Rifkin.[1] The second divides up the world into the "is"
and the "oughts," where science is concerned with objectivity and facts while
religion belongs to the part of our culture that deals with values.

Each of these two story lines has contributed to the rationalistic histories that
have been written about the relationship between eugenics and Catholicism. In
most of these accounts, Anglo-American religious communities have been leading opponents of the study of the wellborn. The stand that Catholics have taken

against compulsory sterilization has usually been considered positive proof that this community was univocally opposed to all forms of eugenics. In this chapter, I challenge these traditional fables and argue that Catholic religious figures and their audiences helped to reconstruct the science of eugenics in a number of complicated ways. I begin my narrative by looking at England because it was the home of the supposed founder of eugenics, Francis Galton.

Anti-Catholicism and the English Eugenics Movement

In the latter part of the nineteenth century and the early part of the twentieth century, British hard-line eugenicists often identified Catholics with the unfit who lacked either foresight or self-control.[2] From the very beginning of the British eugenics movement, Catholics found themselves characterized in the scientific journals and in the popular press as members of the uneducated classes or as dogmatists who could be grouped together with Jews, paupers, and other members of the "residuum" who had not learned the immutable laws of Victorian society.[3] For example, in a series of articles on "Physical Degeneracy or Race Suicide?" printed in the *London Times* in October 1906, the influential Sidney Webb lamented that

> In Great Britain, at this moment, when half or perhaps two-thirds, of all the married people are regulating their families, children are being freely born to the Irish Roman Catholics and the Polish, Russian, and German Jews, on the other hand, and to the thriftless and irresponsible—largely the casual labourers and the other denizens of the one-roomed tenements of our great cities—on the other. This particular 25 percent of our population, as Professor Karl Pearson keeps warning us, is producing 50 percent of our children. This can hardly result in anything but national deterioration; or, as an alternative, in this country gradually falling to the Irish and the Jews.[4]

Webb and other Fabians used the issue of the differential birth rate to craft stories that created social boundaries between different races, classes, and ethnic communities in English society.[5] Hierarchies were created to measure the relative "efficiency" of particular groups.

Webb's symbolic universe was representative of the elaborate Victorian and Edwardian eugenical stories that were fabricated in ways that marginalized Catholics and placed them in the camp of the dysgenic. Like many hard-line eugenics advocates, Webb invited his audiences to believe in an England divided biologically into two worlds—the "fit" race composed of "self-controlled and foreseeing members" and the ignorant, lower classes.[6] Stories of race degeneration had been a staple in the arts and sciences for years, but the rise of eugenics seemed to offer new and improved ways of dispassionately assessing the worsening social conditions that demanded some social response. While many writers during the period following the Boer War had pessimistic visions of the future, Webb optimistically hoped for a revolution in human morality that would help with the production of "healthy, moral, and intelligent" citizens. In his eugenic tale, he invited readers to join him in dreaming of a world where in the best English society, "Once set free from the overwhelming economic penalties with which it is at present visited, the rearing of a family may gradually be rendered part of the code of the ordinary citizen's morality. The natural repulsion to interference in marital relations will have free play. The mystic obligations of which the religious-minded feel the force will no longer be confronted by the dead wall of economic necessity."[7] By "ordinary" Webb seemed to be referring to those members of the " 'middle' and professional classes" who had learned that a baby meant "the probability of there being less food, less clothing, less house room, less recreation, and less opportunity for advancement for every member of the family."[8] To encourage the thoughtful, Webb asked his audience to consider the possibility of rewarding those Protestant mothers who understood the importance of "motherhood."[9]

Webb's diatribe against Catholic overpopulation by itself might have been worrisome—he was after all a member of the government's Poor Law Commission—but the problem was exacerbated by the fact that it linked Catholics to the "lower classes," so that more general statistics that applied to non-Catholics could nevertheless be used to indict Catholics for some non-Catholic characteristics. In the same year that Webb was writing about national deterioration in the *London Times*, David Heron, a fellow in the newly established eugenics laboratory in University College of London, claimed that statistical correlations were showing that "the wives in the districts of least prosperity and culture have the largest families, and the morally and socially lowest classes in the community are those which are reproducing themselves with the greatest rapidity."[10] In light of Webb's explicit attack on Catholics, Heron's more general language could be taken, by those so inclined, to include Catholics. As a whole, these writers began to contribute to a discursive tapestry that perpetuated myths about the link between Catholicism and drink, immigration, and fantastic fecundity. English Catholics found themselves attacked not only on the front pages of the nation's leading newspapers but in several leading Fabian tracts of the day. Webb, in his *The Decline in the Birth Rate*, combined his work with Heron's studies and claimed that Irish Catholics were helping to distort the figures of birth-rate differentials.[11] In the first decade of this century, Webb's tract was widely read by the public and reviewed by the press, and even Karl Pearson acknowledged that *The Decline in the Birth Rate* had helped focus attention on the issue of differential reproduction.[12] Webb's work was not only extensively reviewed but quoted for years. The heroes in his story were those skilled artisans, mechanics, and responsible small shopkeepers who collectively composed the most prudential part of English society.[13] When the English Eugenics Society was formed in 1907, it contributed to this fable by warning readers that the problem of the differential birth rate meant that the nation was in danger of being swamped by prostitutes, wastrels, Jews, and Catholics.[14]

In England and Ireland, strict hereditarian eugenics narratives were proclaimed even by bishops of the Church of England. These members of the clergy joined with doctors, social scientists, and politicians in believing that the eugenics movement would be one of the best forces for improving social morality. Many letters supporting the protection of the wellborn were sent to the editor of the *London Times* by Baptists, Congregationalists, and Anglicans. During the first quarter of the twentieth century, one of the most prominent defenders of the movement was the Very Reverend W. R. Inge, dean of Saint Paul's, who became famous for his broadcasts and public statements on eugenics. Many of these eugenicists, although politically conservative, were considered to be part of the modernism movement in theology. Inge, along with the bishop of Exeter and Frederick D'Arcy, the bishop of Down, published materials that were in the tradition of liberal Protestantism and that tried to bring together science and religion, especially evolutionary biology.[15] For example, Bishop Barnes of Birmingham was both a eugenicist and a vocal supporter of sterilization.[16] These writers provided their readers with stories of how new legislation would help protect "honest" British workers from the dependency of the reckless and incompetent. These different church organizations supported the eugenicists at two crucial political junctures in the quest for the legitimacy of the movement—during the debate over the Mental Deficiency Bill in 1912, and when the British government was petitioned to allow the voluntary sterilization of the unfit in 1929.[17]

In many ways, the arguments crafted by the British Eugenics Society were structural inversions of the tenets of Roman Catholicism. In place of charity and the protection of the weak, strict hereditarians wanted to protect the wellborn and expend fewer resources on the unfit. Instead of a society governed by abstract natural law principles that were used to support a redistribution of income for all human beings, many eugenicists argued for family allowances and higher wages only for the deserving few who merited attention. In place of church dogma writers like Galton and Pearson wanted a society that was willing to be "efficiently" regulated by a "new religion" based on the sound biological principles of eugenics. In place of decadent discussions of liberalism and the rights of humanity, eugenicists wanted the state to take control of a variety of social functions. If Nietzsche had lived a few more years, he would have found that a movement had been created that seemed to put into practice what he had been preaching concerning the need for a "transvaluation" of values.[18]

Eugenics, Nativism, and American Catholicism

America, like England, had a long discursive history of anti-Catholic rhetoric. As early as 1835, Samuel F. B. Morse, in his *Immigration Dangers to the Institutions of the United States through Foreign Immigration,* was warning that the "ignorant and the vicious," as well as the "priest-ridden slaves of Ireland and Germany," were a part of the "outcast tenants of the poorhouse and prisons of Europe."[19] Political organizations like the Know-Nothing Party sprang up during the middle of the nineteenth century as Americans began to feel the social and economic pressures that came from growing numbers of immigrants. Just before World War I, more than a million people a year were coming from Eastern Europe and other lands and to many nativists they seemed a race apart, new immigrants who had a germplasm that was drastically different from that of the "old" ones. Generally poor and Catholic or Jewish, they were often portrayed in the pages of respected magazines like the *Saturday Evening Post* as illiterate, unskilled, and prone to segregate themselves in the cities.[20] Earlier depictions of Irish and German immigrants had often been just as racist, but they were frequently accompanied by discussions of how these groups needed to be assimilated into the American culture, and charity organizations focused on the possibilities of redeeming the new arrivals. The new wave of immigrants were not so fortunate. Many of them were said to be permanent parasites on the American body politic, forever tainted by their blood and incapable of having their condition ameliorated. Hiram Evans spoke for many white, native-born Americans when he wrote in the *North American Review* in 1926 that "The real indictment against the Roman Church is that it is, fundamentally and irredeemably . . . alien, un-American and usually anti-American. The old stock Americans . . . see in the Roman Church today the chief leader of alienism, and the most dangerous alien power with a foothold inside our boundaries."[21] Evans, the leader of the growing KKK, claimed that he was simply articulating aloud what many Americans were already thinking.

In the first decade of the twentieth century, many nativists who joined anti-Catholic associations were also eugenicists who associated the "rising tide" of immigration with attempts by the pope to rule America.[22] To the modern ear much of this rhetoric sounds like blatant ethnocentrism, but to Americans living during this period, it was those who objected to immigration restrictions who were letting their passions overrule good rational judgment in the face of the threat of "bad germplasm."[23] While some organizations like the American Protective Association and the Ku Klux Klan were explicitly racist and nativist, the eugenics creed offered its advocates a more nuanced discourse that often provided a veneer of respectability to restrictionist schemes. As one scholar has observed, "eugenic arguments provided apparently new, objective scientific justifications for old, deep-seated racial and class assumptions."[24] Many Catholics during the 1920s scrambled to find ways of dealing with a materialist philosophy of life that challenged those who believed in charity and helping the "necessitous."

An analysis of the rhetoric of the 1930s reveals that Catholics were faced with a resurgence of eugenics discussions. While scholars who have written on the subject are correct in their assessment that there was a great deal of support for eugenics in general in the years before World War I, in other historical periods an emphasis was placed on a particular type of eugenic activity. Following *Buck v. Bell* (1927) there was renewed interest in certain forms of eugenics—particularly sterilization—on the part of some public health officials, social workers, lawyers, judges, and other opinion leaders.[25] Articles favoring eugenics appeared in regional journals like the *Virginia Medical Monthly* and in the prestigious pages of the *New England Journal of Medicine*. Leading gynecologists like Robert Dickinson became members of the Committee on Maternal Health of the American Eugenics Society.[26] For every Madison Grant or Harry Laughlin, there were dozens of minor government officials in bureaus of vital statistics, welfare offices, and police stations who shared the concerns of the eugenicists. Catholics in America found that their attempts to provide charity for the poor were regarded as short-sighted, sentimental acts that were contributing to the degeneration of civilization.

Catholic Interpretations of Eugenics in Anglo-American Discourse

In Victorian England, the threat posed by the feebleminded and other members of the "residuum" brought calls for "colonisation" of the paupers, segregation, marriage restrictions, sterilization, and poor-law reforms. The articulation of eugenical concerns provided many English writers with ways of discussing a number of social problems that came with the rise of capitalism, urbanization, and imperialism. Many nervous British Catholics contributed their fair share to the tales of "degeneration" and "race suicide," but they voiced their sentiments in ways that were drastically different from the claims of hard-line eugenics.[27] At times Catholics may have sympathized with efforts to improve the marriages of the poor or to enforce the segregation of the unfit, but they argued that some eugenics proposals were simply violations of natural rights.

Many Catholic writers, rather than completely denying the relevance of eugenics to Christian teachings, simply redefined the term to make it more compatible with Catholic doctrines. Some explicitly argued that the burden was on the hard-liners to show that reforms like sterilization were "necessary." Thomas Gerrard, after examining the English Majority and Minority Reports of the Poor Law Commission, argued in 1911 that

> The moment these remedies are named [sterilization and segregation] there is a clash of interests, ideals, and sentiments. To allow the feebles unrestrained liberty would appear to be a menace to the freedom of the community, whilst to subject them to all the remedies proposed would seem to be an unnecessary violation of their rights, and perhaps an infliction of unwarranted cruelty. We must move warily and scientifically. In the first place, it must be granted as a principle that the government of a country has a right to have recourse to compulsory segregation and surgery if such action is necessary for the good of the community. The State hangs people, shuts them up in the gaol, in lunatic asylums and in inebriate homes. On the same principle, it can, if necessary, carry out the eugenic reforms proposed. The question is whether all such drastic measures are *necessary* [emphasis mine].[28]

While many other Catholics were not willing to go as far as granting such "necessary" powers to the state, this article included a pattern of argument that would continue for decades—surgery was considered to be the last resort of the state. Gerrard, for example, quoted Saleeby's remark that it was "necessary to be reasonable" and that in "seeking the superman, to remain at least human."[29] In place of sterilization, Gerrard claimed that society needed to concentrate on the "acquired" hereditary traits within a population, and he claimed that the Church was doing its best to get rid of race poisons, pauperism, immorality, and unemployment. In this eugenics narrative, most of England's unfit could be taken care of if they were only educated. People like Gerrard may have accepted the need to stop the propagation of some of the unfit, but they thought that this could be accomplished through placement of the feebleminded in institutions like "Waverley, Ursberg, Sandlebridge, and White House."[30]

In place of strictly hereditarian schemes for the wellborn, Catholics created what they called a "supernatural eugenics," which purposely blurred the line between "nature" and "nurture." Some Catholics joined English public health officials in criticizing the work of Galton and Pearson and in claiming that it was the environment of the poor that caused their "demoralisation" and "degradation." One such critic noted that

> Feeble-mindedness is so often a cause of poverty, and poverty so often a cause of feeble-mindedness, that there is a danger of confusing one with the other. Catholics, therefore, need to exercise a strong vigilance lest, under pretence of eugenic reform, the rights of the poor are infringed. Poverty is no bar to the sacrament of marriage. The poor, and even the destitute, as such, have every right to the joys and protection of married life. Destitution is largely due to economic causes. In so far as the poor are the victims of these causes and are not subject to the racial defects mentioned above, so far must they be protected against the indiscriminate zealot who would deprive them of their most precious rights. Sufficient has been said now to justify a general statement as to the chief difference between the eugenics of the Galton school and the eugenics of the Catholic Church. The Galton school is not simply ultimate enough. It does not realize how far-reaching is its much vaunted principle that there are causes of causes.[31]

This Catholic rhetoric operated to circumscribe tightly the territory in which eugenics could be applied. It denied that poverty per se was a sign of genetic flaws, and it suggested alternative causes of degeneration that were not addressed by the "Galton school" of eugenics.

Catholic writers did not simply critique the Galtonian rhetoric of hard-line eugenics: they also crafted their own approaches to dealing with the "necessitous" through the use of eugenics. One of the best examples of this type of narrative reconstruction can be found in the work of Gerrard, who kept track of the work of both the Christian Social Unions in England and the rhetoric of moderate eugenicists like Saleeby.[32] In June 1912, when eugenics discourse was at one of its peaks in England, Gerrard reminded his readers that public criticism had forced the "professional eugenist" to modify some of the claims that had initially been advanced in the new movement for race culture. In an article in the *Catholic World* titled "Eugenics and Catholic Teaching," Gerrard shared the belief that most eugenicists had been trying to create standards of "civil worth" that were means oriented and not ends oriented. Materialist eugenicists thus had as "many opinions on the point as there are eugenists." Gerrard invited his readers to consider that the best form of eugenics could be found within the standards provided by the Catholic Church. On the question of the unfit, Gerrard asked: "Who is to decide the standard code? Is the predominant impulse to be the standard, as it is asserted by Nietzsche and his followers? Is mere reason to be the standard as proposed by the rationalists? Or is the standard to be that which is set up by the Catholic Church, namely right reason duly informed by the Divine Will?"[33]

Gerrard argued that people needed to move away from modernistic eugenical schemes that required marriage certificates for the unfit to a selection process that was based on control of the passions, which he argued would be the "supreme eugenic value." Characterizing these theological virtues as habits of the heart and mind that would bring about the real sound principles of "positive eugenics," Gerrard then claimed that "The cultivation of noble men and women, the populating of heaven with immortal saints, is all absolutely dependent on one elemental fact, namely, the existence of babies. Race suicide is the first and most alarming phenomenon which threatens all efforts in race culture."[34] Gerrard's story is an example of how the meaning of eugenics promoted by hard-liners could be managed rhetorically by co-opting rather than taking head-on certain eugenical creeds. Gerrard's work, which appeared on both sides of the Atlantic, informed readers of the latest views of both eugenicists like Pearson and Webb and members of the local health boards. Many of these health workers held views on the issues of charity, sanitation, and the poor laws that were much more closely aligned with Gerrard's interpretation of eugenics than with Pearson's. If eugenics meant the welfare of children, then Gerrard could and did persuasively argue that the "anti-eugenical acts of gluttony, drunkenness, intemperance, idleness, bad company and neglect of prayer" were what prevented the children of England from learning about the importance of "supernatural prudence." While agreeing with many of the arguments posed by moderate eugenicists like Saleeby, Gerrard claimed that too few eugenical scientists understood the importance of the spiritual factor and treated the Church as a hindrance rather than as a help in solving the problems of the wellborn.[35]

In Catholic narratives about race degeneration and the unfitness of the poor, the adversaries in society were not the scientists but the material abuses that took place in English society under the name of eugenics. Gerrard lamented the fact that the British Eugenics Education Society tried to limit the definition of the word "eugenics" to simply mean "good breeding" because this reduced the study of agencies and social control to the arena of the barnyard, where humans were treated like race horses.[36] George Bernard Shaw was ridiculed for suggesting that people should have the freedom to mate outside the confines of marriage.[37] When Anglican Church leaders like Inge spoke out in favor of hereditarian interpretations of eugenics, they were attacked in the Catholic press as representatives of movements that had to deal with the "opposition of public opinion."[38]

Many Catholics felt that they had to respond to Inge because under the veil of eugenics he often attacked many of the Catholic Church's traditions as being anti-eugenical in nature. Gerrard quoted Inge as having said that "We do not think it wicked to encourage a beautiful and glorious specimen of womanhood to become a nun or sister of mercy, with vows of perpetual virginity. Here, surely, is a case in which the Eugenics Education society ought to have something to say. A man or woman belonging to a good stock ought to be told by public opinion that it is a duty to society for him or her to marry and have children."[39] For more than four decades English society had been exhorted about the necessity for interventionist programs that would encourage the wellborn to reproduce while prohibiting the unfit from perpetuating their kind. Catholics realized that this enabled their Protestant critics to condemn their religion in two ways: they could be chastised for encouraging the masses to reproduce and at the same time for cloistering their most intelligent members in convents or monasteries. Catholics responded to these attacks by turning some of the eugenics arguments on their head. On the issue of positive eugenics, one commentator claimed that

> Guided by this supernatural principle of selection, aiming solely at the development of the spiritual life, the Church is able to carry out her own system of eugenics. She is able in the first place to promote and control the eugenic principle of selection in marriage. Sir Francis Galton need not have gone to such pains to demonstrate that rational selection in marriage is possible. It is obvious. The Church promotes it and controls it perhaps more effectually than any other organization on the earth. . . . As a matter of positive eugenics she teaches that marriage is a sacrament through which is conveyed a divine strength enabling the married pair to perform all the duties of the state.[40]

Furthermore, the Catholic Church was said to be not only the protector of the inebriates and the diseased—it also worked to improve the wages of the worker and went beyond the "temporary palliatives" advocated by the materialists.[41] Quoting Goddard, Somerville would argue in his "Eugenics and the Feebleminded" that some eugenicists were focusing too much on the concept of "fixed" intelligence and not enough on "social necessity."[42] At the same time, Gerrard claimed that "Sir Francis Galton, then, and Dr. Saleeby and Dean Inge would seem to have made the most anti-eugenic stroke of all in striking at the Church's practice of celibacy and virginity . . . if so much depends on environment and education, and if heredity is nothing without it, then the monks and nuns of the dark ages did the best possible thing for race culture in retiring to such places where they could train themselves in art and literature. . . . Moreover, the strong and intellectual parents of those ages did not send *all* their children into the cloister."[43] In their defense of the activities of the Catholic Church, some Catholic rhetors were willing to discuss eugenics in order to defend their faith and their social welfare activities. Even Saleeby, having written about the importance of nature and nurture, found himself assailed by Catholics who pointed out some of the contradictions in his own rhetoric.

Yet Catholic rhetors were not on the defensive in all forms of eugenical argumentation. There were fragments of even hard-line rhetoric that Catholic communities could live with. Before World War I, most of the debates that took place over eugenics seemed to focus on the issues of education, marriage, and segregation, and the Catholic community did not yet feel compelled to deny all of the assumptions that were circulating under the eugenics rubric. For example, some opponents of proposals for sterilization had accepted the possibility of restricting the marriage of the feebleminded and of state regulation of prostitutes. Yet when the government tried to pass the Mental Deficiency Bill in 1913, Catholic radicals like Cecil Chesterton helped organize campaigns against the act.[44]

After World War I, Catholic eugenicists and anti-eugenicists found themselves labeled as reactionaries and dogmatists who hindered the progress of true eugenical reforms. Alliances were formed between members of the "birth control" and hard-line eugenical communities, and new discourses were created that placed Catholic eugenics on the periphery of eugenical discussions. As negative eugenics took center stage, debates over marriage restrictions were replaced with vocabularies that focused on the needs of the state in the area of mandatory sterilization and segregation.[45] This temporary alliance between advocates of "birth selection" and "birth control" meant that Catholics now found that their attacks on these birth control schemes were *welcomed* as evidence of the progressive nature of hard-line eugenics.[46] Marie Stopes, for example, counterattacked in court and in print by railing against the "malevolent and perfidious R.C.s."[47] Catholics in England thus found themselves accused of standing in the way of all eugenical schemes.

England's Catholic leaders used several different strategies to combat these "birth control" and hard-line eugenical movements. The two most popular approaches in the 1920s and 1930s involved either broadening the scope of eugenics (for example to include marriage restriction or help for the poor in the form of increased wages) or abandoning all forms of eugenics. The first strategy meant that Catholics would attempt to align themselves with more moderate eugenicists, while the second strategy meant admitting that the hard-liners controlled the public usages of "eugenics."

By broadening the range of social reforms covered by the term "eugenics," Catholic writers in England tried to move the study of the wellborn away from the fledging birth control movement in England. Some of these intellectuals reminded the hard-line eugenicists that just a few years ago they too had been against artificial birth control, and they added the threat of depopulation to their litany of the evils of contraception. By accepting some forms of "birth selection" rather than "birth control," Catholics were able to combine discussions of "race suicide" with the citations to theological pronouncements and papal encyclicals. Within these narratives, birth control became the peril rather than the promise of the English race. For example, both Cardinal Bourne, the archbishop of Westminster, and Dr. Downey, the archbishop of Liverpool, could use the authority of the registrar-general in arguing that the British were "a vanishing race."[48]

A second Catholic strategy involved abandoning the term "eugenics" to the enemy camp. Some Catholic writers were convinced that after the mid-1920s most members of the English community would forever associate eugenics with sterilization. Since the time of Galton, the state had been an important part of many eugenical reforms, and now Catholics were able to portray eugenics as a weapon of secular governments for protecting the upper classes. Chesterton, for example, in his *Eugenics and Other Evils*, likened eugenics to Prussianism, claiming that such bullying bureaucracies had led nations into war. Playing on patriotic sentiments, Chesterton claimed that the tyranny of eugenics meant that people would try "to reach the secret and sacred places of personal freedom, where no sane man ever dreamed of seeing it, especially the sanctuary of sex."[49] Audiences of all classes were now presented with pictures of an omnipotent government that could *force* eugenical marriages, and Chesterton reminded his readers that such statutes could reach "every rustic who is eccentric" and that normal people could be subject to laws "designed for homicidal maniacs."[50]

In sum, Catholics became anti-eugenic when that word was associated in the popular literature with sterilization. As long as eugenicist advocated some form of segregation they were on safe ground with some Catholics. But when it came to sterilization—even voluntary sterilization—the hard-liners found themselves facing vocal Catholic communities intent on maintaining traditional notions of charity and aid for the "necessitous."

American Catholicism and the Appropriation of Eugenics for the "Necessitous"

American Catholics were having to cope with some of the same social pressures that hindered English Catholics—immigration, nativism, and rapid urbanization. Yet some internal changes within the Catholic Church hierarchy complicated matters in the United States, and Catholic communities in the early decades of the twentieth century were torn over what to do about eugenics for several reasons. Some Catholics supported Americanist movements that claimed that the future of Catholicism depended on the United States and not the Vatican. Other Catholics recognized that Church doctrines needed to cope with scientific advances, and they watched as modern doctors, jurists, and social workers seemed to medicalize the issue of the feebleminded.[51] Some worried that the Church should attend to the needs of the laity, and if this meant appearing "progressive," so be it. Other Church leaders thought that the concept of eugenics could help improve the health conditions of new immigrants. For example, people like James Walsh suggested that modern organizers of care for the insane and defectives might emulate the way these groups were treated by the Church in the Middle Ages.[52] Finally, many Catholics recognized the fact that eugenics—especially calls for sterilization—were supported by Protestant Anglo-Saxons who vilified the Eastern Europeans who became a growing part of the Catholic and Jewish communities.[53]

Much like their British counterparts, American Catholics preferred the segregation of the unfit to the sterilization of the dysgenic.[54] For decades, Catholics in the United States were recognized as some of the most vocal opponents of hard-line eugenics. At first glance one might expect that American Catholics might have been univocal in their attitudes toward sterilization, but an analysis of the American Catholic discourse of the first decades of the twentieth century reveals that the solidification of opinion within the Catholic community did not occur overnight. Although some articles claimed that all Church leaders spoke out against sterilization from the beginning, a review of the rhetoric of the times indicates that there were heated debates over how to approach the problem of the feebleminded.[55] Some American Catholics agreed with the hard-line eugenicists who believed that sterilization was the scientific answer to the problems of the mentally and morally deficient. For example, Samuel Donovan, of Saint Bonaventure's Seminary in New York, reasoned that if society was sufficiently threatened by large numbers of criminal degenerates, then it should be morally permissible for the state to sterilize them.[56] Donovan argued that if Catholic theology allowed capital punishment, then it was also necessary to permit sterilization, and he could point to several other Catholic scholars who shared this opinion.[57] During the period between 1910 and 1913, more than twenty-four articles appeared in the *Ecclesiastical Review* discussing the legitimacy of sterilization.[58]

Yet the majority of American Catholic rhetors were against compulsory sterilization by the state, and these commentators created several different rhetorical strategies to counteract the influence of the hard-line nativist eugenicists. One involved a reconceptualization of eugenics that attempted to move audiences away from hard-line eugenical creeds. Another involved undermining the scientific ethos of nativist eugenicists. A third strategy was to deny the social and legal "necessity" for eugenical sterilization.

Many American Catholic writers in the first decades of the twentieth century tried to claim that the broad scope of eugenics included more than racially oriented reforms. Commentators like Conway invited readers to accept the need for a "remolding of life after the Christian pattern," which promised to "do infinitely more for the elimination of racial poisons and the improvement of the race than all hysterical eugenic agitations."[59] Catholics found that they could agree with eugenicists on the need for race "betterment" but that this concession did not justify the drastic measures advocated by those favoring sterilization of the unfit. Conway in the *Catholic World* proudly proclaimed, "The Catholic Church yields to no one in her zeal for the betterment of the race, but she uncompromisingly sets her face against all materialistic social experiments that outrage human dignity, go counter to elemental ethics . . . and lead to a callous disregard of the weak elements of the community."[60] American Catholics were willing to admit that there might be a need to stop social degeneration, but many believed the materialist hard-liners were merely leading people astray.

In place of the hard-line eugenical creed, American Catholics joined their British neighbors in offering their own rendition of eugenics. This form of eugenical discourse amalgamated spiritual and material aspects of human nature. Instead of admitting any need for birth control or sterilization of the unfit, Catholic eugenic stories focused on the ways in which social orders and economic disparities were linked to the problems of the poor. At the same time that hard-line eugenicists were claiming that genetic factors and germplasm were the paramount indicators of racial health, Catholics like Walter Kennedy were calling for a living wage to help the needy. Kennedy reminded readers that "the proponents of the Minimum Wage law have it in the words of an English jurist, spoken in 1762, but just as true today; 'Necessitous men (and we may add women) are not, truly freemen.' "[61] These strands of neo-Lamarckism allowed Catholics to battle for environmental rather than germinal changes in society.

While hard-liners were trying to convince Congress and the United States Supreme Court of the "necessity" of sterilization, Catholic critics of racist eugenics were imploring their readers to remember the influence of social conditions on human health. One critic of the social Darwinistic elements of hard-line eugenics was John Lapp, who in columns of the *Catholic Charities Review* passionately attacked the materialist creeds that blamed the feebleminded for the many ills of society. Lapp attacked Chicago organizations that believed in the survival of the fittest, and he asked: "Is a person who is sick from overwork or contagion unfit to survive? Is the man whose morale has been broken by fruitless searches for work or for a living wage unfit for survival? Is he who has been crippled by an accident unfit? Is the individual who loses everything in the failure of a bank or a business or a corporation thereby unfit to survive?"[62]

In Lapp's Catholic story, it was the artificial organization of society that had created the squalid poverty of the poor. To counter claims of hard-line eugenicists that at least 80 percent of the causes of pauperism or feeblemindedness were genetic in nature, Catholic writers like Lapp usually called attention to external circumstances like war, floods, sickness, unemployment, and inadequate wages, arguing that they accounted for "ninety percent or more of all the poverty in the United States.[63] Like other Catholic intellectuals, Lapp argued that the edicts of Pope Leo XIII meant that justice required protecting the poorer classes that needed help. In place of the survival of the fittest Lapp wanted "social justice."[64]

A second tactic used by American Catholics in combating hard-line eugenical discourse involved undermining the scientific ethos or credibility of the hardliners. Catholic writers were among the first to attempt to delegitimate the "science" of racist eugenics. As more and more geneticists, biologists, and social scientists began to question some of the Mendelian assumptions of leading eugenicists like Davenport and Laughlin, American readers were continually being briefed by Catholic intellectuals on the latest logical fallacies in the science of the wellborn. Writers like Pearl, Meyerson, S. J. Holmes, and Newman found themselves quoted extensively in newspapers, scientific journals, and articles in the Catholic and popular press. Ignatius Cox, for example, told his readers how even the British government in its report to the Committee on Sterilization had concluded in 1933 that the "supposed abnormal fertility of defectives is, in our view, largely mythical and results from the accidents" that occurred from time to time.[65]

One aspect of this attempt to undermine the ethos of the hard-line eugenicists involved reminding audiences of the political and social forces that were operating behind the scene. Hard-liners believed themselves to be objective researchers, but Catholic writers noted that much of this research was being funded by wealthy patrons. At the same time that they defended the supposedly unfit, Catholic critiques lampooned the notion that the wealthy or intelligent were necessarily the "fit" of America. While the hard-line eugenicist painted a graphic picture of the poor as thoughtless contributors to the stream of bad germplasm, Catholic commentators claimed that the poor in cultural communities were cooperative and "unselfish in regard to the sharing of the necessaries of life. . . . The poor are by no means the least 'rich towards God.' "[66] These critics of mainline eugenics closed the distance between the eugenicists and the people that they were trying to sterilize and constantly lamented the fact that the economically distressed were being treated as if they were a race outside of civilization. For example, Somerville argued that many intellectual geniuses could not "manage their affairs with ordinary prudence" and therefore they were the ones who ought to be classified as feebleminded.[67] Other critics tried to undermine some of the old Malthusian arguments. Ryan, for example, defended the right of parents to have children:

> Why did these ancestors of the present generation bring into the world children whom they could afford neither to educate nor to train for some occupation the products of which are sufficient in demand to make a living wage easily secured? Why indeed! . . . Here we have an excellent example of "visiting the iniquity of the father upon the children unto the third and fourth generations." . . . This statement is not only shallow and inhuman, but disgustingly pharisaical; for it intimates that these ancestors, who made sacrifices of all sorts to care for all the children that God sent them, exercised less sexual self-control than those more cultured persons who limit the number of their offspring.[68]

At the same time, Catholic writers ridiculed hard-line elitists for forgetting their social responsibilities. For Windle, the people who were warning Americans about the prevention of the marriage of the feebleminded and the other defectives were taking an approach that was "hardly a charitable attitude toward the afflicted."[69] Another critic complained that "It is the way with some eugenists to judge *eugenic value* by *social standing, economic competency,* and the amount of *formal education* received. Social standing, however, is not virtue; economic competency may imply crime; and formal education has cultivated at times some shady acquaintances" (emphasis in the original).[70] These writers highlighted what was continually being denied by the hard-liners—that much of their eugenical rhetoric was being produced by spokespersons for particular class interests.

Other critics attacked the ethos of hard-line eugenics by claiming that the hard-liners were falling behind the latest in genetical research and that they were using outdated information. One writer asked his audience to believe that "Modern scientific findings do not support the eugenists' claim that the births of feebleminded children will be greatly reduced by the sterilization of all mental defectives."[71] While hard-line eugenicists focused on the hereditarian elements that caused mental deficiency, some Catholics pointed out that the newest investigations were taking into account the role of the environment as well as heredity in the creation of problems for the poor. One writer observed that "insane departments of the poorhouses" were discovering the "nearly one hundred thousand cases of pellagra in our Southern States hidden away in the county insane asylums and the poorhouses, and the disease has evidently been in existence for at least one hundred years."[72] This focus on the environment directly challenged the claim of many eugenicists that germplasm was primarily responsible for human progress.

Sometimes the credibility of hard-line eugenics was subverted by portraying sterilization as an unnatural practice that robbed civilization of some of its greatest people. Hard-liners often claimed that sterilization was a simple medical procedure, but in the Catholic narratives these same activities were described as dehumanizing. One writer declared that "Nature is far wiser than the eugenicist, who breeds for points like the breeders of cattle. She seeks to develop all the faculties of man and to prevent all onesidedness. If the eugenicists had been in power down the ages, the world would have been robbed of many a genius who came from the most unpromising antecedents."[73] In this narrative, Catholics subtly invited readers to contemplate the possibility that perhaps eugenicists empowered throughout the ages would have enacted programs that violated the natural rights protected by the Catholic Church.

The third rhetorical strategy used by Catholic Americans in their campaign against sterilization involved the denial that eugenical surgery was a "necessity."[74] When the hard-liners failed in their attempts to persuade American audiences of the need for coercive marriage regulation, they turned to sterilization as an effective and inexpensive means of reducing the number of unfit. At first Catholic critics of hard-line eugenics simply ridiculed the exaggerated dangers that came from the feebleminded. One commentator noted that America showed no signs of imminent decay and "consequently the right of national self-preservation may not be invoked."[75] Many hard-liners disagreed, and massive immigration in the first two decades of the twentieth century seemed to provide further evidence that feeblemindedness was becoming a national responsibility.

Another element of the Catholic attack on the "necessity" of sterilization involved providing counter-characterizations of the people who underwent eugenical surgery. While mainstream eugenicists presented American audiences with mountains of statistics and examples of degenerate families like the Jukes and Kallikaks, Catholic writers were humanizing the men and women who were declared to be feebleminded and unfit. What the eugenicist characterized as a biologically unfit person was viewed by the Church as a child of God, possessing an immortal soul and entitled to the dignity of natural "rights."[76] Commentators ridiculed the notion that there existed any one economic "test for sterilization" that was for the "good of the community."[77]

Catholics objected to the "necessity" of hard-line eugenics on patriotic as well as religious grounds. Americans were admonished to remember that this was an issue of human rights that could not be taken lightly. One editorial in *Catholic World* defended the immigrant and vilified the Anglo-Saxons who followed the writings of Gino Speranza.[78] Another commentator observed that "The eugenists, with their division of human into the 'fit' and 'unfit' deny the fundamental principle of the American Constitution. They take upon themselves to say who shall have life and liberty, who shall marry and have children, and who shall be denied these human rights, who shall be treated as belonging to stocks that society must exterminate."[79] One critic remarked that if "these immoral faddists" had their way, the Statue of Liberty would become a "monument in memory of our dearly departed."[80] Another claimed that Galton's notion of probability as the foundation of eugenics was an insufficient basis for action when the life or liberty of an individual was at stake.[81] Most Catholic theologians opposed sterilization on the grounds that it destroyed a "natural faculty" and allowed for the voluntary "mutilation" that violated "bodily integrity."[82] American audiences were reminded that this "kind of outrage on human rights in the name of social benefit is what Christianity has fought since the days of pagan Rome."[83]

By the second half of the 1920s, the Catholic eugenical strategies in the legal and the larger rhetorical culture had produced mixed results. They succeeded in helping to undermine some of the credibility of the more racist hard-liners and they offered constructive social reforms, but they failed to stop the passage of "progressive" eugenical legislation. Prior to the *Buck* case, Catholic rhetors helped create an interesting political cycle of events. Influential hard-line eugenicists would help gain the passage of state sterilization laws, but courts and members of the executive branches of the states and municipalities would either veto or leave unenforced the most offensive parts of these statutes. One writer claimed that "as a result we have had a series of gubernatorial vetoes, and decisions holding asexualization laws unconstitutional" and "all of them betrayed dread and repulsion, and a dislike not only of the legislation proposed or passed, but of the proponents of it."[84] In 1927 the governor of Colorado vetoed a sterilization bill, in part owing to opposition from the Holy Name Society and the Denver Knights of Columbus. The Denver Diocesan Holy Name Union attacked the sterilization bill as a violation of natural law and because humans had an "inability to pass judgment on human mentality."[85] One writer ridiculed state leaders who were trying to sterilize people who had been "convicted of murder . . . rape, highway robbery, chicken stealing, bombing, or theft of automobiles."[86] Catholics at times were ambivalent about the need for marriage restrictions or the segregation of the unfit, but they often agreed that sterilization was counterproductive.

With the conclusion of the *Buck* case, Catholic writers stepped up their attacks on the credibility of the hard-liners and the legitimacy of sterilization. Like their English counterparts, American Catholics were objecting to the *means* that were being used in defenses of eugenical legislation. As Ignatius Cox argued in an article entitled "The Folly of Human Sterilization," no sensible person "can be opposed to the aim of eugenics, the health and happiness of future generations. The attempt, however, to attain this end by a means unjustifiable on scientific or moral grounds, and hence, fundamentally on legal grounds—namely, by human sterilization—will meet the opposition of those who give the subject profound considerations."[87] For many Catholics, there was simply not enough scientific evidence to prove the "necessity" of legal sterilization. Too many questions could not be answered by the hard-liners on the nature, scope, and limits of eugenical sterilization. For example, Cox, commenting in *Scientific American*, argued that it was extremely difficult to decide just who were the "undesirable elements."[88] For Catholic intellectuals, eugenical sterilization was the antithesis of Christian charity.

By the end of the 1920s, Americans seemed to be evenly divided on the issue of eugenical sterilization. Local Catholic communities had voiced their opposition to it, but hard-liners like Popenoe claimed that the Catholic Church had not definitively decided about eugenics. This may have helped influenced the pope to speak out on eugenical sterilization. In December 1930 Pope Pius XI commented on the problems of eugenics along with divorce, birth control, and the celebration of materialist passion in films and theaters.[89] The Casti Connubii, like earlier Catholic commentaries, argued that the *aims* of eugenics were good but that the *means* of putting them into effect were sometimes evil.[90] The contents of Pope Pius's encyclical were published in the *New York Times*, where millions of Americans could read the pope's attack on the eugenicists' abuse of "the Law of Extreme Necessity." Pope Pius focused attention on the abuses of sterilization and proclaimed: "Magistrates have no direct power over the bodies of their subjects. Therefore, when no crime has taken place, they can never directly harm or tamper with the integrity of the body, either for reasons of eugenics or any other reason."[91] The pope's stance simply reiterated what Catholic writers had been arguing for decades—that eugenics itself was not necessarily immoral, but when sterilization tampered with the "integrity of the body" this was an illegitimate abuse of state power.

By the mid-1930s, many Anglo-Americans began to echo the complaints of the Catholic community on the issue of sterilization. Collectivist notions that social "necessity" should override the rights of the individual were prominent in the first quarter of the twentieth century, but the Catholic stand on sterilization gained in credibility as more and more Americans became aware of the abuses that took place under the guise of medicine after Germany passed its sterilization laws in the early 1930s. Catholic writers were some of the first to question the wisdom of the German legislation. Commentators like James Walsh warned readers of the *Commonweal* about the possible political abuses that came from laws that dealt with the feebleminded. He admonished his audience to remember that this type of statute had the "tendency to neglect or minimize certain of the inviolable rights of man."[92] Many of these warnings would become commonplace in the years ahead.

By the end of the 1930s, Catholics gained much ground in their quest to stop the practice of sterilization. Scholars writing on the abuses of eugenics have tended to emphasize the success of the advocates of eugenical sterilization, but the hard-liners faced stiff opposition. After the pope's warning about being "oversolicitous for the cause of eugenics," many organizations like the Knights of Columbus responded to homilies by Catholic bishops. At the same time, the papal encyclical discouraged some liberal Catholic theologians who had earlier expressed views that were at odds with the Casti Connubii.[93] These discussions

at the higher levels of the Catholic hierarchy were not simply metaphysical debates over the theory of eugenic sterilization, they were guidelines for practical
public action and were often used by Catholic leaders in mobilizing opposition
to sterilization. Even when mainline eugenicists like Laughlin argued that the
United States had settled the issue of the legitimacy of sterilization in the case of
Buck v. Bell, these advocates soon found that the Holmes decision had energized
not only the American Eugenics Society but the opposition as well.

In New Jersey, even the support of the League of Women Voters and the Fed-
eration of Women's Clubs could not overcome Catholic opposition.[94] Roswell
Johnson, one of the leading eugenicists and editor of the *Eugenics* newsletter, at-
tributed the New Jersey loss to "religious prejudice," a hardly "veiled reference
to the Catholic Church, a perennial adversary."[95] Elsewhere Johnson, who moni-
tored legislative developments for his magazine, noted that the Roman Catholics
had "furnished the main opposition to the New York and Connecticut birth control bills."[96] According to a contemporary critic in one local dispute "A priest
called upon an assemblyman and told him that he controlled 1,200 votes in his
parish, and that these votes would be necessary for his re-election and that only
by voting against the sterilization bill could he hope to be returned to the Assembly. Another assemblyman was threatened with a boycott of his store by all
Catholics in his district if he continued to favor the bill. Another assemblyman
who was in the insurance business was told that the policies he had written on a
Catholic Church would not be renewed if he voted for the bill."[97] Yet Catholic
pressure on hard-line eugenics did not come just from priests and other leaders
of the community. It also came from the laity. Marion Olden, the executive secretary of Birthright, claimed that "Whenever sterilization bills were introduced,
the Catholics descend upon the capitol in numbers—priests, nuns and laity—
and attack the bill as 'against the will of God' and 'an attack on the American
Home.' . . . A Catholic physician testified at the hearings that States with a law,
including California, have ceased to use it and that the operation robs a man of
virility! . . . The tactics used in Wisconsin were not wanting in Alabama."[98]

In the decade that followed the Casti Connubii, hard-liners in Maine, Arizona,
Alabama, Wisconsin, and elsewhere had to deal with powerful religious opposition to eugenics.[99] Just as strict hereditarian eugenicists kept track of the victories
for the proponents of sterilization, Catholic writers reminded their audiences of
the ways in which local organizations in many states were stopping the carnage
of human mutilation. One editor in the *Commonweal* told how in New Jersey
a proposed sterilization bill was being bitterly debated before the state senate's
Public Health Committee. In this confrontation, "Major" Eugene F. Kincade

was said to oppose the bill in the name of "1,000,000 Catholics."[100] In describing disputes in Iowa, the same critic mentioned that local newspapers including the Dubuque *Telegraph Herald* and the *Times Journal* were joining forces with "the diocesan organ, the *Witness*" in pointing out "fallacies in the arguments for a sterilization law."[101] Readers were told tales of how men and women had been "forced" by relief workers, under penalty of being denied relief, to submit to sterilization operations in California and Ohio.[102] Even when Catholic communities couldn't stop the passage of sterilization legislation, their protests worried many of the officials who were responsible for enforcing the statutes. In Kansas, for example, the state legislature had passed an aggressive sterilization policy in the mid-1920s, but commentators worried about the large number of protests that came from "those of the Catholic faith who claim it is against their religious teachings to interfere with nature."[103] These types of charges reminded readers that compulsory sterilization was not just a medical issue.

Other eugenical accounts support this view of the impact of Catholic activity. In May of 1939, the American Eugenics Society held a conference that was supposed to be on eugenics and its relation to the church. Conference leader Frederick Osborn was exasperated when the conference focused most on sterilization and the ethics of negative eugenics instead of the problem of the disintegrating family value among the best stocks. The conference was attended by more than 135 leaders in religion, eugenics, birth control, and philanthropy. Urban Catholics found themselves agreeing with rural Baptists that sterilization was not the answer.[104] An obviously shaken Osborn, after listening to some of these speeches, claimed that he had never been more "bitterly discouraged." He implored his audience to remember that "If the Churches cannot teach us the true value of life . . . where are we going to learn this lesson?"[105]

By the end of the 1930s, Catholic writers found that they had allies in their antisterilization campaign. Some of these writers shared enthusiasm for schemes for the "living wage," but more often they joined in the attack on the credibility of the hard-line eugenicists. Social scientists and biologists (Boas, Pearl, Jennings, and Huxley, for example) began to write books, articles, and speeches on the limitations of eugenics, and sterilization was one of the primary topics under debate. Many of them wrote about the difficulty of defining the term "eugenics," but few would credit the Catholics for having expanded the term to include traditional notions of charity, child welfare, maternal benefits, and higher wages. By this time hard-liners were infuriated when in the Catholic stories of eugenics the term was used to justify the very programs that they thought were "dysgenic." In the Catholic narratives of the 1930s, the best type of eugenics did not involve birth control clinics but rather improvements in social justice. One commentator went so far as to claim that what people needed to remember was that there were two legitimate and effective measures which

> are the elimination of war and social injustice. . . . War is disgenic [*sic*]. It brings with it an ever-widening trail of death, disease, insanity, neuroses, economic and financial confusion. Social injustice is, in large measure, responsible for our slums, for disease, for helplessness in human life, for despondency and consequent neuroses. In this country it is possible to produce enough that all may live well, if the wealth we produce is properly distributed through a cultural wage, and not allowed to concentrate in the hands of the few. And notice this: that war and social injustice are too often the result of the leadership of those who are supposed to be of the best eugenic breed: the educated, those of social standing and economic competency. To pass over war and social injustice in the hope of eradicating human ills by sterilization may be good propaganda; certainly it is bad eugenics.[106]

For many Catholics, attitudes toward eugenics depended on what *type* of eugenics was being advocated.

Of all vulgar modes of escaping from the consideration of the effect of social and moral influences on the mind, the most vulgar is that of attributing the diversities of conduct and character to inherent natural differences.

John Stuart Mill

The superficially sympathetic man flings a coin to a beggar; the more deeply sympathetic man builds an alms house for him so that he need no longer beg; but perhaps the most radically sympathetic of all is the man who arranges that the beggar shall not be born. **Havelock Ellis**

Liberal and Socialist Interpretations of Eugenics

In histories of the eugenics movement written in the 1940s, 1950s, and 1960s, the primary advocates of the eugenics creed were depicted as conservative reactionaries out of touch with the real world. In these orthodox scholastic accounts, the controversial writings of people like Pearson, Davenport, Laughlin, Wiggam, and Stoddard became prototypical examples of the antidemocratic rhetoric that supposedly represented the core of eugenical argumentation.[1] In the historical accounts of such writers as Mark Haller, Kenneth Ludmerer, and Daniel Kevles, conservative hard-liners formed the vanguard of those interested in the science of the wellborn until the advent of reform eugenics in the late 1920s and early 1930s.[2] As Diane Paul has recently observed, the "history of eugenics has been presented so often as though it were simply the extension of nineteenth-century social Darwinism, reflective of the same conservative values and the interests of the identical social groups, that we have nearly lost sight of the fact that important segments of the Left . . . were once also enthusiastic about the potential uses of eugenics."[3] "Eugenics" was in fact a much more ambiguous term.

In this chapter, I look at the ways eugenical arguments were deployed in Anglo-American discourse by liberals and socialists in their political debates with conservatives.[4] I will illustrate how British and American leftists had their own interpretations of eugenics, which helped popularize forms of eugenical argumentation long before the appearance of reform eugenics.

Liberal Interpretations of Eugenics

While scholars interested in eugenics usually trace the origins of the movement to conservative forces influenced by Francis Galton, the study of the wellborn had multiple origins. Beginning in the early 1880s, stories circulated in the British press about the birthrates of the poor and the quality of the average English citizen (see chapter 3), but it was not until the nation collectively perceived the need for massive change in its overall *biological* composition that readers would take seriously the exhortations of Galton, Pearson, and the Webbs.

Those who worried about the differential birthrate and the existence of the residuum included not only conservative members of the upper class but middle-class liberals as well. By 1904 many English social workers, politicians, and philanthropists believed that the nation was in a state of emergency requiring some rational program of "efficiency," and they were unwilling to allow the paupers and casual workers of their nation to languish and reproduce themselves endlessly in workhouses, jails, inebriate homes, and other institutions.[5] Members of the middle class worried about the effect of the growing number of the unfit on the tax rates, and they encouraged the government to take a more active role in reducing the numbers of "inefficient" Britons. A Royal Commission on the Care and Control of the Feebleminded was established, and for four years this group studied in detail the conditions that went into the creation of the necessitous.[6]

For centuries stories had been circulating in liberal circles that attempted to find ways of discriminating between the truly necessitous and the idle masses who abused private and governmental aid, but at the turn of the century, liberal reformers found a new way of helping Edwardian England cope with the residuum. They discovered the existence of a class known as the "feebleminded" who resided among the poor. The feebleminded were those close-to-normal denizens of the lower classes who had once been thought of as victims of the Industrial Revolution but were now seen as doomed by their heredity to live a life of mental deficiency.[7] While the term "feebleminded" had been in the English philanthropy literature at least since 1876, it was this Royal Commission of 1904 and the British press coverage that it received that popularized the concept.[8] One of the goals of the commission was to determine "what constitutes such weakness of mind as to necessitate a person to be taken care of."[9]

Socialists and labor leaders would accuse the commission of victimizing the poor; but for the conservatives and liberals who accepted its findings, the discovery of the extent of feeblemindedness among the pauper classes helped to explain the failure of social reforms that had been initiated within capitalist frameworks in the nineteenth century. While the commission studied a variety of causes of both pauperism and feeblemindedness, some British writers began to focus on biological explanations of poverty in the midst of plenty. While some British conservatives continued to believe in a minimalist, laissez-faire approach to the feebleminded and other necessitous groups, others reluctantly joined with moderate liberal reformers in supporting the Royal Commission's efforts at categorizing the poor for possible government intervention.[10] The Royal Commission's reports were discussed in the *London Times*, the *Manchester Guardian*, *Eugenics Review*, the *Charity Organisation Review*, and other publications. Commission members included representatives from the British Medical Association, the National Vigilance Association, and the Ladies Samaritan Societies. One editorial in the *London Times* (subsequently cited in the *Eugenics Review*) commented that there was a "definite race of chronic paupers . . . breeding in and through successive generations."[11]

While the term "eugenics" had existed in the British public vocabulary since at least the early 1880s, it was the discovery of the menace of the feebleminded that spurred the creation of the eugenics movement. Several years after the Royal Commission findings, local and national eugenical organizations had formed across England. Many eugenicists began to argue that the commission had proved that "inefficient" philanthropy simply added to the ranks of the pauper class. The Royal Commission's study of more than fifty thousand children in various sections of London seemed to reinforce liberal perceptions that the unfit could not control their reproductive habits.[12] An argument that often appeared in the popular press contrasted "normal" families who had four children with "degenerates" who had more than seven.[13] The *London Times* reported that "Especially in view of the evidence concerning fertility, the prevention of mentally defective persons from becoming parents would tend largely to diminish such persons in the population . . . the evidence strongly supports measures . . . for placing mentally defective persons in institutions where they will be employed and detained . . . and kept under effectual supervision so long as may be *necessary.*[14] Liberals joined the ranks of those who were convinced that some government measures were needed in order to combat the growing numbers of the unfit.

The discovery of the feebleminded provided British liberals with a rhetorically powerful classification that could be used to legitimate the extension of government into what some had thought of as the private sphere without becoming involved in schemes for the redistribution of income. At the same time British liberals could use eugenical arguments to disseminate information to the working classes on how they should behave biologically for their own benefit and that of the English "race." In the first two decades of the twentieth century, the term "feebleminded" was employed to identify anyone who did not fit middle-class standards of physical, mental, and social fitness. For example, a woman who bore a child out of wedlock was considered to have the "weakness of mind" that indicated a "lack of moral fibre."[15] The term stigmatized hundreds of thousands of individuals who were said to have failed in their attempts to adapt to society, and it shifted attention away from the economic plight of those who languished in squalor and poverty.[16] The existence of feeblemindedness could also be used by Fabians and other liberals to explain why representative democracies needed an elite cadre of leaders to implement social reforms devised by the genetically superior intellectual classes. Furthermore, liberals who worried that Britain was becoming "socialistic" could argue that children who failed to profit from educational programs had a variety of physical and mental problems that prevented them from succeeding in either school or society.[17]

Less than a decade after the creation of the first eugenical societies in England, politicians and other government officials began to use eugenical arguments in defense of liberal social reforms. These moderates joined British conservatives in looking for ways of helping the "residuum," who did not share in the economic benefits that naturally came to the more meritorious working poor. Representatives of the middle classes began to complain that the feebleminded were reproducing at rates that overwhelmed the supporting taxpayers. One critic, for example, declared that it was repugnant to see that the "strong should be overwhelmed by the feeble, ailing and unfit."[18] Winston Churchill, England's Home Secretary in 1910 and 1911, wrote to the prime minister that the "multiplication of the unfit" was a "very terrible danger to the race."[19] As one member of the Poor Law Commission commented in 1909, England needed a "strong and capable service" that would deal with "destitute or 'necessitous' persons." [20] Many speakers and writers in the Anglo–Saxon community thought that it was time to recognize that the existence of the "feebleminded" among the pauper classes was an emergency requiring that the necessities of the state be balanced against the liberties of the individual.

British liberals in the prewar years were divided in their response to the proposals of the hard-line eugenicists. Traditionalists tended to side with the conservatives, while members of the "new liberalism" movement wanted more moderate eugenical reforms. While hard-liners were predisposed to offer strong hereditarian interpretations of eugenics, writers like Leonard Hobhouse argued that these hard-liners were forgetting that some of the poor law commissions were based on "the assumption that the pauper was a normal person made necessitous by circumstance." [21] These proponents of the "new liberalism" in England believed in the importance of eugenics, but they thought that hard-liners were forgetting the important cultural influences on the "social fabric." Hobhouse, for example, spoke for many of his colleagues when he claimed that

> The older Galtonian view working with small variations leads to the suggestion that natural selection is a permanent necessity of racial progress; it desires to subordinate the social structure in general to that end, and would, if consistently pushed through, lead to the permanent suppression, generation after generation of the weaker stocks. The newer view points in quite another direction. It finds the basis of racial progress in definite mutations, which if not destroyed by an unfavorable environment, establish themselves. . . . On this view it may be said that the most fundamental necessity from the point of view of racial progress is to maintain an environment in which any new mutation of promise socially considered may thrive and grow, and by this line of argument we arrive once more at the conclusion that liberty, equality of opportunity, and the social atmosphere of justice and considerateness are the most eugenic of agencies.[22]

While the new liberals continued to emphasize the importance of character in human evolutionary development, they believed that the hard-liners were ignoring the fact that some social changes were beyond the control of the individual. While agreeing with the Galtonians that there were "hereditary paupers," new liberals like Hobhouse tended to use neo-Lamarckian explanations focusing on the "social environment" that turned human beings into "wastrels" and "degenerate stock." [23] These liberals did not deny the existence of paupers or the feebleminded; they simply disagreed with other liberals and with conservatives on the causes of need.

The existence of this more moderate form of British eugenics meant that a variety of social reformers—including public health officials, philanthropists, and members of Parliament—could use forms of eugenical arguments to rationalize the health insurance acts, child labor laws, new poor laws, and other measures that hard-liners claimed were dysgenic in nature.[24] Liberals who shared Hobhouse's perspective could thus use eugenical arguments without having to quote the hard-line members of the Eugenics Education Society. Decades before the advent of what Kevles has called reform eugenics, these liberals appropriated much of the language of the hard-liners in order to help the lower classes benefit from the fruits of capitalism. They helped to popularize eugenics by making four important changes in the eugenics vocabulary. First, they insisted that the government had to take a more active role in highlighting the social conditions that contributed to the growing numbers of the feebleminded. Second, they expanded the definition of eugenics to include the influences of both nature and nurture. Their third alteration was a shift in emphasis from compulsory to voluntary eugenical schemes. Finally, they worked to redefine "feeblemindedness" so that fewer working poor would be classified as "mental defectives."

In the early years of the twentieth century, English liberals allied themselves with those who believed that nationalism and collectivism could augment individualism in combating social problems.[25] Some of these rhetors were eager to employ the "rational" powers of the state in promoting "natural selection" among the unfit. These writers insisted that the government should take a more active role in reducing the numbers of the feebleminded. "No consistent eugenist can be a 'Laisser Faire' " wrote Sidney Webb, "unless he throws up the game in despair. He must interfere, interfere, interfere!"[26] Many new liberals believed that if the intelligent members of the upper and middle classes helped their more unfortunate brothers and sisters, they might begin to restore the balance in capitalist society between natural and social evolution. Caleb Williams Saleeby spoke for many liberal eugenicists when he wrote exuberantly in 1909 that "the present writer believes that eugenics is going to save the world."[27] World War I would dash the hopes of some of these reformers, but in the prewar years, the progress of science seemed to demand that the British government get involved in the collective affairs of the imperial race.

The second major change initiated by liberal eugenicists was to redefine eugenics to include both hereditarian and environmental concerns. As I indicated in chapter 2, eugenics could be interpreted in a variety of ways, but hard-liners were vehement in insisting on strict, Galtonian interpretations of human nature. These more conservative eugenicists thus labeled liberal interpretations of eugenics as *anti*-eugenical, even when liberal writers claimed to be using eugenical arguments or when they acknowledged their debt to Galton or Pearson. At the same time that political conservatives were discussing the national necessities that demanded the implementation of coercive eugenical policies, one group of liberal social reformers was more interested in identifying and controlling the environmental causes of pauperism. Unlike the hereditarian eugenicists, these more moderate Edwardian liberals were interested in economic and social necessities as well as biological ones. Although some liberals directly attacked the very existence of eugenics, many influential elites of the period were more interested in redefining the study of the wellborn to include environmental influences. They co-opted the social Darwinistic rhetoric of the hard-liners and turned this discourse into a more palatable form of eugenics.

The third significant alteration crafted by liberals was to move Britain away from the hard-line schemes of eugenical legislation and toward more voluntary orientations. Many liberals opposed compulsory restrictions on marriage and argued that voluntary improvements in sanitation and in prenatal and medical care would reduce infant mortality rates. At least in the early years, liberals were convinced that persuasion and public education would significantly improve the welfare of the feebleminded.

The liberals' fourth substantive change in eugenical argumentation involved a redefinition of unfitness. Perhaps nothing revealed the importance of deciding who was unfit better than the narratives that were constructed when the Mental Deficiency Bills were presented to Parliament in 1912 and 1913.[28] Some writers, like Larson, have argued that in spite of the efforts of members of the Eugenic Education Society, "their doctrines had little impact on Parliament."[29] Yet much of Larson's own research reveals that there were a variety of eugenical interpretations of the Mental Deficiency Acts, and even when the legislators tried to distance themselves from the eugenicists, the debates were framed in eugenical terms. An ideographic analysis of the discussions that took place over the Mental Deficiency Acts shows the way many rhetors and writers—including moderate and radical liberals—took for granted some of the biological explanations of human conduct that governed a variety of social relationships.

In the English Parliament of 1912, both conservative and liberal members supported the passage of the Mental Deficiency Bill.[30] Gershom Stewart, a conservative, brought before Parliament the Eugenic Education Society's Feeble-Minded Control Bill, observing that it had "originated, after due consideration, with the scientific and benevolent people who have been trying to grapple with this problem." Avoiding any direct reference to eugenics itself, Stewart remarked that he would not "theorize as to the cause of this disease" other than to note that "no 'feeble-minded' person can ever be made an effective citizen, and two feeble-minded parents can never have a normal child."[31] The liberal Union Member of Parliament Alfred Lyttelton would insist that the danger of racial degeneration was "now scientifically established beyond doubt."[32] The 1912 bill called for segregation of the mentally defective in order to halt the regressive social trend they represented and to protect both the defective individuals and society.

Yet as Larson has pointed out, members of Parliament in 1912 and 1913 were still leery of using the term "eugenics" in their legislative deliberations.[33] Liberals wanted to join conservatives in voting for early versions of the Mental Deficiency Bill, but some radicals like Josiah Wedgwood convinced more moderate liberals that using the language of eugenics meant accepting legislation that threatened the liberties of poor persons who were not mentally deficient. Charles Roberts warned, "I would ask people before they make up their minds as on the latest novelty of the eugenics theory to be a little cautious."[34] Advocates of the mental deficiency legislation compromised by arguing in Parliament and in the press that it was based on accepted knowledge ("common sense," in press accounts) and was not necessarily tied to any new experimental science. Leslie Scott, for example, represented the views of many conservatives and liberals when he wrote a letter to the editor of the British *Nation* defending the Mental Deficiency Act. Scott countered Wedgwood's contentions by claiming:

> We do not know exactly what causes deficiency to develop in the first place. . . . But we do know that its presence indicates such a degeneration of the stock that it is not possible for a person affected by it to procreate a whole family of healthy children. There is no more doubt about it than there is about the consequences of breeding with other diseases. It is not a question of eugenics at all; it is a question of common sense. No man would ever let his daughter marry a man who was so diseased that he could not possibly procreate healthy children. . . . While it would not be easy to define a rhinoceros in an Act of Parliament, it is perfectly easy for anyone who has ever seen a rhinoceros to recognize one when he meets it in the street. So the difficulty of defining a feeble-minded person does not arise from any difficulty in identifying mental defect when it is seen.[35]

Some members of the House of Commons were willing to explain in great detail why the first Mental Deficiency Bill was necessary. One argued that "more than half the people in our inebriate homes are not drunkards, but feebleminded."[36] In the stories that were told by the defenders of the measure, no "sane person" became feebleminded because of "starvation, neglect, or misery." Instead, the growing numbers of defectives came from "inherited" feeblemindedness. As Scott would insist,

> There is no case of a feeble-minded person being cured of his defect by treatment or training. You can no more cure a man with half a mind than you can cure one with half a leg. Lastly, the children of defectives always suffer from an hereditary taint. A large proportion will be themselves mentally affected; the others will hand on the taint to their children. To the third and fourth generation they will work out, in misery and in crime, the evil effects of their ancestral taint. The liberty of the subject, for which Mr. Wedgwood contends, is, in the last resort, merely the liberty to die in the workhouse, the brothel, or the gaol.[37]

For many members of Parliament, some form of hereditarian argument was clearly operative in English society.[38]

Yet not all liberals were willing to accept this form of eugenical legislation. While the majority of moderate liberals favored passage of the Mental Deficiency Bill, there were radical liberals like Josiah Wedgwood who refused to compromise. Wedgwood crafted a narrative that vilified the defenders of a tyrannical bill. On the floor of Parliament, he indignantly announced that

> the spirit at the back of the Bill is not the spirit of charity, not the spirit of the love of mankind. It is a spirit of the horrible Eugenic Society which is setting out to breed up the working class as though they were cattle. . . . This incarceration of people who have committed no crime is bad enough, but it is particularly dangerous when you allow people to be incarcerated on the dictum of the specialist. Here you are alienating these powers, powers which were possessed by the Holy Inquisition, and you are going to entrust them to a body of specialists whose absolute remedies for disease change every year, and who invent year after year new fungoid growths, or something of the kind which may be stamped out by science only if you give them a free hand.[39]

Building on a common Enlightenment theme, Wedgwood's speeches were considered at the time to be radical in their sentimentalism, and he was fighting an uphill battle in questioning some of Britain's highest medical authorities.[40] Typical of Wedgwood's remarks were the claims that he made in Parliament when that body was debating whether doctors or magistrates should determine who fell under the scope of the Mental Deficiency Bill. Wedgwood believed that "The Royal Commission consisted of specialists, many of them members of the Eugenics Society, all of them people who have one aim and object, and only one, and that is the materialistic one of improving the race and the breed of people in the country. I submit our object as politicians in a democratic country is not first and foremost to breed the working class as though they were cattle."[41] Wedgwood's tirade moved few of his comrades in the legislature, but it was an important part of the debates that took place in the popular press.[42]

In 1913, moderate liberals negotiated the Mental Deficiency Bill through Parliament by deftly removing some of its more objectionable parts. Any hint of a connection between care for the feebleminded and the hard-line Eugenics Education Society was removed, although this group had been one of the prime movers in having this legislation submitted to Parliament. When Wedgwood claimed that the bill violated English principles of "liberty," pro-eugenics legislators like Dr. William Chapple responded that the power to decide who was eugenically unfit would rest with learned "magistrates" and not the doctors. With these and other changes (the definition of feeblemindedness was significantly narrowed), the Mental Deficiency Act went into effect before the advent of World War I.

Wedgwood's brand of liberalism exceeded that of Hobhouse in denying the legitimacy of any form of Galtonian eugenics. Wedgwood ultimately failed to prevent the passage of the Mental Deficiency Bill, but in its altered form the amended bill looked more like a piece of negotiated "reform" eugenics legislation than any hard-line eugenical measure. Conservative eugenicists hailed it as a significant step toward creating a eugenical society, but even they acknowledged that this second bill had been watered down significantly. The revisions to the Mental Deficiency Acts reflected all four of the liberal changes noted above. The government took a more active role in dealing with the feebleminded, and the bill was said to be more "voluntary" than coercive. Parliamentary debates on the role of heredity took into account the importance of the environment, and the definition of feeblemindedness that was finally accepted represented a liberal interpretation of the term.

The passage of the Mental Deficiency Bill occurred in spite of the divisions within the English liberal community, yet when we compare the debates that took place in the popular press with those in Parliament, we find that the radical liberals may have been correct in their belief that English "liberty" had saved the day. Radical critics of the Mental Deficiency Bills in the British popular press attacked both the goals and the scientific soundness of hard-line eugenics.[43] For example, one writer in the *Athenaeum* ridiculed the parliamentary legislation for being based on a "eugenics" science that did not have a "secure foothold."[44] The influential *Manchester Guardian* noted that the early versions of the Mental Deficiency Bill followed "half-baked" scientific theories.[45] One radical liberal writer referred to the Acts as the "spiritual mutilation" of the poor and lamented that

Parliament did not do more about tuberculosis, the "white scourge" that was "most common amongst the poor, who are often unable to procure the necessaries of life."[46] In place of "coercive philanthropy" some liberals wanted homes for the poor on a "voluntary" basis.[47] In a series of editorials, the *Nation* echoed the claims of Wedgwood and argued that eugenics was being advanced by "experts" who were using the "name of science and efficiency" to enslave a very poorly defined community.[48] Writing on the "Crime of Being Inefficient," one angered commentator charged that "no minimising speech can conceal the fact that this is a large and ambitious Bill. It is the first essay in legislation of the Eugenist School. It has its origin in a vicious theory of social development, and it embodies in its pages, not latent or concealed, but legible and conscious, an undermining of liberty, which threatens dangers to the community incomparably graver than the undisciplined lives and uncontrolled multiplication of the unfit."[49] More moderate liberals were willing to accept the Mental Deficiency Bill as long as some changes were made to protect the rights of the "feebleminded," but more radical liberals were unwilling to accept these eugenical measures.

These radical and liberal British magazines created narratives that highlighted what hard-line eugenicists had consistently denied—that there was an intimate connection between heredity and the environment. The editors of the *Nation* invited their readers to identify with those British citizens who understood the real necessities of nature and the economic laws that came with privation and class distinction. One critic wrote that "Bad heredity is almost *necessarily* associated with bad environment. The child of a defective mother is nearly always reared under the worst possible conditions of care, education, nutrition, and housing. Even if statistics showed that in nine cases out of ten a defective child had a defective mother, it would still be possible to argue that the cause of the deficiency was in the environment, and could be removed with proper care."[50] These types of arguments were effective because they did not dispute the existence of defectiveness or feeblemindedness but instead highlighted the conditions that were "nearly always" associated with mental deficiency. One commentator remarked that "The real enemy of human development is the bad environment which social politics attempt too slowly and too partially to transform. It is the despair of impatience which would 'segregate' the mother, when we ought rather to reform the nursery. The short cut to efficiency through the back-yard of the house of detention, would leave us still the slum and the sweating-den where 'deficiency' is bred. The race would still degenerate, and degenerate no less swiftly because liberty had gone."[51] For many radical liberals, the true economic necessities were left untouched by legislation that merely offered a quick biological fix for a complicated social problem. Segregating the feebleminded might prove to be genetically effective, but at what social cost? In the eyes of British radicals, the race would continue to degenerate as long as human beings were placed back in the slum that bred degeneracy.

Many of the debates in Parliament over the role of the state in controlling the feebleminded seemed to be conducted in antiseptically clinical language, but radical liberals were offended by the way in which parliamentary members characterized the poor and the unfit. Many of the early hard-line eugenical narratives contained definitions of feeblemindedness that seemed to be based on the principles of social Darwinism. Leftist journalists who felt that they were representing "the people" resented the suggestion that the lower or working classes were inherently inferior or subnormal because of the size of their pocketbooks. One writer opined that it was "no longer necessary for a man to prove that he is capable of 'competing on equal terms with his normal fellows' in order to escape the imputation of feeblemindedness."[52] An editorial in the *Nation* pointed out some of the sexism that lay hidden in the Mental Deficiency Bill when it claimed that "down to the last generation" women were supposed to be "incapable of managing their own affairs except under suitable supervision." This commentator astutely observed that the term "feeblemindedness" was subject to both narrow and wide interpretation, depending on whether one was eager to "shut up anyone and everyone to whom the terms of the definition might be made to apply."[53]

While hard-line eugenicists in the popular and scientific presses constantly talked about the "necessities" of the state, liberal writers countered with claims that strictly hereditarian measures violated English traditions that respected the balance between individual liberties and collective duties. From the radical liberal perspective, a feebleminded person needed the "power of leaving the institute" as a "weapon" or defense against maltreatment.[54] One editorial written in April 1913 lamented the fact that "A somewhat pallid and bloodless re-incarnation of the Mental Deficiency Bill has appeared on the Parliamentary scene. The genius of Eugenics and the closely associated spirit of the Ratepayers' Defence Association has been exorcised, and the Avatar emerges from the brain of Mr. McKenna purified from those elements of spiritual contagion. . . . The original Bill was . . . supported by the serried ranks of Toryism, and the plaudits of the 'Times.' It embodied the wisdom of the physical science. It took its definitions from the Royal College of Physicians. It translated Eugenics into action."[55] Having been defeated on the floors of Parliament, the radical liberals looked for symbolic victory in the popular press. Some writers noted that "in these days compulsion is the major word for everyone," and they consoled themselves that they had to be "thankful for having reduced the sphere of arbitrary action so far as has been done." [56] While few in number, the opponents of the Mental Deficiency Bill had been vociferous, and these radicals prided themselves on the stand that they had taken in the name of liberty against state "tyranny."

Yet it would be a mistake to claim that the support for the Mental Deficiency Act was anti-eugenic in nature.[57] This may have been the perspective of the radical conservatives and liberals in Parliament and in the popular press, but it was not the position of either the Eugenics Education Society or moderate liberals, who thought that "common sense" dictated the recognition that feeblemindedness caused pauperism. This was a debate over different forms of eugenics and hereditarian arguments. Even the most vehement critics of the Mental Deficiency Bill were willing to allow that some classes of people could be truly classed as "feebleminded"; they were simply arguing over who belonged in this category. Some wanted the feebleminded to be cared for in "homes" and not detention centers. These supposedly mentally deficient people were still treated as members of a class or even a race apart; they were still considered necessitous and at the mercy of the state. The issue often presented even by radicals was not whether the state could or would intervene but how it would intervene. As one editor wrote in the *Manchester Guardian* of July 31, 1913, "we have never denied that legislation was necessary." [58] One editorial agreed that "feebleminded girls deserve the protection against men" who might turn them into mothers living on "the rates." [59] By making a choice on how to attack the Mental Deficiency Bill, the members of the liberal and radical press in some ways were conceding the importance of hereditarian explanations—and objecting merely to the hard-line legislation framed in the language of the Eugenic Education Society.

In the 1920s and 1930s, the eugenical arguments of the liberals would be picked up by other influential social actors who disagreed with conservative eugenicists. Some of the most powerful critics of hard-line eugenics in England were not scientists or eugenicists but the labor representatives who recognized that support for sterilization measures was coming largely from the middle and upper classes.[60] In northern urban areas where the Labour Party was powerful, many people were either hostile to or uninterested in eugenical sterilization.[61] Most of the opposition came from the Labour Party M.P.'s including Herbert Morrison.[62] Another vocal opponent of sterilization was George Gibson, general secretary of the Mental Hospital Workers' Union, which represented many of the auxiliary staff who worked in mental hospitals. Gibson's union was responsible for publishing the *Mental Hospital Workers' Journal*, which covered many of the major speeches and publications on the subject of sterilization. Besides writing journal articles, laborites also lobbied politicians. In 1929, the British minister of health received several memos on sterilization. One was from a division of the Birmingham branch of the Distributivist League, which was influenced by G. K. Chesterton's social philosophy, and the other was from the Public Health Advisory Committee of the Labour Party's Research Division.[63] One of these documents noted that "there is a popular belief that the biologists are in possession of a great body of exact knowledge concerning the transmission of diseases and deficiency which only sentimental or religious prejudice prevents being put into practical use. This is complete delusion."[64] The memorandum went on to attack the exaggerated numbers of people that were included in the definitions of mental deficiency, observing that sterilization "would in practice only be applied to the poor."[65] At the same time that some doctors were writing in favor of sterilization in the *British Medical Journal* and the *Journal of the American Medical Association,* the *Mental Hospital Workers' Journal* was publishing cartoons ridiculing the Nazi laws of 1934.[66] Gibson's speeches against sterilization were noticed by Blacker and other eugenicists, and it was because of Gibson's work that the Trade Union Congress passed a motion against sterilization in October 1934.[67] After Labour Party speakers like Gibson had helped defeat the first British Sterilization Bill in 1931, the younger eugenicists began to realize that people like McBride, Inge, and Schiller were not going to get sympathy of the working classes by speaking "about them as dregs and scum."[68]

American Liberals and Eugenics

In America hundreds of speeches and articles claimed that it was Francis Galton who rediscovered the modern study of the wellborn, but even so there had been abundant commentary on the relationship between poverty, the differential birth rate, unfitness, and other topics long before the revival of the eugenics movement at the end of the nineteenth century.[69] Sociologist Lester Ward once observed that long before the word "eugenics" made its appearance, the word "stirpiculture" was "quite common in America."[70] As early as 1837, people like John Humphrey Noyes, a free church minister, indicated their interest in stirpiculture, or the process of selective breeding.[71] Espousing his theories of "perfectionism," the founder of the Oneida Community convinced some of his followers that the best way to move away from the problems of the orthodox Christian world was to establish a communistic society whose members were not bound by the restrictions of monogamous marriage. Noyes was able to convince dozens of his followers to study and practice what would later be called the genetic laws of breeding. In the Oneida Community, fifty-eight children were born to parents who claimed that they had the "best possible offspring."[72] When Galton's work was popularized in America, Noyes would borrow from Galton, but he lambasted the Englander for not practicing what he preached.

Few hard-line eugenicists would concede that anyone prior to Galton had engaged in truly scientific analysis.[73] The hard-line Galtonians tried to distance themselves from the disreputable activities of radical leftists and rebels who did not appreciate the importance of marriage and human decency. When Victoria Woodhull began writing on the relationship between eugenics, sexuality, equality, and free love, her invocation of "science" was considered a perversion of the true laws of human inheritance.[74] For such American conservatives as Charles Davenport and Paul Popenoe, the science of eugenics was rediscovered when Mendelian genetics came to the attention of the scientific community.

When liberal Americans were exposed to eugenical arguments at the beginning of the twentieth century, they were unsure what to make of this novel science. On the one hand, they welcomed "progressive" measures that followed the laws of genetics (see chapter 2). On the other hand, they were skeptical when they saw how some of these biological theories were applied. Like their British neighbors, liberals worried about the social consequences of compulsory marriage laws, segregation restrictions, and sterilization statutes.[75] What complicated matters was the fact that there were more hard-line eugenicists in America than there were in England.

In America, liberals interested in critiquing eugenics adopted one of two rhetorical approaches. One group took the route of reforming eugenics rather than denying the legitimacy of the new science. The second accepted the goals of eugenics but questioned the efficacy of the science of the wellborn.

Most American liberals followed their English counterparts in believing that eugenics could be rehabilitated, but they wanted the new science to move away from the racist views of the American nativists. To counter the tales of degeneracy and pessimism circulated by more conservative eugenicists, some liberals countered that a proper interpretation of eugenics could lead the masses out of despair. Some writers believed that certain types of eugenics did not recognize the significance of differential opportunity among the American public.[76] Instead of assuming the genetic inferiority of the poor, many reform eugenicists insisted that a leveling of the social playing field would show which groups were truly biologically inadequate. Jennings, for example, attacked the hard-line eugenicists for claiming that biology "requires an aristocratic constitution of society."[77] Huxley argued from a similar stance when he asserted that there were "vast reservoirs of innate intelligence untrained in children from the lower social strata."[78] Like their British counterparts, American liberals were finding a way to discriminate between aristocratic and democratic forms of eugenics.

Some American liberals thought that the best forms of eugenics were egalitarian rather than hierarchial in nature. Lester Ward, for example, suggested,

> it is said that society is doomed to hopeless degeneracy. Is it possible to take another view? I think it is, and the only consolation, the only hope, lies in the truth that, so far as the native capacity, the potential quality, the "promise and potency" of a higher life are concerned, those swarming, spawning millions, the bottom layer of society, the proletariat, the working classes, the "hewers of wood and drawers of water," nay, even the denizens of the slums—that all these are by nature the peers of the boasted "aristocracy of brains" that now dominates society and looks down upon them, and the equals in all but privilege of the most enlightened teachers of eugenics.[79]

This reformist approach to eugenics involved accepting some of the biological arguments of the hard-liners but supplementing them with discussions of the influence of social influences. Ward, for example, was sympathetic to interpretations of eugenics like those of Caleb Saleeby (see chapter 2), but he refused to believe that the world was composed of masses of defectives. Ward once remarked that "to read the eugenic literature one would infer that the majority of mankind are defectives."[80] He and other liberals thought that both the geniuses and defectives within society were substantially fewer in number than what was claimed by many hard-liners. In place of the older forms of eugenics, Ward asked his readers to find a way to combine studies of heredity with those of the environment so that eugenics could find itself supplemented with "euthenics."[81] In one important work, Ward lamented the fact that "The present eugenic movement is one of distrust of nature, of lack of faith in great principles, of feverish haste to improve the world, or egotism in the assumption of a wisdom superior to nature. If it could have its way it would thwart and distort the spontaneous upward movement, and create an artificial race of hydrocephalous pygmies. Fortunately, its power is limited, and can produce only a ripple on the surface of society."[82]

Ward was not alone in this assessment. Building on the work of Saleeby, MacBride, and other eugenicists, these liberals brought together Galtonian and neo-Lamarckian ideas concerning nature and nurture. An especially important part of their work was an acknowledgment of the importance of the "race poison" studies that already existed on the periphery of mainstream eugenics discourse. Leftists in their tales brought these concerns to the foreground and argued that the studies on alcohol and syphilis pointed the way for true eugenicists to be concerned with both heredity and the environment. Much of this discourse re-cast the classical Lamarckian environmental terms in more modern lexicons.[83] Many biologists, geneticists, and other scientists began to discuss the need for "social hygiene" to complement the work of heredity in human reproduction. A decade later hard-line eugenicists would be able to muster more than a "ripple" of power in passing sterilization laws and immigration restrictions, but people like Ward created liberal interpretations of eugenics that helped to dilute some of the power of the hard-liners.[84]

Some reform eugenicists combined a defense of the poor in American with an attack on the upper classes who funded hard-line eugenical research. While the hard-liners drew attention to the spread of feeblemindedness among the poor, the liberals reminded their audiences of the ways in which the upper classes were subverting the democratic process. Some public defenders of the working classes claimed that the rich had just as many mentally defectives as the poor but that the well-to-do had the means to hide their deficiencies. As Jennings would argue in a response to Laughlin's work: "Would not statistics from expensive private institutions in all probability show a reversal in the proportion of native-born and foreign-born?"[85] Liberals thus lampooned the hard-liners who thought that their privileged social status came from biological superiority.

Many liberal Americans attempted to defend eugenics by lambasting strict hereditarians for using the new science as a means of questioning the viability of democracies. An entire subgenre of eugenical tales had been written by hard-line eugenicists who thought that giving the vote to the masses would only per-petuate state interference in the processes of natural selection, and reformists responded to these claims by pointing out the healing powers of assimilation. Where hard-liners rarely questioned the "necessity" of the state to impose its will on individuals who threatened the survival of the nation, liberal reformists defended the American liberties that were enshrined in the Constitution. Even H. L. Mencken would come to admit that the "sharecropper, though he may appear to the scientist to be hardly human, is yet as much under the protec-tion of the Bill of Rights as the president of Harvard."[86] Some of these writers came to the defense of "the people" who were targeted for segregation and sterilization.[87] Another liberal would write that the advent of eugenics brought with it "tyranny."[88] Clarence Darrow observed in 1926 that if state officials were allowed to use eugenics, it would "inevitably direct human breeding" so that "big business would create a race in its own image . . . breeding would be controlled for the use and purpose of the powerful and unintelligent."[89] One critic, Robert Lowie, asked: "What is to prevent the eugenist, when in possession of the State machinery, from legislating out of their procreative rights any class of whose tenets or characters he may disapprove?"[90] In sum, liberals supported forms of eugenical legislation, but they were hesitant to place unlimited power in the hands of either hard-line eugenicists or government officials.

One of the greatest differences between hard-line and reform eugenicists was in their attitudes toward immigration to America. Although American eugenicists were not supposed to be as class conscious as their European counterparts, some liberals writing in the first decades of this century were sensitive to the fact that the tales of degeneration produced by Grant, Wiggam, and Davenport were used to attack democratic notions of the "melting pot" and the easy assimilation of immigrants into the United States. One writer voiced his opinion that the hard-line eugenicist "forgets that the jails of Europe were opened to populate America, and that we are the proud sons and daughters of a refuge-seeking ancestry, of times of doubtful character. The views on immigration are not those of a biologist, but those of a 100 per cent American, who fears that we are selling 'our birth right for a mess of pottage' to the immigrant people of the world."[91] Many of these immigrants were members of the poor or working classes, and they were easy targets for nativist eugenicists. Yet these groups did have their defenders. As one commentator observed, "If there are any signs of decadence anywhere they are not in the proletariat. They are to be found among the pampered rich and not among the hampered poor. These who, though ill bred, are well born; the infusion into the population imparts to it a healthy tone. It constitutes the hope of society."[92] Hard-liners cringed when they read such rhetoric, for they believed that this defense of the poor was based on outdated neo-Lamarckian beliefs in the limitless power of education and reformation of character.

Finally, there were some American liberals who agreed with the utopian goals of positive or negative eugenics but simply thought that the science was too immature for society to begin applying its principles. By the early 1920s, some of the same newspapers that had applauded the growth of the eugenics movement were now printing articles that criticized the feasibility of some of its recommendations.[93] After the passage of the Immigration Act of 1924, a growing number of social scientists and journalists began weaving together a plethora of stories that attacked the legitimacy of some forms of eugenics.[94] Some critics were primarily concerned with making sure that the new science was not using "false biology."[95] Harvard geneticist William Castle, an early eugenics supporter, worried that some of these activities were making members of the movement look "ridiculous."[96] Some academicians also lamented the introduction of the principles of hard-line eugenics into the public forum. Charles Emerson noted in July 1926, that "Unfortunately, eugenics now has reached popular literature, and books have been published, written in convincing style, by those who have only an academic knowledge of biology and no accurate first-hand acquaintance with chromosomes, genes. . . . Studies of families have been made by those who trust the family traditions of ignorant grandchildren and the gossip of neighbors, but who could not tell a moron or a child with dementia precox from one with adenoids."[97] Eugenicists at the turn of the century had hoped that the popular imagination would take up the cause of their creed. They got more than they bargained for.

By 1929, the advent of the Great Depression meant that aristocratic forms of eugenics were no longer credible when millions of hardworking Americans found themselves in financial straits. The crash of the stock market greatly altered the composition of audiences willing to listen to mainline eugenical speculations.[98] As one writer would observe, the genetically "fit" and "unfit" shared the misfortunes that came with the stock market crash.[99] When both second-generation immigrants and native Anglo-Saxons suffered with the rest of the social order, the calls for the sterilization of tens of millions of Americans fell on deaf ears. While the turbulence of the Depression did not totally eliminate eugenical arguments, it did force both the hard-line and moderate eugenicists to alter their appeals to both the scientific community and the broader public audiences.[100]

Socialism and Eugenics

At the same time that liberals in England were attacking hard-line eugenicists for abusing the democratic processes of parliamentary government, there were socialist writers who believed that all capitalist forms of eugenics were inherently flawed. For socialist eugenicists, the economic disparities of capitalism that created divisions between entrepreneurs and wage slaves hindered eugenical progress. While more moderate liberals tried to balance the influence of nature and nurture, individualism and collectivism, and tradition with reform, many socialists claimed that only revolutionary change would bring about lasting eugenical changes. In many ways, the strict environmentalism of the socialists was just as deterministic as the hereditarianism of the hard-line eugenicists. When mainstream eugenicists tried to discuss the relative merits of segregation and sterilization, socialist critics in England used these debates to comment on the evils of nationalism, imperialism, "wage slavery," and capitalism in general. In place of hard-line legislation that looked at ways of controlling the reproductive habits of the poor, the socialists tried to use eugenics to rein in the abuses of the rich, and they talked about the importance of factory legislation, child-labor regulation, and women's suffrage. What socialists shared with radical liberals was a belief that economic necessities were responsible for the plight of the pauper classes. One speaker urged his listeners to remember that "In the classless society far-reaching eugenic measures could be enforced by the state with little injustice. Today, this would not be possible. We do not know in most cases, how far social failure and success are due to heredity and how far to environment. And environment is the easiest of the two to improve."[101] For socialists, the key to eugenical reform involved finding that "classless society."

After World War I, socialists joined liberals in discussing the importance of eugenical policies, and these writers looked for ways of creating a science that could be implemented without class or race bias. One of the earliest contributors to this British socialist attack on the racial aspects of hard-line eugenics was Lancelot Hogben.[102] In one article Hogben would claim that "Eugenic social propaganda" had been "dominated by an explicit social bias which in England can only serve to render the eugenic standpoint unpalatable to a section of the community which for good or evil seems to be assuming the role of a governing class. The greatest obstacle to a sane eugenic point of view is the eugenists themselves. By recklessly antagonizing the leaders of thought among the working classes, the protagonists have done their best to make eugenics a matter of party politics with results which can only delay the acceptance of a national minimum of parenthood."[103] Hogben joined critics like Huxley, Haldane, and Crew in their attempts to transform eugenics into a more palatable form of politics. Hogben's stance was typical of the generation of English social scientists and intellectuals in the mid-1920s who began to have reservations about the polemics of the English Eugenics Society. Liberal social scientists and geneticists who had once readily accepted strong hereditarian interpretations of social problems were now skeptical of hard-line claims that feeblemindedness could disappear in a few generations.

Many of these writers began to popularize some of the arguments that had been created decades earlier during the debates over marriage restriction and mental deficiency. Most of these liberal critics defended nonracial eugenics but, as noted earlier, hard-liners interpreted these attacks as *anti*-eugenical commentaries. One hard-line eugenicist, Carr-Saunders, anxiously wrote a colleague that "a man of some eminence" told him that "he understood that Hogben had knocked the bottom out of eugenics."[104] Yet liberal writers constantly argued that they were saving eugenics from its supposed hard-line friends. Radical commentators constantly complained that strict hereditarian eugenicists represented the political views of a condescending upper class that seemed to scorn the really meritorious that could be found in all social classes. Hogben and other leftists vilified the Whethams, Major Darwin, and other hard-line eugenicists who had attacked the provision of scholarships for children outside of the professional classes, and Hogben charged that the hard-line stance represented a "system of ingenious excuses for combating the amelioration of working class conditions."[105] Many of these arguments resembled those used by Wedgwood and his supporters in the radical attacks on the Mental Deficiency Bills.

At the same time, drastic changes had taken place both within and outside of the field of genetics in the 1920s that affected the scientific ethos of the hard-liners. Many of the more conservative eugenicists had based their social claims on Mendelian pedigree charts that were now considered by biologists and geneticists to be hopelessly inadequate. A decade earlier, Wedgwood had been fighting the hereditarian "common sense" of the community, but later rhetors like Hogben were armed with the power of science itself in debates with the hard-liners. Racial and class prejudices that were once thought to be an immutable part of nature were now called into question by liberal researchers who portrayed the hard-liners as propagandists. One critic thought that it "might take years to purge the word 'eugenics' of associations which are inimical to the thought of this generation."[106] Another commentator in the *Lancet* thought that the "story of human genetics should be removed from the atmosphere of the drawing room" and taken to the laboratory, where "sincere investigation should replace amateur political speculation."[107]

Although these reform eugenicists continually claimed that they were engaged in dispassionate research, their rejection of the hard-line interpretations was itself politically motivated. These socialist eugenicists were unwilling to use the traditional biological idioms that excluded millions of working class British children from the benefits of a progressive science. By stressing the infinite variety of genetic configurations and the presence of "mutations," socialist researchers undermined the credibility of some of the earlier hard-line research that depended on antiquated Mendelian "unit" traits. Hogben, for example, ridiculed the belief of some eugenicists that genes had "characters" like "sobriety" and "improvidence" that could be transmitted from generation to generation.[108] Haldane argued that if eugenicists were really concerned with finding accurate definitions of human fitness, they needed to look at the reports of the bankruptcy courts, which showed that a "considerable number of the nobility are incapable of managing their own affairs."[109] Writers like Bertrand Russell invited audiences to think of how "the established order showers knighthoods and fortunes upon the men of science, who become more and more determined supporters of the injustice and obscurantism upon which our social system is based."[110] Haldane reported in 1926 that the "growing science of heredity is being used in this country to support the political opinions of the extreme right" and this meant that eugenics was becoming "abhorrent to many democrats."[111] One writer in the *New Statesman and Nation* was even more specific when he noted some of the errors of the hard-line Eugenics Education Society:

> When they assume a simple genetic character for such complicated combinations of heredity and environmental ingredients as produce feeble-mindedness, criminality, and even pauperism, boldly confusing economic and biological factors to prove that the poor should be sterilized, the scientific mood has deserted them. Political bias, social prejudice and ethical predilections which have no connection with science have fathered assumptions about the rate and extent of selection which J. B. S. Haldane has shown by mathematical analysis have no grounds. . . . They have filled the bookshelves of the world with the deadweight of hearsay, sham expert opinion and doubtful conclusions, based on sufficiently entertaining family histories illustrated by neat little genealogical trees.[112]

For many of these socialist writers, hard-line eugenicists represented the worst abuses of scientific investigation.

English socialists found reason to worry about the hard-liners because in the later part of the 1920s, the Eugenics Education Society conducted an all-out campaign to encourage Parliament to pass an act for the sterilization of defectives. The publication of the Wood Report in 1929 was interpreted by hard-liners as a vindication of their views on the rising costs to society that came from the growing ranks of the feebleminded. In the October issue of the *Eugenics Review*, these English eugenicists announced the creation of a "Social Problem Group" Investigation Committee that was going to examine the connection between the defective and criminality, unemployment, prostitution, inebriety, vagrancy, and epilepsy.[113] When government committees were formed in order to investigate the viability of sterilization as an option, eugenicists kept in touch with chairs of some of these committees, like Lawrence Brock, and let them know about eugenics publications that were being released at the same time as some of the commission reports.[114]

When hard-line eugenicists began to concentrate their efforts on passing sterilization legislation, many English socialists thought that the conservatives in their country were trying to follow in the footsteps of American extremist eugenicists who argued for the "necessity" of compulsory sterilization (see chapter 5).[115] Questions of race and class bias once again came to the forefront of eugenical discussions. One influential leftist commentator, Joseph Needham, criticized the eugenicist MacBride for his attacks on the "Iberian" elements of the population, and he questioned the "fitness" of the shareholders of companies who derived their incomes from the labors of other human beings. Needham also rejected the claims of the hard-liners that two million unemployed in Britain needed to be punished by sterilization.[116] In the end, the efforts of the hard-liners to pass compulsory sterilization failed miserably in England.

By the early 1930s, socialists were joined by Marxist eugenicists who now called for new economic and social opportunities as eugenical prerequisites.[117] For some commentators, only with the coming of a classless society would it be possible to have "far reaching eugenic measures."[118] While not totally agreeing with the "Jeffersonian doctrine of equality," Haldane argued that social justice demanded "from each according to his ability, to each according to his needs."[119]

A typical example of socialist attitudes toward eugenics can be found in the influential writings of H. J. Muller. In comparison with other eugenic publicists, Muller can be regarded as a "fairly extreme environmentalist."[120] Muller asked British audiences to believe that without a proper environment, even the best of genes would be wasted. Muller dreamed of a world in which an improvement in economic opportunity would bring with it a truly eugenical community. In his seminal *Out of the Night*, Muller invited his readers to share in a utopian vision where women living in an "enlightened community devoid of superstitious taboos and sex slavery" would be eager to "bear and rear a child of Lenin or of Darwin!"[121] Muller, like other socialists and Marxists, was convinced that without any economic or social revolution there would be no "revolution in our attitudes towards sex and reproduction."[122]

American Socialists and Eugenics

In the decade prior to World War I, American socialists expressed their feelings on the issue of eugenics in their own newspapers and journals. The discursive images created in these texts provide us with a vastly different picture of the life of the necessitous than the one depicted by American hard-liners like Charles Davenport and Harry Laughlin. Like their British counterparts, many Ameriᴬn socialists thought that most eugenical creeds were nonsense. Yet there were socialists who believed that some forms of eugenics were compatible with socialistic ideals. Eden and Cedar Paul, for example, claimed that "unless the socialist is a eugenist as well, the socialist state will speedily perish from racial degradation."[123] Years later, Huxley would ask readers to think of the possibility that the world might be witnessing the "emergence of a theory and practice of biological socialism" that would treat the "best" gametes as the "communal possession as well as the equal birthright of every child that is born."[124]

At the same time that hard-line eugenicists were trying to popularize the science of the wellborn, some American socialists objected to both the goals and means of eugenics. They used the science of the wellborn as a foil for their commentary on capitalist government abuses. They tried to collapse all forms of eugenics into a single perspective, biological eugenics, which ignored the role of both the environment and economic relations. Radical newspapers and journals conjured up pictures of wealthy eugenicists joining hands with scientific experts in order to turn American workers into "wage slaves," and they lashed out at the physical "mutilation" of the poor. One of the most famous and representative of these works was Eva Trew's "Sex Sterilization," published in the *International Socialist* in May 1913. Trew provided a narrative that was typical of socialist and Marxist literature of the period. She warned her readers that "Asexualization, or sterilization of undesirables is the recent cure-all advanced by science and millionaire philanthropists as a solution for what they believe to be the greatest menace to society, namely — the increasing number of defectives, incapables, and paupers."[125] While liberals were willing to admit that eugenics was the province of the middle-class professional communities, radicals tended to create a world that was polarized between the rich and poor, between the haves and have-nots. When American states in the early 1910s were slowly adopting laws that restricted marriages and allowed for eugenical sterilization, hard-liners complained about the states' lack of "progress." Socialists and other radicals interpreted these events differently. While liberals were sometimes willing to accept some form of eugenics as long as they were supported by progressive science, more radical critics simply saw these activities as examples of tyrannical programs that were being used by greedy rich humans who were in a hurry to sterilize the poor.[126]

Radical speakers and writers used the debates over the soundness of eugenics as a means of pointing out some of the contradictions inherent in the goals of capitalism. While many mainstream newspapers like the *New York Times* generally supported eugenics activities, the radical press used these discussions of biological necessities to vilify the magnates who were thought to be destroying modern civilization. American readers of newspapers like the *New York Call* were constantly kept informed of the many local and international eugenical meetings. In July 1912, for example, one writer wrote about how the "superior classes" were being urged to procreate. Yet within the same article, the author reminded readers that some people buried in Westminster Abbey had been the seventh, eighth, ninth, and even seventeenth children born in their families.[127]

Some radicals claimed that if there were any "fit" Americans, then it would be the hardy workers and not the rich who should be considered genetically well-endowed. Famous eugenicists like Charles Davenport were chastised for blaming the victims of poverty. One radical writer opined that at the same time that the rich and their representatives were vilifying the poor for their lack of "instinct" for the accumulation of property, they were claiming that it was a mark of being "unfit" to "invade the stores of others."[128] While most eugenicists saw themselves as genetic pioneers presaging a new era of planning, socialists claimed that the new science merely reflected innovative expressions of some very old themes. One socialist remarked, "It is interesting to note that while the remedy to be applied is modern, the offense to be eradicated is as old as the history of private property,—namely, poverty and its effects. . . . In a country that has so unmistakably enthroned the dollar above all else, it is scarcely to be wondered if the distinguishable mark of imbecility is for one not to know 'what shall be for his profit or his loss.' "[129] Socialists writers invited their readers to believe that any sign of communal sharing on the part of the masses was seen by capitalists as evidence that they lacked some mental capability. Cartoons and stories in the radical press depicted the rich as the exploiters of the poor, and the feebleminded who lived in institutions were said to provide cheap labor for the capitalists.

Many radicals objected to marriage restrictions, mental classifications, and other eugenics measures, but what was the most unpardonable sin of the hard-liners was the means that they used to accomplish their goals. Capitalist eugenicists were condemned for their incessant calls for the sterilization of the unfit. Trew, like many other socialists and Marxists, argued that it would be the poor and the propertyless—and not the real "unfit" in society—who would be marked for sterilization. She warned her reading public that: "in view of the fact that our wealth is being concentrated in the hands of the few, with an increasing tendency to lessen the number in control, a corresponding increase in the number of property-less persons, or those who, seemingly 'have not developed the sense of property rights' will be marked as candidates for sterilization."[130] Hard-line

...ugenicisr believed that the poor were burdening the upper and lower classes, but the socialists hammered away at the "propertyless" state of the poor. For the many readers of these socialist publications, the advent of eugenics brought not hope but peril. It meant that the rich had one more weapon in an already well-stocked arsenal with which they could profit from the necessities of the masses.

While hard-liners like Grant and Stoddard prided themselves on their patriotic attempts at preserving the American germplasm, socialists condemned eugenics as just one more form of domestic and colonial imperialism. One contributor to the *New York Call* compared the traditional eugenics narrative with the military stories of Moltke, Steinmetz, and Bernhardi, who had claimed that the competition of war meant that "though the best of blood of nations was destroyed, the biological advantages gained by victory of superior forces led to the development of a superior race."[131]

The Discursive Compromise: The Crafting of "Reform" Eugenics

By the early 1930s, strictly hereditarian eugenicists in both England and in the United States found themselves under siege. They felt that they were being attacked from the right by Catholics who did not understand the difference between eugenical sterilization and castration and from the left by socialists and liberals claiming that their family studies were pseudoscientific in nature. While the flagging spirits of the hard-liners were bolstered by the immigration restrictions of 1924 and the Supreme Court decision of *Buck v. Bell*, they still recognized that some of the most popular interpretations of eugenics did not reflect the hard-line hereditarian stance.[132] Rhetorically what happened was that a compromise took place; eugenics remained a viable science but one that recognized the importance of both heredity and the environment in the creation of human character. In the 1930s, the necessitous in England and in the United States, who were once considered to be feebleminded, now found themselves assigned to "social problem" groups that were subjected to "reform" eugenics.[133]

On the right, hard-line eugenicists began to admit that perhaps nurture did have some influence in the creation of the necessitous. Unlike earlier eugenicists, the new conservatives took into account the environment: They now simply claimed in their stories that the character of the poor created the slums, or that regardless of cause the best prevention still involved changing the reproductive *habits* of the poor. These hard-line eugenicists, while dwindling in number, persisted in reminding their peers of the importance of hereditarian principles.[134]

Liberal reformers contributed their share to reform eugenics by demanding that eugenics be voluntary, respectful of individual liberties, and nonbiased. With the rise of Nazism, racial and class-based eugenical schemes were no longer politically acceptable, and fewer members of the lower classes could be characterized as feebleminded. Liberals joined conservatives in insisting that biology could not be ignored, but they asked that critics remember the importance of balancing hereditarianism with environmentalism, social evolution with biological evolution, liberty with necessity. While conservatives fought for coercive marriage restrictions, segregation, and sterilization, liberals forced a negotiation that allowed for eugenical sterilization as long as it was a last resort and voluntary. The power of this liberalization of eugenics is evidenced by the fact that even after the publication of the Brock Report in 1934—it seemed to favor some forms of coercive sterilization—the British Ministry of Health and other governmental agencies avoided instituted policies of sterilization as long as they remained morally controversial.[135]

Within the professional ranks, liberals worked to undermine the credibility of the hard-liners. Some of these writers continued to argue that the field was still too new to have produced enough information about the origins of "mental defectiveness." When the term "feeblemindedness" was abandoned, this spelled a symbolic victory for the liberals because it considerably *narrowed* the number of people who would be subject to sterilization even if legislation was passed.[136] People now talked about thousands of mental defectives rather than millions. Other reforms influenced the direction of eugenics by pointing out that the "mentally deficient" were not a danger to society, and even if they were, it was cultural deficiency that helped create this exigency and this was not a problem of the lower social orders exclusively.[137] When conservatives like Hilda Pocock engaged in public debates over eugenical sterilization, they found that their liberal opponents were scoring points by arguing that sterilization would be useless in helping the working classes.[138] Several of these liberals attacked the older form of eugenics because it sought an aristocracy rather than a meritocracy, and they objected to the fact that economic and social conditions needed to provide for equalization of opportunity before attention was turned to the sterilization of the mentally deficient.[139]

The Human Genome Project is both science and metaphor. It will create a track in dense social vapor. It will confront us with our own assumptions about what it is to be human, to be ill, to be perfect, to be monster, and to be wise. The Human Genome Project is culture-saturated science.
Howard Stein, 1992

Will the Nazi program to eradicate Jewish or otherwise "inferior" genes by mass murder be transformed here into a kinder, gentler program to "perfect" human individuals by "correcting" their genomes in conformity, perhaps, to an ideal, "white, Judeo-Christian, economically successful" genotype? **Salvador Luria, 1989**

7

The Return of Eugenics: Ideographic Fragments and the Mythology of the Human Genome Project

Within rhetorical cultures, the key ideographs that represent a society's collective commitments change over time, and with them change the justifications that are given for social activities that are conducted in the name of liberty, equality, or privacy.[1] In the 1910s, 1920s, and 1930s, many Anglo-Americans were ostracized, segregated, or sterilized because their neighbors believed that there were some social necessities that demanded the relinquishment of some rights for the greater good of the race or nation. In the years prior to World War II, the restriction of reproductive rights was rationalized on the basis of myriad medical, social, economic, and political considerations.[2]

Yet with the rise of Nazism, conservatives, liberals, and radicals around the world watched with horror as some of these same arguments were appropriated and reconfigured to legitimate the creation of the ultimate eugenic state. Initially, many eugenicists on both sides of the Atlantic viewed these Nazi programs as excellent examples of medical progress, but as Europe prepared for war the Allies distanced themselves from the "abusers" of the science of eugenics or genetics. Anglo-Americans wishing to avoid the Nazi tyranny engaged in a process of cultural amnesia, and the histories of many biological sciences were rewritten in order to distance pure genetics from its eugenical shadow.

At the same time, the anti-hard-line eugenical arguments of feminists, African-Americans, Catholics, and others could no longer be ignored. Anyone interested in eugenics after 1940 heard demands that the science be nonracist and that no single culture should be singled out for amelioration. At the same time, liberal communities insisted that the working class could no longer be considered dysgenic. The old eugenicists who had justified the use of coercion in the name of the state found themselves vilified as antidemocratic.[3]

For almost four decades, anyone interested in publicizing genetics had to cope with a rhetorical culture filled with stories on the virtues of being nonracist and egalitarian. Geneticists, doctors, and other supporters of race "betterment" found themselves having to explain that their basic and applied research programs were voluntary in nature. In earlier years the ambiguity and capaciousness of the word "eugenics" had allowed both hard-liners and reformers to employ the term, but now the word was associated with fascism, and researchers scrambled to find ways of erasing any ideological links between their agendas and that of the Nazis.[4] Buildings that were once occupied by scholars interested in the biological "inequality" of the races now housed investigators who spoke of "race betterment." Within genetic textbooks, chapters on hard-line eugenical ideas disappeared, and "voluntariness" was in the air.[5] So thorough was this ideographic transformation that Ludmerer could write in 1972 that "in the last three decades, the eugenics movement, like the science of human genetics, has undergone its scientific reconstruction."[6] Environmental and cultural influences were soon considered to be as (or more) important than heredity.[7] Within the academy, scholars who still believed in genetic predestination found themselves outnumbered by humanists, behaviorists, and cultural determinists who talked incessantly about genetic fallacies.[8] Eugenics — which at one time seemed to be on the threshold of being recognized as a premier mode of inquiry — was now lampooned and lumped together with the pseudosciences of astrology and phrenology.

In the 1980s and 1990s, the rhetoric of eugenics returned with a vengeance out in a radically altered form. Cracks began to develop in the thick discursive wall of arguments that had been created in response to overt racism. The passage of time brought changes in both the technical and public spheres that allowed new questions to be raised about the purported "equality" of human beings. In fields like molecular biology, the study of human pathology and traits focused attention on the differences in our genes, and sciences like sociobiology and genomics rose from the ashes and gained impressive explanatory power.[9] Outside the halls of science, anxious middle-class taxpayers began to worry about the growing federal deficit. Generations that had grown up listening to arguments about the right of privacy or equal access to government facilities now heard narratives highlighting the failures of the New Deal, the welfare system, and affirmative action. Some commentators both in scientific communities and in the larger rhetorical culture began to suggest that too many scarce resources had been allocated on the basis of false notions of equality. As Hubbard and Wald commented in 1993, this "shift is due in part to a conservative backlash against the gains of the civil rights and women's rights movements. These and similar movements have emphasized the importance of our environment in shaping who we are, insisting that women, African-Americans, and other kinds of people have an inferior status in American society because of prejudices against them, not because of any natural inferiority. Conservatives are quick to hail scientific discoveries that seem to show innate differences which they can use to explain the current social order."[10] Yet genetic arguments appeal to liberals and moderates as well. With the growing complexities and apparent intractability of problems like violence, racial disharmony, and gender inequities, calls for possible limitations on individual rights and liberties seem to make sense.[11] Some commentators have even had the audacity to claim that the ancient controversy between nature and nurture has finally been resolved in favor of nature. Within this cultural milieu the rhetoric of eugenics has flourished.[12]

Although the growing influence of eugenics can be felt on many fronts, perhaps the best example of the recurrence of some of these arguments can be found in the debates over the Human Genome Project (HGP).[13] Both advocates and opponents of this initiative have taken up many of the positions that were created by hard-liners and reform eugenicists in the late nineteenth and early twentieth centuries. Throughout this book, my contention has been that the most popular forms of eugenics that circulated in the public sphere in England and the United States were not always the hard-line tales constructed by people like Francis Galton, Karl Pearson, Harry Laughlin, and Charles Davenport. Rather, the interpretations of eugenics that were most common in the popular press seemed to be neo-Lamarckian in nature, where rhetors asked audiences to engage in a variety of social reforms that touched people's lives from "the cradle" to "the grave."[14] If this claim has merit, then we need to reassess the importance of the Human Genome Project by going beyond claims that this type of research has everything or nothing to do with Nazi tyrannies. In order to sensitize ourselves to the polysemic ways that eugenics can enter our lives, we need to review the ways in which contemporary discussions of programs like the Human Genome Project recapitulate many of the arguments of earlier eugenical movements.[15]

The Rhetorical Construction of the "New" Eugenics and the Promotion of the Human Genome Project

For any research program to establish itself as capable of advancing epistemic knowledge and worthy of public funding, it must convince many skeptics that the allocation of financial resources will have benefits for both scientists and members of the public. Very often the trajectory of particular research disciplines depends on both the internal discoveries that are found within a community as well as the external symbolic practices that alter perceptions of certain lines of scientific inquiry.[16] Charles Taylor has remarked that the demarcations that exist between the realm of society and science are created through discursive activities that depend on the constitutive authority of particular social communities.[17]

One project involved in this type of boundary work is the new Human Genome Project, a $3 billion program aimed at mapping and sequencing the genes that control our heredity. In the early stages of funding the project, a plethora of rationalizations were used for creating this "big science project." Some officials in Congress and the Department of Energy saw the program as a way to employ researchers who had previously been involved in defense-related activities. Other advocates of government support for the project used nationalistic claims and argued that this type of research would show the world that America could compete with Japan. Scientists who campaigned for the Human Genome Project focused attention on the ways in which the mapping and sequencing of the genes could contribute to our understanding of everything from aggression to cystic fibrosis.[18] One exuberant fan of the endeavor articulated his belief that decoding the genetic messages within our DNA molecules would "provide the ultimate answers to the chemical underpinnings of human existence. They will not only help us understand how we function as healthy human beings, but will also explain, at the chemical level, the role of genetic factors in a multitude of diseases, such as cancer, Alzheimer's disease, and schizophrenia, that diminish the individual lives of so many millions of people."[19]

Throughout the 1980s, the search for the human genome was making daily news, and Americans were bombarded with stories telling how researchers were finding the genes that made us musical geniuses, Olympic athletes, alcoholics, manic-depressives, or homeless.[20] For one Nobel Prize–winning genetic pioneer, the 1990s genetic research represented an extension of American mapping efforts that began with the Declaration of Independence in 1776.[21] Armed with new information on the causes of genetic diseases, researchers participating in the genome project urged their listeners to think of benefits that would come from the identification of carriers of certain hereditary diseases. Like the early hard-line eugenicists who ridiculed the Lamarckian beliefs of nineteenth-century educators, the proponents of the Human Genome Project claimed that genetical researchers would no longer have to conduct biomedical research with "one hand tied' behind their back.[22] Defenders of the project had no qualms about asking governments around the world to fund a project "akin to the Manhattan Project that led to the atomic bomb and the Apollo Project that landed men on the moon."[23] Euphoric publicizers of the project Jerry Bishop and Michael Waldholz have argued in their book, Genome, that gene identification or mapping "cannot be stopped any more than the technology of the automobile, the machine gun, or the atomic bomb were stopped."[24] Senator Gore lavished praise on the new project by proclaiming that the human genome initiative was the "birth of a new revolution" in science." By 1993, one commentator observed that "genetics has become a coffee-table science and the gene, a ubiquitous popular image. We encounter the gene in supermarket tabloids and soap operas, in television sitcoms and talk shows."[26] Genetic investigations were once again in fashion.

Yet for any scientific program to flourish it must have a broad-based appeal within a number of communities, and the advocates of the Human Genome program have had to search for ways of legitimating a project that seems to threaten some of the most basic liberal principles of Anglo-American societies. Some critics ask: If genes truly are our destiny or our fate, then what happens to our notions of human agency, free will, and liberty? When we support the Genome Project, aren't we funding a program that resembles that of the Nazis?

Proponents of the HGP have answered these critics by invoking the importance of choice in democratic nations.[27] Like the earlier hard-line eugenicists, geneticists argue that the new knowledge gained from the Genome Project will help citizens cope with the hard realities of nature. In these new renditions of the tale, there will be no government intervention or coercion because geneticists have learned from the past and have willingly set aside funds to study beforehand the social, ethical, and legal ramifications of gene therapy and other controversial subjects. Within these new mythic accounts, history has taught researchers the limitations of strict biological determinism and that the politically correct way to talk about the relationship between nature and nurture is to assign some percentage of influence to both. Defenders of the project continually emphasize the difference between an acceptable notion of "predisposition" and unacceptable claims of biological "predestination." In these powerfully alluring narratives, participants in genomic research are portrayed as public servants who merely provide a service that responds to the needs of purportedly millions of people.

The functional appropriation of "choice" as the new ideographic term of these researchers is rhetorically important because it counters the claims of opponents who believe that an unbroken line exists between the old and new eugenics. Many supporters of the grandiose Human Genome Project are ever mindful of the negative images of genetics that circulate in countless media stories that almost always mention the history of eugenics.[28] By arguing that patients' choices will be expanded through an acceptance of biological necessities, genome enthusiasts accomplish two tasks. First, the emphasis on choice allows them to argue that the very concept of a modern form of eugenics is an impossibility because the older study of the wellborn asserted the rights of society over those of the individual. Alternatively, proponents of the Genome Project can defend the existence of a pristine form of eugenics that has nothing to do with racism or any historical coercion that was carried out in the name of eugenics. In either case, participants in the project can now present themselves as rational human beings prepared to "proceed with caution."[29] Within these tales, the question of governmental oversight or regulation can be defined as unwarranted interference with "freedom of expression" or the right to be left alone.[30] For some researchers involved in genomic projects, the greatest danger is that some people might try to stop their kind of scientific inquiry.[31] Skeptics who do not appreciate the difference between science and pseudoscience are thus characterized as well-meaning but misguided humans who have confused the possibility of gene therapy with crude forms of eugenical sterilization or "playing God."[32]

Advocates of the Human Genome Project thus claim that their views are accepted by the majority of thoughtful human beings. In many of the articles produced for technical and public consumption, a balanced view of the project is interpreted as one that at least mentions the speculative possibility of the "abuse" of genetics and then goes on to show how these claims are exaggerated.[33] One historian, Daniel Kevles, has recently argued that the mere existence of democratic institutions of government would prevent the abuse of science in the "name" of eugenics.[34] James Watson, one of the former directors of the HGP, made a similar argument when he remarked that the way to prevent the recurrence of eugenic atrocities was by making sure that scientists, doctors, and the public at large refused to "cede control of genetic discoveries to those who would misuse them." [35] Within this rhetorical construct, advocates of the Human Genome Project would be the last parties who would be interested in trying to breed superior human beings. [36] Any traces of the intimate relationship between genetics and applied eugenics are erased in historical constructions that begin with either Mendel or Watson and Crick and the discovery of the DNA double helix.

The defenders of the Human Genome Project thus attempt to gain the rhetorical high ground by acknowledging the potential dangers of the program while at the same time denying any links between their research agendas and the prejudices, politics, and vagaries of the times. [37] The early hard-line eugenicists supposedly had preconceived ideas about genetic inferiority that tainted their results, while more modern researchers are able to maintain their objectivity and healthy skepticism. [38] Sinsheimer once opined that "It is worthwhile to consider specifically wherein the potential of the new genetics exceeds that of the old. To implement the older eugenics of Galton and his successors would have required a massive social program carried out over many generations. Such a program could not have been initiated without the consent and cooperation of a major fraction of the population, and would have been continuously subject to social control. In contrast, the new genetics could, at least in principle, be implemented on a quite individual basis, in one generation, and subject to no existing social restrictions." [39] Unlike the old eugenics, which focused on "culling the unfit," the new eugenics is said to "permit in principle the conversion of all of the unfit to the highest genetic level." [40]

The Performance of Eugenics and the Human Genome Project

Although molecular biologists, geneticists, and other scientists involved in the Genome Project constantly discuss the importance of value-free research, their descriptions of what constitute "natural" genetic facts and "normal" behaviors are selective discursive fragments that often provide us with clues to how citizens might be expected to live in a genomic universe. [41] In hundreds of lectures, conventions, pamphlets, and books, audiences are warned of the dire consequences that come from paying too much attention to nurture and too little to the power of the omnipotent gene. Like the hard-line and "reform" eugenicists before them, many of these researchers exhort their audiences to remember the importance of the germplasm to future generations. The old pedigree charts that were used in the 1910s, 1920s, and 1930s to show the prevalence of feeble-mindedness in families have now been refurbished to chart an ever increasing number of diseases that are supposedly caused by "defective" genes.[42] New texts are circulated to allow even the youngest of schoolchildren to see how "Cells Are Us."[43]

While almost every participant in the Genome Project is cognizant of the dangers of politically mixing the pseudoscience of eugenics with the science of genetics, what they often ignore are the ways eugenics may be *performed* in the media, in the halls of Congress, and even in the laboratory. The rhetoric of eugenics is not something that is simply discussed—it is a way of living—and in many ways some modern researchers knowingly or unknowingly act out eugenical story lines that have venerable roots. By creating elitist hierarchial structures that discriminate between the "geniuses" in the field and the rest who are clamoring for their share of funding, the project carries out what Francis Galton would have called a program of "positive" eugenics: scarce funds are allotted to the "wellborn." The very process of defining who will be considered "normal," or the carrier of a "disease" or "trait," is not only a scientific issue: it is also a matter of power relationships.[44] In the act of creating genome stories, defenders and opponents of the HGP tell us a great deal about themselves and their worldviews. For example, when citizens do not avail themselves of opportunities to use the new methods of genetic screening and "therapy," they are depicted as uneducated and primitive people who do not truly understand the meaning of choice or what it means to have the ability to control your genetic "fate."[45] Disagreement with proponents of the project on goals and methods becomes positive proof of the amount of ignorance that presently exists within the public and scientific community.[46]

Even more revealing are the genetic characterizations, ideographs, narratives, and myths that are used to explain why everyone in England and America needs genetic mapping and sequencing. A representative example of the social vision that informs some of these perspectives can be found in the rhetoric of James Watson, world-famous codiscoverer of the structure of DNA and the first director of the Human Genome Project.[47] Watson never tires of reminding us of the existence of a special taskforce within the HGP that is responsible for monitoring the ethical, legal, and social implications of this type of research, and an analysis of his rhetoric reveals just why we need these safeguards.[48] His speeches and articles are filled with discussions of how individuals and families have to use genetics in order to decide issues such as whom to marry or what genes should be removed from the gene pool. In a presentation delivered in 1993 as part of a symposium celebrating the fortieth anniversary of the discovery of the double helix, the former head of the Human Genome Project claimed that now "developmental biologists, who do not think in terms of DNA, are relics of the past with little likelihood to influence the future."[49]

Thus in discussing the limitations of the environment, we are exhorted to believe that genes are the predominant factor in human development. In the same speech, we are told that "any prospective child" carrying certain genes would be born without any "opportunity for a meaningful life."[50] Watson does not hesitate to take this argument to its logical conclusion. He proceeds to advise anyone interested in preventing the spread of these conditions.[51]

In Watson's social Darwinian world, "justice" demands the universal availability of genetic diagnosis. Like the hard-line eugenicists before him who saw sterilization as a medical practice that would bring "liberty" to those confined to institutions, Watson sees the work of geneticists as a part of a larger mission, one that ironically cannot extricate itself from the language of eugenics. Watson's reductionist definition of eugenics sees problems with a "Hitler-like leader" using genetics, but he sees no inherent problems in his defense of modern therapies, and he is willing to defend his views in spite of their potential unpopularity. Waxing eloquent on the benefits of a pragmatic stance, he warns his listeners that "there might exist some future moments in human existence where germ line gene modification might be perceived as necessary weapons for human survival."[52] For Watson and other members of the Human Genome Project who share his hope and aspirations, a genetic way of thinking is more than a scientific process or method of inquiry—it also contains normative political, social, and economic assumptions.[53]

In the process of creating and defending the Genome Project, advocates like Watson end up deploying a rhetoric that reconfigures much of the ground covered by the earlier eugenical movements. While earlier hard-liners like Grant, Holmes, and Davenport talked about the overriding importance of race and the "necessity" of controlling the reproductive habits of the feebleminded, more nuanced accounts today talk about the "individual" responsibility of parents in contributing to the survival of nations. Now all persons have the right of "choice," but it is important that they make the *right* choice.[54] Instead of basing their decisions on speculative fears and anxieties, laypersons are supposed to use "therapeutic" frames of reference. Older tales of negative eugenics are now transformed into geneticized accounts of how society profits from having educated citizens who no longer question the desirability or feasibility of human gene therapies. The progress of science is seen as depending on the continued support of the Human Genome Project.

Oppositional Rhetoric and the Denigration of the Human Genome Project

Promoters of the new Genome Project like to give the impression that after the initial congressional debates over the funding of the project, meaningful debate within the scientific community ceased and a "mandate" was given to the researchers involved in the HGP, but an analysis of the literature in both the public and scientific spheres reveals the controversial nature of this program.[55] Like many of the older critics of hard-line racist eugenics, opponents of the project argue that very few diseases have an exclusively genetic component, and they highlight the political and economic motivations behind the support for the project.[56] Some supporters of the HGP are attacked for circulating "genetic stories" in an effort to convince us that mapping and sequencing our genes will somehow be "the" best method of relieving human suffering and disease.[57] For many of these critics, speculation that "presymptomatic" individuals may in the future have particular "predispositions" has little to do with the provision of daily health care.[58] Instead, individuals who have histories of family problems may find themselves socially stigmatized and unable to get adequate work or insurance.[59]

In both England and the United States, opponents of the Genome Project claim that the geneticization of social problems will help create a public consciousness that places responsibility on the individual rather than society for problems like homelessness, poor diets, and inadequate prenatal care. Some critics worry about the erosion of programs that have been developed over the years in order to cope with poverty, racism, and sexism.[60] Others complain that the exaggerated claims of proponents of the Genome Project help maintain the illusion that most if not all of society's problems can be managed or prevented through the use of neuroscientific and other biological advances.[61] As Nelkin recently opined, the use of reductionist genetic metaphors entices us into believing that the human body is simply a composite set of "genetic instructions" that are transmitted from generation to generation and that the decipherment of this text will allow us to reconstruct the "essence" of our existence.[62] Genetic research thus appears to be at the vanguard of social change, and complex human conditions are presented as simply matters of reading the genes and not necessarily as issues of power or allocation of resources.[63]

Other commentators have initiated a more radical campaign, and the stories of Daedalus and Frankenstein have been recycled by critics who warn that the Human Genome Project is simply the latest in a long line of destructive myths that have promised scientific progress and instead delivered social perils.[64] While these dystopic visions are rhetorical genres that are generally available to critics who lament the existence of technologies gone awry, they have special relevance in the realm of genetic research.[65] The Human Genome Project has brought with it the issue of whether it is a "new eugenics program in the making."[66] For example, Ari Berkowitz recently asked, "What about the much more likely possibility that the power to alter human genes will encourage well-meaning re-searchers and statesmen [sic] to create human beings with characteristics they see as beneficial, something along the lines of Aldous Huxley's *Brave New World?* How would the cost of dehumanization inherent in the fabrication of people compare with the benefits of eradicating certain disease?"[67]

While defenders of the HGP cloak themselves with the mantle of scientific neutrality, their opponents constantly equate the mapping and sequencing of genes with the eugenics sterilization programs in the United States and the German Holocaust of the 1930s and 1940s. The hard-line eugenics narratives certainly provided ample ammunition for those who objected to any form of ge-netic manipulation. Just as early critics of eugenics had questioned the ability of eugenicists to distinguish between the fit and unfit in society, now some ques-tioned the ability of geneticists to differentiate between the "enhancement" of the gene pool and the removal of diseases. Jack Kirwan, for example, noted the difficulty of drawing the line between the need to conquer genetic diseases and the identification of those merely susceptible to particular diseases.[68] For those opposed to genetic manipulation, the Human Genome Project meant a revival of eugenics in the form of state control of reproductive technology.

In order to provide a brief example of some of the controversies that await us, I will briefly discuss some of the class, racial, and gender issues associated with the new forms of geneticization.

The Human Genome Project and the Creation of the "Underclass"

Although proponents of the HGP contend that the goal of mapping and se-quencing of the genes is to provide all citizens equally with information that they can use to create genetic profiles, opponents warn us that this knowledge has the potential of creating a new underclass.[69] For some of these commentators, the advent of the Genome Project spelled the widening rather than the narrowing of class divisions. People who were once characterized as belonging to a race of the feebleminded are now considered to be the unlucky victims of a genetic lottery that has brought them bad fortune. Defenders of the project, like their predecessors reform eugenicists, often contend that increased genetical knowledge can bring new profiles that warn consumers that they need to change their behaviors or lifestyles, but critics respond that much of the funding for such projects comes from private companies who are primarily interested in finding ways of cutting down expenses. Laying off workers is said to be justified as a "health" measure, and insurance companies back testing and screening as a means of weeding out expensive clients. While supporters of the HGP see the expanding list of diseases amenable to genetic analysis as evidence of progress, their opponents argue that these supposed "therapies" are products in search of markets. For example, one ethicist recently remarked that "people can be made to *want*" screening, and "even to insist on it as their right."[70] Detractors become infuriated when they see terms like "autonomy," "the right of privacy," and "choice" used to rationalize social inequities.

Yet many of the most vehement defenders of the Human Genome Project see these revolutionary changes in the funding of the program as an opportunity to solve the problems of the lower classes. Daniel Koshland, one of the editors of the prestigious magazine *Science*, wrote in the late 1980s that

> The benefits to science of the genome project are clear. Illnesses such as manic depression, Alzheimer's, schizophrenia, and heart disease are probably all multigenetic and even more difficult to unravel than cystic fibrosis. Yet these diseases are at the root of many social problems. The costs of mental illness, the difficult civil liberties problems they cause, the pain to the individual, all cry out for an early solution that involves prevention, not caretaking. To continue the current warehousing or neglect of these people, many of whom are in the ranks of the homeless, is the equivalent of providing iron lungs to polio victims at the expense of working on a vaccine.[71]

Koshland's diatribe is just one example of many speeches that make a distinction between the needs of scientists and "these people." From within this common eugenical tale, what is implied is that any money spent on amelioration rather than prevention of a condition is a waste of precious resources. Like sterilization, the use of germ-line therapy becomes a means of ensuring that we have fewer generations of unfortunates.

Linking mental illness to homelessness is controversial in and of itself, but it is simply one claim of many that seem to echo the lamentations of the earlier eugenics. Perhaps even more debatable in modern-day discussions have been arguments about the quantity and quality of populations. In attempting to legitimate the goals or methods of genetics and the genome program, many normative judgments have been made on the reproductive habits of the underclass. While the early eugenicists called for sterilization and segregation, the new gene prophets admonish their audiences to use this information "voluntarily" in order to avoid unwise marriages or disrespect for the rights of future generations.[72] A common thread running through many of these tales is that individuals have rights of autonomy over their own "somatic" genes, but as soon as one enters the area of "genomic" inheritance, proprietary interests somehow change. The very existence of new screening methods for diseases like cystic fibrosis is viewed as creating a mandate that this technology be used. Citizens who do not take advantage of the new screening methods are characterized as ignorant, uncaring, or irresponsible.

Many of these supposedly new rationales for novel therapies and screening methods echo the arguments of those eugenicists who advocated governmental and societal restrictions on marriage and reproduction of the unfit. For example, in 1988 the United States Congress published a report from the Office of Technology Assessment claiming that "Human mating that proceeds without the use of genetic data about the risks of transmitting diseases will produce greater mortality and medical costs than if carriers of potentially deleterious genes are alerted to their status and encouraged to mate with noncarriers or to use artificial insemination or other reproductive strategies."[73] Just which class should engage in this type of mating is not specified, but the language of this report reminds us of an earlier time. Instead of the U.S. Supreme Court's acceptance of Virginia's depiction of Carrie Buck as a "probable potential parent of socially inadequate offspring," we now have "carriers of potentially deleterious genes." Some rhetors who defend the Human Genome Project make even more interesting comparisons to the earlier eugenics movement. One government report claimed that "new technologies for identifying traits and altering genes make it possible for eugenical goals to be achieved through technological as opposed to social control."[74] Blending together rhetorics of social control and humanitarianism, many of these new accounts portray a utopian world in which massive screening for deleterious genes will mean that even those who lack monetary assets may possess genetic wealth in that their children will be born "normal" and eugenically fit.

Some proponents of the HGP go as far as to argue that it would be unethical *not* to use the knowledge gained from scientific advances. One defender of the project asserted that "Sequencing the human genome puts us on the threshold of great new benefits and some real but avoidable risks. There are immoralities of commission that we must avoid. But there is also the immorality of omission—the failure to apply a great new technology to aid the poor, the infirm, and the underprivileged."[75] Koshland is not alone in his call for immediate application of the newest genetic advances.[76] In November 1993, a British editorial writer remarked in *New Scientist* magazine that while "most people wince at the mere mention of the word eugenics" this was not the time to maintain taboos about applications of some of the new germ-line therapies.[77] While admitting that these technologies might be used by "governments" to create a "super race" or "designer babies," the writer went on to argue that this kind of research represented the only hope for some couples who wanted to bear a "healthy child." The editorial argued further that doctors "necessarily have a moral obligation to try to offer the best possible treatment to their patients."[78] Audiences who read about the "astonishing" Genome Project are told that these new technologies will in the foreseeable future allow young couples to determine as early as the eighth week of pregnancy whether their future child will be subjected to the "nightmare" of schizophrenia, manic-depressive illness, cancer, or multiple sclerosis.[79] The fruits of genome research are said to provide "freedom" from uncertainty and a relief from the "terribly burdensome anxiety, fear, and worry" that come with the game of "genetic roulette."[80] Readers are reminded that if future generations are able to select genetically determined traits for their children, then society may be able to experience the benefits of a "hereditary meritocracy."[81]

These appeals are rhetorically alluring in that they create the impression that by participating in the screening and therapy processes, individuals are not only helping themselves but also showing concern for society's burdens and the rights of future generations. Enormous social pressure obviates the need for government coercion. The symbolic power of the Human Genome Project comes from its ability to transform controversial social positions into unassailable arguments supposedly based on natural, indisputable facts. The project employs a new, more acceptable form of eugenics based on the most believable claims of the older eugenicists. In the new narratives, members of the American public—especially the poor—"need" the genetic information from these government projects in order to do a better job of controlling their fate. The knights in quest of the "holy grail" are willing to overcome whatever obstacles are necessary in order to maintain civilization's progress toward a more perfect genetic society.

Genomics, Violence, and Racial Issues

The Human Genome Project has also revived debates about the relationship between genetics and race. In many circles race is still a taboo subject, and researchers talk about studying large aggregates of "individuals," but critics of geneticism respond that this rhetorical shift does little to dispel concerns about the dangers of new forms of racism.[82] In the 1970s, the African-American community had to cope with the ill-fated sickle-cell screening programs, and these historical anxieties have resurfaced.[83]

Although these fears have manifested themselves in a number of ways, it has been the resurgence of interest in the link between violence, crime, and race that has occupied the attention of many African-Americans and other minorities. At least since the time of Galton and Lombroso, there have been officials interested in exploring the relationship between heredity and crime, and the return of eugenics has brought with it renewed interest in finding ways of preventing or controlling violence. The early hard-line eugenicists once argued that blacks, immigrants, "white trash," and other "unfit" groups were predestined to engage in criminal activities, but the newer forms of racism are much more subtle.[84] People are no longer predestined to be criminals—they may simply be "predisposed" to commit crimes.[85]

Defenders of genomic research often argue that this genetic research raises no new ethical or legal issues, but this stance often ignores the social consequences of publicizing this type of research. In the early 1990s, two events threatened to undermine the renewed interest shown by the federal government in understanding the link between genetics and crime. The first controversy erupted when the American press began reporting the existence of a "human violence initiative."[86] Members of the African-American community became concerned when Frederick Goodwin, a high-ranking federal health official, made a remark during a speech that seemed to "liken violence by inner-city youth to the behavior of 'male monkeys' in the jungle."[87] The *Detroit Free Press* reported that Goodwin's comments "hang like a cloud over the federal government's plans to spend $400 million over five years to try to reduce violence among young people. Opponents call the project racist and promise a furious fight if it comes before

Congress for funding next year. If opposition doesn't kill it, the Department of Health and Human Services in 1994 will launch the Youth Violence Initiative, an unprecedented nationwide effort to identify youths at risk of committing violence and finding ways to prevent it."[88] While Goodwin was reprimanded and assigned to another post, his remark caused a fury of protest and brought some of the potential dangers of this violence link to the attention of Congress and marginalized communities, which saw this as a racial attack.[89] Senator Edward Kennedy and Representative John Dingell wrote letters that appeared in the public press that claimed that "primate research is a preposterous basis for discussing crime and violence that plagues our country today."[90] Outside of the halls of Congress, individuals like Peter Breggin and Ronald Walters created organizations geared toward stopping the human violence initiative.

Ideographically, the debate over the links between genetics and crime pitted the language of what Beckwith has called "genetic essentialism" against the egalitarian vocabulary of civil rights ("equality" versus "necessity"). Like the hard-line eugenicists in the 1910s and 1920s, researchers involved in violence studies contend that they have a right to freedom of expression and inquiry and that it is a disservice to the nation to ignore the genetic roots of crime. Many saw this type of work as redressing the balance between nature and nurture, and they argued that as long as no single race was singled out as potential carriers of defective genes, there could be no true discrimination.

To add to the tension, a second and related controversy sprang up when an entire National Institutes of Health convention came under attack for attempting to explore the links between the human genome and violent behavior. A brochure written for an NIH conference on "Genetic Factors in Crime" (which was subsequently postponed) argued that "genetic research holds out the prospect of identifying individuals who may be predisposed to certain kinds of criminal conduct."[91] Immediately the conference came under attack by critics like Peter Breggin, who argued that seeking genetic markers for criminal behavior deserved to be discussed about as much as Nazi Germany ought to discuss whether Jews were genetically inferior.[92] A social drama unfolded as the scientific and public presses used the debate between Goodwin and Breggin as a way of helping scientists and the public determine what type of applied research would be acceptable.[93] One writer for the *New Scientist* claimed that

> In a society terrified by wanton violence and deeply divided by race, the study of inheritance is a political minefield. . . . The combination of genetics and prejudice has already been the source of much evil in this century. . . . Some reasons for

opposing this conference are bad ones. Judging by the planned schedule and list of participants, it was not going to advance the cause of eugenics. And there was no evidence that it would promote a plan allegedly hatched by the National Institute of Mental Health to combat crime by identifying young men who are biologically predisposed to violence. . . . Yet there is a deeper, and more justified reason why the conference set off protests within the American scientific community. Put simply, the U.S. government has lost the confidence of people most directly affected by violent crime.[94]

Not all commentators are so sanguine.[95] Geneticism is inviting for those interested in taking "preemptive action" in order to reduce crime. As one enthusiast has remarked, it "seems pointless to wait until high-risk prospects actually commit crimes before trying to do something to control them."[96] It doesn't take much imagination to guess which individuals will be perceived as being predisposed to criminal activity.

The Human Genome Project, Sexuality, and the Reconfiguration of Gender

Since long before the arrival of the Genome Project, feminists have waged a discursive battle against eugenical claims that biology is destiny.[97] Like the earlier eugenical templates, the modern rhetorics of genetics are now being redeployed to support traditional biases, sexual stereotypes, and "prevailing ideologies." In the first quarter of the twentieth century, British and American women were constantly being admonished that entire races depended on motherhood and preservation of the germplasm. Today, this language has been modified to include discussions of "genetic rights" of the unborn and the importance of maintaining traditional family values.[98]

Within a rhetorical culture that emphasizes the role of the environment or acculturation, women are considered to be autonomous persons who possess equal abilities and rights. Yet the return of eugenics may take us back to a time when reproduction was women's defining social activity.[99] Countless media stories about the biological differences between the genders invite us to believe that women are predisposed to their "natural role of nurturance" while boys are "genetically programmed" to be aggressive.[100] Hubbard warns that now "scientists and physicians are in a position to provide the means with which to act on the eugenic prejudices of the society which they share. And once a technique exists to identify a fetus that will be born with a particular disability, individual women and families become responsible for acting out these prejudices."[101] As researchers create a discursive fabric that constantly narrows the purported influence of "fate," they will expand the number of diseases or behaviors that are considered to be under human control. Doctors fearing malpractice suits and companies interested in selling tests will join other interested parties in pushing for "voluntary" or even mandatory screening. By June 1994, one observer noted that "new genetic tests roll off the conveyor belt of the Human Genome Project almost once a week."[102]

Nor are heterosexuals the only people that will be affected by the rise of genetic essentialism. At the same time that investigators search for the genes responsible for hereditary disease, they have looked for genetic explanations of purported "abnormal" sexual behavior.[103] Some researchers hope that scientific evidence of a genetic cause for homosexuality will mean that homophobic societies will become more accepting of it, but critics complain that many of these correlational studies are meaningless.[104] Legal studies that have surveyed the impact of the Genome Project warn us about the dangers that come from popularizing this type of genetic determinism. Just one example of the portentous impact of these novel genetic explanations comes from England, where a lord of the British Commonwealth argued in July 1993 that "If we could by some form of genetic engineering eliminate those [homosexual] trends, we should — so long as it is done for a therapeutic purpose."[105] Biological arguments can be used in a number of ways, but the history of eugenics reminds us of some of the *predominant* uses of this information. If biology becomes destiny, we have a good idea of what will be considered "sexually unhealthy" behavior.[106]

Assessment: The Future of the Human Genome Project and the Rhetoric of Eugenics

More than a century ago, Francis Galton and other eugenicists dreamed of the day that the study of the wellborn would become part of the secular religion of developed countries. That time has come.[107] In the Western world, the genetic revolution has brought new rhetorics of eugenics that celebrate the rise of new sciences like "genomics" and the development of new ways of assuring "perfect" babies. The media remind English and American audiences of the power of genetics to explain everything from divorce to rising crime rates. The dense, discursive mythologies and narratives that once demanded the containment of racism and affirmed the inherent equality of all persons have been augmented with new lexicons that remind us of differences that are "hardwired."

The quest for the human genome will not bring with it a new Frankenstein monster in the form of forced eugenics, but neither will it provide cures for all the complex diseases and social conditions that confound us. Some argue that this type of research could have been conducted without all of the hyperbole and reductionism that have given the public distorted images of science.[108] Yet the really explosive results of this research will come when doctors begin justifying massive screening in the name of public health and societal wellbeing. The dangers we will have to confront will come not in the form of overt racism but when insurance companies justify discriminatory practices on the basis of mere susceptibility to disease.

In coping with these complexities, we will have to do more than try to find independent commissions or increase the amount of money spent on ethics investigations. We will need to hear the views of a variety of public communities whose interests may not be reflected in the arguments advanced by elites. In dealing with the ambiguities of eugenics, we need to understand the ways that the ideographs of "choice" and "necessity" are constantly being reappropriated to fit particular political and social agendas.

Compromises will have to be made between two extreme forms of determinism—genetic and cultural. Scientists in the future may be allowed to engage in both somatic and gene-line therapy, but only so long as changes are made in society. There will have to be greater access to health care, laws passed against discrimination and invasions of privacy, and better prenatal care.[109] Researchers will be allowed freedom of expression in conducting controversial studies on violence, but only so long as these investigations do not claim to have discovered a single racial gene responsible for a single trait. Doctors and investigators can talk about the importance of preventive medicine, but they claim as China did in December 1993 that "more than 10 million disabled persons" had been born who could have been "prevented through better controls."[110]

In sum, what we will have to deal with is a return visit by a revised form of eugenics that is just beginning to be critiqued. Some critics have argued that the press and public need to stay out of this debate because of their ignorance of genetics, but this assumes that technically competent officials and investigators within our society are the most responsible of citizens. Historical evidence shows otherwise. All of the sciences and humanities have biases and assumptions that reflect and influence the problems and interests of larger rhetorical cultures. Like all discursive constructs, the modern eugenical tales are selective reconfigurations made from materials handed down from generation to generation. As I indicate throughout this book, the study of the wellborn in the past did not come into being or disappear simply because of the activities of a few enlightened scientists. The popularity of eugenics depends on what all of us in the public sphere—women, African-Americans, Catholics, and the rest of us—are willing to accept as a part of our culture. The arrival of the Human Genome Project has brought new challenges that invite us to grapple with complex issues like poverty, gender selection, mandatory testing, screening, and health insurance.[111] The choices are ours to make.[112]

Appendix:

Terms of Art in

Rhetorical Analyses

Ideology. Ideology in its broadest sense may be defined as the use of symbol systems to influence social change. From an ideographic perspective, ideologies are made up of ideographs, narratives, myths, characterizations, and other discursive units. This discursive approach to ideology combines the insights of the materialism of the neo-Marxists with some of the arguments of symbolic interactionists. A critic engaged in ideographic research would agree with the Marxists that there are "givens" within the human environment that "impinge" on the use and development of language but would reject the view that this means that discourse cannot influence economics. A critic would also agree with the symbolist who regards humans as symbol-using, myth-creating animals but might reject the argument that reality is nothing but myth. An ideographic analysis combines the two perspectives and argues that symbols and material realities operate in a *recursive,* mutually reinforcing manner. In other words, humans, in their use of ideographs, do influence social action, and material conditions in turn affect the way in which we create our symbol systems.[1]

The discursive units of a public vocabulary have usages that help individuals and communities rhetorically construct "peoples," "nations," and "races."[2] Ideologies work to *condition* (rather than cause—humans still have volition) human beings to accept particular warrants or excuses for action or belief.[3] An ideographic approach is closer to the ideal of humans working through culture in order to create laws and other social constructions.[4] The power of an ideology is that it may obviate the need for coercion, if public actors come to act on the basis of their beliefs in the ideographs. For an ideographic analysis, an ideology is not something that contributes to "false consciousness" but is an essential ingredient in the value structure of a particular community.[5]

Narratives. Narratives are the stories that are used in the formation of ideologies.[6] Narratives are different from ideographs in form and function. While ideographs are single, highly evocative words, narratives consist of more elaborate story forms with structured plots. Narratives are accounts of deeds or actions that are meant to be constantly retold.[7] Social actors identify themselves with particular collectives by choosing between competing stories. For example, communities that see immigrants as welcome additions to the assimilating "melting pot" are going to be treated differently than if they are characters in a tale about "foreign parasites" invading the purity of American shores. Another example would be the discursive battles waged between fulfilling material and moral dimensions of the "American Dream."[8]

Characterizations. These are the subcomponents that make up the substantive elements of narratives and other discursive structures.[9] Descriptions are made of agents, acts, scenes, and purposes, and when these descriptions are accepted as fairly accurate depictions of a class, a characterization is the result. The "Founders," "Boy Scouts," or "Know-Nothings" are examples of discursive units that are characterizations.[10] For the purposes of rhetoric, the importance of a characterization is not necessarily its truth or falsity according to some standard outside of the narrative but rather the potency of the characterization to audiences who identify with particular stories.[11] For example, if Americans are to accept immigrants as part of the polity, discourses have to be crafted to persuade native communities that the new arrivals need not be characterized as members of a different nationality, race, or species.

Myths. Closely related to narratives, myths also play a central role in defining the way we think about ourselves and our "liberties," "freedoms," and "duties." Lewis noted that myths are stories of origins and destinies, explanations or pedagogic images of nature and humanity.[12] Our myths about the Founders and the origins of constitutional government justify particular social structures and provide us with ways of making sense of our lives.[13] Myths may perhaps be narratives that have stood the test of time. They allow different historical communities to form discursive bonds with each other. For example, myths about fighting tyranny and oppression may help collectives cope with recurring obstacles and solve similar social problems. Southern myths about the "glorious cause" might be a recurring theme built on mythic foundations.[14]

One fruitful method of unpacking the complexities and contradictions within any particular culture is to explore the "culturetypal" and countercultural elements that exist within discursive communities. Culturetypal rhetorics are the dominant, legitimate, and controlling interpretations that help articulate the core values that are accepted by most members of any cultural community.[15] In any civic polity, the culturally established narratives, characterizations, and ideographs provide both advocates and their audiences with an established public vocabulary.[16] The stories that we tell are symbolic interpretations of the world that are shaped by history, culture, and character.[17] These narratives are a form of discourse that allows advocates to make suggestions about our moral and political values.[18] Rhetors working within the orthodox lexicon have the advantage of speaking to listeners who are familiar with the interpretations and rhetorical depictions portrayed in culturetypal discourse. Unlike archetypes, which are timeless and cross-cultural in their power, culturetypal principles are embedded in specific, temporal contexts.[19]

Countercultural rhetorics operate outside of the central tenets of the mainstream of a community and have to work for legitimacy in order to effect some significant social change. Unlike popular culturetypal discourse, countercultural lexicons are marginalized codes often providing an alternative voice that "shadows" the culturetypal rhetoric.[20] Rhetors who advance countercultural perspectives have the choice of accepting, modifying, or rejecting the narratives and histories advanced by culturetypal speakers.[21] Presentations made from a countercultural stance may reinterpret and rearrange the narratives, characterizations, and ideographs that are part of the traditional public usages.[22]

Notes

Chapter 1: The Significance and Origins of the Rhetoric of Eugenics

1. For several excellent discussions of the polysemous nature of "eugenics," see Elof Axel Carlson, "Ramifications of Genetics," *Science* 232 (1986): 531–32; Diane Paul, "Eugenic Anxieties, Social Realities, and Political Choices," *Social Research* 59 (1992): 663–83. One of the earliest studies of eugenics can be found in Nicholas Pastore, *The Nature-Nurture Controversy* (New York: King's Crown Press, 1949). For a literature review that is extremely helpful in tracking down some of the early work, see Lyndsay A. Farrall, "The History of Eugenics: A Bibliographic Review," *Annals of Science* 36 (1979): 111–23.

2. Francis Galton, quoted in Paul, "Eugenic Anxieties" 666.

3. Kevles has argued that the "shadow" of eugenics looms over human genetic research. Daniel Kevles, "Controlling the Genetic Arsenal," *Wilson Quarterly* 16 (1992):

68–76, 68. For an example of literature that distinguishes between eugenics and genetics, note the seminal work of Bentley Glass, "Geneticists Embattled: Their Stand against Rampant Eugenics and Racism in America during the 1920s and 1930s," *Proceedings of the American Philosophical Society* 130 (1986): 130–54. Some have argued that genetics is the science of heredity while eugenics is merely a "philosophical position concerning the values and methods of improving the quality of human life by genetic means." Arthur R. Jensen, "Objectivity and the Genetics of I.Q.: A Reply to Stephen Selden," *Phi Delta Kappan* 66 (1984): 284–86, 285.

4. For some interesting interpretations of the importance of the earlier eugenicists, see Charles B. Davenport, *Heredity in Relation to Eugenics* (New York: Henry Holt, 1911). Galton has been a popular figure to study. Notice the work of Ruth Schwartz Cowan, "Sir Francis Galton and the Study of Heredity in the Nineteenth Century" (Ph.D. diss., University of Michigan, 1969); C. P. Blacker, *Eugenics: Galton and After* (Cambridge, Mass.: Harvard University Press, 1952); Carl Jay Bajema, ed., *Eugenics: Then and Now* (Stroudsburg, Pa.: Dowden, Hutchinson, and Ross, 1976).

There is also a vast literature on the founders of English eugenics. Gilbert K. Chesterton, *Eugenics and Other Evils* (London: Cassell and Co., 1922); G. R. Searle, *Eugenics and Politics in Britain, 1900–1914* (Leyden: Noordhoff International, 1976); Harvey G. Simmons, "Explaining Social Policy: The English Mental Deficiency Act of 1913," *Journal of Social History* 11 (1978): 387–403; Donald MacKenzie, "Eugenics in Britain," *Social Studies of Science* 6 (1979): 499; David Barker, "How to Curb the Fertility of the Unfit: The Feebleminded in Edwardian Britain," *Oxford Review of Education* 9 (1983): 197–211; L. A. Farrall, *The Origins and Growth of the English Eugenics Movement, 1865–1925* (New York: Garland, 1985); Greta Jones, *Social Hygiene in Twentieth Century Britain* (London: Croom Helm, 1986); David Barker, "The Biology of Stupidity: Genetics, Eugenics, and Mental Deficiency in the Inter-War Years," *British Journal of the History of Science* 22 (1989): 347–75; Edward J. Larson, "The Rhetoric of Eugenics: Expert Authority and the Mental Deficiency Bill," *British Journal for the History of Science* 24 (1991): 45–60; Pauline M. H. Mazumdar, *Eugenics, Human Genetics and Human Failings* (London: Routledge, 1992).

While this book focuses on the meanings of eugenics within Anglo-American communities, a growing number of studies illustrate the international dimensions of eugenical argumentation. Note the work of William Schneider, "Toward the Improvement of the Human Race: The History of Eugenics in France," *Journal of Modern History* 54 (June 1982): 268–91; Paul Weindling, "Weimar Eugenics: The Kaiser Wilhelm Institute for Anthropology, Human Heredity, and Eugenics in Social Context," *Annals of Science* 42 (1985): 303–18; Robert Lifton, *The Nazi Doctors: Medical Killing and the Psychology of Genocide* (New York: Basic Books, 1986); Sheila F. Weiss, "The Race Hygiene Movement in Germany," *Osiris* 3 (1987): 193–236; Benno Müller-Hill, *Murderous Science* (Oxford: Oxford University Press, 1988); Robert N. Proctor, *Racial Hygiene: Medicine under the Nazis* (Cambridge, Mass.: Harvard University Press, 1988); Peter Weingart,

"German Eugenics: Between Science and Politics," *Osiris* 5 (1989): 260–82; Paul Weindling, *Health, Race, and German Politics between National Unification and Nazism, 1870–1945* (Cambridge: Cambridge University Press, 1989); Mark B. Adams, ed., *The Wellborn Science: Eugenics in Germany, France, Brazil, and Russia* (New York: Oxford University Press, 1990).

5. For a summary of the early literature on the eugenics movement, see S. J. Holmes, *A Bibliography of Eugenics* (Berkeley: University of California Publications in Zoology, 1924).

6. An illuminating discussion of the relationship between the earlier eugenical laws and modern-day genetics issues can be found in George J. Annas, "Who's Afraid of the Human Genome?" *Hastings Center Report* 19 (1989): 19–21. See also Barry A. Mehler, "A History of the American Eugenics Society, 1921–1940" (Ph.D. diss., University of Illinois at Urbana, 1988) 8.

7. Richard J. Herrnstein and Charles Murray, *The Bell Curve* (New York: Free Press, 1994). Herrnstein and Murray seem to have mixed feelings about past eugenical creeds. While they deplore the unscientific "perversion" of eugenics (343), at the same time they note that "at the bottom, the Victorian eugenicists and their successors had detected" a certain "demographic pattern that seems to arise with great (though not universal) consistency around the world" (343). Astonishingly, Herrnstein and Murray talk about how abuses wiped the idea of "eugenics" from the "public discourse in the West" (343) while at the same time they defend many of the early studies of "dysgenesis." This term appears to be a modern word for genetic unfitness.

8. Carl Degler has recently advanced the interesting argument that the role of ideology pervaded not only biological but *cultural* explanations of human behavior. Carl N. Degler, *In Search of Human Nature: The Decline and Revival of Darwinism in American Social Thought* (New York: Oxford University Press, 1991) viii.

9. Abby Lippman, "Led (Astray) by Genetic Maps: The Cartography of the Human Genome and Health Care," *Social Science and Medicine* 35 (1992): 1469–76, 1470.

10. At times we have simply changed our forms of discrimination.

11. For a history of the notion of value-free science, see Robert N. Proctor, *Value-Free Science: Purity and Power in Modern Knowledge* (Cambridge, Mass.: Harvard University Press, 1991).

12. For interesting contrasting discussions of "race" in genetic research, compare Nancy Stepan, *The Idea of Race in Science: Great Britain, 1800–1960* (Hamden, Conn.: Archon, 1982), with *Shockley on Eugenics and Race*, ed. Roger Pearson (Washington: Scott-Townsend, 1992).

13. Donald K. Pickens, *Eugenics and the Progressives* (Nashville, Tenn.: Vanderbilt University Press, 1968) 5–70. On Charles B. Davenport, see Charles E. Rosenberg, "Charles B. Davenport and the Beginning of Human Genetics," *Bulletin of the History of Medicine* 35 (1961): 266–76. For a discussion of Laughlin, see Frances Hassencahl, "Harry Hamilton Laughlin, Expert Eugenics Agent for the House Committee on Im-

migration and Naturalization, 1921–31" (Ph.D. diss., Case Western Reserve University, 1970); Randy Bird and Garland Allen, "Sources in the History of Eugenics: The Harry Hamilton Laughlin Papers in Kirksville, Missouri," *Journal of the History of Biology* 14 (1981): 339–53. For an intriguing discussion of some of the early work of the eugenicists, see Barbara A. Kimmelman, "The American Breeders' Association: Genetics and Eugenics in an Agricultural Context, 1903–1913," *Social Studies of Science* 13 (1983): 163–204. On the role of physicians in the eugenics movement, a good place to start is Philip Reilly's "The Surgical Solution: The Writings of Activist Physicians in the Early Days of Eugenics Sterilization," *Perspectives in Biology and Medicine* 26 (1983): 637–56.

14. See Daniel Kevles, *In the Name of Eugenics: Genetics and the Uses of Human Heredity* (New York: Alfred A. Knopf, 1985). Other researchers, like Pickens, argued that it was the "economic crash and subsequent depression from 1929 to 1940" that was "the death knell of Galtonian eugenics in the United States" (see Pickens, *Eugenics and the Progressives* 205). Pickens also believed that with the coming of the New Deal, the Depression affected the biologically fit and unfit (205).

15. Germans often expressed envy at the rate of eugenics progress in America, and American laws on sterilization served as models for the Nazis. For example, Popenoe's model laws written in the early 1920s served as models for Nazi sterilization laws.

16. See, for example, the discussion of eugenics found in Mark Haller, *Eugenics: Hereditarian Attitudes in American Thought* (New Brunswick, N.J.: Rutgers University Press, 1963). For Haller, society was saved from the most radical of the eugenicists by the presence of a more cautious, sober, and scientific eugenics (3–7).

Another major monograph on the American eugenics movement came nine years later with the publication of Kenneth Ludmerer, *Genetics and American Society: A Historical Appraisal* (Baltimore, Md.: Johns Hopkins University Press, 1972). Ludmerer built on Haller's work, and argued that the eugenicists had misused the science of eugenics to the point that prominent figures in the genetic community were forced to repudiate much of the work of the eugenicists. Ludmerer was careful to distinguish between illegitimate "racist" research and legitimate scientific investigations. He also asked his readers to remember that the early eugenicists might have been racists but that they were living at a time when determinist hereditarian interpretations were dominant. Ludmerer has been criticized for taking a too narrow view of the relationship between eugenics and racism (Mehler, "The American Eugenics Society" 14).

17. While I disagree with the Whiggish views of some of these commentators, their analysis of the politics involved is difficult to ignore. Note, for example, the moving discussion of the "abuses" of eugenics in Clement E. Vose, "The Eugenics Movement," *Constitutional Change: Amendment Politics and Supreme Court Litigation since 1900* (Lexington, Mass.: Lexington Books, 1972); Steven Jay Gould, "Carrie Buck's Daughter," *Natural History* 7 (1984): 14–18; Elazar Barkan, *The Retreat of Scientific Racism: Changing Concepts of Race in Britain and the United States between the World Wars* (Cambridge: Cambridge University Press, 1992).

18. A typical example of this genre can be found in the work of M. F. Ashley Montagu, *Man's Most Dangerous Myth: The Fallacy of Race* (New York: Harper and Brothers, 1952). In his chapter on "Eugenics, Genetics, and 'Race,' " Montagu argued that "The clear stream of science must not be polluted by the murky visions of politicans and the prescriptions of effete castes distinguished by an hypertrophied sense of their own importance" (157).

19. For example, Kevles recently claimed that much of the opposition to the spread of genetic engineering came from "environmentalists, small farmers, clerics, and animal rights activists." This gives the impression that dissenters are simply obstructionists who are outside the public mainstream. Daniel J. Kevles, "Vital Essences and Human Wholeness: The Social Readings of Biological Information," *Southern California Law Review* 65 (1991): 255–78, 269. In contrast, see the work of Keller and Sapp.

20. Some writers have tried to finesse this point by making distinctions between the "old" eugenics movement (1900 to 1925) and the "newer" eugenics movement that emerged between 1925 and 1940. See, for example, Garland Allen, "The Role of Experts in Scientific Controversy," in *Scientific Controversies: Case Studies in the Resolution and Closure of Disputes in Science and Technology,* ed. H. Tristram Englehardt, Jr., and Arthur L. Caplan (Cambridge: Cambridge University Press, 1987) 169–202, 172. But see the recent work that questions the discontinuity between the old and new eugenics. For example, see Elazar Barkan, "Reevaluating Progressive Eugenics: Herbert Spencer Jennings and the 1924 Immigration Legislation," *Journal of the History of Biology* 24 (1991): 91–112.

21. Benno Müller-Hill, "Genetics after Auschwitz," *Holocaust and Genocide Studies* 2 (1987): 3–20, 3.

22. For an equivocal discussion of some of these issues, see Richard J. Neuhaus, "The Return of Eugenics," *Commentary* 85 (1988): 15–26.

23. Most of the eugenic studies seemed to be tailored toward an analysis of the activities of a very small number of individuals. For example, even the discursively sensitive work of Nicole Hahn Rafter calls our attention to the studies of just a few eugenical workers. Nicole Hahn Rafter, *White Trash: The Eugenic Family Studies, 1877–1919* (Boston: Northeastern University Press, 1988). Similarly, Reilly's important work on eugenical sterilization focuses on the views of key doctors, eugenicists, and legislators. Philip R. Reilly, *The Surgical Solution: A History of Involuntary Sterilization in the United States* (Baltimore, Md.: Johns Hopkins University Press, 1991).

If there were any discussions of public argument involving eugenics, they usually took the form of discussing the role of the movement in helping pass the 1924 immigration laws or in sterilization decisions in the courts. Psychologists, educators, social workers, criminal anthropologists, and other social scientists often described eugenics as a pernicious influence within their own disciplines. See for example the debate discussed in Jensen, "Objectivity and the Genetics of I.Q." Some of these studies have focused on the abuse of eugenics in formulating intelligence tests based on race. See Richard Hofstadter,

Social Darwinism in American Thought, 1860–1915 (Philadelphia: University of Pennsylvania Press, 1945); Thomas F. Gossett, *Race: The History of an Idea in America* (New York: Schocken, 1965); Stephen J. Gould, *The Mismeasure of Man* (New York: W. W. Norton, 1981); Steven A. Gelb, "Myths, Morons, Psychologists: The Kallikak Family Revisited," *The Review of Education* 11 (1985): 255–59.

Examples of exceptions to this rule can be found in the work of Garland E. Allen, "Genetics, Eugenics, and Class Struggle," *Genetics* 79 (1975): 29–45; Allen Chase, *The Legacy of Malthus* (New York: Alfred A. Knopf, 1977); Michael Freeden, "Eugenics and Progressive Thought: A Study in Ideological Affinity," *Historical Journal* 22 (1979): 645–71; Greta Jones, *Social Darwinism and Biological Thought* (Sussex: Harvester Press, 1980); Greta Jones, *Social Hygiene in Twentieth Century Britain;* Robert N. Proctor, "Eugenics among the Social Sciences: Hereditarian Thought in Germany and the United States," in *The Estate of Social Knowledge*, ed. JoAnne Brown and David K. Van Keuren (Baltimore, Md.: Johns Hopkins University Press, 1991); Ian Barns, "The Human Genome Project and the Self," *Soundings* 77 (1994): 99–128.

Note also the recent move to place eugenics in the context of a larger feminist movement. See Linda Gordon, *Woman's Body, Woman's Right: A Social History of Birth Control in America* (New York: Grossman, 1976); Linda Gordon, "The Politics of Population: Birth Control and the Eugenics Movement," *Radical America* 8 (1974): 61–97; Linda Gordon, "Birth Control and the Eugenists," *Science for the People* 10 (1977): 8–15; Rosaleen Love, " 'Alice in Eugenics-Land': Feminism and Eugenics in the Scientific Careers of Alice Lee and Ethel Elderton," *Annals of Science* 36 (1979): 145–58; Richard Allen Soloway, *Birth Control and the Population Question in England, 1877–1930* (Chapel Hill: University of North Carolina Press, 1982).

24. Both of these perspectives trivialize the role of rhetoric in its relationship to scientific inquiry. The apologetic texts ignore the influence of discourse, while Luddite tales assume rhetoric's perniciousness. I refuse to subscribe to the position that our lexicons have little or no impact on the selection of research agendas and their implementation. Scientists not only have to argue within the public sphere for precious dollars: they also have to convince both citizens and their peers that they are engaging in activities that can be accepted as legitimate science. For an excellent discussion of how hegemonic discourse works in the everyday world of the new reproductive technologies, see Celeste M. Condit, "Hegemony in a Mass-Mediated Society: Concordance about Reproductive Technologies," *Critical Studies in Mass Communication* 11 (1994): 205–30.

25. Arthur E. Fink, *Causes of Crime: Biological Theories in the United States, 1800–1915* (Philadelphia: University of Pennsylvania Press, 1938) 160.

26. One of the most intriguing studies that has ever been done on eugenics can be found in Donald A. MacKenzie, *Statistics in Britain, 1865–1930: The Social Construction of Scientific Knowledge* (Edinburgh: Edinburgh University Press, 1981).

27. Kevles, *In the Name of Eugenics* x.

28. Troy Duster, *Backdoor to Eugenics* (New York: Routledge, 1990) 4.

29. In using the term "rhetoric," I mean the study of the influence of discursive symbols in maintaining or changing public attitudes. For an introduction to the field, see James L. Golden, Goodwin F. Berquist, and William E. Coleman, eds., *The Rhetoric of Western Thought* (Dubuque, Iowa: Kendall/Hunt, 1983).

30. Prior to the 1970s, few studies even considered the possibility that the sciences were at least in part rhetorically constructed, but this changed with the growing influence of texts like Thomas Kuhn's *The Structures of Scientific Revolutions* (Chicago: University of Chicago Press, 1970). See also the influential work of P. K. Feyerabend, *Against Method* (London: New Left Books, 1975).

As John Lyne once observed, even those scientific texts that purport to be against rhetoric are themselves forms of "antirhetorics" that have an "unavoidable rhetorical character." See Lyne's "Bio-rhetorics: Moralizing the Life Sciences," in *The Rhetorical Turn: Invention and Persuasion in the Conduct of Inquiry*, ed. H. W. Simons (Chicago: University of Chicago Press, 1990) 35–57, 54. Since that time, many more researchers have sought ways of explicating the murky boundaries between the disciplines and have looked for ways of uncovering some of the persuasive strategies at work in the internal and external structures of the sciences. I should note here, though, that opinions are divided even within the field of rhetoric, where many theorists still maintain that a clear division exists between "rhetoric" and "science."

31. Condit recently noted that rhetoric was considered to be the "harlot" of the arts in comparison with "chaste" science. See Celeste M. Condit, "The Birth of Understanding: Chaste Science and the Harlot of the Arts," *Communication Monographs* 37 (1990): 323–27. For an example of a more moderate stance within the field of communication, see Lawrence Prelli, "Rhetorical Perspective and the Limits of Critique," *Southern Communication Journal* 58 (1993): 319–27.

32. Scholars from a number of disciplines have indicated a renewed appreciation of the role of rhetoric in the construction of the goals, theories, and tactics of the human and natural sciences. For an excellent overview of attitudes within a number of disciplines toward rhetoric, epistemology, and the sciences, see Steve Fuller, *Philosophy, Rhetoric, and the End of Knowledge* (Madison: University of Wisconsin Press, 1993). For Fuller's discussion of the relevance of McGee's work, see especially chapter 1.

Broadly defined, many researchers treat rhetoric as simply discourse or ideology. See, for example, the excellent work of Stanley Aronowitz, *Science as Power: Discourse and Ideology in Modern Society* (Minneapolis: University of Minnesota Press, 1988). Close relatives of rhetorical perspectives can be found in the social studies of science and technology movements. Note here the work of Barry Barnes, *Scientific Knowledge and Sociological Theory* (London: Routledge and Kegan Paul, 1974); *Natural Order: Historical Studies of Scientific Culture*, ed. Barry Barnes and Steven Shapin (London: Sage, 1979); David Bloor, *Knowledge and Social Imagery* (London: Routledge and Kegan Paul, 1976); Bruno Latour, *Science in Action: How to Follow Scientists and Engineers through Society* (Cambridge, Mass.: Harvard University Press, 1987).

33. Celeste M. Condit and John L. Lucaites, *Crafting Equality: America's Anglo-American Word* (Chicago: University of Chicago Press, 1993) ix. A new subdiscipline has emerged within the field of communications that explores the "rhetoric of the sciences." See P. N. Campbell, "The Persona of Scientific Discourse," *Quarterly Journal of Speech* 61 (1975): 391–405; Philip Wander, "The Rhetoric of Science," *Western Journal of Speech Communication* 40 (1976): 226–35; W. B. Weimer, "Science as a Rhetorical Transaction: Toward a Nonjustificational Concept of Rhetoric," *Philosophy and Rhetoric* 10 (1977): 1–29; Alan G. Gross, "Public Debates as Failed Social Dramas: The Recombinant DNA Controversy," *Quarterly Journal of Speech* 70 (1984): 397–409; Trevor Melia, "And Lo the Footprint . . . Selected Literature in Rhetoric and Science," *Quarterly Journal of Speech* 70 (1984): 303–13; S. M. Halloran, "The Birth of Molecular Biology: An Essay in the Rhetorical Criticism of Scientific Discourse," *Rhetoric Review* 3 (1984): 70–83; Thomas M. Lessl, "Science and the Sacred Cosmos: The Ideological Rhetoric of Carl Sagan," *Quarterly Journal of Speech* 71 (1985): 175–87; John A. Campbell, "Scientific Revolution and the Grammar of Culture: The Case of Darwin's *Origin*," *Quarterly Journal of Speech* 72 (1986): 351–76; John Lyne and H. Howe, " 'Punctuated Equilibria': Rhetorical Dynamics of a Scientific Controversy," *Quarterly Journal of Speech* 72 (1986): 132–47; John S. Nelson, Allan Megill, and Donald M. McCloskey, eds., *Rhetoric of the Human Sciences: Language and Argument in Scholarship and Public Affairs* (Madison: University of Wisconsin Press, 1987); R. M. Bokeno, "The Rhetorical Understanding of Science: An Explication and Critical Commentary," *Southern Speech Communication Journal* 52 (1987): 300–321; Thomas M. Lessl, "Heresy, Orthodoxy, and the Politics of Science," *Quarterly Journal of Speech* 74 (1988): 18–34; Lawrence J. Prelli, *A Rhetoric of Science: Inventing Scientific Discourse* (Columbia, S.C.: University of South Carolina Press, 1989); Carolyn R. Miller, "The Rhetoric of Decision Science, or Herbert A. Simons Says," *Science, Technology, and Human Values* 14 (1989): 43–46; H. W. Simons, ed., *Rhetoric in the Human Sciences* (London: Sage, 1989); Lawrence J. Prelli, "Rhetorical Logic and the Integration of Rhetoric and Science," *Communication Monographs* 57 (1990): 315–22; Alan G. Gross, *The Rhetoric of Science* (Cambridge, Mass.: Harvard University Press, 1990); Charles A. Taylor, "Defining the Scientific Community: A Rhetorical Perspective on Demarcation," *Communication Monographs* 58 (1991): 402–20; Henry Howe and John Lyne, "Gene Talk in Sociobiology," *Epistemology* 6 (1992): 109–63; Kenneth S. Zagacki and William Keith, "Rhetoric, Topoi, and Scientific Revolutions," *Philosophy and Rhetoric* 25 (1992): 59–78; Dilip P. Gaonkar, "The Idea of Rhetoric in the Rhetoric of Science," *Southern Communication Journal* 58 (1993): 258–95; Michael J. Hyde, "Medicine, Rhetoric, and Euthanasia: A Case Study in the Workings of a Postmodern Discourse," *Quarterly Journal of Speech* 79 (1993): 201–24.

34. Jacques Derrida, *Dissemination*, trans. Barbara Johnson (Chicago: University of Chicago Press, 1981); Michel Foucault, *Power/Knowledge: Selected Interviews and Other Writings, 1972–1977*, ed. Colin Gordon (New York: Pantheon Books, 1980); Evelyn F. Keller, *Reflections on Gender and Science* (New Haven: Yale University Press, 1985); E. F.

Keller, "Fractured Images of Science, Language and Power: A Postmodern Optic, or Just Bad Eyesight?" *Poetics Today* 12 (1991): 227–43.

For an interesting extension of Gramsci's work, see JoAnne Brown, *The Definition of a Profession: The Authority of Metaphor in the History of Intelligence Testing, 1890–1930* (Princeton, N.J.: Princeton University Press, 1992).

35. One of the best examples of the interdisciplinary interest in rhetoric can be found in the attention that has been given to the University of Iowa's Rhetoric of Inquiry Program. For a sample of discussions of the relationship between rhetoric and history, law, anthropology, mathematics, and other sciences, see Nelson, Megill, and McCloskey, *The Rhetoric of the Human Sciences*.

36. Lessl, "Heresy, Orthodoxy," 18.

37. For an insightful criticism of this stance, see Christopher Norris, *Uncritical Theory: Postmodernism, Intellectuals and the Gulf War* (Amherst: University of Massachusetts Press, 1992). While I do not share all of Norris's views on postmodernity, I do think he makes a strong case for recognizing the limits of critique.

38. As McGuire and Melia recently note, it would be a "mistake" to "replace an arrogant scientism with a rampant rhetoricism." J. E. McGuire and Trevor Melia, "Some Cautionary Strictures on the Writing of the Rhetoric of Science," *Rhetorica* 7 (1989): 87–99. While I do not agree with the extent to which McGuire and Melia domesticate rhetoric, I do agree that there is a line that can be crossed. I disagree with their contention that there is a "world of meaning and system which is highly immune to the vagaries of the larger culture within which the science is pursued" (94). The difficult question is whether this world of meaning is *legitimately* kept from public critique. Note also the work of Peter Slezak, "The Social Construction of Social Constructionism," *Inquiry* 37 (1994): 139–57; Proctor, *Value-Free Science?* x.

39. Within the field of communication, we have had a series of lively debates on what it means for rhetoric to be "epistemic." See Thomas Farrell, "From the Parthenon to the Bassinet: Along the Epistemic Trail," *Quarterly Journal of Speech* 76 (1990): 78–84.

40. Ideographs are *one* of the discursive units that make up ideologies (see the appendix for some of the other discursive units of analysis). These are abstract value terms that serve as powerful warrants when members of a collective are willing to take some social action because of their beliefs (Celeste M. Condit, "Democracy and Civil Rights: The Universalizing Influence of Public Argumentation," *Communication Monographs* 54 [1987]: 1–18). Throughout this book I use quotation marks to indicate their existence. Examples of ideographs include the "rule of law," "right of privacy," "liberty," and "equality." McGee explained how terms like "freedom of speech" become the building blocks of "ideology," where single words or phrases may come to symbolize an orientation within a culture. Michael Calvin McGee, "The 'Ideograph' as a Unit of Analysis in Political Argument," in *Proceedings of the Summer Conference on Argumentation*, ed. Jack Rhodes and Sara Newell (Annandale, Va.: Speech Communication Association, 1980) 68–87. Not all words or terms of value are ideographs. For example, legal texts may de-

scribe "political autonomy," but if the members of the public have never heard of or used that term in their lexicon, it would not be an ideograph. See Celeste M. Condit, "Rhetorical Criticism and Audience: The Extremes of Leff and McGee," *Western Journal of Speech Communication* 54 (1990): 330–45, 332.

41. For a discussion of the difference between rhetorical histories and other types of analysis, see Condit and Lucaites, *Crafting Equality* ix–xxi. In their analysis of the importance of "equality" in African-American discourse, Condit and Lucaites point out that rhetors use ideographs in public discourse in order to gain the warranted assent of public citizens (*Crafting Equality* xiv).

42. For discussions of the importance of criticism in scientific investigations, see Proctor, *Value-Free Science;* W. S. Lee, "Social Scientists as Ideological Critics," *Western Journal of Communication* 57 (1993): 221–32, 223. "Critical Science" is an approach to the sciences that investigates the relationship between the knowledge claims of scientific disciplines and their historical and discursive presuppositions. While the roots of "critical science" have ancient origins, moderns critiques of science adopt theoretical postures that reject the notion of neutrality in science (Proctor, *Value-Free Science* 232). Scholars who adopt this perspective may or may not be interested in the "truth" claims of particular theories or methodologies, but they would be concerned with the political and ethical implications of engaging in concrete social practices (Proctor, *Value-Free Science* 232). For example, a researcher adopting this perspective might wonder how the advocacy of particular scientific visions has altered the way in which individuals and societies think about race, gender, or class. Any theoretical approach based on developing a "critical science" could build on the works of rhetoricians who have already uncovered some of the inventional topoi of science (Prelli, Zagacki, and Keith) by illustrating how these discursive units were deployed in concrete public settings. The goal here would be to go beyond mere description of the rhetorical or persuasive elements in scientific discourse in order to find those constructive alternatives that may have been left behind.

43. Michael C. McGee, "The 'Ideograph': A Link between Rhetoric and Ideology," *Quarterly Journal of Speech* 66 (1980): 1–16.

44. I. K. Zola, "In the Name of Health and Illness: On Some Socio-Political Consequences of Medical Influence," *Social Science and Medicine* 9 (1975): 83–87, 83.

45. Keller, "Fractured Images of Science" 228.

46. Brown, *The Definition of a Profession* 33. Brown contends that two metaphorical vocabularies, that of medicine and engineering, were used by American psychologists as a means of creating a professional community that excluded other vocabularies and voices (33–34). I would argue that it is not only metaphors but other discursive units that frame our political and social values. As Flower and Health explain, even a "document" that is hypostatized "as fact" often contains evidence of "earlier inscriptions" that have their own histories. "Michael J. Flower and Deborah Health, "Micro-Anatomo Politics: Mapping the Human Genome Project," *Culture, Medicine and Psychiatry* 17 (1993): 27–41, 28.

47. McGee, "The 'Ideograph'" 1–16.

48. Condit, "Democracy and Civil Rights" 2.

49. For example, note the attitude toward the masses of someone like Walter Bagehot, who envisioned a public composed of an ignorant mass constantly being duped by an intellectual elite. See Andrew King, "The Rhetoric of Power Maintenance: Elites at the Precipice," *Quarterly Journal of Speech* 62 (1976): 127–34, 127.

50. For a discussion of the role of Locke in communication studies, see John Durham Peters, "John Locke, the Individual, and the Origin of Communication," *Quarterly Journal of Speech* 75 (1989): 387–99.

51. Commenting on the work of historians R. G. Collinswood and Herbert J. Muller, McGee has argued that words like "freedom" and "progress" are examples of ideographs that are cherished parts of our discursive heritage. McGee, "The 'Ideograph'" 11. See R. G. Collinswood, *The Idea of History* (1946; rpt. London: Oxford University Press, 1972) 302–34; Herbert J. Muller, *The Uses of the Past* (New York: Oxford University Press, 1952) 37–38.

52. James W. Carey, "The Press and the Public Discourse," *Center Magazine* (1987): 4–32.

53. The concept of "fragment" I appropriate from Michael McGee "Text, Context, and the Fragmentation of Contemporary Culture," *Western Journal of Speech Communication* 54 (1990): 274–89. See also Dominick LaCapra, *History and Criticism* (Ithaca, N.Y.: Cornell University Press, 1985).

54. LaCapra, *History and Criticism* 11.

55. Ana Maria Alonso, "The Effects of Truth: Re-Presentations of the Past and the Imagining of Community," *Journal of Historical Sociology* 1 (March 1988): 33–57.

56. Because ideographs are the units that make up the material for ideologies, tracing ideographs allows an investigator to follow the ways in which social change is affected when people gain a new or modified social consciousness. Advocates engaged in public deliberation can become influential when they help change social vocabularies or create different interpretations for the words that make up the ideographic components of ideologies.

57. For some seminal discussions of the way in which critics can help appropriate some of these new constructs see the work of Stuart Hall. Hall once claimed that "historically-elaborated discourses" have left us a "reservoir of themes." Stuart Hall, "The Rediscovery of 'Ideology': Return of the Repressed in Media Studies," in *Culture, Society, and the Media*, ed. Michael Gurevitch et al. (London: Methuen, 1982) 56–90, 73.

58. Gross, *The Rhetoric of Science* 53.

59. For discussions of "liberty" and "equality" see the work of Condit and Lucaites. The term "necessity" is an especially powerful ideograph because it serves several different rhetorical functions in the history of Western civilization. John Stuart Mill once noted just some of these meanings when he claimed that "the word Necessity . . . sometimes

stands only for Certainty, at other times for Compulsion; sometimes for what cannot be prevented." John Stuart Mill, *A System of Logic, Ratiocinative and Inductive,* ed. J. M. Robson (Toronto: University of Toronto Press, 1974) 814.

From a rhetorical perspective, what is important about ideographs is that they allow us to see the ways in which these salient terms are deployed and reemployed in several different political settings to convince historical audiences of the existence of resource scarcity. Foucault once opined that "Need is also a political instrument, meticulously prepared, calculated and used." Michel Foucault, *Discipline and Punish: The Birth of the Prison,* trans. Alan Sheridan (New York: Vintage, 1979) 26, quoted in Nancy Fraser, "Struggle over Needs: Outline of a Socialist-Feminist Critical Theory of Late-Capitalist Political Culture," in *Women, the State, and Welfare,* ed. Linda Gordon (Madison: University of Wisconsin Press, 1990) 199. Whether an individual perceives a condition of necessity depends in part on the persuasiveness of the discourse employed. Vico argued that some of the first humans on earth were poets who used their power of imagination [*fantasia*] to grasp the "necessities and utilities" of life and became the first creators of nations, formal contracts, and legal codes. J. Samuel Prues, "Spinoza, Vico, and the Imagination of Religion," *Journal of the History of Ideas* 50 (1989): 71–93, 92.

In recent years, several scholars have begun to investigate isolated examples of historical uses of the "necessity plea." Michael McGee, for instance, warns us of the way in which this ideograph is used in times of national emergency. McGee gave a classic example of the power of the term "necessity" when he argued that we "make a rhetoric of war to persuade us of war's necessity, but then forget that it is a rhetoric—and regard negative popular judgments of it as unpatriotic cowardice" ("The 'Ideograph'" 6). Although McGee does not elaborate on the ways in which "necessity" can be rhetorically deployed, he recognizes the existence of the term as an ideograph. Scholars in other fields have also started to warn us of some of the ways in which public officials employ this dynamic ideograph. Richard Epstein, for instance, recently claimed that "One reason for constitutional government is to create a situation in which we make sure that government does not use the plea of necessity with such promiscuity that it will then erect whole series of repressive statutes, which turn out to be the very evil which we're fighting against" ("Proceedings of the Conference on Takings of Property and the Constitution," *University of Miami Law Review* 41 [1986]: 49–222, 50). Another legal commentator, Roberto Unger, recently admonished his readers to be aware of the ways in which false claims of "necessity" are sometimes employed in legal and social discourse in order to impose constraints on radical social changes (Roberto Mangabeira Unger, *False Necessity: Anti-Necessitarian Social Theory in the Service of Radical Democracy* [Cambridge: Cambridge University Press, 1987] 1).

60. Proctor, *Value-Free Science.*

61. Richard C. Lewontin, Steven Rose, and Leon Kamin, *Not in Our Genes* (New York: Pantheon Books, 1984).

62. Proctor, *Value-Free Science.* In the words of Professor Alan Gross, the "objectivity

of scientific prose is a carefully crafted rhetorical invention" (*The Rhetoric of Science* 15).

63. Aronowitz, *Science as Power* viii.

64. Taylor, "Defining the Scientific Community" 403.

65. Proctor, *Value-Free Science* 230.

66. Proctor, *Value-Free Science* 230.

67. Ann Fausto-Sterling, *Myths of Gender: Biological Theories about Women and Men* (New York: Basic Books, 1985); Elizabeth Fee, "Women's Nature and Scientific Objectivity," in *Woman's Nature: Rationalizations of Inequity,* ed. Marian Lowe and Ruth Hubbard (New York: Pergamon Press, 1983).

68. I am not suggesting that this is the only fruitful rhetorical approach. When faced with particular scientific controversies in the area of genetic research, rhetoricians and other researchers interested in the sciences have several ways to evaluate legitimate or illegitimate lines of inquiry. One is to stay on the sidelines of particular controversies by creating descriptive studies that avoid taking sides in normative debates. This seems to be the most common posture within the rhetoric of science community. At other times, analysts have provided us with much-needed insight into the intricacies of a debate, like Lessl's study of scientific creationism, where we get some implicit indications of the feelings of the writer. On rare occasions, scholars have combined descriptive with prescriptive critique. One common strategy in these types of analyses involves maintaining a sharp distinction between "true" science and an abusive imposter. For example, some research has focused attention on the dissimilarities between genetics and "eugenics" (Kevles, *In the Name of Eugenics*), or astronomy and astrology. Still other commentators have chosen to critique the rhetorics of science by illustrating how the language of one discipline has been misappropriated by another, as in the case of sociobiology and population genetics (Howe and Lyne). Yet as I argue here, too often these types of inquiries domesticate rhetoric by narrowing the audiences that are considered to be participants in the creation of legitimate science. For a discussion on the potential of inclusivity to enhance objectivity, see Helen E. Longino, "Multiple Subjects and the Diffusion of Power," *Journal of Philosophy* 88 (1991): 666–74.

69. Unfortunately, traditional divisions between the "scientific" and the "social" often hinder such a move. Oftentimes this type of approach is treated as "secondary" literature because it often involves public interpretations of "primary" eugenical studies. Throughout this book, I purposely blur the line between these sources of eugenic material because I am trying not to privilege the writings of the eugenicists.

70. If the "rhetoric of science" is ever to impact the way in which we conduct science, it needs to be sensitive to the ways in which it can be a part of a larger interdisciplinary attempt to make scientists accountable to the societies that provide them nourishment and autonomy.

71. See Hyde, "Medicine, Rhetoric, and Euthanasia," 201–24. In a postmodern world, scientific investigators have had to cope with a difficult dilemma. Theorists and practitioners of science are supposed to be free to engage in scientific inquiry, and yet at

the same time they are supposed to be accountable for their activities. They need public support to garner funds in the era of "big science" (super colliders, space stations), yet they frequently complain that the involvement of "the public" spells the introduction of Luddites or zealots who are merely interested in halting the progress of science.

72. For a trenchant critique of this division between rhetorical and scientific discourse, see Carolyn R. Miller, "Reviews: Some Perspectives on Rhetoric, Science, and History," *Rhetorica* 7 (1989): 101–20.

73. Donna Haraway, "Situated Knowledges: The Science Question in Feminism and the Privilege of Partial Perspective," *Feminist Studies* 14 (1988): 575–99; Helen E. Longino, *Science as Social Knowledge: Values and Objectivity in Scientific Inquiry* (Princeton, N.J.: Princeton University Press, 1990); Helen E. Longino, "Feminist Standpoint Theory and the Problems of Knowledge," *Signs* 19 (1993): 201–12; Sandra Harding, "After the Neutrality Ideal: Science, Politics, and 'Strong Objectivity,'" *Social Research* 59 (1992): 568–87; *The "Racial" Economy of Science: Toward a Democratic Future*, ed. Sandra Harding (Bloomington: Indiana University Press, 1993). Of these four writers, Longino takes the most moderate stance, claiming that through the use of critical social processes we improve our objective knowledge. "Knowledge, Bodies, and Values: Reproductive Technologies and Their Scientific Context," *Inquiry* 35 (1992): 323–40, 331. While I agree with Longino on the need for more inclusive approaches in scientific inquiry, I do share her optimism regarding the search for consensual objective knowledge.

74. Abir-Am Pnina, "Themes, Genres and Orders of Legitimation in the Consolidation of New Scientific Disciplines: Deconstructing the Historiography of Molecular Biology," *History of Science* 23 (1985): 72–115.

75. Hahn, *White Trash*, ix. For an elaboration of this "constructionist" analysis, see Nicole H. Rafter, "Claims-Making and Socio-Cultural Context in the First U.S. Eugenics Campaign," *Social Problems* 39 (1992): 17–34.

One of the most radical and insightful discussions of the relationship between power and the construction of selective hereditarian sciences can be found in Jan Sapp, *Beyond the Gene: Cytoplasmic Inheritance and the Struggle for Authority in Genetics* (New York: Oxford University Press, 1987).

76. Joel Best makes a similar point about the relationship between discourse and social problems when he argues that "claims-making" is a persuasive activity, subject to "rhetorical analysis." Joel Best, "Rhetoric in Claims-Making: Constructing the Missing Children Problem," *Social Problems* 34 (1987): 101–21. Best laudably sees the importance of discursivity, but he relies on the static tools of Toulmin's categories, which sometimes miss the dynamic nature of rhetoric.

77. Hahn, *White Trash* 2.

78. Hahn, *White Trash* 7. On the power of official scientific reports in framing our ethical perspectives, see Martha Solomon, "The Rhetoric of Dehumanization: An Analysis of Medical Reports of the Tuskegee Syphilis Project," *Western Journal of Speech Communication* 49 (Fall 1985): 233–47.

79. Scholars often write about the need for alternative views of science, but these discussions often focus on neglected views of other scientists rather than take public argumentation seriously. For a discussion of how even empathic critiques sometimes neglect the multiplicity of marginalized voices, see Ruth Frankenberg, *White Women, Race Matters: The Social Construction of Whiteness* (Minneapolis: University of Minnesota Press, 1993) 10.

80. One of the few explicitly ideographic studies of scientific discourse can be found in Michael Altimore, "The Social Construction of a Scientific Controversy: Comments on Press Coverage of the Recombinant DNA Debate," *Science, Technology, and Human Values* 7 (1982): 24–31. While Altimore does a good job of explaining McGee's theoretical position, his analysis of newspaper coverage of the R-DNA controversy does not give us any extended discussion of how particular configurations empowered different audiences.

81. Recent scholarship reveals the way in which the eugenic claims of reducing the numbers of the unfit through legal initiatives had an appeal for liberals and socialists as well as reactionaries (see Mazumdar, *Eugenics*).

82. One of the best investigations into this continuity can be found in Charles E. Rosenberg, *No Other Gods: On Science and American Social Thought* (Baltimore, Md.: Johns Hopkins University Press, 1976).

83. Plato, *The Republic of Plato*, trans. Francis M. Cornford (London: Oxford University Press, 1971) 106–7.

84. For discussions by scholars of the influence of the pre-Socratics and Plato, see Degler, *In Search of Human Nature* 4; Kevles, "Controlling the Genetic Arsenal" 68.

85. See Ivan Hannaford, "The Idiocy of Race," *Wilson Quarterly* 18 (1994): 8–35.

86. Bernard Mandeville, *The Fable of the Bees; or, Private Vices, Public Benefits*, ed. Douglas Garman (London: Wishart and Co., 1934). This work was first published in 1714.

87. William Godwin, *Enquiry Concerning Political Justice*, ed. K. Codell Carter (Oxford: Clarendon Press, 1971) xi. For other influences on Godwin, see James Preu, "Swift's Influence on Godwin's Doctrine of Anarchism," *Journal of the History of Ideas* 15 (1954): 371–83.

88. Thomas R. Malthus, *An Essay on the Principle of Population; or, A View of Its Past and Present Effects on Human Happiness*, 9th ed. (London: Reeves and Turner, 1888). Some of the best analyses of Malthus's work can be found in D. V. Glass, *Introduction to Malthus* (London: Watts and Co., 1953) 185–205; Patricia James, *Population Malthus: His Life and Times* (London: Routledge and Kegan Paul, 1979); Gertrude Himmelfarb, "Malthus: Political Economy De-Moralized," in *The Idea of Poverty: England in the Early Industrial Age* (New York: Alfred A. Knopf, 1984). Eugenicists like Henry Fairfield Osborn would later admit that the "idea of the Survival of the Fittest came to Darwin only through the suggestion of Malthus, who, in turn, probably borrowed it from Buffon." Henry Fairfield Osborn, *From the Greeks to Darwin* (New York: Macmillan, 1908) 239.

89. For other discussions of the importance of this "goad of necessity," see Arthur E.

Walzer, "Logic and Rhetoric in Malthus's *Essay on the Principle of Population,* 1798," *Quarterly Journal of Speech* 73 (1987): 1–17, 11.

90. Malthus quoted in John R. Poynter, *Society and Pauperism: English Ideas on Poor Relief, 1795–1834* (London: Routledge and Kegan Paul, 1969), 157.

91. Sir Thomas Malthus, "An Essay on the Principle of Population" (1830), parts reprinted in *On Population: Three Essays* (New York: Mentor Books, 1960) 14, 34. Almost a century before the advent of eugenics, one French physician, Pierre-Jean-Georges Cabanis, provided similar commentary when he lamented that, "After we have occupied ourselves so minutely with the means of making better and stronger races of animals and useful and agreeable plants; after we have done a hundred times over the race of horses and dogs; after we have transplanted, grafted, worked over fruits and flowers in every manner, why is it not shameful to have totally neglected the human race!—as though it were more distant!—as if it were more essential to have large strong cattle, than healthy, vigorous men, good smelling peaches and speckled tulips, than wise and good citizens. Quoted in Victor Hilts, "Obeying the Laws of Hereditary Descent: Phrenological Views on Inheritance and Eugenics," *Journal of the History of the Behavioral Sciences* 18 (1982): 62–77, 64.

92. Malthus, *On Population: Three Essays* 32.

93. Malthus, *On Population: Three Essays* 33. Perhaps even more controversial was Malthus's notorious parable of "nature's feast," which he used to show the inherent material constraints that were placed on the voracious appetites of the poor. He argued that "a man born into a world already possessed . . . has no claim of right to the smallest portion of food, and in fact, has no business to be where he is. At nature's mighty feast there is no cover for him." Malthus, quoted in Poynter, *Society and Pauperism,* 163. This discussion of "nature's feast" was withdrawn from the 1806 and subsequent editions.

94. Malthus, *The Principle of Population* 473.

95. Malthus, quoted in Poynter, *Society and Pauperism* 163.

96. Thomas Jarrold, quoted in Poynter, *Society and Pauperism* 169.

97. Mary Wollstonecraft, quoted in G. J. Barker-Benfield, "Mary Wollstonecraft: Eighteenth-Century Commonwealthwoman," *Journal of the History of Ideas* 50 (1989): 95–115, 106.

98. Herman Ausubel, "William Cobbett and Malthusianism," *Journal of the History of Ideas* 13 (1952): 250–56, quoted also in Poynter, *Society and Pauperism* 175.

99. William Hazlitt, quoted in Poynter, *Society and Pauperism* 177.

100. Merle Curti, "Human Nature in American Thought: The Age of Reason and Morality, 1750–1860," *Political Science Quarterly* 68 (1953): 354–75; Hilts, "Obeying the Laws of Hereditary Descent."

101. Curti, "Human Nature in American Thought" 361.

102. Hilts, "Obeying the Laws of Hereditary Descent" 62.

103. Franz Joseph Gall, quoted in Hilts, "Obeying the Laws of Hereditary Descent" 62.

104. Jean-Baptiste Lamarck was a French naturalist philosopher who helped construct a pre-Darwinian theory of evolution. According to Lamarck, evolutionary change occurred as a consequence of an organism's effort to improve the situation in its habitat. Degler, *In Search of Human Nature* 20.

105. Hilts, "Obeying the Laws of Hereditary Descent" 64.

106. Hilts, "Obeying the Laws of Hereditary Descent" 64. Almost one hundred years later, in *Buck v. Bell*, Oliver Wendell Holmes, Jr., would allow the sterilization of a woman by the name of Carrie Buck and claim that "three generations of imbeciles" were enough. See Marouf Hasian, Jr., and Earl Croasmun, "The Legitimizing Function of Judicial Rhetoric in the Eugenics Controversy," *Argumentation and Advocacy* 28 (1992): 123–34, 130.

107. Spurzheim, quoted in Hilts, "Obeying the Laws of Hereditary Descent" 66.

108. Hilts, "Obeying the Laws of Hereditary Descent" 66.

109. Hilts, "Obeying the Laws of Hereditary Descent" 67–68.

110. Hilts, "Obeying the Laws of Hereditary Descent" 68.

111. Cynthia Eagle Russett, *Darwin in America: The Intellectual Response, 1865–1912* (San Francisco: W. H. Freeman, 1976) 88–90; Degler, *In Search of Human Nature* 11.

112. George W. Julian, "Is the Reformer Any Longer Needed?" *North American Review* 127 (1878): 237–60.

113. Degler, *In Search of Human Nature* 32.

114. Degler, *In Search of Human Nature* 20.

115. Warner, quoted in Haller, *Eugenics* 60.

116. Joseph Le Conte, quoted in Degler, *In Search of Human Nature* 23.

117. See for example the claims that as a result of some of these new biological arguments "Lamarckism collapsed" both as a science and as a "cultural movement." Peter J. Bowler, *The Eclipse of Darwinism* (Baltimore, Md.: Johns Hopkins University Press, 1983) 221. I disagree. Several different competing strands of hereditarian arguments have continued to exist side by side, and neo-Lamarckism constantly resurfaces.

118. Stepan, *"The Hour of Eugenics": Race, Gender, and Nation in Latin America* (Ithaca: Cornell University Press, 1992) 1; Degler, *In Search of Human Nature* 41.

119. An excellent early illustration of how Galton was working within a climate of discourse can be found in James A. Field, "The Progress of Eugenics," *Quarterly Journal of Economics* 26 (November 1911): 1–67.

120. Kevles, "Controlling the Genetic Arsenal" 68.

121. Stepan, *"The Hour of Eugenics"* 1–2.

122. Degler, *In Search of Human Nature* 41; Kevles, "Controlling the Genetic Arsenal" 68.

123. Barry Mehler has presented us with a systematic analysis of the leadership of American and international eugenics ("A History of the American Eugenics Society").

124. Allen, "The Role of Experts in Scientific Controversy" 172.

125. "Germplasm" was the term that was used to describe the hereditary matter trans-

mitted across generations. For introductions to the study of American eugenics, Pickens, *Eugenics and the Progressives;* Bird and Allen, "Sources in the History of Eugenics: The Harry Hamilton Laughlin Papers in Kirksville, Missouri," *Journal of the History of Biology* 14 (1981): 339–53; Philip Jenkins, "Eugenics, Crime, and Ideology: The Case of Progressive Pennsylvania," *Pennsylvania History* 51 (1984): 64–78; R. B. Kershner, Jr., "Degeneration: The Explanatory Nightmare," *Georgia Review* (1986): 416–44; Edward J. Larson, "Belated Progress: The Enactment of Eugenics Legislation in Georgia," *Journal of the History of Medicine and Allied Sciences* 46 (1991): 44–64.

126. Degler, *In Search of Human Nature* 20.

127. Hard-line eugenicists often objected to many of these social reforms. They argued that many officials still operated under the "assumption that the pauper is a normal person made necessitous by circumstances." "Eugenics and Pauperism," *London Times,* November 7, 1910: 13–14, 14.

128. Bowler, *The Eclipse of Darwinism* 133.

129. This is not to say that elites themselves agreed over the meaning of eugenics or its use in making public policy decisions. Dorothy Porter has argued that in Britain, the influence of the eugenicists was countered by the work of public officials concerned with environmental factors. Dorothy Porter, " 'Enemies of the Race': Biologism, Environmentalism, and Public Health in Edwardian England," *Victorian Studies* 34 (1991): 159–78.

130. Stepan, *"The Hour of Eugenics"* 14. Other scholars have also lamented the fact that we seem to be focusing exclusively on the work of elites. Marshall Hyatt, for example, recently complained that Barkan's work "pays little attention to the growth in blacks' struggle for equality, which had important ideological, social, and political implications for the intellectual repudiation of racism." Marshall Hyatt, "Review of Elazar Barkan's *The Retreat of Scientific Racism,*" *Anthropological Quarterly* (1993): 106–7, 107.

131. See, for example, Michael Calvin McGee, "In Search of 'The People': A Rhetorical Alternative," *Quarterly Journal of Speech* 61 (1975): 235–49; McGee, " 'The Ideograph' " 4; Stephen Depoe, " 'Qualitative Liberalism': Arthur Schlesinger, Jr., and the Persuasive Uses of Definition and History," *Communication Studies* 40 (1989): 81–96; Celeste Michelle Condit and John Louis Lucaites, "The Rhetoric of Equality and the Expatriation of African-Americans, 1776–1826," *Communication Studies* 42 (Spring 1991): 1–21.

Chapter 2: From Cradle to Grave: The Popularization of Eugenics within the Rhetorical Sphere, 1900–1940

1. The term "gene" did not enter into the Anglo-American vocabulary until 1909.

2. E. A. Ross, "Turning towards Nirvana," *Arena* 4 (1891): 736–43, 737.

3. I. W. Howerth, "War and the Survival of the Fittest," *Scientific Monthly* 3 (1916): 488–97, 491. Sociologist Robert Hoxie described how the common American laborer dur-

ing the Progressive period felt when he wrote: "It is not merely in his view the world of material things and the relations of man to these things that fall under the domination of the laws of physical force. According to his experience also the relations of man to man is thus determined. His action as an individual is controlled by the character of the machinery with which he works; the individual machine stands definitely related by mechanical *necessity* to the whole machinery of the individual, industrial process. . . . These laws, the worker's experience teaches him, are blind, unmoral. . . . he grows fatalistic, atheistic" (my emphasis). Robert F. Hoxie, "Class Conflict in America," *American Journal of Sociology* 13 (1908): 776–81, 777.

4. Henry H. Goddard, "The Elimination of Feeble-Mindedness," *Annals of the American Academy of Political and Social Science* (1911): 261–72, 272.

5. William J. Fielding, "The Morality of Birth Control," *Birth Control Review* 4 (November 1920): 12–13, 12.

6. Harold Laski, "The Scope of Eugenics," *Westminster Review* 174 (1910): 25–34, 34.

7. For discussions of various "Progressive" philosophies, see Carl Resek, ed., *The Progressives* (Indianapolis: Bobbs-Merrill, 1967).

8. James H. Timberlake, *Prohibition and the Progressive Movement, 1900–1920* (Cambridge, Mass.: Harvard University Press, 1963) 27.

9. As historian Carl Degler recently explained, "Unlike social Darwinism, which sought to defend the status quo, eugenics was reformist in intention, a movement that sought to improve society through the application of the latest scientific knowledge. Again, contrary to social Darwinism, eugenics looked to the intervention of the state in society; in effect it repudiated laissez faire. In the name of its philosophy, it put society's good above that of the individual; it countered selfish individualism with social responsibility. Thus it is not accidental that eugenics did not come into its own as a movement in the United States until early in the twentieth century" (Carl N. Degler, *In Search of Human Nature: The Decline and Revival of Darwinism in American Social Thought* [New York: Oxford University Press, 1991] 42). As I illustrate below, there were interpretations of eugenics that were very much Social Darwinian.

10. See for example G. H. Parker, "The Eugenics Movement as a Public Service," *Science* 41 (March 5, 1915): 344; J. H. Landman, *Human Sterilization* (New York: Macmillan, 1932) 21; Donald Pickens, *Eugenics and the Progressives* (Nashville, Tenn.: Vanderbilt University Press, 1968) 21.

11. Martin Barr, quoted in Paul A. Lombardo, "Eugenic Sterilization in Virginia: Aubrey Strode and the Case of *Buck v. Bell*" (Ph.D. diss., Department of Education, University of Virginia, 1982) 86.

12. Joseph DeJarnette, quoted in Lombardo, "Eugenic Sterilization in Virginia" 112.

13. Maynard M. Metcalf, quoted in Degler, *In Search of Human Nature* 44.

14. One example of the kinds of alternatives that were contemplated was provided by a geneticist who claimed that the "restriction of undesirable additions to our human stock may be partially accomplished, at least in America, by employing the following agencies:

control of immigration; more discriminating marriage laws; a quickened eugenic sentiment; sexual segregation of defectives; and finally, drastic measures of asexualization when *necessary*. Providing for the eugenic elimination of defectives is as truly a civic duty as administering charity to them after they are born" (emphasis mine). Herbert E. Walter, *Genetics: An Introduction to the Study of Heredity* (New York: Macmillan, 1928) 322.

15. For example, improving the education of the unfit would be dysgenic from within this perspective because once a person was born genetically unfit, no amount of education or "moralising" could supply the missing "germplasm."

16. See Mark Haller, *Eugenics: Hereditarian Attitudes in American Thought* (New Brunswick, N.J.: Rutgers University Press, 1984) 8.

17. Pearson and some of the other eugenicists often thought that this national regeneration could come about through the acceptance of a new eugenic creed that might become a national secular religion. See Kenneth M. Ludmerer, "American Geneticists and the Eugenics Movement: 1905–1935," *Journal of the History of Biology* 2 (1969): 337–62, 341.

In the eugenical literature, the term "race" could refer to the white race, the British race, the human race. Some insightful comments on the ambiguity of the term can be found in M. F. Ashley Montagu, *Man's Most Dangerous Myth: The Fallacy of Race* (New York: Harper and Brothers, 1952); Thomas F. Gossett, *Race: The History of an Idea in America* (New York: Schocken, 1963); Stephen Steinberg, *The Ethnic Myth: Race, Ethnicity, and Class in America* (New York: Atheneum, 1981).

18. Some of the earliest followers of Galtonian ideas believed that Indians and African-Americans would simply die out over time. See Henry W. Holland, "Heredity," *Atlantic Monthly*, October 1883: 447–52; Pickens, *Eugenics and the Progressives* 35. Holland argued that "Galton's law is squarely across their path, and the sooner they die quietly out the better and to assist them to multiply becomes as wrong as keeping the filthy and effete Turk in Europe for the sake of enfeebling Russia" (Pickens, *Eugenics and the Progressives* 35).

19. Francis Galton, quoted in Pickens, *Eugenics and the Progressives* 30.

20. In the 1910s and 1920s, eugenicists would claim that they were not ignoring the environment—they were simply redressing the balance by reminding scientists and other interested parties that genetics could not be ignored. Typical of these arguments were those of Paul Popenoe, who wrote in 1915 that "we are far from denying that nurture has an influence on nature, but we believe that the influence of nurture, the environment, is only a fifth or perhaps a tenth that of nature—heredity" (Popenoe, quoted in Ludmerer, "American Geneticists and the Eugenics Movement" 350).

21. For example, Francis Galton argued that "Eugenics co-operates with the workings of nature by securing that humanity shall be represented by the fittest races. What nature does blindly, slowly, and ruthlessly, man may do providently, quickly, and kindly" (Galton, quoted in Pickens, *Eugenics and the Progressives* 27).

22. Karl Pearson, for example, thought that living eugenically meant accepting the fact that the "power intellect shall determine whether the life-calling of a man is to scavenge the streets or to guide the nation" (Daniel J. Kevles, *In the Name of Eugenics: Genetics and the Uses of Human Heredity* [New York: Alfred A. Knopf, 1985] 24). Many eugenicists abhorred the concept of egalitarian democracy, and they believed that only by having enlightened experts in charge of science and government could a nation begin to deal with the criminals, mentally retarded, and the impoverished who were the dregs of society (Haller, *Eugenics* ix).

23. Quoted in E. Alec-Tweedie, "Eugenics," *Fortnightly Review* 97 (1912): 854–65, 855.

24. Kevles, *In the Name of Eugenics* ix.

25. Alternatively, some researchers contend that eugenics was never really popular. For example, Haller once wrote that "despite the widespread influence of eugenics upon educated Americans, many eugenists eventually despaired that their views could ever gain mass support" (Haller, *Eugenics* 6).

26. Note here the work of Bentley Glass, "Geneticists Embattled: Their Stand against Rampant Eugenics and Racism in America during the 1920s and 1930s," *Proceedings of the American Philosophical Society* 130 (1986): 130–54. Contrast Glass's work with that of David Barker, "The Biology of Stupidity: Genetics, Eugenics and Mental Deficiency in the Inter-War Years," *British Journal of the History of Science* 22 (1989): 347–75.

27. For discussions of this division between the early mainline and "reform" eugenicists, see Haller, Ludmerer, and Kevles. For a short but insightful discussion of the differences between the two, see Elazar Barkan's review of Richard Soloway's *Demography and Degeneration* (*Journal of Interdisciplinary History* 21 [1991]: 672–75).

28. Some writers are willing to acknowledge that eugenics was extremely popular, but they argue that this popularity came by way of perverting eugenics. Kevles, for example, has argued that most of the coercive or otherwise objectionable parts of this discourse came in "the name" of eugenics (*In the Name of Eugenics*). Greta Jones and others have argued that an exclusive focus on the influence of eugenical leaders is due to the "intellectual" fallacy, whereby we as scholars focus almost exclusively on the rhetoric of scientists or other intellectuals. See Jones's review of Mazumdar's *Eugenics, Human Failings: The Eugenics Society, Its Sources and Its Critics in Britain* (*British Journal for the History of Science* 25 [1992]: 486–87, 487).

29. See, for example, the link between neo-Lamarckism and eugenics in France and Latin America. William H. Schneider, *Quality and Quantity: The Quest for Biological Regeneration in Twentieth-Century France* (Cambridge: Cambridge University Press, 1990); Nancy L. Stepan, "Eugenics in Brazil, 1917–1940," in *The Wellborn Science: Eugenics in Germany, France, Brazil, and Russia*, ed. Mark B. Adams (New York: Oxford University Press, 1990). It is of course my contention that this was perhaps the most popular form of eugenics worldwide, including Anglo-American eugenics.

30. I am not arguing that other scholars have not noticed these links between eugenics

and other social movements. I am simply claiming that these usages are often compared with the discovered "intentions" of the eugenical leaders to see if they can accurately be termed "eugenical."

31. Caleb Saleeby would contend that religion and science should "join hands in the coming time over the cradle of the unborn, and a little child shall lead them." C. W. Saleeby, *The Methods of Race-Regeneration* (New York: Moffat, Yard, 1911) 64. For a discussion of Saleeby's relationship with Galton and Pearson, see G. R. Searle, *Eugenics and Politics in Britain, 1900–1914* (Leyden: Noordhoff International Publishing, 1976).

32. Quoted in Daniel Kevles, "Annals of Eugenics, A Secular Faith—II," *New Yorker,* October 15, 1984: 52–125.

33. Percy Andreae, *The Prohibition Movement* (Chicago: Felix Mendelsohn, 1915) 400.

34. Kevles, "Annals of Eugenics" 52.

35. The term "race poison" referred to any type of substance or hazard that could harm one's genetic health. Building on the work of the neo-Lamarckians, many doctors, social workers, and other intellectuals often wrote about the need for adequate neonatal care. For example, alcohol and tobacco were considered to be "race poisons." Eugenicists were certainly not alone in commenting on the dangers of the bottle. See Hester Pendleton, *The Parent's Guide: or, Human Development through Inherited Tendencies* (New York: S. R. Wells, 1871; rpt. New York: Garland, 1984) 32–55; T. D. Crothers, "Heredity," *The Cyclopedia of Temperance and Prohibition* (New York: Funk and Wagnalls, 1891) 204–7; "Alcoholism and Degeneration," *Current Literature* 38 (1905): 361.

Crothers would ask readers of *The Cyclopedia of Temperance and Prohibition* to "Observe the direful results to individuals in typical cases of intemperance—the loss of health, character, position, wealth, integrity, morals, means of support, and happiness; understand that these results are, in eight cases in ten, visited upon the wretched sufferers because of the conscious or unconscious sins of ancestors, and all will be ready to grant that the evils entailed by drink through the laws of heredity may not be described in words too profuse or too vivid" (207).

36. For some of the best work in this area, see Bartlett C. Jones, "Prohibition and Eugenics, 1920–1933," *Journal of the History of Medicine and Allied Sciences* 18 (1963): 158–72.

37. See Irving Fisher, *Prohibition at Its Worst* (New York: Macmillan, 1926).

38. Albert Wiggam, quoted in Jones, "Prohibition and Eugenics" 158. Several years later, Wiggam would elaborate on these views by noting the role of alcohol in human evolution. Albert E. Wiggam, "The Rising Tide of Degeneracy: What Everybody Ought to Know about Eugenics," *World's Work* 53 (1926): 25–33.

39. This is not to say that older eugenicists ignored the children. Galton, in a letter to the *London Times* of June 18, 1909, reported that new inquiries had determined that the nation was showing signs of degeneration because children had problems with their teeth, hearing, eyesight, and other "malformations" (Galton quoted in Searle, *Eugenics and Politics* 21).

40. Searle, *Eugenics and Politics* 2–3.

41. Searle, *Eugenics and Politics* 3.

42. Timberlake has speculated that it was the millions of unorganized workers who were against prohibition. Mostly unskilled, non-Protestant, and of foreign stock, these groups had less enthusiasm than the middle class for the movement (*Prohibition and the Progressive Movement* 98–99).

43. Fisher, *Prohibition At Its Worst* 138.

44. Fisher, *Prohibition At Its Worst* 103, 106.

45. Fisher, *Prohibition At Its Worst* 4.

46. On the political and social symbolism involved in the complex temperance movement, see Joseph R. Gusfield, *Symbolic Crusade: Status Politics and the American Temperance Movement* (Urbana: University of Illinois Press, 1986), 1.

47. John Kobler, *Ardent Spirits: The Rise and Fall of Prohibition* (New York: G. P. Putnam's Sons, 1973) 57.

48. Kobler, *Ardent Spirits* 142. Alcohol could also be linked to "all sorts of illness, shocks, and misfortune" (Samuel J. Holmes, *The Eugenic Predicament* [New York: Harcourt, Brace, 1933] 18).

49. Kobler, *Ardent Spirits* 148.

50. Kobler, *Ardent Spirits* 168.

51. Wiggam, "The Rising Tide of Degeneracy" especially 27–31. These arguments on the use and abuse of alcohol were often vague and contradictory. Wiggam covered a lot of territory when he claimed that "It seems evident, then, that it is civilization with its luxury, comfort and ease, with its reversal and defiance of natural selection, its reckless and ignorant tinkering with the human germ-plasm, which makes eugenics a superlative necessity. . . . Are the present objects of civilization worth the price? The American Indian, for example, in his wide, open life and in his old happy hunting ground, was probably a better, happier organic being than is the Indian to-day, with his tuberculosis, measles, tailored clothes, automobiles, telephones, radio, reading, writing, arithmetic, alcohol, and cancer" (27, 31).

52. Kobler, *Ardent Spirits* 183; Timberlake, *Prohibition and the Progressive Movement* 139.

53. Kobler, *Ardent Spirits* 183.

54. Kobler, *Ardent Spirits* 199.

55. Kobler, *Ardent Spirits* 200.

56. Senator Sheppard, quoted in Timberlake, *Prohibition and the Progressive Movement* 177.

57. Kobler, *Ardent Spirits* 202. The popularity of some of these arguments can also be inferred from some of the remarks of opponents of this eugenical position. In 1922, even William Jennings Bryan complained that "Darwin rightly decided to suspend his doctrine, even at the risk of impairing the race. But some of his followers are more hardened. A few years ago I read a book in which the author defended the use of alcohol on

the ground that it rendered a service to society by killing off the degenerates. And this argument was advanced by a scientist in the fall of 1920 at a congress against alcohol." William Jennings Bryan, *In His Image* (New York: Fleming H. Revel Co., 1922) 110.

58. Kobler, *Ardent Spirits* 206. For other views of Leonard Wood on the need for character development, see David I. MacLeod, *Building Character in the American Boy* (Madison: University of Wisconsin Press, 1983) 179.

59. See Henry Smith Williams, "The Scientific Solution of the Liquor Problem," *McClure's* 32 (1909): 419–26; Timberlake, *Prohibition and the Progressive Movement* 60.

60. "Eugenics and Happiness," *The Nation*, July 25, 1912: 75–76.

61. Ethel Alec Tweedie, quoted in "Eugenics and Happiness" 75.

62. Michael Calvin McGee, "The 'Ideograph': A Link between Rhetoric and Ideology," *Quarterly Review of Speech* 66 (1980): 1–16, 11.

63. Ethel Alec Tweedie, quoted in "Eugenics and Happiness" 75.

64. See Steven Selden, "Biological Determinism and the Normal School Curriculum, Helen Putnam and the N.E.A. Committee on Racial Well-Being, 1910–1922," *Journal of Curriculum Theorizing* 1 (1979): 105–22.

65. Selden, "Biological Determinism" 107.

66. Putnam, quoted in Selden, "Biological Determinism" 116.

67. Dean M. Freeman, quoted in Selden, "Biological Determinism" 105.

68. Selden, "Biological Determinism" 118.

69. Selden, "Biological Determinism" 119.

70. Steven Selden, "The Use of Biology to Legitimate Inequality: The Eugenics Movement within the High School Biology Textbook, 1914–1949," in *Equity in Education,* ed. Walter G. Secada (New York: Falmer Press, 1989) 124.

71. George William Hunter, quoted in Selden, "The Use of Biology" 129.

72. Selden, "The Use of Biology" 131.

73. See Allan Chase, *The Legacy of Malthus* (New York: Alfred A. Knopf, 1977).

74. See "Eugenics and Happiness" 75.

75. For a study of American college textbooks and eugenics, see Steven Selden, "Educational Policy and Biological Science: Genetics, Eugenics, and the College Textbook, c. 1908–1931," *Teachers College Record* 87 (1985): 35–51.

76. Fitzgerald, quoted in Kevles, "Annals of Eugenics" 52.

77. Kevles, "Annals of Eugenics" 52.

78. Kevles, "Annals of Eugenics" 52.

79. Kevles, "Annals of Eugenics" 52.

80. Kevles, "Annals of Eugenics" 53.

81. Kevles, "Annals of Eugenics" 53.

82. Kevles, "Annals of Eugenics" 54.

83. Kevles, "Annals of Eugenics" 54.

84. Kevles, "Annals of Eugenics" 54.

85. Rosenthal has argued that the study of the scouts movement would help him to

"read" the culture of Edwardian England through one of its representative institutions. Michael Rosenthal, *The Character Factory: Baden-Powell and the Origins of the Boy Scout Movement* (New York: Pantheon, 1986) 1. One article claimed that by 1913, millions of boys were interested in scouting: "Boy Scouts and Their Periodicals," *Outlook* 105 (October 25, 1913): 387.

86. Rosenthal, *The Character Factory* 1.

87. Baden-Powell was a popular figure on both sides of the Atlantic. See for example, "Sir Robert Baden-Powell's Adventures as a Spy," *Everybody's Magazine* 32 (1915): 184–92. The ideological underpinnings of the early scout movement and their relationship to social Darwinism are still subjects of scholastic debate. See John Springhall, "Baden-Powell and the Scout Movement before 1920: Citizen Training or Soldiers of the Future?" *English Historical Review* 102 (1987): 934–42; Allen Warren, "Sir Robert Baden-Powell, the Scout Movement and Citizen Training in Great Britain, 1900–1920," *English Historical Review* 101 (1986): 376–98.

88. Rosenthal, *The Character Factory* 6.

89. After the first two years of the scouting movement, Baden-Powell could boast that there were 350,000 scouts in England, Canada, Germany, France, and Australia. Boy Scouts of America, *Handbook for Scoutmasters: A Manual of Leadership*, 2d ed. (New York: Boy Scouts of America, 1922) 472.

90. Baden-Powell, quoted in Rosenthal, *The Character Factory* 6.

91. Rosenthal, *The Character Factory* 6–7.

92. Arnold Freeman, quoted in Rosenthal, *The Character Factory* 8–9.

93. Baden-Powell, quoted in Rosenthal, *The Character Factory* 8.

94. Rosenthal, *The Character Factory* 116. Part of the power of this rhetoric came from its ability to build on three strands of citizen training—"the militaristic, the educational, and the Christian" (Warren, "Sir Robert Baden-Powell" 390). The eugenical movement was similarly constructed.

95. Rosenthal, *The Character Factory* 118.

96. Rosenthal, *The Character Factory* 135. This was the figure that was usually discussed in the British press around the turn of the century during the Boer War. For a contrasting view on this deterioration, see "The Report of the Privy Council upon Physical Deterioration," *The Lancet* (August 6, 1904): 390–92.

97. Rosenthal, *The Character Factory* 297.

98. Pearson, quoted in Rosenthal, *Character Factory* 158.

99. C. W. Saleeby, *The Progress of Eugenics* (London: Cassell, 1914) 84.

100. Caleb Saleeby, quoted in Rosenthal, *The Character Factory* 159. Saleeby's work combined nature with nurture and was extremely popular in many different communities. Saleeby and Pearson often quarreled over the direction that British eugenics should take. At one point, Saleeby, a physician, claimed that: "The asserted opposition between eugenics and social reform, eugenics and education, eugenics and philanthropy, does not exist. The eugenist must welcome all agencies that make for better nurture, alike for rich

and poor, born and unborn" (*The Progress of Eugenics* 24; Rosenthal, *The Character Factory* 158). Saleeby would also claim that a careful reading of Galton's earlier work would show that Galton intended to include both nature and nurture and that when Galton later adopted a definition that omitted reference to nurture, this must be because of Galton's older age (Saleeby, *The Progress of Eugenics* 56).

101. Saleeby, quoted in Rosenthal, *The Character Factory* 159.

102. R. F. Horton, *National Ideals and Race Regeneration* (London: Cassell, 1912) 38; Rosenthal, *The Character Factory* 159.

103. Arnold White, "Eugenics and National Efficiency," *The Eugenics Review* 1 (July 1909): 111.

104. Rosenthal, *The Character Factory* 178–79.

105. Rosenthal, *The Character Factory* 305. Later on, the scouts would try to win over both unions and the socialists. See Harold P. Levy, *Building a Popular Movement: A Case Study of the Public Relations of the Boy Scouts of America* (New York: Russell Sage Foundation, 1944) 25.

106. Boy Scouts of America, *Handbook for Scoutmasters* 588, 589.

107. Sometimes eugenicists like Henry Fairchild of New York University would make inquiries into whether the scouting movement had succeeded in developing socially useful "character traits." Levy, *Building a Popular Movement* 88.

108. Boy Scouts of America, *Handbook for Scoutmasters* 479, 482.

109. Boy Scouts of America, *Handbook for Scoutmasters* 496.

110. Boy Scouts of America, *Handbook for Scoutmasters* 271. More than a decade later one critic could still write that "One still hears the phrases so beloved of our forefathers — 'criminal tendencies,' 'Original sin,' 'born to the gallows,' etc. etc., phrases which were responsible for the wholesale transportations and exterminations of criminals in bygone years." H. S. Bryan, *The Troublesome Boy* (London: C. Arthur Pearson, 1936) 27.

111. Rosenthal, *The Character Factory* 2.

112. Obviously, not all of the aims of the movement were either militaristic or eugenical in nature. For one contemporary account of some of the purposes of the movement, see Norman E. Richardson and Ormond E. Loomis, *The Boy Scout Movement Applied by the Church* (New York: Charles Scribner's Sons, 1915) 19.

113. Boy Scouts of America, *Handbook for Scoutmasters* 4.

114. Boy Scouts of America, *Handbook for Scoutmasters* 280.

115. Boy Scouts of America, *Handbook for Scoutmasters* 272.

116. Boy Scouts of America, *Handbook for Scoutmasters* 293.

117. Boy Scouts of America, *Handbook for Scoutmasters* 309.

118. See for example Levy's claim that "Ernest Thompson Seton, naturalist writer and one of the originators of the Boy Scout movement in America, drew a sad contrast between the New England workers of the 1900s who 'fairly represent the average population' and the virile 'fighting fathers of the Revolutions' who had relied mainly on their out-of-door training in their relentless physical struggle for American independence" (*Building a Popular Movement* 16).

119. Richardson and Loomis, *The Boy Scout Movement* 304. Decades later Levy would explain that the idea of scouting flourished at a time when frontiers were vanishing and large segments of the people expressed a "restive nostalgia for the old life of the outdoors" (Levy, *Building a Popular Movement* 16). See also Henry S. Curtis, *The Play Movement and Its Significance* (New York: Macmillan, 1917), who argued that a return to nature would stop the breeding of idleness, weakness, and delinquency (251).

120. Richardson and Loomis, *The Boy Scout Movement* 25.

121. Richardson and Loomis, *The Boy Scout Movement* 75, 227.

122. Richardson and Loomis, *The Boy Scout Movement* 304.

123. Richardson and Loomis, *The Boy Scout Movement* 305.

124. Richardson and Loomis, *The Boy Scout Movement* 351, 359.

125. David Procter, "The Dynamic Spectacle: Transforming Experience into Social Forms of Community," *Quarterly Journal of Speech* 76 (1990): 117–33.

126. Murray Edelman, *Constructing the Political Spectacle* (Chicago: University of Chicago Press, 1988) 10.

127. Thomas B. Farrell, "Media Rhetoric as Social Drama: The Winter Olympics of 1984," *Critical Studies in Mass Communication* 6 (1984): 158–82, 160.

128. Sometimes even novels and films were based on eugenical themes. Erling Holtsmark argues that Edgar Rice Burroughs's Tarzan is based in part on Darwinian themes: Erling B. Holtsmark, *Tarzan and Tradition: Classical Myth in Popular Literature* (Westport, Conn.: Greenwood Press, 1981) 147. More recently, Holtsmark has remarked that, "Burroughs's fascination with eugenics is undoubtedly tied to his strong interest in Darwinism. Tarzan himself is often said to be the end-development of generations of British aristocratic stock, representing what Burroughs seems to have conceived of as the *ne plus ultra* of eugenic perfection" (Erling Holtsmark, *Edgar Rice Burroughs* [Boston: Twayne Publishers, 1986] 49).

129. Kathleen M. Blee, *Women of the Klan: Racism and Gender in the 1920s* (Berkeley: University of California Press, 1991) 20. Decades later, the Klan would hold baby contests in several places, including Kokomo in 1925.

130. One of the few scholars who has called attention to these displays is Daniel Kevles. For the congressional display, see Chase, *The Legacy of Malthus*.

131. Kevles, "Annals of Eugenics" 54. See also Jones, "Prohibition and Eugenics" 158.

132. Kevles, "Annals of Eugenics" 54.

133. Kevles, "Annals of Eugenics" 54.

134. For a description of a typical test, see Kevles, "Annals of Eugenics" 57; Ida Clarke, "Kansas Has a Big Idea," *Pictorial Review* 26 (1925): 20, 72.

135. Kevles, "Annals of Eugenics" 57.

136. Kevles, "Annals of Eugenics" 57.

137. Kevles, "Annals of Eugenics" 57.

138. Kevles, "Annals of Eugenics" 57.

139. Kevles, "Annals of Eugenics" 57.

140. "The Exhibit 'On the Road,'" *Eugenics Review* 24 (1932): 24–25, 24.

141. "The Exhibit 'On the Road' " 24.

142. "The Exhibit 'On the Road' " 24.

143. "The Exhibit 'On the Road' " 25.

144. James Marchant, quoted in Richard A. Soloway, *Birth Control and the Population Question in England, 1877–1930* (Chapel Hill: University of North Carolina Press, 1982) 65.

145. Soloway, *Birth Control and the Population Question* 160. This report was part of a much larger debate on the existence and causes of the decline. For examples of some of the other influences that supposedly contributed to this decline, contrast the views of William McDougall, *National Welfare and National Decay* (London: Methuen, 1921) and Halliday Sutherland, *Control of Life* (London: Burns, Oates, and Washbourne, 1944).

146. Soloway, *Birth Control and the Population Question* 160.

147. For "liberal" discussions of some of these reforms, see Kathleen Jones, *The Making of Social Policy in Britain, 1830–1990* (London: Athlone, 1991).

148. Soloway, *Birth Control and the Population Question* 161.

149. Soloway, *Birth Control and the Population Question* 161.

150. Marchant, for example, estimated that contraception had contributed to the loss of about twenty million potential lives since the Knowlton trial of 1877 (Soloway, *Birth Control and the Population Question* 161). In the contemporary literature, it was often Annie Besant and Charles Bradlaugh who were accused of popularizing artificial birth control and contributing to this loss of lives.

151. Soloway, *Birth Control and the Population Question* 167.

152. Soloway, *Birth Control and the Population Question* 167. See also Paul Crook, "War as a Genetic Disaster? The First World War Debate over the Eugenics of Warfare," *War and Society* 8 (1990): 47–70.

153. Leonard Darwin, quoted in Soloway, *Birth Control and the Population Question* 168.

154. Caleb Saleeby, quoted in Soloway, *Birth Control and the Population Question* 169.

155. Michael Pearlman, *To Make Democracy Safe for America: Patricians and Preparedness in the Progressive Era* (Urbana: University of Illinois Press, 1984).

156. Note here the work of John P. Finnegan, *Against the Specter of a Dragon: The Campaign for American Military Preparedness, 1914–1917* (Westport, Conn.: Greenwood Press, 1974).

157. Pearlman, *To Make Democracy Safe* 5. On the importance of morality for some of these communities living in urban areas, see Paul Boyer, *Urban Masses and Moral Order in America, 1820–1920* (Cambridge, Mass.: Harvard University Press, 1978).

158. Pearlman, *To Make Democracy Safe* 3.

159. Theodore Roosevelt, "Twisted Eugenics," *Outlook* 106 (1914): 30–34, 31.

160. Pearlman, *To Make Democracy Safe* 18.

161. Leonard Wood, quoted in Pearlman, *To Make Democracy Safe* 38.

162. Charles W. Burr, quoted in Pearlman, *To Make Democracy Safe* 45.

163. Pearlman, *To Make Democracy Safe* 48.

164. Pearlman, *To Make Democracy Safe* 128. As Roosevelt would argue in "Twisted Eugenics," "To advocate reforms in land tenure, or the holding of property, or the use of railways, or the suffrage, is easy for any man; but to front [*sic*] the vital problems of the perpetuation of the best race elements seems to demand more courage and farsightedness than the reformer usually possesses" (32). Note also the insightful work of Thomas G. Dyer, *Theodore Roosevelt and the Idea of Race* (Baton Rouge: Louisiana State University Press, 1980).

165. For a discussion of how eugenics influenced immigration, see Alan M. Kraut, *Silent Travelers: Germs, Genes, and the "Immigrant Menace"* (New York: HarperCollins, 1994) 253–54.

166. Henry Stimson, *Issues of the War* (New York: National Security League, n.d.) 16.

167. Nicholas Ray Butler, *A World in Ferment* (New York: Scribners, 1917) 179.

168. See also Barbara Solomon, *Ancestors and Immigrants: A Changing New England Tradition* (Chicago: University of Chicago Press, 1971).

169. Pearlman, *To Make Democracy Safe* 5.

170. Leonard Wood, quoted in Pearlman, *To Make Democracy Safe* 38.

171. Pearlman, *To Make Democracy Safe* 44.

172. See John Garry Clifford, *The Citizen Soldiers: The Plattsburg Training Camp Movement, 1913–1920* (Lexington: University Press of Kentucky, 1972).

173. Raymond Pearl, quoted in Kevles, *In the Name of Eugenics* 122.

Chapter 3: Race and African-American Interpretations of Eugenics

1. As Christina Simmons has remarked, African-Americans are usually examined as objects in traditional narratives. "African Americans and Sexual Victorianism in the Social Hygiene Movement, 1910–1940," *Journal of the History of Sexuality* 4 (1993): 51–75, 51. This problem is being partially remedied with the publication of texts like Sandra Harding's collection of essays in *The "Racial" Economy of Science: Toward a Democratic Future* (Bloomington: Indiana University Press, 1993).

The absence of black rhetoricians may be partly due to the exclusivity of scientific organizations at the turn of the century. Other causes include the lack of health facilities for African-Americans during these years and the prevalent belief that all blacks simply imitated their white counterparts. For a discussion of the treatment of African-Americans in the 1930s, see Steven Noll, "Southern Strategies for Handling the Black Feeble-Minded: From Social Control to Profound Indifference," *Journal of Policy History* 3 (1991): 130–51. One insightful discussion that comments on the sterilization of minority women is in Patricia Williams, "On Being the Object of Property," *Signs* 14 (1988): 5–24.

2. Frederick Bancroft, quoted in Robert G. Weisbord, *Genocide? Birth Control and the Black American* (Westport, Conn.: Greenwood Press, 1975) 25–26.

3. Frederick Douglass, quoted in Weisbord, *Genocide?* 26.

4. Weisbord, *Genocide?* 27.

5. See, for example, Richard Sutch, "The Breeding of Slaves for Sale and the Westward Expansion of Slavery, 1850–1860," in *Race and Slavery in the Western Hemisphere: Quantitative Studies,* ed. Stanley L. Engerman and Eugene D. Genovese (Princeton, N.J.: Princeton University Press, 1975) 173–98.

Slave owners themselves sometimes deplored their social and economic system. In her diary, Mary Boykin Chesnut blamed the system of slavery for producing infidelity among white men and "prostitution" among the women: "In Slavery, we live surrounded by prostitutes . . . God forgive us, but ours is a monstrous system, a wrong an iniquity. Like the patriarchs of old, our men live in one house with their concubines; and the mulattoes one sees in every family partly resemble the white children." (Quoted in Shirley J. Yee, *Black Women Abolitionists: A Study in Activism, 1828–1860* [Knoxville: University of Tennessee Press, 1992] 43.)

6. See "Liberty and Government," *De Bow's Review* 30 (1861): 198–203, 199.

7. George Fitzhugh, "The Conservation Principle; or, Social Evils and Their Remedies," *De Bow's Review* 22 (1856): 419–30, 422.

8. Thomas S. Szasz, "The Sane Slave," *American Journal of Psychotherapy* 25 (1971): 228–38.

9. For example, William T. Harris believed that blacks in America had "acquired our Anglo-Saxon consciousness in its American type through seven generations of domestic servitude in the family of a white master" (Harris, quoted in Harvey Wish, "Negro Education and the Progressive Movement," *Journal of Negro History* 49 (1964): 184–200, 191.

For other discussions of the role of neo-Lamarckian analyses that were egalitarian in nature, see Edward H. Beardsley, "The American Scientist as Social Activist: Franz Boas, Burt G. Wilder, and the Cause of Racial Justice, 1900–1915," *Isis* 64 (1973): 50–66.

10. These arguments were surprisingly resilient. In the late 1920s, African-Americans still felt compelled to respond to claims that the race was dying out. See, for example, "The Depopulation Spectre," *The Broad Axe* [Chicago], June 25, 1927: 3; Kelly Miller, "Is the Negro a Living or Dying Race," *Afro-American* [Baltimore], September 10, 1927: 7.

11. For some of the best work on Spencer and social Darwinism, see Richard Hofstadter, *Social Darwinism in American Thought, 1860–1915* (Philadelphia: University of Pennsylvania Press, 1945).

12. See for example the arguments in Nathaniel Shaler, "The Negro Problem," *Atlantic Monthly,* November 1884: 696–709.

13. Carol M. Taylor, "W. E. B. Du Bois's Challenge to Scientific Racism," *Journal of Black Studies* 11 (1981): 449–60, 450. Taylor's work on Du Bois and his rhetorical contributions to the discursive battle over eugenics is one of the few scholastic works that have considered in any detail the role of African-Americans in deconstructing racial eu-

genics. For an excellent critique of modern biological threats, see Patricia A. King, "The Dangers of Difference," *Hastings Center Report* 22 (1992): 35–38.

14. Galton, quoted in Taylor, "W. E. B. Du Bois's Challenge" 452. Galton was not alone in his thinking. The eugenicist psychologist Lewis Terman claimed that the new experimental methods would show that there were enormous differences in the general intelligence of races that "cannot be wiped out by any scheme of mental culture." Quoted in William B. Thomas, "Black Intellectuals' Critique of Early Mental Testing: A Little Known Saga of the 1920s," *American Journal of Education* (1982): 258–92, 262.

15. Frederick Hoffman, *Race Traits and Tendencies of the American Negro* (New York: Macmillan, 1896), quoted in Taylor, "W. E. B. Du Bois's Challenge" 451. Hoffman's work did not go unchallenged. Kelly Miller wrote a paper for the American Negro Academy contesting many of his claims. See Thomas, "Black Intellectuals' Critique" 264.

16. Taylor, "W. E. B. Du Bois's Challenge" 450.

17. Jacques Barzun, *Race: A Study in Superstition* (New York: Harper and Row, 1965) 184.

18. Edward M. East, quoted in Thomas, "Black Intellectuals' Critique" 271. For other authors writing in this vein, see Lothrop Stoddard, *The Rising Tide of Color against White World Supremacy* (New York: Charles Scribner's Sons, 1921); and Earnest Sevier Cox, *White America* (Richmond, Va.: White America Society, 1923), and *The South's Part in Mongrelizing the Nation* (Richmond, Va.: White America Society, 1926).

19. Terman, quoted in Thomas, "Black Intellectuals' Critique" 262.

20. Madison Grant, *The Passing of the Great Race* (New York: Scribner's, 1918) 226, quoted in Taylor, "W. E. B. Du Bois's Challenge" 453.

21. Madison Grant, quoted in Taylor, "W. E. B. Du Bois's Challenge" 453.

22. See, for example, W. A. Plecker, "Virginia's Attempt to Adjust the Color Problem," *American Journal of Public Health* 15 (January 1925): 111.

23. Taylor, "W. E. B. Du Bois's Challenge" 449.

24. Senator Walter F. George of Georgia, quoted in James Weldon Johnson and Herbert Seligmann, "Legal Aspects of the Negro Problem," *Annals of the American Academy of Political and Social Science* 140 (1928): 90–97, 90–91.

25. David C. Jones, quoted in Frank F. Arness, "The Evolution of the Virginia Anti-miscegenation Laws" (M.A. thesis, Department of History, Old Dominion College, 1966) i.

26. Thomas, "Black Intellectuals' Critique" 264.

27. Arthur de Gobineau, *The Inequality of Human Races* (Los Angeles: Noontide Press, 1966).

28. Strong, quoted in Hofstadter, *Social Darwinism* 153–55.

29. Max Nordau, quoted in Hofstadter, *Social Darwinism* 147.

30. August Meier, "Negro Racial Thought in the Age of Booker T. Washington, circa 1880–1915" (Ph.D. diss., Department of Political Science, Columbia University, 1957) 58.

31. Meier, "Negro Racial Thought" 59.

32. Gobineau, *The Inequality of Human Races* 37.

33. Herbert Miller, "The Myth of Superiority," *Opportunity* 1 (1923): 228–29, 228.

34. Miller, "The Myth" 228.

35. Miller, "The Myth" 229.

36. Howard Long, "On Mental Tests and Racial Psychology—A Critique," *Opportunity* 3 (May 1925): 134–38, 138.

37. Du Bois, quoted in Taylor, "W. E. B. Du Bois's Challenge" 457. Frazier once noted that these eugenical arguments were nothing new. He would argue in 1928 that prejudice against blacks was at least as old as Gall and phrenology. E. Franklin Frazier, "The Mind of the American Negro," *Opportunity* 6 (1928): 263–66, 263.

38. Du Bois, *The Crisis*, May 1911: 21, quoted in Taylor, "W. E. B. Du Bois's Challenge" 458.

39. Taylor, "W. E. B. Du Bois's Challenge" 453. Particularly galling to many African-Americans was what some eugenicists called the "mulatto hypothesis"—the belief that any superior performance on the part of blacks was simply due to admixture between the races and the presence of white blood. See William B. Thomas, "Black Intellectuals, Intelligence Testing in the 1930s, and the Sociology of Knowledge," *Teachers College Record* 85 (1984): 477–501, 485.

40. Du Bois, *The Crisis*, May 1914: 24, quoted in Taylor, "W. E. B. Du Bois's Challenge" 454–55.

41. John Dewey, quoted in William B. Thomas, "Black Intellectuals' Critique" 268.

42. Herbert Aptheker, ed., *A Documentary History of the Negro People in the United States*, 2 vols. (New York: Citadel Press, 1969) 2: 925.

43. At its peak circulation the *Crisis* reached about a hundred thousand Americans, about 80 percent of whom were black. Taylor, "W. E. B. Du Bois's Challenge" 450. For a discussion of the growing influence of groups like the NAACP, see C. F. Kellogg, *NAACP* (Baltimore, Md.: Johns Hopkins University Press, 1967).

44. Herbert Miller, quoted in Thomas, "Black Intellectuals' Critique" 269.

45. Albert Sidney Beckham, "Applied Eugenics," *The Crisis* (1924): 177–78, 177.

46. William Pickens, "The Ultimate Effects of Segregation and Discrimination," *The Ultimate Effects of Segregation and Discrimination: The Seldom Thought in the Negro Problem* (published by the author, 1915), reprinted in Aptheker, *A Documentary History of the Negro People* 84.

47. William Pickens, quoted in Aptheker, *A Documentary History of the Negro People* 84.

48. Pickens, quoted in Aptheker, *A Documentary History of the Negro People* 84–85.

49. Kelly Miller, "Government and the Negro," *Annals of the American Academy of Political and Social Science* 140 (1928): 98–104, 102.

50. See, for example, Cox, *White America* 248–49.

51. Joseph C. Carroll, "The Race Problem," *Sociology and Research* 11 (1927): 266–71, 268–69.

52. Carroll, "The Race Problem" 269. Anglo-Saxon clubs were influential private organizations that sought to maintain the purity of the races.

53. Carroll, "The Race Problem" 271.

54. Carroll, "The Race Problem" 270. Both the Rhinelander and Sweet cases were considered by contemporaries to be seminal examples of racism.

55. Beckham, "Applied Eugenics" 177. The army tests were intelligence examinations that were given to millions of Americans during World War I.

56. Carroll, "The Race Problem" 270.

57. Thomas, "Black Intellectuals' Critique" 266.

58. Thomas, "Black Intellectuals' Critique" 272.

59. Thomas, "Black Intellectuals' Critique" 272.

60. Thomas, "Black Intellectuals' Critique" 276.

61. Beckham, "Applied Eugenics" 177–78.

62. Beckham, "Applied Eugenics" 177.

63. Beckham, "Applied Eugenics" 178.

64. Beckham, "Applied Eugenics" 178.

65. Beckham, "Applied Eugenics" 178.

66. "Miscegenation" as a descriptive term first originated in the "miscegenation hoax" in the national election of 1864. See Sidney Kaplan, "Miscegenation Issue in the Election of 1864," *Journal of Negro History* 34 (July 1949): 277.

67. For example, in New York in 1910, there was an unsuccessful attempt to establish a state law barring intermarriage between the races. The proposed "Act to Amend the Domestic Relations Law, in Relation to Miscegenation" proposed to void all marriages "contracted between a person of white or Caucasian race and a person of the negro or black race." Gilbert Osofsky, *Harlem: The Making of a Ghetto* (New York: Harper and Row, 1966) 42. For a discussion of some of the work of the NAACP in effectively opposing miscegenation laws, see Albert E. Jenks, "The Legal Status of Negro-White Amalgamation in the United States," *American Journal of Sociology* 21 (1915): 666–78.

68. Miller, "Government and the Negro" 102.

69. Eugene Gordon, "The Negro Press," *American Mercury* 8 (May 1926): 207–15, 209.

70. One local newspaper, the *Richmond Planet*, warned state legislators that the "white folks" had better let well enough alone. "They are liable by 'a scratch of a pen' to be putting white folks over on the Negro side of the racial fence and colored folks over on the white folks['] side of the same dividing line. Only God can unerringly trace the racial blood in a man or a woman, and he is not in that business right through here now" ("Too Much Digging," *Richmond Planet*, March 15, 1924: 1, quoted in Arness, "The Evolution of Virginia Antimiscegenation Laws" 42).

71. For one typical discussion of the miscegenation law in the popular press, see "Fellow Caucasians! Virginia Law on Racial Integrity," *The Nation* 118 (April 1924): 388.

72. Miller, "Government and the Negro" 103.

73. *The Searchlight* [Atlanta], April 1, 1922, quoted in Guy B. Johnson, "The Race Philosophy of the Ku Klux Klan," *Opportunity* 1 (1923): 268–70, 267. Blacks realized the effect that their claims of improvement had on whites. Guy Johnson, for example, argued that "The progress of the Negro, then, with his increasing race consciousness, faces the white man with a problem of adjustment; he must either adapt his views to the changing condition and grasp the higher concepts in race relations, or he must hold to his traditional views. The Klan represents that body of Americans who have taken the latter course" (278).

74. Kelly Miller, "The Historical Background of the Negro Physicians," *Journal of Negro History* 1 (1916): 99–109, 100.

75. Miller, "The Historical Background" 108. See also Kelly Miller, "Eugenics of the Negro Race," *Scientific Monthly* 5 (1917): 57–59.

76. African-American newspapers were said to have a readership of nearly five million readers. Gordon, "The Negro Press" 207.

77. Some racists were interested in these laws for reasons that went beyond racial inequality. Apparently some nativists still believed that in the long term, blacks would leave the United States. Brian William Thomson, "Racism and Racial Classification: A Case Study of the Virginia Racial Integrity Legislation" (Ph.D. diss., Department of Sociology, University of California Riverside, 1978) 1.

78. W. E. B. Du Bois, quoted in Arness, "Evolution of the Virginia Antimiscegenation Laws" i.

79. Johnson and Seligmann, "Legal Aspects of the Negro Problem" 97.

80. For an excellent discussion of the salience of race, class, and gender for African-Americans in the related social hygiene movement, see Christina Simmons, "African-Americans and Sexual Victorianism in the Social Hygiene Movement, 1910–1940," *Journal of the History of Sexuality* 4 (1993): 51–75. My research supports Simmons's assertion that middle-class leaders were trying to mobilize Victorian values in order to challenge white racism (75).

81. Arness, "Evolution of the Virginia Antimiscegenation Laws" 40.

82. Quoted in Arness, "Evolution of the Virginia Antimiscegenation Laws" 40–41.

83. Arness, "Evolution of the Virginia Antimiscegenation Laws" 41.

84. The association between blood and race pride had divided African-Americans for decades. Compare the words of John Smith and Frederick Douglass. Smith claimed in 1887 that "The Negro is now a distinct, and ever will be a distinct race in this country. Blood — not language and religion — make social distinctions. We are therefore bound by every drop of blood that flows in our being, and by whatever of self-respect you and I individually and collectively possess, to make ourselves . . . a great people" (quoted in Meier, "Negro Racial Thought" 130). Contrast this with the statement of Frederick Douglass two years later: "Do we not know that every argument we make, and every pretention we set up in favor of race pride is giving the enemy a stick to break our own heads?" (quoted in Meier, "Negro Racial Thought" 213).

85. Elmer Carter, "Eugenics for the Negro," *Birth Control Review* 16 (1932): 169–70, 170.

86. Beckham, "Applied Eugenics" 177.

87. W. E. B. Du Bois, "Black Folk and Birth Control," *Birth Control Review* 16 (1932): 166–67, 166. Years earlier, Beckham had made a similar claim: "It is fundamental to note that persons of like undesirable traits should not mate. Persons of the best blood as evidenced by mental, moral, and physical life should mate if possible. This would insure an eugenic product of the highest type. It is to be regretted that at present the birth rate of the best blood barely suffices that lost by death" ("Applied Eugenics" 178).

88. Charles Johnson, "A Question of Negro Health," *Birth Control Review* 16 (1932): 167–68, 67.

89. Du Bois, "Black Folk and Birth Control" 167.

90. Carter, "Eugenics for the Negro" 169.

91. Thomas R. Garth, "Eugenics, Euthenics, and Race," *Opportunity* 8 (July 1930): 206–7, 206.

92. Beckham, "Applied Eugenics" 178.

93. William A. Robinson, quoted in Thomas, "Black Intellectuals, Intelligence Testing" 495.

94. Du Bois, quoted in Taylor, "W. E. B. Du Bois's Challenge" 459.

Chapter 4: Women and the Eugenics Movement

1. In recent years some writers have been more sensitive to the role of women in the eugenics debate. See, for example, Nicole Hahn Rafter, *White Trash: The Eugenic Family Studies, 1877–1919* (Boston: Northeastern University Press, 1988).

2. Linda Gordon, *Woman's Body, Woman's Right: A Social History of Birth Control in America* (New York: Grossman, 1976) 117.

3. Gordon, *Woman's Body* 144.

4. Gordon, *Woman's Body* 112.

5. Gordon, *Woman's Body* 121.

6. For a discussion of the relative merits of segregation and sterilization, see Florence Mateer, "Mental Heredity and Eugenics," *Psychological Bulletin* 10 (1913): 224–29.

7. For a discussion of the importance of eugenical arguments in our "public memory," see Elazar Barkan, *The Retreat of Scientific Racism: Changing Concepts of Race in Britain and the United States between the World Wars* (Cambridge: Cambridge University Press, 1992) 279–340.

8. Herbert Spencer, *The Study of Sociology* (New York, 1893) 373, quoted in Jill Conway, "Stereotypes of Femininity in a Theory of Sexual Evolution," *Victorian Studies* (1970): 47–62, 48.

9. Conway, "Stereotypes of Femininity" 48.

10. See Anna Davin, "Imperialism and Motherhood," *History Workshop* 5 (1978): 9–65.

11. For a discussion of the fears that came from perceptions of differential birth rates, see Richard Allen Soloway, *Birth Control and the Population Question in England, 1877–1930* (Chapel Hill: University of North Carolina Press, 1982) xi.

12. Davin, "Imperialism and Motherhood" 10.

13. Davin, "Imperialism and Motherhood" 12.

14. Davin, "Imperialism and Motherhood" 12.

15. Davin, "Imperialism and Motherhood" 13.

16. See, for example, the discussions of Caleb Saleeby.

17. Halford, quoted in Angus McLaren, *Birth Control in Nineteenth-Century England* (New York: Holmes and Meier, 1978) 207.

18. For a discussion of some of the variants of this "progressiveness," see Michael Freeden, "Eugenics and Progressive Thought: A Study in Ideological Affinity," *Historical Journal* 22 (1979): 645–71.

19. Francis Galton, quoted by James Field, "The Progress of Eugenics," *Quarterly Review of Economics* 26 (November 1911): 1–67, 23.

20. McLaren has argued that "All feminists agreed on one thing: motherhood had to be voluntary" (*Birth Control* 197).

21. Other more radical feminists, like F. W. Stella Browne, worried that eugenical calls for maternity endowment might be used to shift attention away from the essential right of the woman not to have children and would be another "engine of exploitation and oppression" (McLaren, *Birth Control* 206).

22. Frances Swiney, "An Ethical Birth Rate," *Westminster Review* 199 (1901): 550–54.

23. James Marchant, quoted in McLaren, *Birth Control* 198.

24. Olive Schreiner, for example, opined in her *Woman and Labour* that "the New Woman's conception of parenthood differs from the old in the greater sense of the gravity and obligation resting on those who are responsible for the production of the individual life, making her attitude toward the production of her race widely unlike the reckless, unreasoning, maternal reproduction of the woman of the past." (Quoted in McLaren, *Birth Control* 203.)

25. See Ann Martin, "The Mother and Social Reform," *Nineteenth Century and After* 73 (1913): 1060–79.

26. See Eden Paul and Cedar Paul, eds., *Population and Birth Control: A Symposium* (New York: Critic and Guide, 1917) 254. For a contrasting view of the role of women, see Grant Allen, "Plain Words on the Woman Question," *Fortnightly Review* 52 (1889): 448–58.

27. Alice B. Stockham, quoted in McLaren, *Birth Control* 203.

28. Clapperton, quoted in McLaren, *Birth Control* 205.

29. McLaren, *Birth Control* 199.

30. See, for example, Arnold L. Gesell, "The Village of a Thousand Souls," *The American Magazine* 76 (October 1913): 11–15.

31. Rafter, *White Trash* 1.

32. Gertrude Davenport, "Society and the Feebleminded," *The Independent*, April 27, 1914: 170.

33. Rafter, *White Trash* xi.

34. Even hard-line British eugenicists winced when they heard how some American eugenicists were using some of this research.

35. Interestingly, many of these studies comparing good and bad strains within families focused on demonstrating the constancy of men's germplasm and showing that women's germplasm seemed to carry most of the taints. See also Elizabeth S. Kite, "Two Brothers," *Survey* 27 (1912): 1861–64.

36. Some wondered about the extent of this illegitimacy and its relation to feminist movements. See George B. Mangold, "Unlawful Motherhood," *Forum* 53 (1915): 335–43. For an insightful discussion of the relationship between feeblemindedness and prostitution, see Margaret J. Kavounas, "Feeblemindedness and Prostitution: The Laboratory of Social Hygiene's Influence on Progressive Era Prostitution Reform" (master's thesis, Sarah Lawrence College, 1992).

37. Gesell, "The Village of a Thousand Souls" 14

38. Harvey W. Wiley, "The Rights of the Unborn," *Good Housekeeping*, October 1922: 32.

39. See also J. David Smith, *Minds Made Feeble: The Myth and Legacy of the Kallikaks* (Rockville, Md.: Aspen Publications, 1985).

40. For one of the best accounts of the collection of this information, see Nicole Rafter's *White Trash*.

41. Many of these workers were women who were not allowed to work as scientists, so this research provided them with a form of economic mobility.

42. Elizabeth Kite claimed that only a "trained eye" could detect the "deficiency" in an "attractive" defective who could potentially tempt a "clean youth" (Elizabeth Kite, "Unto the Third Generation," *Survey* 28 [1912]: 789–91, 91). Kite went on to argue that "something must be done and done at once, if this girl and thousands of similar defective girls are to be saved from themselves, and society saved from the evils they unwittingly engender" (791).

43. See, for example, Elizabeth Kite, "The 'Pineys,'" *Survey* 31 (1913): 7–13, 38–40, 10. Kite complained that families like the Pineys were trying to get these necessities without "entering into life's stimulating struggle" (10).

44. This also meant that women needed to be aware that they were going to be scrutinized by men. See Nellie M. L. Nearing and Scott Nearing, "When a Girl is Asked to Marry," *Ladies Home Journal*, March 1912: 7, 69–70. The Nearings tried to warn their readers about the need for marrying correctly by contrasting the famous Jukes and Edwards families (70).

45. Elizabeth Kite, "The 'Pineys'" 10. Kite was from the Training School at Vineland, New Jersey. For other examples of her influential work, see Elizabeth S. Kite, "Two Brothers" and "Unto the Third Generation."

46. Edward J. Larson, "Issues in the Southern Eugenics Movement" (paper presented to the University of Georgia History Department, 1993).

47. Women were also part of the audiences that heard addresses that linked Klan goals with typical eugenical claims. Klan leaders like Hiram Evans spoke on the importance of a genetically "good stock of Americans." In November 1923, the *New York Times* reported that Evans gave an address in Fort Wayne where he told five thousand assembled Klans members that "We have our Hester Streets and our box car flats and shacks in every industrial center . . . unsanitary, unwholesome, uninspirational; the national habitation and breeding place of the moron, nomad, and criminal." Kathleen M. Blee, *Women of the Klan: Racism and Gender in the 1920s* (Berkeley: University of California Press, 1991) 23, 172.

48. In the early 1910s Tyler would help start the "better babies" movement (Blee, *Women of the Klan* 20). Decades later, the Klan would hold baby contests in several places, including Kokomo in 1925. These better-baby contests were exceedingly popular ways of circulating eugenic information. See for example, George E. Dawson, "100 Superfine Babies: What the Science of Eugenics Found in the Babies of Our Contest," *Good Housekeeping*, February 1912: 238–41.

49. Blee, *Women of the Klan* 18, 23.

50. I am not claiming that popular accounts in women's journals ignored the role of race or class—these were just not the only issues addressed.

To help make sure that American women knew just what to avoid, eugenical writers in the women's magazines created vivid illustrations of the type of people who either ignored the warnings of the eugenicists or defied the laws of biological destiny. One wanted to "beg my readers never to forget the indelible, ineffaceable influence of the primary stress of heredity." Another asked his readers to remember that Americans were being faced with a new source of pollution of the germplasm—the immigrant: "There is menace in alien blood. Fourteen thousand insane aliens are in the hospitals of one state, New York. More than 88% of the insane patients admitted to the New York City hospitals last year were aliens. Exceeding great care must be taken not to turn these streams of disease into floods of disaster by scattering them among our native population. One drop of tainted blood inherited by your child may blight his life." Stoddard Goodhue, "Do You Choose Your Children?" *Cosmopolitan*, July 1913: 148–57, 155.

51. Goodhue, "Do You Choose Your Children?" 148–57.

52. Goodhue, "Do You Choose Your Children?" 148.

53. Goodhue, "Do You Choose Your Children?" 148.

54. Wiley, "The Rights of the Unborn" 173.

55. Goodhue, "Do You Choose Your Children?" 150.

56. Goodhue, "Do You Choose Your Children?" 150.

57. Ella Wheeler Wilcox, "The Forecast," *Good Housekeeping*, July 1912: 130.

58. This new mix of hereditary and environmental arguments in the 1920s created what Gordon has called a "popular" eugenics tradition that emphasized the need for

programs that would prevent birth defects, including prenatal medical care for women (Gordon, *Woman's Body: Woman's Right* 260–80).

59. Wiley, "Rights of the Unborn" 170.

60. In the 1870s, the ideograph of "voluntary motherhood" symbolized the notion that women, although divided into many loose reform tendencies, still had a coherent ideology on the major issues of suffrage, employment opportunities, marriage, and divorce (Gordon, *Woman's Body, Woman's Right* 95).

61. Quoted in Sidney Ditzion, *Marriage, Morals and Sex in America* (New York: Bookman Associates, 1953) 300.

62. The attitudes of women toward eugenics usually broke down along class lines. Middle- and upper-class Protestant women often supported some form of hard-line eugenics, while the poorer classes (at least in urban areas) were generally opposed to schemes for reducing the number of the "unfit."

63. Gordon, *Woman's Body, Woman's Right* 179.

64. Gordon, *Woman's Body, Woman's Right* 130.

65. Margaret Sanger, "Birth Control and Race Betterment," *Birth Control Review* 3 (1919): 11–12.

66. Gordon, *Woman's Body, Woman's Right* 134. For a contemporary discussion of mothers as "mere breeding machines" see Margaret Sanger, "Woman and War," *Birth Control Review* 1 (June 1917): 5.

67. For an example of the importance of "voluntary motherhood" to the birth control movement, see Margaret Sanger, "Shall We Break This Law?" *Birth Control Review* 1 (January 1917): 4–5. Sanger continued to stress the importance of "voluntary choice" in the decades ahead when many eugenicists were calling for coercive sterilization measures. See "Editorial," *Birth Control Review* 12 (March 1928): 73–74, 74.

68. Emma Goldman, "The Social Aspects of Birth Control," *Mother Earth* 11 (1916): 468–75, 471. For an analysis of the influence of Goldman, see Martha Solomon, *Emma Goldman* (Boston: Twayne Publishers, 1987).

69. Nancy Woloch, *Women and the American Experience* (New York: Alfred A. Knopf, 1984) 367; John M. Murphy, "'To Create a Race of Thoroughbreds': Margaret Sanger and *The Birth Control Review*," *Women's Studies in Communication* 13 (1990): 23–45, 28.

70. Sanger, quoted in Gordon, *Woman's Body, Woman's Right* 276–77. Although there are more recent feminist examinations of eugenics, I believe that Gordon's work still provides one of the best accounts of the early eugenics discussions in America.

Initially, Margaret Sanger emphasized the need for revolutionary social change, and she often spoke for the poor and working class and protested their treatment at the hands of the other classes. For example, Sanger started her own newspaper, the *Woman Rebel*, and in it she included articles on contraception, family limitation, and health issues of the time (Murphy, "'To Create a Race of Thoroughbreds'" 24, 28).

71. Murphy, "'To Create a Race of Thoroughbreds'" 25. See also Gordon, *Woman's Body, Woman's Right* 281.

72. Margaret Sanger, "Birth Control and Race Betterment" 12.

73. Gertrude Davenport, "The Eugenics Movement," *The Independent*, January 18, 1912: 146–48.

Chapter 5: Catholic Interpretations of Eugenics Rhetoric

1. See, for example, the influential Andrew D. White, *A History of Warfare of Science and Theology in Christendom*, 2 vols. (1896; rpt. New York: Dover, 1960).

2. Angus McLaren, *Our Own Master Race: Eugenics in Canada, 1885–1945* (Toronto: McClelland and Stewart, 1990) 15. For a discussion of anti-Catholicism in England, see Edward R. Norman, *Anti-Catholicism in Victorian England* (London: George Allen and Unwin, 1968).

3. For discussions of the "residuum," see Pauline M. H. Mazumdar, *Eugenics, Human Genetics, and Human Failings* (London: Routledge, 1992). Decades later, eugenicists would call the paupers and other undesirables in Britain the "social problem group."

4. Sidney Webb, "Physical Degeneracy or Race Suicide?" *London Times*, October 16, 1906: p. 7 col. 1.

5. For some of the best studies of the influence of degeneration during this period, see Gareth Stedman Jones, *Outcast London* (Oxford: Clarendon Press, 1971), and Richard Allen Soloway, *Demography and Degeneration: Eugenics and the Declining Birth Rate in Twentieth-Century Britain* (Chapel Hill: University of North Carolina Press, 1990).

6. Webb, "Physical Degeneracy" 7.

7. Webb, "Physical Degeneracy" 7.

8. Webb, "Physical Degeneracy" 7.

9. Soloway, *Demography and Degeneration* 156.

10. Quoted in Soloway, *Demography and Degeneration* 14.

11. Soloway, *Demography and Degeneration* 14.

12. Soloway, *Demography and Degeneration* 14–15.

13. Soloway, *Demography and Degeneration* 14.

14. Stephen Trombley, *The Right to Reproduce* (London: Nicolson, 1988) 38.

15. Greta Jones has remarked that it was surprising that many of the other denominations in England supported different interpretations of eugenics. In the first several decades of the twentieth century, Dean Inge was considered to be one of the most influential popularizers of the hard-line eugenics movement, and his speeches were often publicized on both sides of the Atlantic. Greta Jones, *Social Hygiene in Twentieth Century Britain* (London: Croom Helm, 1986) 47–48.

16. Even in 1950, Barnes was still talking about eugenics, warning English readers that "inferior stocks are increasing far too rapidly and are a menace to the future." E. W. Barnes, "Science, Religion, and Moral Judgments," *Nature* 166 (1950): 455–57, 457, 456.

17. Jones, *Social Hygiene in Twentieth Century Britain* 47–48.

18. For an insightful discussion of how eugenicists read and quoted Nietzsche's work, see Mazumdar.

19. Quoted in V. F. Calverton, "The Myth of Nordic Superiority," *Current History* 24 (1926): 671–77, 676.

20. Carl N. Degler, *In Search of Human Nature: The Decline and Revival of Darwinism in American Social Thought* (New York: Oxford University Press, 1991) 153. See also Robert Divine, *American Immigration Policy, 1924–1952* (New Haven: Yale University Press, 1951).

21. Hiram W. Evans, "The Klan's Fight for Americanism," *North American Review* 223 (1926): 33–63, 45.

22. See Donald Kinzer, *An Episode in Anti-Catholicism: The American Protective Association* (Seattle: University of Washington Press, 1964).

23. For a general overview of anti-Catholic sentiment, see the work of Philip Perlmutter, *Divided We Fall: A History of Ethnic, Religious, and Racial Prejudice in America* (Ames: Iowa State University Press, 1992) 202–20.

24 Angus McLaren, *Our Own Master Race* 49.

25. *Buck v. Bell* was the first case on sterilization that came before the U.S. Supreme Court. For an excellent overview of *Buck* and the history of sterilization in America, see Philip R. Reilly, *The Surgical Solution: A History of Involuntary Sterilization in the United States* (Baltimore: Johns Hopkins University Press, 1991). In *Buck*, Oliver Wendell Holmes, Jr., wrote an opinion for the U.S. Supreme Court that upheld the constitutionality of a Virginia statute allowing the sterilization of Carrie Buck. Buck was described as the "feebleminded daughter of a feebleminded mother and is herself the mother of an illegitimate feebleminded child." John A. Ryan, "Unprotected Natural Rights," *The Commonweal*, June 15, 1927: 151–52, 151.

While hard-line eugenicists celebrated this case as a watershed event in the progress of their science, Catholics for decades would see *Buck* as an example of the dark forces threatening humanitarian natural rights. David H. Burton, "Justice Holmes and the Jesuits," *American Journal of Jurisprudence* 27 (1982): 32–45. See also Jacob B. Aronoff, "The Constitutionality of Asexualization Legislation in the United States," *St. Johns Law Review* 1 (1927): 146–74; J. E. Coogan, "Eugenical Sterilization Holds Jubilee," *Catholic World* 177 (1953): 44–49; Daniel J. Kevles, *In the Name of Eugenics: Genetics and the Uses of Human Heredity* (New York: Alfred A. Knopf, 1985) 118.

26. Reilly, *Surgical Solution* 89.

27. Cardinal Bourne, a leader of the two and a half million Catholics in Britain, worried about what would happen to this minority when as many as thirteen million people would disappear over the next thirty years (Soloway, *Demography and Degeneration* 265).

28. Thomas Gerrard, "The Catholic Church and Race Culture," *Dublin Review* 149 (1911): 49–68, 58.

29. Gerrard, "The Catholic Church and Race Culture" 59.

30. Gerrard, "The Catholic Church and Race Culture" 61.

31. Gerrard, "The Catholic Church and Race Culture" 62.

32. For an example of Gerrard's critique of Saleeby and his "doctrine of materialism," see Gerrard, "The Catholic Church and Race Culture" 49–68.

33. Thomas Gerrard, "Eugenics and Catholic Teaching," *Catholic World* 95 (June 1912): 289–304, 290, 293.

34. Gerrard, "Eugenics and Catholic Teaching" 297, 299.

35. Gerrard, "Eugenics and Catholic Teaching" 300–302.

36. Gerrard, "The Catholic Church and Race Culture" 49.

37. Gerrard, "The Catholic Church and Race Culture" 53.

38. Gerrard, "The Catholic Church and Race Culture" 54.

39. Quoted in Gerrard, "The Catholic Church and Race Culture" 55.

40. Gerrard, "The Catholic Church and Race Culture" 64.

41. Gerrard, "The Catholic Church and Race Culture" 64–65.

42. Henry Somerville, "Eugenics and the Feeble-minded," *Catholic World* 105 (1917): 209–18, 213.

43. Gerrard, "The Catholic Church and Race Culture" 67. Emphasis in the original.

44. Greta Jones, *Social Hygiene in Twentieth-Century Britain* 49.

45. In the 1930s, eugenics advocates began arguing that marriage restrictions and segregation of the necessitous alone had been ineffective.

46. Degler has argued, "That the socially conservative Roman Catholic church invariably opposed all sterilization laws whenever they might be proffered further convinced many reform-minded or Progressive Americans that permanently preventing the unfit from procreating was forward-looking as well as socially necessary" (*In Search of Human Nature* 46).

47. Soloway, *Demography and Degeneration* 265.

48. Soloway *Demography and Degeneration* 264.

49. Kevles, *In the Name of Eugenics* 120.

50. G. K. Chesterton, *Eugenics and Other Evils* (London: Cassell and Company, 1922) 21.

51. As one historian has remarked, doctors and welfare workers were overrepresented in the eugenics movement "not simply because they thought they knew something about inherited disabilities; eugenics was an ideology that exalted both professions as playing potentially crucial roles in protecting social stability" (McLaren, *Our Own Master Race* 114).

52. James J. Walsh, "The Story of Organized Care of the Insane and Defectives," *Catholic World* 104 (November 1916): 226–34.

53. One question in this debate was how accurate eugenical tests were in determining who was unfit. See Somerville, "Eugenics and the Feeble-minded" 208.

54. Many Catholic commentaries concentrated on the dangers of negative rather than

positive eugenics. Somerville, for example, wrote in 1917 that "There has been much talk of eugenics among Catholics, but we have been prone to fix our attention on its more impossible and absurd claims, and we have felt satisfied in laughing it out of court. . . . There is little chance that what is called 'positive eugenics' will ever have any wide application; but there is a real and even immediate danger from 'negative eugenics' " ("Eugenics and the Feebleminded" 217).

55. In Europe, especially during the latter part of the 1920s, some Catholic scholars also advocated the use of eugenic sterilization. See Joseph Mayer, "Eugenics in Roman Catholic Literature," *Eugenics* 3 (1930): 43–51, quoted in Reilly, *Surgical Solution* 119. Eugenicists on both the East and West Coasts looked for examples of Catholic rhetoric supporting eugenics and sterilization, and they included such material in thousands of newsletters, articles, and books that were distributed nationwide.

In 1932, Landman would argue that "Of course, the cacogenic people have their staunch friends in the religionists. Organized religion, especially the Roman Catholic Church, is opposed to any form of interference with the natural procreation of the race, whether the progenitors be ideal parents or not. Continence for the married laity is considered irreligious. It is an interference of God's will that we procreate. There is, however, a liberal Roman Catholic Movement that permits human sterilization for therapeutic purposes and even for eugenic purposes, where the cacogenic progenitors and their progeny are a burden to themselves and to society. Some of the Protestant churches have in recent times registered approval of discriminatory procreation." J. H. Landman, *Human Sterilization* (New York: Macmillan, 1932) 9.

See the encyclical Casti Connubii of Pope Pius XI, "On Christian Marriage in Relation to Present Conditions, Needs and Disorders of Society" of January 9, 1931, in *Current History* 33 (1931): 797; the Federal Council of the Churches of Christ, representing twenty-seven Protestant churches, "Moral Aspects of Birth Control," *Current History* 34 (1931): 97–100.

56. For the debate over Donovan's position, see Stephen M. Donovan, "The Morality of the Operation of Vasectomy," *Ecclesiastical Review* 44 (1911): 571–74; "The Morality and Lawfulness of Vasectomy," *Ecclesiastical Review* 44 (1911): 562–71.

For years, hard-line eugenicists in America tried to capitalize on the eugenics debate within the Catholic community. See Paul Popenoe, "A Roman Catholic View of Sterilization," reprinted in *Collected Papers on Eugenics Sterilization in California* (Pasadena: Human Betterment Foundation, 1930) 186–89.

57. S. M. Donovan, quoted in Reilly, *Surgical Solution* 118. See also "The Morality and Lawfulness of Vasectomy" 562–65.

58. See John A. Ryan, "Sterilization," *Ecclesiastical Review* 84 (1931): 267–71. In his review of all these articles, Ryan admonished his readers to remember that the "great majority" of these contributors thought that sterilization was "intrinsically wrong." He reminded his audience that they needed to remember the papal encyclicals of Pope Leo

on the conditions of labor and the "necessaries of life," which focused not on hereditary feeblemindedness but on "charity" and the need to convince the rich to contribute some of their "abundance of this world's goods" (Ryan, "Sterilization" 270).

59. Bertrand L. Conway, "The Church and Eugenics," *Catholic World* 123 (1928): 148–55. Note the similarities between the definition of eugenics offered by Saleeby and some of these Catholic interpretations.

60. Conway, "The Church and Eugenics" 154.

61. Walter B. Kennedy, "The Supreme Court and Social Legislation," *Catholic Charities Review* 7 (1923): 208–12, 210.

62. See John A. Lapp, "Justice First," *Catholic Charities Review* 11 (127): 201–9, 207.

63. Lapp, "Justice First" 207.

64. Lapp, "Justice First" 209.

65. Ignatius W. Cox, "The Folly of Human Sterilization," *Scientific American* 151 (1934): 188–90, 189.

66. Bertram C. A. Windle, "A Rule of Life," *Catholic World* 103 (August 1916): 577–87, 579. See also John A. Ryan, *A Living Wage* (New York: Macmillan, 1906).

67. Somerville, "Eugenics and the Feeble-minded" 212.

68. John A. Ryan, "Family Limitation," *Ecclesiastical Review* 54 (1916): 684–96, 694.

69. Windle, "A Rule of Life" 583.

70. Cox, "The Folly" of Human Sterilization" 188.

71. Lawrence J. Coleman, "Is the Eugenist Scientific?" *Modern Schoolman* 12 (1934): 3–6, 6.

72. James J. Walsh, "The Story of Organized Care" 226.

73. Conway, "The Church and Eugenics" 151.

74. One unnamed writer claimed that there was no imminent danger to the state in *Buck* and that it had "another and more effective means of protecting itself, namely, segregation." "A Far-Reaching Decision," *Catholic Charities Review* 11 (1927): 225–26, 226. From the very beginning of the twentieth century, Catholics contrasted the Church's doctrine of charity and "free will" with the "necessity" of sterilizing or discriminating against the unfit (Kevles, *In the Name of Eugenics* 118).

75. Conway, "The Church and Eugenics" 154.

76. Kevles, "In the Name of Eugenics" 119.

77. Somerville, "Eugenics and the Feeble-Minded" 211.

78. "Editorial Comment," *Catholic World* 118 (December 1923): 401–7.

79. Somerville, "Eugenics and the Feeble-minded" 217.

80. Conway, "The Church and Eugenics" 153.

81. Somerville, "Eugenics and the Feeble-minded" 208.

82. This is not to say that all Catholics were opposed to sterilization. In 1927, John Ryan, a professor of theology at Catholic University and a spokesman for the Vatican on policy issues in the United States, was said to have "broken ranks with his more reform-minded colleagues on the National Catholic Welfare Council" and condemned eugenical

sterilization as a violation of the "intrinsic sacredness of the person." See F. L. Broderick, *Right Reverend New Dealer: John A. Ryan* (New York: Macmillan, 1963) 148–50. Yet, as Reilly noted, even Ryan did not exclude the possibility that there might be certain circumstances when the public welfare might require some form of involuntary sterilization (Reilly, *Surgical Solution* 118).

83. Somerville, "Eugenics and the Feeble-minded" 218.

84. Aronoff, "The Constitutionality of Asexualization Legislation" 148–49.

85. Reilly, *Surgical Solution* 118.

86. Landman, *Human Sterilization* 259.

87. Cox, "The Folly of Human Sterilization" 188.

88. Cox, "The Folly of Human Sterilization" 188.

89. Kevles, *In the Name of Eugenics* 119.

90. Reilly, *Surgical Solution* 119.

91. "Full Text of Pope Pius's Encyclical," *New York Times,* January 9, 1931, 14–15: 15.

92. James J. Walsh, "Race Betterment," *The Commonweal* 19 (1934): 371–72, 372.

93. Reilly, *Surgical Solution* 120.

94. Reilly, *Surgical Solution* 89.

95. Roswell Johnson, quoted in Reilly, *Surgical Solution* 89.

96. R. H. Johnson, quoted in Reilly, *Surgical Solution* 118.

97. Marion Olden, quoted in Reilly, *Surgical Solution* 120. For a discussion of the stand of the Catholic Church by the end of the 1930s, see Edgar Schmiedeler, *Sterilization in the United States* (Washington, D.C.: National Catholic Welfare Conference, 1943).

98. Reilly, *Surgical Solution* 121.

99. For a discussion of Catholic opposition to sterilization in Wisconsin, see Trombley, *The Right to Reproduce* 58.

100. "Sterilization Conflicts," *The Commonweal,* April 12, 1935: 680–81, 681.

101. "Sterilization Conflicts" 681.

102. "Sterilization Conflicts" 681.

103. Reilly, *Surgical Solution* 85. Although many eugenicists liked to think of themselves as progressives, some Catholics denied that the adherents of the sterilization movement deserved that appellation. Lawrence Coleman, for example, writing in 1934, noted that "Many institutions, therefore, now endeavor to fit the feebleminded for life in the community and by selective parole offer to many of them a chance for social rehabilitation. It is noteworthy that the states in which such progressive work is being accomplished *are not in favor of sterilization* and have no sterilization laws" (Lawrence J. Coleman, "Is the Eugenist Scientific?" 6).

104. Barry A. Mehler, "A History of the American Eugenics Society, 1921–1940" Ph.D. diss., University of Illinois at Urbana, 1988) 284–88, 284.

105. Mehler, "History of the American Eugenics Society" 287.

106. Cox, "The Folly of Human Sterilization" 190.

Chapter 6: Liberal and Socialist Interpretations of Eugenics

1. For examples of more conservative eugenical discourse, see Madison Grant, "Discussions of Article on Democracy and Heredity," *Journal of Heredity* 10 (1919): Lothrop Stoddard, "Does Democracy Fit Most Peoples?" *World's Work* 50 (1925): 57–62; Robert DeC. Ward, "Our Immigration Laws from the Viewpoint of Eugenics," *American Breeder's Magazine* 3 (1912): 20–26; Robert DeC. Ward, "The Second Year of the New Immigration Law," *Journal of Heredity* 18 (1927): 3–18; Albert E. Wiggam, "The Rising Tide of Degeneracy: What Everybody Ought to Know about Eugenics," *World's Work* 53 (1926): 25–33.

For an insightful overview of the impact of racial arguments during this period, see Jacques Barzun, *Race: A Study in Superstition* (New York: Harper and Row, 1965). For an elaboration of the lasting effect of social Darwinistic arguments, note the work of Stephen Steinberg, *The Ethnic Myth: Race, Ethnicity, and Class in America* (New York: Atheneum, 1981).

A word of caution is needed here. It is notoriously difficult to label the political proclivities of some of these eugenicists. For a trenchant critique of the inherent difficulty of classifying eugenicists as either hereditarian "conservatives" or environmental "progressives," see Jonathan Harwood, "Nature, Nurture and Politics: A Critique of the Conventional Wisdom," in *The Meritocratic Intellect*, ed. James V. Smith and David Hamilton (Aberdeen: Aberdeen University Press, 1980) 115–209. For example, Karl Pearson has been called everything from a hard-line conservative to a reluctant Marxist. In my own narrative construction I take a functional approach that looks at the policies advocated by these rhetors.

2. None of these writers ignore non-hard-line eugenical arguments; they simply place them on the periphery of discussion until the mid-1920s.

3. Diane Paul, "Eugenics and the Left," *Journal of the History of Ideas* (1984): 567–90, 568–69.

4. For some of the earliest discussions of leftist eugenics, see the work of Loren Graham, "Science and Values: The Eugenics Movement in Germany and Russia in the 1920s," *American Historical Review* 82 (1977): 1133–64; Loren Green, *Between Science and Values* (New York: Columbia University Press, 1981) 217–56; Diane Paul, "Eugenics and the Left" 567–90.

As Ray has recently argued, some of the eugenicists did seem to be "conservative" or "aristocratic," but at other times their movement was "critical of prevailing political institutions." L. J. Ray, "Eugenics, Mental Deficiency and Fabian Socialism between the Wars," *Oxford Review of Education* 9 (1983): 213–25. See also Greta Jones, *Social Hygiene in Twentieth Century Britain* (London: Croom Helm, 1986).

5. Control of reproduction did not necessarily mean sterilization. In 1908, when the Royal Commission on the Care and Control of the Feebleminded was considering its op-

tions in dealing with the mentally defective, only three out of twenty-one witnesses who mentioned sterilization as an alternative were in favor of it (Jones, *Social Hygiene* 88).

6. See Harvey G. Simmons, "Explaining Social Policy: The English Mental Deficiency Act of 1913," *Journal of Social History* 11 (1978): 387–403, 397.

7. For a discussion of feeblemindedness and normality, see Simmons, "Explaining Social Policy" 388.

8. Simmons argues that the term "feebleminded" may have been used first by Sir Charles Trevelyan, a member of the Council of the Charity Organization Society, who used the term to refer to "improvable idiots" ("Explaining Social Policy" 388). For an illustration of how the "feebleminded" were described in the contemporary popular press, see R. Brudenell Carter, "The Feeble-Minded," *London Times*, November 29, 1912: 6.

9. Simmons, "Explaining Social Policy" 391.

10. England's upper classes had their own interpretations of the Royal Commission report. For conservatives, it indicated that liberals had been in charge of private and governmental policies for too long. Private charity had been found wanting, and sentimentalists had failed abysmally in their use of the available resources.

11. Simmons, "Explaining Social Policy" 395.

12. The more conservative members of the eugenics community focused on the need for positive eugenical schemes that would encourage the reproduction of geniuses, and their narratives were filled with stories of how the economically successful were the "fit" members of society. More liberal eugenicists objected to some of these early eugenical tales because at times these conservative narratives tended to exclude even members of the middle class. What united British eugenicists was their common concern that the lower classes were outbreeding the "better" classes.

13. Tredgold, quoted in Simmons, "Explaining Social Policy" 394.

14. Simmons, "Explaining Social Policy" 394; emphasis mine.

15. Mary Dendy, a worker in the area of mental deficiency in Manchester and a founder of the Lancashire and Cheshire Society for the Permanent Care of the Feebleminded, quoted in Simmons, "Explaining Social Policy" 392.

16. One of the most popular definitions of the "feebleminded" used by the Royal Commission came from the prestigious Royal College of Physicians, which claimed that the term applied to any person "capable of earning a living under favourable circumstances, but . . . incapable from mental defect existing from birth or from an early age (a) of competing on equal terms with his normal fellows; or (b) of managing himself and his affairs with ordinary prudence" (Simmons, "Explaining Social Policy" 392). As I indicate below, this definition would become a major source of controversy in the parliamentary debate over the Mental Deficiency Bills.

17. Simmons, "Explaining Social Policy" 388.

18. Arnold White, quoted in Simmons, "Explaining Social Policy" 390.

19. Winston Churchill to Asquith, December 1910, quoted in G. R. Searle, *Eugen-*

ics and Politics in Britain, 1900–1914 (Leyden: Noordhoff International Publishing, 1976) 107. Churchill's views on eugenics are still controversial. See Alexander Cockburn, "Memory," *The Nation* 255 (1992): 618–19.

20. Bernard Bosanquet, "The Reports of the Poor Law Commission, I. The Majority Report," *Sociological Review* 2 (1909): 109–26, 111.

21. Leonard T. Hobhouse, *Social Evolution and Political Theory* (New York: Columbia University Press, 1928) 73.

22. Hobhouse, *Social Evolution* 71.

23. Hobhouse, *Social Evolution* 74.

24. For an interesting discussion of the debate over the role of public health in Edwardian England, see Dorothy Porter, " 'Enemies of the Race': Biologism, Environmentalism, and Public Health in Edwardian England," *Victorian Studies* 34 (1991): 159–78, 173.

25. For a wonderful discussion of the balancing of these tensions, see Stefan Collini, *Liberalism and Sociology* (Cambridge: Cambridge University Press, 1979).

26. Sidney Webb, quoted in Diane Paul, "Eugenics and the Left" 570.

27. Saleeby, quoted in Searle, *Eugenics and Politics in Britain* 1.

28. It is perhaps no coincidence that these measures were being debated at the same time that the First International Eugenical Congress was being held in London in 1912. The conference was widely publicized in English newspapers.

29. Edward J. Larson, "The Rhetoric of Eugenics: Expert Authority and the Mental Deficiency Bill," *British Journal for the History of Science* 24 (1991): 45–60, 47.

30. Larson, "The Rhetoric of Eugenics" 52.

31. Gershom Stewart, quoted in Larson, "The Rhetoric of Eugenics" 52.

32. Alfred Lyttelton, quoted in Larson, "The Rhetoric of Eugenics" 53.

33. This was because the term "eugenics" was still primarily associated with conservatives in British society like the Eugenics Education Society.

34. Charles Roberts, quoted in Larson, "The Rhetoric of Eugenics" 53.

35. Leslie Scott, "The Mental Deficiency Bill," letter to the editor, the *Nation* [London], November 16, 1912: 310–11, 311. (The British journal the *Nation* is not the same as the American journal of the same name.)

Compare this statement with an editorial written in the summer of 1912 claiming that Parliament was confusing economic with medical tests of fitness and arguing that the Mental Deficiency Bill covered all of the "failures of our competitive society, all who cannot satisfy a standard of efficiency which the struggle for existence tends continually to raise. The shiftless, the casual worker, the tramp, the genius, and the witlessly incompetent are all in danger. . . . Assume that the cult of Eugenicism and the zeal for efficiency makes way under official patronage among doctors, magistrates, and relieving officers, and this Bill may be used to deprive the liberty and reduce to servitude any man or woman who can be accused of marked incompetence. . . . their liberty is in graver peril than that of a Russian moujik or a Mexican plantation serf. . . . It looks like a harmless proposal for segregating idiots. It really is a first essay in the scientific breeding of the poor" ("The Crime of Being Efficient," *The Nation*, June 15, 1912: 390–92, 391).

36. Scott, "The Mental Deficiency Bill" 311.

37. Scott, "The Mental Deficiency Bill" 311.

38. Part of the reluctance of the moderates in Parliament to acknowledge the influence of eugenics may have stemmed in part from the ready availability of neo-Lamarckian explanations of feeblemindedness.

39. Josiah Wedgwood, quoted in Larson, "The Rhetoric of Eugenics" 53.

40. Liberal Home Secretary Reginald McKenna noted that even the Royal Commission supported the Mental Deficiency Bill.

41. Josiah Wedgwood, quoted in Larson, "The Rhetoric of Eugenics" 54. For an interesting discussion of some of the doctors' interpretations of morals and mental deficiency, see Patricia Potts, "Medicine, Morals and Mental Deficiency: The Contribution of Doctors to the Development of Special Education in England," *Oxford Review of Education* 9 (1983): 181–96.

42. The *London Times* was generally supportive of the Mental Deficiency Bills. See "Proposed Legislation for the Feebleminded," *London Times*, May 20, 1912: 9.

43. Larson, "The Rhetoric of Eugenics" 56.

44. "Science," *The Athenaeum*, June 1, 1912: 625.

45. "The Mental Deficiency Bill," *Manchester Guardian*, July 20, 1912: 8. For a more ambivalent liberal perspective, see J. A. Hobson, "Race Regeneration," *Manchester Guardian*, October 10, 1911: 6.

46. "Science," *The Athenaeum*, June 1, 1912: 625. This was supposed to be a review of Charles Benedict Davenport's book *Heredity in Relation to Eugenics*, but it turned into a diatribe against the Mental Deficiency Bill.

47. "Coercive Philanthropy," *Manchester Guardian*, July 31, 1913: 6b.

48. See "The Crime of Being Inefficient," *The Nation* [London] 11 (1912): 276–77; "The Crime of Being Inefficient," *The Nation* [London] 12 (1912): 390–92; "The Dangers of the Mental Deficiency Bill," *The Nation*, October 26, 1912: 168–69.

49. "The Crime of Being Inefficient" 390.

50. "The Crime of Being Inefficient" 392.

51. "The Crime of Being Inefficient" 392.

52. The vague phrase "competing on equal terms with his normal fellows" caused a great deal of debate both in Parliament and in the press. See "The Dangers of the Mental Deficiency Bill" 168.

53. "The Dangers of the Mental Deficiency Bill" 168, 169.

54. "The Dangers of the Mental Deficiency Bill" 169.

55. "Second Thoughts on Mental Deficiency," *The Nation*, April 5, 1913: 8–9, 8.

56. "Second Thoughts on Mental Deficiency" 8.

57. Some scholars claim that some liberals and conservatives "rejected eugenics *in*

toto" (Diane Paul, "Eugenics and the Left" 571). Paul includes some social Darwinists, liberals like J. A. Hobson, and Catholics like G. K. Chesterton. Paul sees Hobhouse as a critic who made arguments that resembled the socialist stance.

58. "Coercive Philanthropy" 6b.

59. "The Dangers of the Mental Deficiency Bill" 169.

60. Jones, *Social Hygiene* 99. This was even the conclusion of some of the eugenicists themselves. C. P. Blacker and Cecil Binney in 1956 would look back and claim that the labor movement was one of the reasons for the campaign defeat (Jones, *Social Hygiene* 98–99).

61. Jones, *Social Hygiene* 101.

62. Eugenics was clearly a divisive issue for the Labour Party.

63. Jones, *Social Hygiene* 102.

64. Jones, *Social Hygiene* 102.

65. Jones, *Social Hygiene* 102.

66. Jones, *Social Hygiene* 102.

67. Jones, *Social Hygiene* 102.

68. C. P. Blacker, quoted in Jones, *Social Hygiene* 103. In private correspondence, Blacker commented that the protectors of the wellborn needed to be careful about questioning the intelligence of the working class. He wrote, "It is safe of course to write these things in the sanctity of one's study. But is it safe to say them to audiences of working or unemployed men, in a big industrial centre?" (quoted in Jones, *Social Hygiene* 109).

69. Much of Galton's popularity was due to the influence of Karl Pearson. For key discussions of some of Pearson's views, see Donald MacKenzie, "Karl Pearson and the Professional Middle Class," *Annals of Science* 36 (1979): 125–43; and Nicholas Pastore, *The Nature-Nurture Controversy* (New York: King's Crown Press 1949): 29–41. Pastore claims that Pearson was a socialist environmentalist before 1900 and a conservative hereditarian after 1900, but MacKenzie sees more continuity in Pearson's arguments (MacKenzie, "Karl Pearson" 136).

70. Lester Ward, "Eugenics, Euthenics, and Eudemics," *American Journal of Sociology* 18 (1913): 737–54, 739.

71. Searle, *Eugenics and Politics* 5.

72. Searle, *Eugenics and Politics* 5.

73. Most of the hard-liners liked to talk about Plato or Sparta and then they would take a huge historical leap to the modern eugenics movement inaugurated by Galton.

74. Searle, *Eugenics and Politics* 5.

75. In 1913, at a time when some states were passing marriage laws based on eugenics, the *Nation* argued that the regulations would bring "evasion," "false swearing," and "maladministration." *The Nation*, August 14, 1913: 138, quoted in Daniel J. Kevles, *In the Name of Eugenics: Genetics and the Uses of Human Heredity* (New York: Alfred A. Knopf, 1985) 120.

76. A. B. Wolfe, "Is There a Biological Law of Human Population Growth?" *Quarterly Journal of Economics* 41 (1927): 593–95.

77. Quoted in Kevles, *In the Name of Eugenics* 128.

78. Kevles, *In the Name of Eugenics* 145.

79. Ward, "Eugenics, Euthenics, and Eudemics" 754.

80. Ward, "Eugenics, Euthenics, and Eudemics" 742.

81. The term "euthenics" was never as popular as "eugenics," but it did occasionally appear in the popular press. For example, in a letter to the editor in October 1926, Joseph Krisses argued that in the debate between eugenics and euthenics, too "little attention had been given to the environment" ("Eugenics and Euthenics," *New York Times*, October 24, 1926: 16, col. 7. Like Ward before him, Krisses attacked those in the press who had placed too much emphasis on eugenics and not enough on euthenics. After discussing the Darwin, Jukes, and other families that had been written about in the press, he observed that "no one has ever taken an Edwards baby and reared it in a Jukes environment."

82. Ward, "Eugenics, Euthenics, and Eudemics" 746.

83. My review of the literature places me in agreement with Mazumdar, who has argued that leftist eugenics contained a "touch of Lamarckianism." Right-wing eugenicists in a variety of countries were quick to point out this connection. In 1921, Fritz Lenz claimed that the left clung to Lamarckism because it was politically advantageous (Pauline Mazumdar, *Eugenics, Human Genetics and Human Failings* [London: Routledge, 1992] 148). As Hitler would later so effectively illustrate, right-wing eugenics could also be popular.

84. There were many different versions of eugenical tales, and many of the arguments that were advanced by these writers were often superficial and contradictory in nature. John A. Glassburg, "Eugenics for the Layman by a Scholar and a Patriot," *New York Call*, September 16, 1923: sec. 2, p. 9.

85. Kevles, *In the Name of Eugenics* 132.

86. H. L. Mencken, quoted by Kevles, *In the Name of Eugenics* 115.

87. Sometimes American audiences were exposed to a series of articles that condemned particular hard-line schemes. For example, an editorial in the *New York Times* ridiculed the plans of Professor William McDougall, who had divided society into three classes depending on their degree of pure Nordic ancestry ("A New Class System," editorial, *New York Times*, April 28, 1923: 12). In another article, the *Times* indicated that McDougall's plan would mean that some criminals and illiterates would be disfranchised and prohibited from intermarriage with the "remaining full citizens" ("Would Reform Society by Marriage Control," *New York Times*, April 26, 1923: 31).

88. Chesterton, quoted in Kevles, *In the Name of Eugenics* 120.

89. Clarence Darrow, quoted in Kevles, *In the Name of Eugenics* 120.

90. "Risks Involved in the Effort to Breed Superior People," *Current Opinion* 69 (October 1920): 499–500, 500.

91. Glassburg, "Eugenics for the Layman" 9.

92. Ward, "Eugenics, Euthenics, and Eudemics" 753.

93. For a discussion of changes that were taking place within the field of heredity itself, see Donald Pickens, *Eugenics and the Progressives* (Nashville, Tenn.: Vanderbilt University Press, 1968) 202; Garland Allen, *Life Science in the Twentieth Century* (New York: Wiley, 1974); Donald A. MacKenzie, *Statistics in Britain, 1865–1900* (Edinburgh: Edinburgh University Press, 1981); Ernst Mayr, *The Growth of Biological Thought* (Cambridge: Belknap Press, 1982).

94. For example, see the work of Walter Lippmann, who ridiculed Army IQ tests that were being used by many eugenicists. Writing in the *New Republic*, Lippmann declared that the claim that the tests measured innate intelligence had "no more scientific foundation than a hundred other fads, vitamins and glands and amateur psychoanalysis and correspondence courses in will power, and it will pass with them into that limbo where phrenology and palmistry and characterology and other Babu sciences are to be found" (Lippmann, quoted in Kevles, *In the Name of Eugenics* 128).

95. Jennings, quoted in Kevles, *In the Name of Eugenics* 132.

96. East, quoted in Kevles, *In the Name of Eugenics* 122.

97. Charles Emerson, "Mental Hygiene: Wise and Unwise Investments," *Mental Hygiene* 10 (1926): 451–63, 452.

98. Pickens, *Eugenics and the Progressives* 202.

99. Pickens, *Eugenics and the Progressives* 205.

100. In some ways the Depression *revived* interest in some forms of eugenics. Now more speakers talked about the importance of sterilization as an alternative to "segregation" or an increase in the number of geniuses. In Britain, the Eugenics Society in 1926 printed tens of thousands of pamphlets discussing the advantages of sterilization (Kevles, *In the Name of Eugenics* 114).

101. J. B. S. Haldane, "My Philosophy of Life," a talk broadcast in November 1929, reprinted in *Inequality of Man and Other Essays* (London: Chatto, 1932) 220.

102. Mazumdar, *Eugenics* 149. See also Paul, "Eugenics and the Left" 571.

103. Lancelot Hogben, *The Nature of Living Matter* (London: Kegan Paul, 1930) 213–14, quoted in Mazumdar, *Eugenics* 149–50. Mazumdar points out that the phrase a "national minimum of parenthood" refers to the work of Beatrice Webb, *The Case for the National Minimum* (London: National Committee for the Prevention of Destitution, 1913).

104. Quoted in Mazumdar, *Eugenics* 171.

105. Lancelot Hogben, quoted in Mazumdar, *Eugenics* 150.

106. Hogben, quoted in Mazumdar, *Eugenics* 171.

107. Mazumdar, *Eugenics* 170.

108. Gary Werskey, *The Visible College: The Collective Biography of British Scientific Socialists of the 1930s* (New York: Holt, Rinehart and Winston, 1978) 107.

109. Kevles, *In the Name of Eugenics* 131. Still other researchers warned that some of

the more affluent families "have got the wind up about sterilisation and prefer to conceal their family histories" (Penrose, October 2, 1931, quoted by Jones, *Social Hygiene* 95).

110. Bertrand Russell, quoted in Werskey, *The Visible College* 19. Russell would also note that eugenical governments might try to "prove imbecility, so that rebels of all kinds will be sterilized" (quoted in Kevles, *In the Name of Eugenics* 120).

111. Werskey, *The Visible College* 96.

112. "Social Biology," *New Statesman and Nation*, December 26, 1931: 816–817, 816.

113. See Bernard Mallet, "The Social Problem Group," *Eugenics Review* 23 (October 1931): 203–6.

114. Jones, *Social Hygiene* 89.

115. For an insightful comparison of the British and American movements, see Kevles, *In the Name of Eugenics*. See also Elazar Barkan, *The Retreat of Scientific Racism: Changing Concepts of Race in Britain and the United States between the World Wars* (Cambridge: Cambridge University Press, 1992). For a much earlier but still relevant critique, see Clarence Darrow, "The Eugenics Cult," *American Mercury* 8 (1926): 129–37.

116. Joseph Needham, quoted in Peter J. Bowler, "E. W. MacBride's Lamarckian Eugenics and Its Implications for the Social Construction of Scientific Knowledge," *Annals of Science* 41 (1984): 245–60, 253.

117. See for example the arguments presented in H. J. Muller, "The Dominance of Economics over Eugenics," *Scientific Monthly* 37 (1933): 40–47.

Some liberal eugenicists were not moved by socialist or Marxist arguments. Keynes would ask in 1925: "How can I adopt a creed [Marxism] which, preferring the mud to the fish, exalts the boorish proletariat above the bourgeois and the intelligentsia, who, with whatever faults, are the quality in life and surely carry the seeds of all human advancement?" (quoted in Werskey, *The Visible College* 29).

118. Haldane, quoted in Werskey, *The Visible College* 97.

119. Haldane, quoted in Mazumdar, *Eugenics* 189.

120. Diane Paul, "Eugenics and the Left" 575.

121. H. J. Muller, *Out of the Night* (New York: Vanguard Press, 1935) 122.

122. Paul, "Eugenics and the Left" 578.

123. Eden Paul and Cedar Paul, "Eugenics, Birth Control and Socialism," quoted in Diane Paul, "Eugenics and the Left" 568.

124. Julian Huxley, "Marxist Eugenics," *Eugenics Review* 28 (1936): 66–68, 68.

125. Eva Trew, "Sex Sterilization," *International Socialist* (1913): 814–17. Contrast this position with that of the hard-liners. Seth Humphrey, for example, believed that "Once the vital necessity for denying parenthood to the unfit is recognized, there need be no battle over methods." Seth K. Humphrey, "Parenthood and the Social Conscience," *The Forum* 49 (April 1913): 457–64, 463.

126. Trew, "Sex Sterilization" 814.

127. "'Superior Classes' Urged to Procreate: Must Have More Numerous Progeny, Professor Tells Eugenists," *New York Call*, July 27, 1912: 3.

128. Trew, "Sex Sterilization" 814.

129. Trew, "Sex Sterilization" 814.

130. Trew, "Sex Sterilization" 814. Contrast this passage with the language of hard-liners writing decades later. Caradog Jones, for example, noted in a speech delivered in the early 1930s that, "Most of us in these days believe in the principle underlying the social services and we realize the benefits which they have brought the working classes; but I think the time has come when one must exercise more refined methods in selecting those families which are to enjoy these benefits. No humane person would wish to see anybody destitute; but we cannot afford to give . . . without reasonable inquiry. . . . In particular, those who have any regard for the future of the race will agree that we should try to put a premium on the prevention of a pauper class" (Caradog Jones, "Mental Deficiency on Merseyside," address to the Annual Conference of Mental Health Workers, April 17, 1932, quoted in Jones, *Social Hygiene* 90).

Some of the highest government officials sympathized with this view. Neville Chamberlain, for example, once argued that the time was fast approaching when "this question of sterilization of the mentally deficient will have to be very seriously considered. . . . It has seemed to me repugnant to common sense that, if a mentally deficient parent or parents on the average, produces or produce similar children the state should allow them to continue to do so" (quoted in Jones, *Social Hygiene* 91).

131. "Eugenics for the Layman," *New York Call*, September 16, 1923: sec. 2, p. 9.

132. Some communities were in favor of mandatory sterilization. A 1937 *Fortune* magazine poll found that 63 percent of Americans endorsed the compulsory sterilization of habitual criminals and that 66 percent favored sterilizing mental defectives (Kevles, *In the Name of Eugenics* 114).

133. C. P. Blacker, ed., *A Social Problem Group?* (Oxford: Oxford University Press, 1937). See also Jones, *Social Hygiene* 89–90. Many of these were collected in E. J. Lidbetter, *Heredity and the Social Problem Group* (London: E. Arnold and Company, 1933).

134. For example, hard-liners still believed in the importance of planning for racial and economic progress by controlling the heredity of the "submerged tenth." In 1931, Blacker would write about the inherent dangers of having to deal with "four million persons (the 10 percent sub-cultural group) in England and Wales who are the purveyors of social inefficiency, prostitution, feeblemindedness and petty crime, the chief architects of slumdom, the most fertile strain in the community. Four million persons forming the dregs of the community and thriving upon it as the mycelium of some fungus thrives upon a healthy vigorous plant. It is difficult to conceive of a more sweeping or socially significant generalization" (Blacker to Penrose, October 1, 1931, quoted in Jones, *Social Hygiene* 95).

135. Jones, *Social Hygiene* 91.

136. At the same time, liberals warned doctors of the consequences of abusing sterilization (Jones, *Social Hygiene* 88–89). Jones notes that the medical profession may have feared lawsuits for damages and malpractice. She observes that in the 1930s, geneticists

like J. B. S. Haldane were attacking sterilization of women as dangerous. See Haldane, *Human Biology and Politics* (London: British Science Guild, 1935) 13. This was a lecture delivered November 28, 1934, at the Goldsmith Hall.

137. See L. S. Penrose, *Mental Defect* (London: Sidgwick and Jackson, 1933); L. S. Penrose, "Mental Deficiency—II. The Sub-Cultural Group," *Eugenics Review* 24 (1933): 289–91.

138. Jones, *Social Hygiene* 97.

139. Jones, *Social Hygiene* 107. Jones astutely notes that for "for all their rhetoric, not one policy promulgated by the Eugenics Society in the 1930s involved an extension of equal opportunity" (107).

Chapter 7: The Return of Eugenics: Ideographic Fragments and the Mythology of the Human Genome Project

1. Celeste Michelle Condit and John Louis Lucaites, *Crafting Equality: America's Anglo-African Word* (Chicago: University of Chicago Press, 1993) xii–xiii. Richard C. Lewontin, one of the most vocal social critics of genetic determinism, characterizes the problem of equality as the "central social agony of American political and social life" ("Women versus the Biologists," *New York Times Book Review*, April 7, 1994: 31–35, 31). Lewontin goes on to explain that the Enlightenment writers helped bring us both the claim for individual rights and the tool for legitimating inequality by making the individual "responsible for causing the unequal situation he or she occupies" (31).

For specific discussions of the relationship between the Human Genome Project and "equality," see Dan W. Brock, "The Human Genome Project and Human Identity," *Houston Law Review* 29 (1992): 7–22.

2. For one of the best discussions of the power of the rhetoric of eugenics in Germany, see Sheila Faith Weiss, *Race Hygiene and National Efficiency: The Eugenics of Wilhelm Schallmayer* (Berkeley: University of California Press, 1987) 157. New laws were passed that restricted marriages between Aryans and Jews, allowed the unfit to be sterilized, and authorized the extinction of those whose lives were medically defined as "not worth living." These "negative" forms of eugenics were supplemented with "positive" or pronatalist projects that encouraged reproduction among the "purer" races of northern Europe.

3. For an example of how some of these histories were being reconfigured, note how *Time* magazine interpreted the eugenics tale in 1940: "Many a sociologist and historian used to agree with Paleontologist Henry Fairfield Osborn that Anglo-Saxons were God's special gift to earth. Osborn was a leading eugenist in the days when many believed that the 'unfit' should be weeded out rather than cared for under public health measures which coddled weaklings, allowed them to reproduce, ultimately lead [*sic*] to an inferior stock. While these ideas have occasionally furnished fodder for opponents of public housing, relief, [and] the New Deal, the only places where they are still flourishing today are

Nazi Germany and Italy. Long before Henry Osborn died in 1935, a new generation was hard at work knocking them down" ("Eugenics for Democracy," *Time*, September 9, 1940: 34). See also Frederick Osborn, "Development of a Eugenic Philosophy," *American Sociological Review* 2 (1937): 389–97.

Yet in the process of "knocking" the old eugenics down, this younger generation of geneticists and other intellectuals filled the popular press and scientific journals with accounts of the arrival of the "new, environmental eugenics" ("Eugenics for Democracy" 34). On the West Coast, eugenicists like Popenoe and Gosney wrote incessantly about the modern eugenics that supported sterilization, while in the East people like Frederick Osborn were claiming that there was a vast difference between a democratic, voluntary eugenics and the "dangerous" compulsory sterilizations that were being advocated by the "older" eugenicists (34).

4. As Keller explains, after World War II, "there was no talk about human genetics. All discussions of genetics were cast in terms of basic science, and scientists were looking at organisms that are very far from humans" (Larry Casalino, "Decoding the Human Genome Project: An Interview with Evelyn Fox Keller," *Socialist Review* 21 [1991]: 111–28, 113).

5. Some eugenicists even began to attack the Nazi sterilization experiments in an effort to distance their field from the few "psychopaths" who had tragically misapplied scientific knowledge. See for example C. P. Blacker, "Eugenic Experiments Conducted by the Nazis on Human Subjects," *Eugenics Review* 44 (1952): 9–19. For a contrasting view of Nazi science, see David G. Horn, "Nazi Science as 'Normal' Science?" *Socialist Review* 19 (1989): 139–42.

By the late 1970s, these historical reconstructions of eugenics had been so successful that Lyndsay Farrall could claim that, "Today, eugenics tends to be dismissed as a pseudo-science or a species of Social Darwinism which received support from political reactionaries or racial bigots" (Lyndsay Farrall, "The History of Eugenics: A Bibliographical Review," *Annals of Science* 36 [1979]: 111–23, 111).

6. Kenneth Ludmerer, *Genetics and American Society* (Baltimore: Johns Hopkins University Press, 1972) 182. Some histories of the sciences have sought to give readers the impression that the "science" of genetics had little to do with the "pseudoscience" of eugenics. Donald Pickens, for example, would claim that "the eugenists were a small group, active in propaganda, who realized some legislative success but without any radical change in current behavior" (Donald K. Pickens, *Eugenics and the Progressives* [Nashville, Tenn.: Vanderbilt University Press, 1968] 215). Other writers, like Bentley Glass, wrote of how "social Darwinists" had used eugenics to "justify every aspect of ruthless industrial oppression and injustice" (Bentley Glass, "Eugenical Implications of the New Reproductive Technologies," *Social Biology* 19 [1972]: 326–35, 328). More recently, the much-acclaimed work of Daniel Kevles seems to ask readers to think of the social evils that took place in the early decades of this century as merely activities that were conducted in "the name" of eugenics (Daniel Kevles, *In the Name of Eugenics* [New York: Alfred A. Knopf, 1985]).

The University of Georgia Press

330 Research Drive   Athens, Georgia 30602-4901 USA

FOR MORE INFORMATION
Tom Payton / Publicity
TEL: 706-369-6160
FAX: 706-369-6131
E-mail: tpayton@uga.cc.uga.edu

A new volume in the
University of Georgia Humanities Center Sseries on Science

The Rhetoric of Eugenics in Anglo-American Thought

Marouf A. Hasian, Jr.

TITLE:
AUTHOR: Marouf A. Hasian, Jr.
ISBN: 0-8203-1771-3
PUBLICATION DATE: May 16, 1996
PRICE: $ 40.00 cloth

Pease send two tearsheets of any review

7. Operating from within an ideographic perspective, I agree with those writers who contend that the ideological expansion of molecular biology did not occur simply because of "internal" scientific advances. See Evelyn Fox Keller, "Nature, Nurture, and the Human Genome Project," in *The Code of Codes*, ed. Daniel J. Kevles and Leroy Hood, Cambridge: Harvard University Press, 1992, 291.

8. Other researchers would rather argue that genomics has come "out of eugenics." See Daniel J. Kevles, "Out of Eugenics: The Historical Politics of the Human Genome," in Kevles and Hood, *The Code of Codes* 3–36.

9. For an insightful introduction to some of the arguments advanced by sociobiologists, see Henry Howe and John Lyne, "Gene Talk in Sociobiology," *Epistemology* 6 (1992): 109–63.

10. Ruth Hubbard and Elijah Wald, *Exploding the Gene Myth* (Boston: Beacon Press, 1993) 9.

11. This use of genetics as a means of expanding our "choices" involves a new form of "geneticization." See Abby Lippman, "Prenatal Genetic Testing and Screening: Constructing Needs and Reinforcing Inequities," *American Journal of Law and Medicine* 17 (1991): 17–50.

Even defenders of the Human Genome Project see problems with some forms of geneticization. Thomas Murray, a former director of one of the task forces for the HGP, recently observed that, "Genetic determinism is one of these simpleminded errors that we were prone to commit when we thought genes linked to diseases in a kind of inevitable, ineluctable fashion" (quoted in John Rennie, "Grading the Gene Tests," *Scientific American* 270 [1994]: 88–97, 91).

12. Keller, "Nature, Nurture, and the Human Genome Project" 282.

13. For a basic introduction to the genome program that includes many statements by its participants, see Necia Grant Cooper, ed., *The Human Genome Project: Deciphering the Blueprint of Heredity* (Mill Valley, Calif.: University Science Books, 1994).

14. The phrase "from cradle to grave" is still used in discussions of genetic diagnostics. See Robert A. Weinberg, "The Dark Side of the Genome," *Technology Review* 94 (1991): 45–51, 48.

15. For a discussion of the relationship between the Human Genome Project and eugenics by the "back door," see Troy Duster, *Backdoor to Eugenics* (New York: Routledge, 1990) 125–29.

16. Alan Gross recently observed that science may be "progressively revealed not as the privileged route to certain knowledge, but as another intellectual enterprise, an activity that takes its place beside, but not above, philosophy, literary criticism, history, and rhetoric itself." Alan Gross, *The Rhetoric of Science* (Cambridge: Harvard University Press, 1990) 3.

17. Charles Taylor, "Defining the Scientific Community: A Rhetorical Perspective on Demarcation," *Communication Monographs* 58 (1991): 402–20, 416.

18. The list of genetic diseases or social conditions that are said to be a part of the province of genomics grows daily, apparently limited only by the human imagination.

As Nelkin complains, this "language of biological determinism" allows researchers to claim that genes are responsible for "obesity, criminality, shyness, intelligence, political leanings, and even preferred styles of dressing—as if complex attributes are transmitted like brown hair or blue eyes" (Dorothy Nelkin, "The Grandiose Claims of Geneticists," *Chronicle of Higher Education,* March 3, 1993: B1–B2, B2).

One critic of this excessive determinism charges that "the recent molecular genetic searches for genes related to such conditions as manic depressive illness, schizophrenia, and alcoholism have suffered from much of the same hastiness and overconfidence that characterized the behavior genetics of the eugenics era" (Jon Beckwith, "A Historical View of Social Responsibility in Genetics," *BioScience* 43 (1993): 327–33, 331).

19. James D. Watson, "The Human Genome Project: Past, Present, and Future," *Science* 248 (1990): 44–48. An entire genre has developed, made up of books and articles that celebrate the arrival of the new science of genomics. For example, see Robert Teitelman, *Gene Dreams: Wall Street, Academia, and the Rise of Biotechnology* (New York: Basic Books, 1989); Joel Davis, *Mapping the Code* (New York: Wiley, 1991); Lois Wingerson, *Mapping Our Genes* (New York: Dutton/Penguin, 1990); Thomas F. Lee, *The Human Genome Project* (New York: Plenum, 1991); Necia Grant Cooper, *The Human Genome Project.*

For an insightful discussion of the role the press plays in pushing genetic products, see Rae Goodell, "The Gene Craze," *Columbia Journalism Review* 4 (1980): 41–45.

20. Keller, "Nature, Nurture, and the Human Genome Project" 281. These "new" eugenical arguments are not being promoted simply by an ignorant public that misunderstands science or a journalistic corps interested in sensational news stories: they can be found within research reports, peer reviews, and governmental assessments.

21. James D. Watson, "First Word," *Omni,* June 1990: 6.

22. James D. Watson, "Looking Forward," *Gene* 135 (1993): 309–15, 313. Scientists interested in legitimizing their research programs have painted an idyllic world that would have made Laughlin and the eugenicists green with envy. Progress is no longer discussed in terms of germplasm; those old, simplistic genetic theories pale by comparison with the promise of the human genome.

23. Jerry E. Bishop and Michael Waldholz, *Genome* (New York: Simon and Schuster, 1990) 21.

24. Bishop and Waldholz, quoted in Jack Kirwan, "Touring the Helix," *National Review,* August 6, 1990: 42–43, 43. Apparently in some nations there are political parties and communities that think it can be stopped. See "Fear of Neo-Eugenics Hits Europe," *New Scientist* 121 (1989): 23.

25. Al Gore, "Human Genome Initiative and the Future of Biotechnology," *Hearings before the Subcommittee on Science, Technology, and Space,* Committee on Commerce, Science and Transportation, U.S. Senate, 100th Congress, First Session, November 9, 1989, 1.

26. Nelkin, "The Grandiose Claims" B1.

27. This move toward expanding "choice" did not begin in the 1980s. For example, Frederick Osborn, writing in January 1939, asked his readers to accept a new eugenical program that "would call for two changes in present conditions, one set of changes directed toward greater freedom in *choice* of parenthood, the other set of changes directed to a larger number of measures which would make for larger families among competent individuals and a society more aware of eugenic needs. . . . Coercive measures could not be applied in the attempt to equalize freedom of parenthood. Nor would the reorientation of educational and emotional influences necessary for the new eugenic motivation result in any arbitrary control over births. . . . Eugenic efforts would be directed to the creation of environmental conditions under which parents would tend to have children in proportion to their mental and physical health, their interest in children, their ability to care for them, and their sense of the contribution they would thus be making to society. It need hardly be pointed out that such a philosophy of eugenics is more appropriate to a democratic than to a totalitarian state." "Social Implications of the Eugenic Program," *Child Study* 16 (1939): 95–97, 96.

28. Nelkin, "The Grandiose Claims" B2.

29. The phrase "proceed with caution" comes from one of the most respected discussions of the promises and perils of modern genetics: Neil A. Holtzman, *Proceed with Caution: Predicting Genetic Risks in the Recombinant DNA Era* (Baltimore: Johns Hopkins University Press, 1989).

30. While Watson was head of the HGP, 3 percent of the entire budget was set aside for studies meant to anticipate ethical, legal, or social problems with the project. Bernard D. Davis thinks setting aside this money was both admirable and "politically shrewd" ("Fervors, Fears, and Manageable Realities," *Science* 257 (1992): 981–82, 982).

31. For example, in late 1989 Koshland argued that those scientists who were questioning the wisdom of the genome project were members of the "sky is falling" group, who stood in the way of "sequencing the human genome" (Daniel E. Koshland, Jr., "Sequences and Consequences of the Human Genome," *Science*, October 13, 1989: 189. See also Bishop and Waldholz, *Genome* 305.

32. In the scientific literature, two groups of people are usually labeled as extremists because of their accusations that scientists are "playing God"—religious leaders and critics like Jeremy Rifkin. The strategic containment of dissent within the scientific and public communities shifts our gaze away from many substantive concerns about the program. Evelyn Fox Keller, "Genetics, Reductionism and the Normative Uses of Biological Information: Responses to Kevles," *Southern California Law Review* 65 (1991): 285–91, 286.

33. For example, see Watson, "First Word" 6.

34. See Kevles, *In the Name of Eugenics*. Bishop and Waldholz similarly argue that the public need not be concerned with any dictatorial government reviving the Nazi eugenics program to produce a superior race (*Genome* 314).

35. Watson, "First Word" 6.

36. François Gros, for example, argues that as "long as this knowledge remains in the hands of experts in the subject we don't need to be afraid" ("The Human Genome and the Responsibility of Scientists: Interview with François Gros," *Impact of Science on Society* 161 [1991]: 5–13, 8). Contrast this leap of faith with the accusations of Luria, who charged in 1989 that the Genome Project was being "promoted without public discussion by a small coterie of power-seeking enthusiasts" (Salvadore Luria, "Letters to the Editor: Human Genome Program," *Science* 246 (1989): 873).

37. Furthermore, any nation that fails to participate fully in all HGP activities because of speculative eugenical fears is accused of being behind the times.

38. One of the most vocal critics of the Genome Project, Richard Lewontin, argues that there has been little if any real skepticism coming from proponents of the project. See Richard C. Lewontin, *Biology as Ideology: The Doctrine of DNA* (New York: Harper-Perennial, 1993).

As Keller explains, the rhetorical strategy of narrowly defining eugenics as a means of coercion or repression opens up a space for activities like gene therapy. This hides the definitional processes that are being deployed in articles on the genome that assume fixed meanings for ambiguous terms like "choice," "disease," and "normality" (Keller, "Nature, Nurture, and the Human Genome Project").

39. Robert L. Sinsheimer, "The Prospect of Designed Genetic Change," in *Heredity and Society*, ed. Adela S. Baer (New York: Macmillan, 1977) 436–43, 442.

40. Sinsheimer, "The Prospect of Designed Genetic Change" 442. This focus on providing everyone with the benefits of genetics harkens back to arguments that were used by the reform eugenicists who attacked hard-liners for focusing on the reproductive habits of "defectives" while leaving "normal" people alone (Ruth Hubbard, "Eugenics: New Tools, Old Ideas," *Women and Health* 13 [1988]: 225–35, 227).

Since the "discovery" of the double-helix structure of DNA in the 1950s by Watson and Crick, researchers in these modern tales have sought ways to predict who among the normal people might be carriers of "defects" so as to prevent them too from having children (Hubbard, "Eugenics: New Tools" 227).

41. For an excellent introduction to ways in which eugenical arguments influence our views of "normality," see Ruth Hubbard, Elijah Wald, and Nicholas Hildyard, "The Eugenics of Normalcy: The Politics of Gene Research," *The Ecologist* 23 (1993): 185–91.

Some critics even argue that the "facts" that go into these symbolic constructs are partially created. As Richard Lewontin argues, "facts in science do not present themselves in a preexistent shape. Rather it is the experimental or observational protocol that constructs facts out of an undifferentiated nature. And if we do not like what we see, we can rearrange the description of nature to have a more pleasing aspect." Richard C. Lewontin, "Facts and the Factitious in the Natural Sciences," *Critical Inquiry* 18 (1991): 140–53, 147.

42. Just what constitutes a "disease" is both a scientific and social construct. See I. K. Zola, "In the Name of Health and Illness: On Some Socio-Political Consequences of

Medical Influence," *Social Science and Medicine* 9 (1975): 83–87. As Rennie recently lamented, the "truth is that the rules for what constitutes a genetic disease are not clear-cut. If researchers someday find a gene that confers a 60 percent predisposition for gross obesity, is that a genetic defect? What about a gene that gives a 25 percent disposition for cardiovascular disease at age 55? Or—moving into an even more ambiguous area—a gene that predisposes to anti-social behavior?" (Rennie, "Grading the Gene Tests" 91).

43. Nelkin recently noted that the children's book *Cells Are Us* was published by one of the key genome institutes, the Cold Spring Harbor Laboratory ("The Grandiose Claims" B1).

The definition of a field of inquiry as respectable science also depends on the next generation, and the proponents of the program have not neglected the power of public education. In early 1994, enthusiasts for the project reported that all fifty-five thousand high school science teachers in the United States would be offered the opportunity to use a "module" explaining the goals and ethics of the HGP (Cooper, *The Human Genome Project* 313).

44. See Michel Foucault, *The Birth of the Clinic* (New York: Vintage Books, 1973). One commentator, Howard Stein, recently argued that the Human Genome Project operates within a cultural milieu that allows a diagnosis to serve as a means of defining abnormality and also confirms that the "diagnostician is not ill" ("Human Genome as Metaphor" *Journal of Family Practice* 35 (1992): 256–58, 257).

45. For example, Billings notes that families afflicted with PKU are said to be "noncompliant" simply because they cannot afford expensive diets (Paul R. Billings, "The Context of Genetic Screening," *Yale Journal of Biology and Medicine* 64 [1991]: 47–52).

46. See "Chromosome Cartography," *Wall Street Journal*, March 16, 1989: 16. This has been a common historical strategy in eugenical argumentation. In the 1920s and 1930s, when institutional inmates or their relatives objected to sterilization in states like California or Virginia, their resistance was taken as proof that they had little understanding of the importance of eugenics.

47. For an interesting discussion of Watson's historical role as advocate, note the essay by Robert Wright, "Achilles' Helix," *The New Republic*, July 9 and 16, 1990: 21–31.

48. For a revealing example of Watson's interpretation of eugenics, see Watson, "First Word" 6.

49. Watson, "Looking Forward" 314.

50. Watson, "Looking Forward" 314.

51. Watson's comments have been circulated in the major scientific journals. Nicholas Short, a biology editor for *Nature* magazine in England, reported that Watson once warned that it would be an "act of true moral cowardice to allow children to be born with known genetic defects." "Forty Years of Molecular Information," *Nature* 362 (1993): 783–84, 784.

52. Watson, "Looking Forward" 315. Watson often identifies himself with Franklin Roosevelt in his speeches and articles. In 1992, in a chapter in *The Code of Codes*, Watson

characterized himself as a "concerned parent" trying to enlist the support of people who would "help us get these genes" (168). Appropriating fragments from a well-known address, he stated that "Deep down, I think that the only thing that could stop our program is fear; if people are afraid of the information we will find, they will keep us from finding it. We have to convince our fellow citizens somehow that there will be more advantages to knowing the human genome than to not knowing it" ("A Personal View of the Project," in Kevles and Hood, *The Code of Codes* 173).

Ironically, many of these claims directly contradict views that Watson himself espoused more than two decades earlier. In 1971 Watson warned that the "new ways of human reproduction" had potential consequences that needed to be investigated. He went on to argue that "This is a matter far too important to be left solely in the hands of the scientific and medical communities. The belief that surrogate mothers and clonal babies are inevitable because science always moves forward, an attitude expressed to me recently by a scientific colleague, represents a form of laissez-faire nonsense . . . if we do not think about it now, the possibility of our having a free choice will one day suddenly be gone" (James D. Watson, "Moving toward the Clonal Man," *Atlantic Monthly* (May 1971): 50–53, 53.

53. Other HGP participants share Watson's belief in the importance of genetics. Robert Sinsheimer once claimed that the DNA sequence "defines a human being," while Paul Berg told one conference that many "if not most human diseases are clearly the result of inherited mutations" (quoted in Beckwith, "A Historical View of Social Responsibility in Genetics," 330).

54. This right choice can have both qualitative and quantitative dimensions. Francis Crick provided an inkling of the concerns of some researchers when he suggested that "All the worries about genetic engineering pale in significance with the question of what you are going to do about there being so many people in the world and the rate at which they increase" (quoted in Leon Jaroff, "Happy Birthday, Double Helix," *Time*, March 15, 1993: 56–59, 59).

55. In 1992, the director of the HGP admitted that "hate letters have made the rounds, including the rounds of Congress, contending that the project is 'bad science'—not only bad, but sort of wicked. The letters say that the project is wasting money at a time when resources for research are greatly threatened. . . . In 1990, someone in my office tried to get a distinguished biologist to help peer-review a big grant application. The biologist said: 'No, not the human genome!' as though he were talking about syphilis" (James D. Watson, "A Personal View of the Project," in Kevles and Hood, *The Code of Codes* 165. Two years later David Cox could still remark that from a "psychological point of view the Project has led to a terrified scientific community" (Cooper, *The Human Genome Project* 82).

This oppositional rhetoric occupies a large number of positions, ranging from concerns that the project will do very little to critiques that it will do too much. The mildest criticisms of the HGP come from critics who simply believe that the project will be ineffectual. Ayala, for example, remarked in 1987 that "The complete nucleotide sequence of the human genome might be helpful to biologists and health scientists as a data base for experiments. But I do not believe that it would contribute any more toward solving major biological or health problems than a computer printout of all the roads in the United States and of all the cars traveling over them in a particular year would help to ascertain the significant causes of highway accidents. The expenditures and human resources required for sequencing the human genome within the next decade or two would amount to a large fraction of those committed to all biological research" (Francisco J. Ayala, "Two Frontiers of Human Biology: What the Sequence Won't Tell Us," *Issues in Science and Technology* 3 [1987]: 51–56, 56).

For an insightful discussion of the many scientific controversies that are involved in the HGP program and a similar evaluation of the program, see Alfred Tauber and Sahotra Sarkar, "The Human Genome Project: Has Blind Reductionism Gone Too Far?" *Perspectives in Biology and Medicine* 35 (1992): 220–35.

56. Other commentators, like Benno Muller-Hill, remind us that many of these genetic conditions are "extremely rare" ("The Shadow of Genetic Injustice," *Nature* 362 [1993]: 491). Contrast this with the claims of Alice Wexler, "Our Genes, Ourselves," *The Nation*, February 4, 1991: 133–36.

57. Abby Lippman, "Led (Astray) by Genetic Maps: The Cartography of the Human Genome and Health Care," *Social Science and Medicine* 35 (1992): 1469–76, 1469.

58. Dorothy Nelkin, "The Social Power of Genetic Information," in Kevles and Hood, *The Code of Codes* 188.

59. Kenneth Garver and Bettylee Garver worry that history shows us how "In the past . . . rather innocuous medical practices or public policies have been distorted or applied as negative eugenics abrogating the rights and privacy of millions of individuals. It is painful to realize how some of our accepted practices today (e.g. prenatal diagnosis and MSAFP/HcG screening) can be considered as negative eugenics. . . . In the future . . . individual patients might lose, in many instances, their right to make a decision" ("Eugenics: Past, Present, and the Future," *American Journal of Human Genetics* 49 [1991]: 1109–18, 1115).

60. Lippman, "Led (Astray)" 1473. Many of these arguments have been heavily influenced by the language of economic liberalism, which prioritizes private rights and personal autonomy.

61. Other complaints include the argument that the project is a costly waste of precious research funds. Martin Rechsteiner, "The Folly of the Human Genome Project," *New Scientist* 127 (1990): 20.

62. Nelkin, "The Grandiose Claims" B1.

63. This is not to say that there are no disorders that have genetic components—cystic fibrosis, Duchenne muscular dystrophy, myotonic dystrophy, and Huntington's disease are examples of ones that do. Kenneth Garver and Bettylee Garver, "The Human Genome Project and Eugenic Concerns," *American Journal of Human Genetics* 54 (1994):

148–58, 148. Critics argue that while these disorders may have simple genetic components, other traits and behaviors are more complex.

64. See Sam N. Lehman-Wilzig, "Frankenstein Unbound: Towards a Legal Definition
of Artificial Intelligence," *Futures*, December 1981: 442–57, 442.

65. See Willard Gaylin, "The Frankenstein Factor," *New England Journal of Medicine*
297 (September 22, 1977): 665–67.

66. Bishop and Waldholz, *Genome* 305.

67. Ari Berkowitz, "Letters," *Science* 246 (1989): 874. For a contrasting perspective,
note the remarks of Koshland: "The argument that dictators would alter genes to convert
their enemies is farfetched. The idea that a Hitler or a Stalin would prefer the engineering of Jews into Aryans or capitalists into communists as cheaper or more satisfying than
killing them (as they did) is absurd. We must be vigilant about ethical concerns but not
paralyzed by outlandish scenarios" (Koshland, "Sequences and Consequences" 189).

68. Kirwan, "Touring the Helix" 42–43.

69. The term "underclass" was perhaps introduced into the literature with the publication of Dorothy Nelkin and Laurence Tancredi's *Dangerous Diagnostics: The Social Power
of Genetic Information* (New York: Basic Books, 1989). This terminology has reached the
halls of Congress. In 1991, Congressman Bob Wise of West Virginia told a House subcommittee of the dangers of creating a "new genetic underclass." See Daniel J. Kevles,
"Social and Ethical Issues in the Human Genome Project," *National Forum* 73 (1993):
18–21, 21.

70. George J. Annas, "Who's Afraid of the Human Genome," *Hastings Center Report*
19 (1989): 19–21, 20. One molecular biologist, Robert Weinberg, told the authors of *Genome* that modern society runs on "the premise that everyone has a biologically equal
chance to be anything he or she wants. But what will happen when, in fact, the scientists
find strong evidence that everyone's fate is greatly affected by the inheritance of a group
of very specific and identifiable genes?" (Kirwan, "Touring the Helix" 43).

71. Koshland, "Sequences and Consequences" 189. For a similar discussion of the
link between genetics and social problems, see U.S. Congress, Office of Technology Assessment, *Mapping Our Genes* (Washington D.C.: Government Printing Office, 1988) 84.
Compare Koshland's statement with the views of Chicago municipal judge Harry Olson,
who commented more than half a century ago that "The enormous burden, economic,
social, and moral, of the defective insane, criminalistic, anti-social and underbred individuals who crowd our courts, jails, penitentiaries, alms houses and insane asylums, who
clog industry and worry relatives, annoy neighbors and work havoc generally in society,
is at last being felt by the general public" (Harry Olsen [Olson], "Check on Society's
Defectives Seen as Urgent Need of Nation," *New York Times*, September 2, 1923: sec. 7,
p. 7).

72. Watson, for example, claims that many "personal tragedies" having to do with alcoholism in families "would not exist" if some generations paid attention to their "choice
in mates" ("Looking Forward" 314).

73. Office of Technology Assessment, *Mapping Our Genes* 84. For a discussion of the importance of this report in legitimating the project, see Keller, "Nature, Nurture, and the Human Genome Project" 281.

Many of these discussions about mating and abortion stem from the fact that so far very little identification of any diseases has resulted, and no cures are yet available. As Leon Jaroff notes, this means that there is "little action the recipient can take, except to avoid having children who might inherit the gene" ("Happy Birthday" 57).

74. Office of Technology Assessment, *Mapping Our Genes,* quoted in Annas, "Who's Afraid of the Human Genome?" 20.

75. Koshland, "Sequences and Consequences" 189. See also "The Genome Project: Pro and Con," *Science* 247 (1990): 270. Koshland's remark about the poor has been one of the most controversial statements ever made in debates over the HGP. Salvador Luria once suggested that Koshland's editorial "hints of a eugenic program" targeted at the poor and the infirm ("Human Genome Program" 873). Several years later, Keller warned that Koshland's arguments leave out the "importance of social, psychological, or political training" (Keller, "Nature, Nurture, and the Human Genome Project" 282). In all fairness, Koshland has elsewhere called for greater assistance for the poor, and he has argued that not all of the homeless are mentally ill. But as Keller points out, just how the "poor, the infirm, and the underprivileged" will be helped out by the HGP is not explained ("Nature, Nurture, and the Human Genome Project" 282). Elsewhere, Beckwith quotes Koshland as saying that the "homeless problem is tractable. One third of homeless are mentally ill—some say 50%. These are the ones who will most benefit from the Genome Project" ("A Historical View" 330).

76. For example, Nancy Wexler argued in 1989 that "For the first time in history, the time is ripe for making major inroads on diseases that wreak havoc not only on one generation but on each subsequent generation. . . . Once we have the capacity to move ahead, however, if we choose not to, we are consigning some people to certain death as actively as if we were to withhold antibiotics or oxygen. The road is before us; we no longer have the excuse that there is nothing to be done" ("The Oracle of DNA," in *Molecular Genetics in Diseases of Brain, Nerve, and Muscle,* ed. Lewis P. Rowland et al. (New York: Oxford University Press, 1989) 440.

77. "Thinking the Unthinkable," *New Scientist* 140 (1993): 3.

78. "Thinking the Unthinkable" 3.

79. Bishop and Waldholz, *Genome* 20.

80. Bishop and Waldholz, *Genome* 267–68.

81. Bishop and Waldholz, *Genome* 321.

82. This does not mean that the new forms of eugenics have totally ignored all of the dangers that come from mixing the "races." Hacker, for example, recently remarked that "In the past, this quest was called 'eugenics' and it had practical as well as scholarly aims. For it hoped to warn people of supposedly superior strains that they should not mate with their genetic inferiors. The fear was of 'mongrelization,' a phrase then commonly used,

wherein the best human breeds would marry down and produce lesser heirs. Today, such sentiments are seldom stated in so direct a way. Rather than counseling against intermarriage, it will be hinted that even social racial mixing can have deleterious effects" (quoted in Garver and Garver, "The Human Genome Project" 152).

83. See Patricia A. King, "The Past as Prologue: Race, Class, and Gene Discrimination," in George Annas and Sherman Elias, eds., *Gene Mapping: Using Law and Ethics as Guides* (New York: Oxford University Press, 1992) 94–111.

84. As Dorothy Nelkin recently explained, the "earlier forms of eugenics are not likely to be duplicated — they reflected specific historical situations" ("Genetic Warnings," *Wilson Quarterly* [1992]: 156). But the "increased visibility of racism coincides with the popular interest in scientific innovations," and the "gene" will be used to "account for an extraordinary range of traits" that are assumed to be "hard-wired" and controlling (156).

85. A typical modern discussion of the link between criminal behavior and "certain alleles" can be found in Christopher Wills, *Exxons, Introns, and Talking Genes: The Science behind the Human Genome Project* (New York: Basic Books, 1991) 311.

86. Some of these controversies begin when grants are obtained to study both the pros and cons of programs like the violence initiative. For an overview of arguments being advanced on both sides of the issue, see John Horgan, "Genes and Crime," *Scientific American* 268 (1993): 24–29. Many officials deny that any "violence initiative" was ever planned in detail, and they deny that it was targeted against blacks in urban communities. See also John Lyne, "Arguing Genes: From *Jurassic Park* to Baby Jessica," in Raymie E. McKerrow, ed., *Argument and the Postmodern Challenge: Proceedings of the Eighth SCA/AFA Conference on Argumentation* (Annandale, Va.: Speech Communication Association, 1993) 437–42.

87. Spencer Rich, "Federal Health Official Resigns, Citing Controversy over Remarks," *Washington Post*, February 28, 1992: A4.

88. Karen Schneider, "Study to Quell Violence Is Racist, Critics Charge," *Detroit Free Press*, November 2, 1992: A1, A11.

89. Goodwin has had his defenders. An editorial in the *Washington Post* in March 1992 noted that while the federal government's top psychiatrist might have been imprudent in some of his remarks, his scientific approaches were considered to be beyond reproach. The editorial claimed that Goodwin was taking "flak for being a biological psychiatrist, though his supporters defend him as balanced in his approach to psychosocial research" ("The Fred Goodwin Case," *Washington Post*, March 21, 1992: A22.

90. Rich, "Federal Health Official Resigns" A4.

91. Dan Charles, "Genetics Meeting Halted amid Racism Charges," *New Scientist* 135 (1992): 4. See also "Criminal Error," *New Scientist* 135 (1992): 3.

92. Charles, "Genetics Meeting Halted" 4. Note also Peter Breggin's comments in "U.S. Hasn't Given Up Linking Genes to Crime," *New York Times*, September 18, 1992: A34; Fox Butterfield, "Dispute Threatens U.S. Plan on Violence," *New York Times*, October 23, 1992: A12; Richard Stone, "Violence Research: NRC Panel Provides a Blueprint,"

Science 258 (1992): 1298; Eliot Marshall, "NIH Told to Reconsider Crime Meeting," *Science* 262 (October 1, 1993): 23–24; Peter Breggin, "Genetics and Crime," *Science* 262 (December 3, 1993): 1498. For discussions of this issue in Europe, see Michael Simms, "Violence Study Hits a Nerve in Germany," *Science* 264 (1994): 653; Steven Rose, "Wishful Thinking," *New Scientist* 141 (March 19, 1994): 52.

93. The debate has not ended. The conference was rescheduled. For detailed explanations, see Jane Ellen Stevens, "The Biology of Violence," *BioScience* 44 (1994): 291–94. Nor is the controversy confined to the scientific community. See Anastasia Toufexis, "Seeking the Roots of Violence," *Time*, April 19, 1993: 52.

94. "Criminal Error" 3.

95. Nelkin worries that if society begins to believe that some people have "criminal genes," this could sanction the use of tests to predict dangerousness, overriding issues of justice or fairness (Nelkin, "The Grandiose Claims" B2).

There are hints that the Genome Project is also contributing to the rich-poor gap between nations. Some critics worry that patenting the products of human genome research will bring new, legally sanctioned forms of neocolonialism (Michael Kirby, "Legal Problems: Human Genome Project," *Australian Law Journal* 67 (1993) 894–903, 901).

96. Nelkin, "The Grandiose Claims" B2.

97. Sexual genetic discrimination has a long history. See Germaine Greer, *Sex and Destiny: The Politics of Human Fertility* (New York: Harper and Row, 1984); Ann Fausto-Sterling, *Myths of Gender: Biological Theories about Women and Men* (New York: Basic Books, 1985); Evelyn Fox Keller, *Secrets of Life, Secrets of Death: Essays on Language, Gender and Science* (New York: Routledge, 1992).

98. Nelkin, "The Grandiose Claims" B2. Weinberg predicts that soon "the birth of a cystic fibrosis child will, in the minds of many, reflect more the negligence of parents than God's will or the whims of nature" ("The Dark Side of the Genome" 48).

99. Feminists argue that part of the problem with the discourse on prenatal diagnosis is that the expertise in the field comes predominantly from white males who have trouble dealing with the "multicultural voices of the women and their families who use, or might use, the new technology." Rayna Rapp, "Moral Pioneers: Women, Men, and Fetuses on a Frontier of Reproductive Technology," *Women and Society* 13 (1988): 101–16, 105. See also Ruth Hubbard, "Science, Facts, and Feminism," *Hypatia* 3 (1988): 5–17.

100. Nelkin, "The Grandiose Claims" B2.

101. Ruth Hubbard, "Eugenics: New Tools" 232. For a contrary view of prenatal diagnosis, see J. M. Friedman, "Eugenics and the 'New Genetics,'" *Perspectives in Biology and Medicine* 35 (1991): 145–54, 149.

102. Rennie, "Grading the Gene Tests" 90. The advances have come so frequently that the Office of Technology Assessment estimates that the number of genetic tests will increase tenfold over the next decade (90). This situation becomes even more complicated when we take into account the commercial pressures involved. In April 1994, an

American university announced that it would try to patent a technique that would allow a father to pass on only "healthy" genes to his descendants. Andy Coghlan, "Outrage Greets Patent on Designer Sperm," *New Scientist*, April 9, 1994: 4.

103. An excellent overview of the scientific and public arguments used in this debate can be found in William Byne, "The Biological Evidence Challenged," *Scientific American* 270 (1994): 50–55. See also Lyne, "Arguing Genes" 440. Lyne worries about the dangers of framing the issue as a contest between "genes" and "choice."

Note that few researchers suggest that finding the genes "for" homosexuality would allow people to *choose* this particular lifestyle.

104. Hubbard and Wald, *Exploding the Gene Myth* 98. Compare Chandler Burr, "Genes and Hormones," *New York Times*, August 2, 1993: A15.

105. Lord Jakobovits, former chief rabbi of the United Hebrew Congregation of the British Commonwealth, quoted in Kirby, "Legal Problems: Human Genome Project," 898. Some members of the Union of Jewish Students of the United Kingdom answered this call by arguing, "As Jews, we find the idea of using genetic engineering to eliminate homosexuality an affront to human rights and dignity. It is disturbing to find fellow Jews advocating something akin to that practiced against our people by the Third Reich" (Kirby, "Legal Problems" 898).

For similar responses, see how even researchers worry about the use of "gay gene" tests. Dean Hamer, considered to be one of the leading researchers in the area, contends that this form of testing would be "wrong, unethical, and an abuse of the research" (quoted in Bob Holmes, "Gay Gene Test 'Inaccurate and Immoral,' " *New Scientist*, March 5, 1994). As Kirby astutely comments, this is just a "warning of the controversies that lie ahead" ("Legal Problems" 898).

106. For discussions of the history of the abuse of this type of information, see Ruth Hubbard, "The Search for Sexual Identity: False Genetic Markers," *New York Times*, August 2, 1993: A15; Jorg Hutter, "The Social Construction of Homosexuals in the Nineteenth Century: The Shift from the Sin to the Influence of Medicine on Criminalizing Sodomy in Germany," *Journal of Homosexuality* 24 (1993): 73–93.

107. Judith Swazey contends that the Genome Project has fused together reductionism and a "secular utopianism" ("Those Who Forget Their History: Lessons from the Recent Past for the Human Genome Quest," in Annas and Elias, *Gene Mapping* 47).

108. Robert N. Proctor, "Genomics and Eugenics: How Fair Is the Comparison?" in Annas and Elias, *Gene Mapping* 57–93.

109. For a good overview of some of the legal issues involved, see Rochelle Cooper Dreyfuss and Dorothy Nelkin, "The Jurisprudence of Genetics," *Vanderbilt Law Review* 45 (1992): 313–48.

110. "Preventing 'Inferior' People in China," *New York Times*, December 27, 1993: A16. Since that time, Chinese officials have changed the name of their eugenic law, calling it the "Natal and Health Care Law" rather than the "Eugenics and Health Protection

Act" (Lincoln Kaye, "Quality Control: Eugenics Bill Defended against Western Critics," *Far East Economic Review* 157 [1994]: 22).

111. As the American Council on Life Insurance warned, genetic testing brings with it issues of profound ethical importance, including concerns about the practice of medicine, procreation, employment, privacy, individual vs. societal rights, confidentiality, the right to know, and the right not to know (Kirwan, "Touring the Helix" 43).

On the other hand, the success of the Human Genome Project and screening for diseases may "ease the way to national health insurance and a national health plan" (John C. Fletcher and Dorothy Wertz, "Ethics, Law, and Medical Genetics: After the Human Genome is Mapped," *Emory Law Journal* 39 [1990]: 747–91, 757).

112. Even if we believe in a distinction between use and abuse of science or technology, as scholars we still have some obligations. As L. C. Dunn once remarked, "the social and political misuse to which genetics applied to man is peculiarly subject is influenced not only by those who support such misuse, but also by those who fail to point out, as teachers, the distinctions between true and false science" (quoted in Ludmerer, *Genetics and American Society* 181).

Appendix: Terms of Art in Rhetorical Analyses

1. The above paragraph is my synthesis of some of McGee's work.

2. Michael C. McGee and Martha Ann Martin, "Public Knowledge and Ideological Argumentation," *Communication Monographs* 50 (1983): 47–65, 47. For an example of the rhetorical construction of the people, see Maurice Charland, "Constitutive Rhetoric: The Case of the *Peuple Québécois*," *Quarterly Journal of Speech* 73 (1987): 133–50; Michael C. McGee, "In Search of 'The People': A Rhetorical Alternative," *Quarterly Journal of Speech* 61 (October 1975): 239.

3. McGee, "The Ideograph" 6.

4. Discourse helps create that culture.

5. John Louis Lucaites, "Flexibility and Consistency in Eighteenth-Century Anglo-Whiggism: A Case Study of the Rhetorical Dimensions of Legitimacy" (Ph.D. diss., University of Iowa, 1984) 20.

6. For discussions of the role of narrative, see Walter R. Fisher, "Clarifying the Narrative Paradigm," *Communication Monographs* 56 (1989): 55–58; Celeste M. Condit, "Crafting Virtue: The Rhetorical Construction of Public Morality," *Quarterly Journal of Speech* 73 (1987): 79–97.

7. Celeste M. Condit, "Democracy and Civil Rights: The Universalizing Influence of Public Argumentation," *Communication Monographs* 54 (1987): 1–18, 4.

8. Walter R. Fisher, "Reaffirmation and Subversion of the American Dream," *Quarterly Journal of Speech* 59 (1973): 160–67.

9. Condit, "Democracy and Civil Rights" 4.

10. See Condit, "Democracy and Civil Rights" 4.

11. Condit, "Democracy and Civil Rights" 4.

12. William Lewis, "Telling America's Story: Narrative Form and the Reagan Presidency," *Quarterly Journal of Speech* 73 (1987): 280–302, 282. Lewis is quoting René Wellek and Austin Warren, *Theory of Literature* (New York: Brace and World, 1956) 119.

13. Robert C. Rowland, "On Mythic Criticism," *Communication Studies* 41 (1990): 101–16, 106. I should note here that I have a more expansive view of myth than Rowland has.

14. See V. William Balthrop, "Culture, Myth, and Ideology as Public Argument: An Interpretation of the Ascent and Demise of 'Southern Culture,'" *Communication Monographs* 51 (December 1984): 339–52.

15. John L. Lucaites and Celeste M. Condit, "Reconstructing <Equality>: Culturetypal and Counter-Cultural Rhetorics," *Communication Monographs* 57 (1990): 5–24, 6. Unlike Lucaites and Condit, I see culturetypes as nonradical in nature and use.

16. These ideographs even influence the relationship between law and public narratives.

17. Walter R. Fisher, *Human Communication as Narration: Toward a Philosophy of Reason, Value and Action* (Columbia, S.C.: University of South Carolina Press, 1989) xiii.

18. Audiences may or may not accept these suggestions.

19. Michael Osborn, "Rhetorical Depiction," in *Form, Genre, and the Study of Political Discourse,* ed. Herbert W. Simons and Aram A. Aghazarian (Columbia, S.C.: University of South Carolina Press, 1986) 82.

20. Lucaites and Condit, "Reconstructing" 6.

21. Lucaites and Condit, "Reconstructing" 6.

22. For an example of the use of oppositional rhetoric, see John L. Lucaites, "Burke's Speech on Conciliation as Oppositional Discourse," in *Texts in Context,* ed. Michael C. Leff and Fred J. Kauffeld (Davis, Calif.: Hermagoras Press, 1989) 81–89.

Bibliography

Journal Articles

Adams, Samuel Hopkins. "Science Has Its Say about Alcohol." *Collier's* 71 (1923): 6.

"Alcoholism and Degeneration." *Current Literature* 38 (1905): 361.

Alec-Tweedie, Ethel. "Eugenics." *Fortnightly Review* 97 (1912): 854–65.

Allen, Garland E. "Genetics, Eugenics, and Class Struggle." *Genetics* 79 (1975): 29–45.

Allen, Grant. "Plain Words on the Woman Question." *Fortnightly Review* 52 (1889): 448–58.

Alonso, Ana Maria. "The Effects of Truth: Re-Presentations of the Past and the Imagining of Community." *Journal of Historical Sociology* 1 (March 1988): 33–57.

Altimore, Michael. "The Social Construction of a Scientific Controversy: Comments on Press Coverage of the Recombinant DNA Debate." *Science, Technology, and Human Values* 7 (1982): 24–31.

Annas, George J. "Who's Afraid of the Human Genome?" *Hastings Center Report* 19 (1989): 19–21.

Aronoff, Jacob B. "The Constitutionality of Asexualization Legislation in the United States." *St. Johns Law Review* 1 (1927): 146–74.

Ausubel, Herman. "William Cobbett and Malthusianism." *Journal of the History of Ideas* 13 (1952): 250–56.

Ayala, Francisco J. "Two Frontiers of Human Biology: What the Sequence Won't Tell Us." *Issues in Science and Technology* 3 (1987): 51–56.

Balthrop, V. William. "Culture, Myth, and Ideology as Public Argument: An Interpretation of the Ascent and Demise of 'Southern Culture.'" *Communication Monographs* 51 (1984): 339–52.

Barkan, Elazar. "Reevaluating Progressive Eugenics: Herbert Spencer Jennings and the 1924 Immigration Legislation." *Journal of the History of Biology* 24 (1991): 91–112.

———. "Review of Richard Soloway's *Demography and Degeneration*." *Journal of Interdisciplinary History* 21 (1991): 672–75.

Barker, David. "The Biology of Stupidity: Genetics, Eugenics, and Mental Deficiency in the Inter-War Years." *British Journal of the History of Science* 22 (1989): 347–75.

———. "How to Curb the Fertility of the Unfit: The Feebleminded in Edwardian Britain." *Oxford Review of Education* 9 (1983): 198.

Barker-Benfield, G. J. "Mary Wollstonecraft: Eighteenth-Century Commonwealthwoman." *Journal of the History of Ideas* 50 (1989): 95–115.

Barnes, E. W. "Science, Religion, and Moral Judgments." *Nature* 166 (1950): 455–57.

Barns, Ian. "The Human Genome Project and the Self." *Soundings* 77 (1994): 99–128.

Beardsley, Edward H. "The American Scientist as Social Activist: Franz Boas, Burt G. Wilder, and the Cause of Racial Justice, 1900–1915." *Isis* 64 (1973): 50–66.

Beckham, Albert Sidney. "Applied Eugenics." *The Crisis* (1924): 177–78.

Beckwith, Jon. "A Historical View of Social Responsibility in Genetics." *BioScience* 43 (1993): 327–33.

Berkowitz, Ari. "Letters." *Science* 246 (1989): 874.

Best, Joel. "Rhetoric in Claims-Making: Constructing the Missing Children Problem." *Social Problems* 34 (1987): 101–21.

Billings, Paul R. "The Context of Genetic Screening." *Yale Journal of Biology and Medicine* 64 (1991): 47–52.

Bird, Randy, and Garland Allen. "Sources in the History of Eugenics: The Harry Hamilton Laughlin Papers in Kirksville, Missouri." *Journal of the History of Biology* 14 (1981): 339–53.

Blacker, Charles P. "Eugenic Experiments Conducted by the Nazis on Human Subjects." *The Eugenics Review* 44 (1952): 9–19.

Bokeno, R. M. "The Rhetorical Understanding of Science: An Explication and Critical Commentary." *Southern Speech Communication Journal* 52 (1987): 300–321.

Bosanquet, Bernard. "The Reports of the Poor Law Commission, I. The Majority Report." *Sociological Review* 2 (1909): 109–26.

Bowler, Peter J. "E. W. MacBride's Lamarckian Eugenics and Its Implications for the Social Construction of Scientific Knowledge." *Annals of Science* 41 (1984): 245–60.

Breggin, Peter. "Genetics and Crime." *Science* 262 (December 3, 1993): 1498.

Brock, Dan W. "The Human Genome Project and Human Identity." *Houston Law Review* 29 (1992): 7–22.

Burton, David H. "Justice Holmes and the Jesuits." *American Journal of Jurisprudence* 27 (1982): 32–45.

Byne, William. "The Biological Evidence Challenged." *Scientific American* 270 (1994): 50–55.

Calverton, V. F. "The Myth of Nordic Superiority." *Current History* 24 (1926): 671–77.

Campbell, John A. "Scientific Revolution and the Grammar of Culture: The Case of Darwin's *Origin*." *Quarterly Journal of Speech* 72 (1986): 351–76.

Campbell, P. N. "The Persona of Scientific Discourse." *Quarterly Journal of Speech* 61 (1975): 391–405.

Carey, James W. "The Press and the Public Discourse." *Center Magazine* (1987): 4–32.

Carlson, Elof Axel. "Ramifications of Genetics." *Science* 232 (1986): 531–32.

Carroll, Joseph C. "The Race Problem." *Sociology and Research* 11 (1927): 266–71.

Carter, Elmer. "Eugenics for the Negro." *Birth Control Review* 16 (1932): 169–70.

Casalino, Larry. "Decoding the Human Genome Project: An Interview with Evelyn Fox Keller." *Socialist Review* 21 (1991): 111–28.

Charland, Maurice. "Constitutive Rhetoric: The Case of the *Peuple Québécois*." *Quarterly Journal of Speech* 73 (1987): 133–50.

Charles, Dan. "Genetics Meeting Halted amid Racism Charges." *New Scientist* September 22, 1992: 4.

Clarke, Ida. "Kansas Has a Big Idea." *Pictorial Review* 26 (1925): 20, 72.

Cockburn, Alexander. "Memory." *The Nation* 255 (1992): 618–19.

Coghlan, Andy. "Outrage Greets Patent on Designer Sperm." *New Scientist* April 9, 1994: 4.

Coleman, Lawrence J. "Is the Eugenist Scientific?" *The Modern Schoolman* 12 (1934): 3–6.

Condit, Celeste M. "The Birth of Understanding: Chaste Science and the Harlot of the Arts." *Communication Monographs* 37 (1990): 323–27.

———. "Crafting Virtue: The Rhetorical Construction of Public Morality." *Quarterly Journal of Speech* 73 (1987): 79–97.

———. "Democracy and Civil Rights: The Universalizing Influence of Public Argumentation." *Communication Monographs* 54 (March 1987): 1–18.

———. "Hegemony in a Mass-Mediated Society: Concordance about Reproductive Technologies." *Critical Studies in Mass Communication* 11 (1994): 205–30.

———. "Rhetorical Criticism and Audience: The Extremes of Leff and McGee." *Western Journal of Speech Communication* 54 (1990): 330–45.

Condit, Celeste M., and John L. Lucaites. "The Rhetoric of Equality and the Expatriation of African-Americans, 1776–1826." *Communication Studies* 42 (1991): 1–21.

Conway, Bertrand L. "The Church and Eugenics." *Catholic World* 123 (1928): 148–55.

Conway, Jill. "Stereotypes of Femininity in a Theory of Sexual Evolution." *Victorian Studies* (1970): 47–62.

Coogan, J. E. "Eugenical Sterilization Holds Jubilee." *Catholic World* 177 (1953): 44–49.

Cook, Walter Wheeler. "Eugenics or Euthenics." *Illinois Law Review* 37 (1943): 287–332.

Coolidge, Calvin. "Whose Country Is This?" *Good Housekeeping* February 1921: 13–14, 106–7.

Cox, Ignatius W. "The Folly of Human Sterilization." *Scientific American* 151 (1934): 188–90.

"The Crime of Being Inefficient." *The Nation* 11 (1912): 276–77.

"The Crime of Being Inefficient." *The Nation* 12 (1912): 390–92.

"Criminal Error." *New Scientist* 135 (1992): 3.

Crook, Paul. "War as a Genetic Disaster? The First World War Debate over the Eugenics of Warfare." *War and Society* 8 (1990): 47–70.

Crow, James F. "Eugenics: Must It Be a Dirty Word?" *Contemporary Psychology* 33 (1988): 10–12.

Curti, Merle. "Human Nature in American Thought." *Political Science Quarterly* 68 (1953): 354–75.

Cushman, Herbert Ernest. "Professor August Weismann." *Outlook* 55 (1897): 252–53.

"The Dangers of the Mental Deficiency Bill." *The Nation* (1912): 168–69.

Darrow, Clarence. "The Eugenics Cult." *American Mercury* 8 (1926): 129–37.

Davenport, Gertrude. "The Eugenics Movement." *The Independent* January 18, 1912: 146–48.

———. "Society and the Feebleminded." *The Independent* April 27, 1914: 170.

Davin, Anna. "Imperialism and Motherhood." *History Workshop* 5 (1978): 9–65.

Davis, Bernard. "Fervors, Fears, and Manageable Realities." *Science* 257 (1992): 981–82.

Dawson, George E. "100 Superfine Babies: What the Science of Eugenics Found in the Babies of Our Contest." *Good Housekeeping* February 1912: 238–41.

Depoe, Stephen. "'Qualitative Liberalism': Arthur Schlesinger, Jr., and the Persuasive Uses of Definition and History." *Communication Studies* 40 (1989): 81–96.

Dewey, John. "The Superstition of Necessity." *Monist* 3 (1893): 362–79.

Donovan, Stephen M. "The Morality of the Operation of Vasectomy." *Ecclesiastical Review* 44 (1911): 571–74.

Dreyfuss, Rochelle Cooper, and Dorothy Nelkin. "The Jurisprudence of Genetics." *Vanderbilt Law Review* 45 (1992): 313–48.

Du Bois, W. E. B. "Black Folk and Birth Control." *Birth Control Review* 16 (1932): 166–67.

Dunn, L. C. "Cross Currents in the History of Human Genetics." *American Journal of Human Genetics* 14 (1962): 1–13.

"Editorial." *Birth Control Review* 12 (1928): 73–74.

"Editorial Comment." *Catholic World* 118 (December 1923): 401–7.

Ellis, Havelock. "Individualism and Socialism." *Contemporary Review* 101 (1912): 527–28.

Emerson, Charles. "Mental Hygiene: Wise and Unwise Investments." *Mental Hygiene* 10 (1926): 451–63.

Epstein, Richard. "Proceedings of the Conference on Takings of Property and the Constitution." *University of Miami Law Review* 41 (1986): 49–222.

"Eugenics and Happiness." *The Nation* 95 (1912): 75–76.

"Eugenics for Democracy." *Time* September 9, 1940: 34.

Evans, Hiram W. "The Klan's Fight for Americanism." *North American Review* 223 (1926): 33–63.

"The Exhibit 'On the Road.'" *Eugenics Review* 24 (1932): 24–25.

Fancher, Raymond E. "Galton in Africa." *American Psychologist* 37 (1982): 713–14.

Farrall, Lyndsay A. "The History of Eugenics: A Bibliographic Review." *Annals of Science* 36 (1979): 111–23.

"A Far-Reaching Decision." *Catholic Charities Review* 11 (1927): 225–26.

Farrell, Thomas. "From the Parthenon to the Bassinet: Along the Epistemic Trail." *Quarterly Journal of Speech* 76 (1990): 78–84.

———. "Media Rhetoric As Social Drama: The Winter Olympics of 1984." *Critical Studies in Mass Communication* 6 (1984): 158–82.

"Fear of Neo-Eugenics Hits Europe." *New Scientist* 121 (1989): 23.

The Federal Council of the Churches of Christ. "Moral Aspects of Birth Control." *Current History* 34 (1931): 97–100.

"Fellow Caucasians! Virginia Law on Racial Integrity." *The Nation* 118 (1924): 388.

Field, James A. "The Progress of Eugenics." *Quarterly Journal of Economics* 26 (November 1911): 1–67.

Fielding, William J. "The Morality of Birth Control." *Birth Control Review* 4 (November 1920): 12–13.

Fisher, Walter R. "Clarifying the Narrative Paradigm." *Communication Monographs* 56 (1989): 55–58.

———. "Reaffirmation and Subversion of the American Dream." *Quarterly Journal of Speech* 59 (1973): 160–67.

Fitzhugh, George. "The Conservation Principle; or, Social Evils and Their Remedies." *De Bow's Review* 22 (1856): 419–30.

Fletcher, John C., and Dorothy Wertz. "Ethics, Law and Medical Genetics: After the Human Genome Is Mapped." *Emory Law Journal* 39 (1990): 747–91.

Flower, Michael J., and Deborah Health. "Micro-Anatomo Politics: Mapping the Human Genome Project. *Culture, Medicine, and Psychiatry* 17 (1993): 27–41.

Frazier, E. Franklin. "The Mind of the American Negro." *Opportunity* 6 (1928): 263–66.

Freeden, Michael. "Eugenics and Progressive Thought: A Study in Ideological Affinity." *Historical Journal* 22 (1979): 645–71.

Friedman, J. M. "Eugenics and the 'New Genetics.' " *Perspectives in Biology and Medicine* 35 (1991): 145–54.

Gaonkar, Dilip P. "The Idea of Rhetoric in the Rhetoric of Science." *Southern Communication Journal* 58 (1993): 258–95.

Garth, Thomas R. "Eugenics, Euthenics, and Race." *Opportunity* 8 (1930): 206–7.

Garver, Kenneth, and Bettylee Garver. "Eugenics: Past, Present, and the Future." *American Journal of Human Genetics* 49 (1991): 1109–18.

———. "The Human Genome Project and Eugenic Concerns." *American Journal of Human Genetics* 54 (1994): 148–58.

Gaylin, Willard. "The Frankenstein Factor." *New England Journal of Medicine* 297 (1977): 665–67.

Gelb, Steven A. "Myths, Morons, Psychologists: The Kallikak Family Revisited." *Review of Education* 11 (1985): 255–59.

Gerrard, Thomas. "The Catholic Church and Race Culture." *Dublin Review* 149 (1911): 49–68.

———. "Eugenics and Catholic Teaching." *Catholic World* 95 (1912): 289–304.

Gesell, Arnold L. "The Village of a Thousand Souls." *American Magazine* 76 (1913): 11–15.

Glass, Bentley. "Eugenical Implications of the New Reproductive Technologies." *Social Biology* 19 (1972): 326–35.

———. "Geneticists Embattled: Their Stand against Rampant Eugenics and Racism in America during the 1920s and 1930s." *Proceedings of the American Philosophical Society* 130 (1986): 130–54.

Goddard, Henry H. "The Elimination of Feeble-Mindedness." *Annals of the American Academy of Political and Social Science* (1911): 261–72.

Goldman, Emma. "The Social Aspects of Birth Control." *Mother Earth* 11 (1916): 468–75.

Goodell, Rae. "The Gene Craze." *Columbia Journalism Review* 4 (1980): 41–45.

Goodhue, Stoddard. "Do You Choose Your Children?" *Cosmopolitan* July 1913: 148–57.

Gordon, Eugene. "The Negro Press." *American Mercury* 8 (May 1926): 207–15.

Gordon, Linda. "Birth Control and the Eugenists." *Science for the People* 10 (1977): 8–15.

———. "The Politics of Population: Birth Control and the Eugenics Movement." *Radical America* 8 (1974): 61–97.

Gould, Steven Jay. "Carrie Buck's Daughter." *Natural History* 7 (1984): 14–18.

Graham, Loren. "Science and Values: The Eugenics Movement in Germany and Russia in the 1920s." *American Historical Review* 82 (1977): 1133–64.

Grant, Madison. "Discussions of Article on Democracy and Heredity." *Journal of Heredity* 10 (1919): 164–65.

Gros, François. "The Human Genome and the Responsibility of Scientists: Interview with François Gros." *Impact of Science on Society* 161 (1991): 5–13.

Gross, Alan G. "Public Debates As Failed Social Dramas: The Recombinant DNA Controversy." *Quarterly Journal of Speech* 70 (1984): 397–409.

Halloran, S. M. "The Birth of Molecular Biology: An Essay in the Rhetorical Criticism of Scientific Discourse." *Rhetoric Review* 3 (1984): 70–83.

Hannaford, Ivan. "The Idiocy of Race." *Wilson Quarterly* 18 (1994): 8–35.

Haraway, Donna. "Situated Knowledges: The Science Question in Feminism and the Privilege of Partial Perspective." *Feminist Studies* 14 (1988): 575–99.

Harding, Sandra. "After the Neutrality Ideal: Science, Politics, and 'Strong Objectivity.' " *Social Research* 59 (1992): 568–87.

Hasian, Marouf, Jr., and Earl Croasmun. "The Legitimating Function of Judicial Rhetoric in the Eugenics Controversy." *Argumentation and Advocacy* 28 (1992): 123–34.

Hatchett, Richard. "Brave New Worlds: Perspectives on the American Experience of Eugenics." *The Pharos* 54 (1991): 13–18.

Hilts, Victor. "Obeying the Laws of Hereditary Descent: Phrenological Views on Inheritance and Eugenics." *Journal of the History of the Behavioral Sciences* 18 (1982): 62–77.

Holland, Henry W. "Heredity." *Atlantic Monthly* October 1883: 447–52.

Holmes, Bob. "Gay Gene Test 'Inaccurate and Immoral.' " *New Scientist* 141 (March 5, 1994): 9.

Horgan, John. "Genes and Crime." *Scientific American* 268 (1993): 24–29.

Horn, David G. "Nazi Science as 'Normal' Science?" *Socialist Review* 19 (1989): 139–42.

Howe, Henry, and John Lyne. "Gene Talk in Sociobiology." *Epistemology* 6 (1992): 109–63.

Howerth, I. W. "War and the Survival of the Fittest." *Scientific Monthly* 3 (1916): 488–97.

Hoxie, Robert F. "Class Conflict in America." *American Journal of Sociology* 13 (1908): 776–81.

Hubbard, Ruth. "Eugenics: New Tools, Old Ideas." *Women and Health* 13 (1988): 225–35.

———. "Science, Facts, and Feminism." *Hypatia* 3 (1988): 5–17.

Hubbard, Ruth, Elijah Wald, and Nicholas Hildyard. "The Eugenics of Normalcy: The Politics of Gene Research." *The Ecologist* 23 (1993): 185–91.

Humphrey, Seth K. "Parenthood and the Social Conscience." *The Forum* 49 (April 1913): 457–64.

Hutter, Jorg. "The Social Construction of Homosexuals in the Nineteenth Century: The Shift from the Sin to the Influence of Medicine on Criminalizing Sodomy in Germany." *Journal of Homosexuality* 24 (1993): 73–93.

Huxley, Julian. "Marxist Eugenics." *Eugenics Review* 28 (1936): 66–68.

Hyatt, Marshall. "Review of Elazar Barkan's *The Retreat of Scientific Racism.*" *Anthropological Quarterly* (1993): 106–7.

Hyde, Michael J. "Medicine, Rhetoric, and Euthanasia: A Case Study in the Workings of a Postmodern Discourse." *Quarterly Journal of Speech* 79 (1993): 201–24.

Jaroff, Leon. "Happy Birthday, Double Helix." *Time* March 15, 1993: 56–59.

Jenkins, Philip. "Eugenics, Crime and Ideology: The Case of Progressive Pennsylvania." *Pennsylvania History* 51 (1984): 64–78.

Jenks, Albert E. "The Legal Status of Negro-White Amalgamation in the United States." *American Journal of Sociology* 21 (1915): 666–78.

Jensen, Arthur R. "Objectivity and the Genetics of I.Q.: A Reply to Stephen Selden." *Phi Delta Kappan* 66 (1984): 284–86.

Johnson, Charles. "A Question of Negro Health." *Birth Control Review* 16 (1932): 167–68.

Johnson, Guy B. "The Race Philosophy of the Ku Klux Klan." *Opportunity* 1 (1923): 268–70.

Johnson, James Weldon, and Herbert Seligmann. "Legal Aspects of the Negro Problem." *Annals of the American Academy of Political and Social Science* 140 (1928): 90–97.

Jones, Bartlett C. "Prohibition and Eugenics, 1920–1933." *Journal of the History of Medicine and Allied Sciences* 18 (1963): 158–72.

Jones, Greta. "Book Review: *Eugenics, Human Failings: The Eugenics Society, Its Sources and Its Critics in Britian*," *British Journal for the History of Science* 25 (1992): 486–87.

Julian, George W. "Is the Reformer Any Longer Needed?" *North American Review* 127 (1878): 237–60.

Kaplan, Sidney. "Miscegenation Issue in the Election of 1864." *Journal of Negro History* 34 (1949): 277.

Kaye, Lincoln. "Quality Control: Eugenics Bill Defended against Western Critics." *Far East Economic Review* 157 (1994): 22.

Keller, Evelyn Fox. "Fractured Images of Science: Language and Power: A Postmodern Optic, or Just Bad Eyesight?" *Poetics Today* 12 (1991): 227–43.

———. "Genetics, Reductionism and the Normative Uses of Biological Information: Responses to Kevles." *Southern California Law Review* 65 (1991): 285–91.

Kennedy, Walter B. "The Supreme Court and Social Legislation." *Catholic Charities Review* 7 (1923): 208–12.

Kershner, R. B., Jr. "Degeneration: The Explanatory Nightmare." *Georgia Review* (1986): 416–44.

Kevles, Daniel. "Annals of Eugenics, A Secular Faith—II." *New Yorker* October 15, 1984: 52–125.

———. "Controlling the Genetic Arsenal." *Wilson Quarterly* 16 (1992): 68–76.

———. "Social and Ethical Issues in the Human Genome Project." *National Forum* 73 (1993): 18–21.

———. "Vital Essences and Human Wholeness: The Social Readings of Biological Information." *Southern California Law Review* 65 (1991): 255–78.

Kimmelman, Barbara A. "The American Breeders' Association: Genetics and Eugenics in an Agricultural Context, 1903–1913." *Social Studies of Science* 13 (1983): 163–204.

King, Andrew. "The Rhetoric of Power Maintenance: Elites at the Precipice." *Quarterly Journal of Speech* 62 (1976): 127–34.

King, Patricia. "The Dangers of Difference." *Hastings Center Report* 22 (1992): 35–38.

Kirby, Michael. "Legal Problems: Human Genome Project." *Australian Law Journal* 67 (1993): 894–903.

Kirwan, Jack. "Touring the Helix." *National Review* August 6, 1990: 42–43.

Kite, Elizabeth S. "The 'Pineys.'" *Survey* 31 (1913): 7–13.

———. "Two Brothers." *Survey* 27 (1912): 1861–64.

———. "Unto the Third Generation." *Survey* 28 (1912): 789–91.

Koshland, Daniel E., Jr. "Sequences and Consequences of the Human Genome." *Science* 216 (October 13, 1989): 189.

Lapp, John A. "Justice First." *Catholic Charities Review* 11 (127): 201–9.

Larson, Edward J. "Belated Progress: The Enactment of Eugenics Legislation in Georgia." *Journal of the History of Medicine and Allied Sciences* 46 (1991): 44–64.

———. "Issues in the Southern Eugenics Movement." Paper presented to the University of Georgia History Department, 1993.

———. "The Rhetoric of Eugenics: Expert Authority and the Mental Deficiency Bill." *British Journal for the History of Science* 24 (1991): 45–60.

Laski, Harold. "The Scope of Eugenics." *Westminster Review* 174 (1910): 25–34.

Lee, W. S. "Social Scientists as Ideological Critics." *Western Journal of Communication* 57 (1993): 221–32.

Lehman-Wilzig, Sam N. "Frankenstein Unbound: Towards a Legal Definition of Artificial Intelligence." *Futures* (1981): 442–57.

Lessl, Thomas M. "Heresy, Orthodoxy, and the Politics of Science." *Quarterly Journal of Speech* 74 (1988): 18–34.

———. "Science and the Sacred Cosmos: The Ideological Rhetoric of Carl Sagan." *Quarterly Journal of Speech* 71 (1985): 175–87.

Lewis, William. "Telling America's Story: Narrative Form and the Reagan Presidency." *Quarterly Journal of Speech* 73 (1987) 280–302.

Lewontin, Richard C. "Facts and the Factitious in the Natural Sciences." *Critical Inquiry* 18 (1991): 140–53.

"Liberty and Government." *De Bow's Review* 30 (1861): 198–203.

Lippman, Abby. "Led (Astray) by Genetic Maps: The Cartography of the Human Genome and Health Care." *Social Science and Medicine* 35 (1992): 1469–76.

———. "Prenatal Genetic Testing and Screening: Constructing Needs and Reinforcing Inequities." *American Journal of Law and Medicine* 17 (1991): 17–50.

Long, Howard. "On Mental Tests and Racial Psychology—A Critique." *Opportunity* 3 (1925): 134–38.

Longino, Helen E. "Feminist Standpoint Theory and the Problems of Knowledge." *Signs* 19 (1993): 201–12.

———. "Knowledge, Bodies, and Values: Reproductive Technologies and Their Scientific Context." *Inquiry* 35 (1992): 323–40.

————. "Multiple Subjects and the Diffusion of Power." *Journal of Philosophy* 88 (1991): 666–74.

Love, Rosaleen. " 'Alice in Eugenics-Land': Feminism and Eugenics in the Scientific Careers of Alice Lee and Ethel Elderton." *Annals of Science* 36 (1979): 145–58.

Lucaites, John Louis, and Celeste M. Condit. "Reconstructing <Equality>: Culture-typal and Countercultural Rhetorics." *Communication Monographs* 57 (1990): 5–24.

Ludmerer, Kenneth M. "American Geneticists and the Eugenics Movement: 1905–1935." *Journal of the History of Biology* 2 (1969): 337–62.

Luria, Salvador E. "Letters to the Editor: Human Genome Program." *Science* 246 (1989): 873.

Lyne, John, and Henry Howe, " 'Punctuated Equilibria': Rhetorical Dynamics of a Scientific Controversy." *Quarterly Journal of Speech* 72 (1986): 132–47.

MacKenzie, Donald. "Eugenics in Britain." *Social Studies of Science* 6 (1979): 499.

————. "Karl Pearson and the Professional Middle Class." *Annals of Science* 36 (1979): 125–43.

Mallet, Bernard. "The Social Problem Group." *Eugenics Review* 23 (October 1931): 203–6.

Mangold, George B. "Unlawful Motherhood." *Forum* 53 (1915): 335–43.

Marshall, Eliot. "NIH Told to Reconsider Crime Meeting." *Science* 262 (1993): 23–24.

Martin, Ann. "The Mother and Social Reform." *Nineteenth Century and After* 73 (1913): 1060–79.

Mateer, Florence. "Mental Heredity and Eugenics." *Psychological Bulletin* 10 (1913): 224–29.

Mayer, Joseph. "Eugenics in Roman Catholic Literature." *Eugenics* 3 (1930): 43–51.

McGee, Michael Calvin. "The 'Ideograph': A Link between Rhetoric and Ideology." *Quarterly Journal of Speech* 66 (1980): 1–16.

————. "In Search of 'The People': A Rhetorical Alternative." *Quarterly Journal of Speech* 61 (1975): 235–49.

————. "Text, Context, and the Fragmentation of Contemporary Culture." *Western Journal of Speech Communication* 54 (1990): 274–89.

McGee, Michael Calvin, and Martha Ann Martin. "Public Knowledge and Ideological Argumentation." *Communication Monographs* 50 (1983): 47–65.

McGuire, J. E., and Trevor Melia. "Some Cautionary Strictures on the Writing of the Rhetoric of Science." *Rhetorica* 7 (1989): 87–99.

Melia, Trevor. "And Lo the Footprint . . . Selected Literature in Rhetoric and Science." *Quarterly Journal of Speech* 70 (1984): 303–13.

Miller, Carolyn R. "Reviews: Some Perspectives on Rhetoric, Science, and History." *Rhetorica* 7 (1989): 101–20.

————. "The Rhetoric of Decision Science, or Herbert A. Simons Says." *Science, Technology, and Human Values* 14 (1989): 43–46.

Miller, Herbert. "The Myth of Superiority." *Opportunity* 1 (1923): 228–29.

Miller, Kelly. "Eugenics of the Negro Race." *Scientific Monthly* 5 (1917): 57–59.

————. "Government and the Negro." *Annals of the American Academy of Political and Social Sciences* 140 (1928): 98–104.

————. "The Historical Background of the Negro Physicians." *Journal of Negro History* 1 (1916): 99–109.

"The Moral Failure of the Modern Cult of 'Efficiency.'" *Current Opinion* 59 (1915): 39–40.

"The Morality and Lawfulness of Vasectomy." *Ecclesiastical Review* 44 (1911): 562–71.

Muller, H. J. "The Dominance of Economics over Eugenics." *Scientific Monthly* 37 (1933): 40–47.

Muller-Hill, Benno. "Genetics after Auschwitz." *Holocaust and Genocide Studies* 2 (1987): 3–20.

————. "The Shadow of Genetic Injustice." *Nature* 362 (1993): 491.

Murphy, John M. " 'To Create a Race of Thoroughbreds': Margaret Sanger and the *Birth Control Review*." *Women's Studies in Communication* 13 (1990): 23–45.

Nearing, Nellie M. L., and Scott Nearing. "When a Girl Is Asked to Marry." *Ladies Home Journal* March 1912: 7, 69–70.

Nelkin, Dorothy. "Genetic Warnings." *Wilson Quarterly* (1992): 156.

————. "The Grandiose Claims of Geneticists." *Chronicle of Higher Education* March 3, 1993: B1–B2.

Neuhaus, Richard J. "The Return of Eugenics." *Commentary* 85 (1988): 15–26.

Noll, Steven. "Southern Strategies for Handling the Black Feeble-Minded: From Social Control to Profound Indifference." *Journal of Policy History* 3 (1991): 130–51.

Osborn, Frederick. "Development of a Eugenic Philosophy." *American Sociological Review* 2 (1937): 389–97.

————. "History of the American Eugenics Society." *Social Biology* 21 (1974): 115–26.

————. "Social Implications of the Eugenic Program." *Child Study* 16 (1939): 95–97.

Parker, G. H. "The Eugenics Movement as a Public Service." *Science* 41 (1915): 344.

Patch, Howard R. "Necessity in Boethius and the Neoplatonists." *Speculum* 10 (1935): 393–404.

Paul, Diane. "Eugenic Anxieties, Social Realities, and Political Choices." *Social Research* 59 (1992): 663–83.

————. "Eugenics and the Left." *Journal of the History of Ideas* (1984): 567–90.

Penrose, L. S. "Mental Deficiency—II. The Sub-Cultural Group." *Eugenics Review* 24 (1933): 289–91.

Peters, John Durham. "John Locke, the Individual, and the Origin of Communication." *Quarterly Journal of Speech* 75 (1989), 387–99.

Plecker, W. A. "Virginia's Attempt to Adjust the Color Problem." *American Journal of Public Health* 15 (1925): 111.

Pnina, Abir-Am. "Themes, Genres and Orders of Legitimation in the Consolidation of New Scientific Disciplines: Deconstructing the Historiography of Molecular Biology." *History of Science* 23 (1985): 72–115.

Pope Pius XI. "On Christian Marriage in Relation to Present Conditions, Needs and Disorders of Society." *Current History* 33 (1931): 797.

Porter, Dorothy. " 'Enemies of the Race': Biologism, Environmentalism, and Public Health in Edwardian England." *Victorian Studies* 34 (1991): 159–78.

Potts, Patricia. "Medicine, Morals and Mental Deficiency: The Contribution of Doctors to the Development of Special Education in England." *Oxford Review of Education* 9 (1983): 181–96.

Prelli, Lawrence. "Rhetorical Logic and the Integration of Rhetoric and Science." *Communication Monographs* 57 (1990): 315–22.

———. "Rhetorical Perspective and the Limits of Critique." *Southern Communication Journal* 58 (1993): 319–27.

Preu, James. "Swift's Influence on Godwin's Doctrine of Anarchism." *Journal of the History of Ideas* 15 (1954): 371–83.

Procter, David. "The Dynamic Spectacle: Transforming Experience into Social Forms of Community." *Quarterly Journal of Speech* 76 (1990): 117–33.

Prues, J. Samuel. "Spinoza, Vico, and the Imagination of Religion." *Journal of the History of Ideas* 50 (1989): 71–93.

Rafter, Nichole H. "Claims-Making and Socio-Cultural Context in the First U.S. Eugenics Campaign." *Social Problems* 39 (1992): 17–34.

Rapp, Rayna. "Moral Pioneers: Women, Men, and Fetuses on a Frontier of Reproductive Technology." *Women and Society* 13 (1988): 101–16.

Ray, L. J. "Eugenics, Mental Deficiency and Fabian Socialism between the Wars." *Oxford Review of Education* 9 (1983): 213–25.

Rechsteiner, Martin. "The Folly of the Human Genome Project." *New Scientist* 127 (1990): 20.

Reilly, Philip. "The Surgical Solution: The Writings of Activist Physicians in the Early Days of Eugenics Sterilization." *Perspectives in Biology and Medicine* 26 (1983): 637–56.

Rennie, John. "Grading the Gene Tests." *Scientific American* 270 (1994): 88–97.

"The Report of the Privy Council upon Physical Deterioration." *The Lancet* (1904): 390–92.

Roosevelt, Theodore. "Twisted Eugenics." *Outlook* 106 (1914): 30–34.

Rose, Steven. "Wishful Thinking." *New Scientist* 141 (March 19, 1994): 52.

Rosenberg, Charles E. "Charles B. Davenport and the Beginning of Human Genetics." *Bulletin of the History of Medicine* 35 (1961): 266–76.

Ross, Edward A. "Turning towards Nirvana." *Arena* 4 (1891): 736–43.

Rowland, Robert C. "On Mythic Criticism." *Communication Studies* 41 (1990): 101–16.

Ryan, John A. "Family Limitation." *Ecclesiastical Review* 54 (1916): 684–96.

———. "Sterilization." *Ecclesiastical Review* 84 (1931): 267–68.

———. "Unprotected Natural Rights." *The Commonweal* 6 (1927): 151–52.

Sanger, Margaret. "Birth Control and Race Betterment." *Birth Control Review* 3 (1919): 11–12.

————. "Editorial." *Birth Control Review* 12 (1928): 73–74.

————. "The Eugenic Value of Birth Control Propaganda." *Birth Control Review* 5 (1921): 5.

————. "Shall We Break This Law?" *Birth Control Review* 1 (1917): 4–5.

————. "Woman and War." *Birth Control Review* 1 (1917): 5.

Schneider, William. "Toward the Improvement of the Human Race: The History of Eugenics in France." *Journal of Modern History* 54 (June 1982): 268–91.

"Science." *The Athenaeum* (1912): 625.

Scott, Leslie. "The Mental Deficiency Bill." *The Nation* (1912): 310–11.

"Second Thoughts on Mental Deficiency." *The Nation* 13 (1913): 8–9.

Selden, Steven. "Biological Determinism and the Normal School Curriculum, Helen Putnam and the N.E.A. Committee on Racial Well-Being, 1910–1922." *Journal of Curriculum Theorizing* 1 (1979): 105–22.

————. "Educational Policy and Biological Science: Genetics, Eugenics, and the College Textbook, c. 1908–1931." *Teachers College Record* 87 (1985): 35–51.

Shaler, Nathaniel. "The Negro Problem." *Atlantic Monthly* November 1884: 696–709.

Short, Nicholas. "Forty Years of Molecular Information." *Nature* 362 (1993): 783–84.

Simmons, Christina. "African-Americans and Sexual Victorianism in the Social Hygiene Movement, 1910–1940." *Journal of the History of Sexuality* 4 (1993): 51–75.

Simmons, Harvey G. "Explaining Social Policy: The English Mental Deficiency Act of 1913." *Journal of Social History* 11 (1978): 387–403.

Simms, Michael. "Violence Study Hits a Nerve in Germany." *Science* 264 (1994): 653.

"Sir Robert Baden-Powell's Adventures As a Spy." *Everybody's Magazine* 32 (1915): 184–92.

Slezak, Peter. "The Social Construction of Social Constructionism." *Inquiry* 37 (1994): 139–57.

"Social Biology." *New Statesman and Nation* December 26, 1931: 816–17.

Solomon, Martha. "The Rhetoric of Dehumanization: An Analysis of Medical Reports of the Tuskegee Syphilis Project." *Western Journal of Speech Communication* 49 (Fall 1985): 233–47.

Somerville, Henry. "Eugenics and the Feeble-Minded." *Catholic World* 105 (1917): 209–18.

Springhall, John. "Baden-Powell and the Scout Movement before 1920: Citizen Training or Soldiers of the Future?" *English Historical Review* (1987): 934–42.

Stein, Howard F. "The Human Genome as Metaphor." *Journal of Family Practice* 35 (1992): 256–58.

"Sterilization Conflicts." *The Commonweal* April 12, 1935: 680–81.

Stevens, Jane E. "The Biology of Violence." *BioScience* 44 (1994): 291–94.

Stoddard, Lothrop. "Does Democracy Fit Most Peoples?" *World's Work* 50 (1925): 57–62.

Stone, Richard. "Violence Research: NRC Panel Provides a Blueprint." *Science* 258 (1992): 1298.

Swiney, Frances. "An Ethical Birth Rate." *Westminster Review* 199 (1901): 550–54.

Szasz, Thomas S. "The Sane Slave." *American Journal of Psychotherapy* 25 (1971): 228–38.

Tauber, Alfred, and Sahotra Sarkar. "The Human Genome Project: Has Blind Reductionism Gone Too Far?" *Perspectives in Biology and Medicine* 35 (1992): 220–35.

Taylor, Carol M. "W. E. B. Du Bois's Challenge to Scientific Racism." *Journal of Black Studies* 11 (1981): 449–60.

Taylor, Charles A. "Defining the Scientific Community: A Rhetorical Perspective on Demarcation." *Communication Monographs* 58 (1991): 402–20.

"Thinking the Unthinkable." *New Scientist* 140 (1993): 3.

Thomas, William B. "Black Intellectuals, Intelligence Testing in the 1930s, and the Sociology of Knowledge." *Teachers College Record* 85 (1984): 477–501.

———. "Black Intellectuals' Critique of Early Mental Testing: A Little Known Saga of the 1920s." *American Journal of Education* (1982): 258–92.

Toufexis, Anastasia. "Seeking the Roots of Violence." *Time* April 19, 1993: 52.

Trew, Eva. "Sex Sterilization." *International Socialist* (1913): 814–17.

Tribe, Laurence. "Technology Assessment and the Fourth Discontinuity: The Limits of Instrumental Rationality." *Southern California Law Review* 46 (1973): 617–60.

Vecoli, Rudolph J. "Sterilization: A Progressive Measure?" *Wisconsin Magazine of History* 43 (1960): 190–202.

Walsh, James J. "Race Betterment." *The Commonweal* 19 (1934): 371–72.

———. "The Story of Organized Care of the Insane and Defectives." *Catholic World* 104 (1916): 226–34.

Walzer, Arthur E. "Logic and Rhetoric in Malthus's *Essay on the Principle of Population, 1798.*" *Quarterly Journal of Speech* 73 (1987): 1–17.

Wander, Philip. "The Rhetoric of Science." *Western Journal of Speech Communication* 40 (1976): 226–35.

Ward, Lester. "Eugenics, Euthenics, and Eudemics." *American Journal of Sociology* 18 (1913): 737–54.

Ward, Robert DeC. "Our Immigration Laws from the Viewpoint of Eugenics." *American Breeder's Magazine* 3 (1912): 20–26.

———. "The Second Year of the New Immigration Law." *Journal of Heredity* 18 (1927): 3–18.

Warren, Allen. "Sir Robert Baden-Powell, the Scout Movement and Citizen Training in Great Britain, 1900–1920." *English Historical Review* 101 (1986): 376–98.

Watson, James D. "First Word." *Omni* June 1990: 6.

———. "The Human Genome Project: Past, Present, and Future." *Science* 248 (1990): 44–48.

———. "Looking Forward." *Gene* 135 (1993): 309–15.

———. "Moving toward the Clonal Man." *Atlantic Monthly* May 1971: 50–53.

Weimer, W. B. "Science as a Rhetorical Transaction: Toward a Nonjustificational Concept of Rhetoric." *Philosophy and Rhetoric* 10 (1977): 1–29.

Weinberg, Robert A. "The Dark Side of the Genome." *Technology Review* 94 (1991): 45–51.

Weindling, Paul. "Weimar Eugenics: The Kaiser Wilhelm Institute for Anthropology, Human Heredity, and Eugenics in Social Context." *Annals of Science* 42 (1985): 303–18.

Weingart, Peter. "German Eugenics: Between Science and Politics." *Osiris* 5 (1989): 260–82.

Weiss, Sheila F. "The Race Hygiene Movement in Germany." *Osiris* 3 (1987): 193–236.

Wexler, Alice. "Our Genes, Ourselves." *The Nation* February 4, 1991: 133–36.

White, Arnold. "Eugenics and National Efficiency." *Eugenics Review* 1 (1909): 111.

Wiggam, Albert E. "The Rising Tide of Degeneracy: What Everybody Ought to Know about Eugenics." *World's Work* 53 (1926): 25–33.

Wilcox, E. Wheeler. "The Forecast." *Good Housekeeping* 1912: 130.

Wiley, Harvey W. "The Rights of the Unborn." *Good Housekeeping* October 1922: 32, 170–73.

Williams, Henry Smith. "The Scientific Solution of the Liquor Problem." *McClure's* 32 (1909).

Williams, Patricia. "On Being the Object of Property." *Signs* 14 (1988): 5–24.

Windle, Bertram C. A. "A Rule of Life." *Catholic World* 103 (1916): 577–87.

Wish, Harvey. "Negro Education and the Progressive Movement." *Journal of Negro History* 49 (1964): 184–200.

Wolfe, A. B. "Is There a Biological Law of Human Population Growth?" *Quarterly Journal of Economics* 41 (1927): 593–95.

Wright, Robert. "Achilles' Helix." *New Republic* July 9 and 16, 1990: 21–31.

Zagacki, Kenneth S., and William Keith, "Rhetoric, Topoi, and Scientific Revolutions." *Philosophy and Rhetoric* 25 (1992): 59–78.

Zola, I. K. "In the Name of Health and Illness: On Some Socio-Political Consequences of Medical Influence." *Social Science and Medicine* 9 (1975): 83–87.

Books

Adams, Mark B., ed. *The WellBorn Science: Eugenics in Germany, France, Brazil, and Russia*. New York: Oxford University Press, 1990.

Allen, Garland. *Life Science in the Twentieth Century*. New York: Wiley, 1974.

———. "The Role of Experts in Scientific Controversy." In *Scientific Controversies: Case Studies in the Resolution and Closure of Disputes in Science and Technology*, ed. H. Tristram Englehardt, Jr., and Arthur L. Caplan, 169–202. Cambridge: Cambridge University Press, 1987.

Andreae, Percy. *The Prohibition Movement*. Chicago: Felix Mendelsohn, 1915.

Annas, George J., and Sherman Elias, eds. *Gene Mapping: Using Law and Ethics as Guides*. New York: Oxford University Press, 1992.

Aptheker, Herbert, ed. *A Documentary History of the Negro People in the United States.* 2 vols. New York: Citadel Press, 1969.

Aronowitz, Stanley. *Science As Power: Discourse and Ideology in Modern Society.* Minneapolis: University of Minnesota Press, 1988.

Bajema, Carl J., ed. *Eugenics: Then and Now.* Stroudsburg, Pa.: Dowden, Hutchinson, and Ross, 1976.

Barkan, Elazar. *The Retreat of Scientific Racism: Changing Concepts of Race in Britain and the United States between the World Wars.* Cambridge: Cambridge University Press, 1992.

Barnes, Barry. *Scientific Knowledge and Sociological Theory.* London: Routledge and Kegan Paul, 1974.

Barnes, Barry, and Steven Shapin, eds. *Natural Order: Historical Studies of Scientific Culture.* London: Sage, 1979.

Barzun, Jacques. *Race: A Study in Superstition.* New York: Harper and Row, 1965.

Bishop, Jerry E., and Michael Waldholz. *Genome.* New York: Simon and Schuster, 1990.

Blacker, C. P., ed. *A Social Problem Group?* Oxford: Oxford University Press, 1937.

Blacker, C. P. *Eugenics: Galton and After.* Cambridge, Mass.: Harvard University Press, 1952.

Blee, Kathleen M. *Women of the Klan: Racism and Gender in the 1920s.* Berkeley: University of California Press, 1991.

Bloor, David. *Knowledge and Social Imagery.* London: Routledge and Kegan Paul, 1976.

Bowler, Peter J. *The Eclipse of Darwinism.* Baltimore, Md.: Johns Hopkins University Press, 1983.

Boyer, Paul. *Urban Masses and Moral Order in America, 1820–1920.* Cambridge, Mass.: Harvard University Press, 1978.

Boy Scouts of America. *Handbook for Scoutmasters, A Manual of Leadership.* New York: Boy Scouts of America, 1922.

Broderick, F. L. *Right Reverend New Dealer: John A. Ryan.* New York: Macmillan, 1963.

Brown, JoAnne. *The Definition of a Profession: The Authority of Metaphor in the History of Intelligence Testing, 1890–1930.* Princeton, N.J.: Princeton University Press, 1992.

Brown, JoAnne, and David K. Van Keuren, eds. *The Estate of Social Knowledge.* Baltimore, Md.: Johns Hopkins University Press, 1991.

Bryan, H. S. *The Troublesome Boy.* London: C. Arthur Pearson, 1936.

Butler, Nicholas Ray. *A World in Ferment.* New York: Scribner, 1917.

Chase, Allan Chase. *The Legacy of Malthus.* New York: Alfred A. Knopf, 1977.

Chesterton, Gilbert K. *Eugenics and Other Evils.* London: Cassell and Co., 1922.

Clifford, John Garry. *The Citizen Soldiers: The Plattsburg Training Camp Movement, 1913–1920.* Lexington: University of Kentucky Press, 1972.

Collini, Stefan. *Liberalism and Sociology.* Cambridge: Cambridge University Press, 1979.

Collinswood, R. G. *The Idea of History.* London: Oxford University Press, 1972.

Condit, Celeste M., and John L. Lucaites. *Crafting Equality: America's Anglo-African Word.* Chicago: University of Chicago Press, 1993.

Cooper, Necia G., ed. *The Human Genome Project: Deciphering the Blueprint of Heredity.* Mill Valley, Calif.: University Science Books, 1994.

Cox, Earnest S. *The South's Part in Mongrelizing the Nation.* Richmond, Va.: White America Society, 1926.

————. *White America.* Richmond, Va.: White America Society, 1923.

Crothers, T. D. "Heredity." *The Cyclopedia of Temperance and Prohibition.* New York: Funk and Wagnalls, 1891.

Curtis, Henry S. *The Play Movement and Its Significance.* New York: Macmillan, 1917.

Davenport, Charles B. *Heredity in Relation to Eugenics.* New York: Henry Holt, 1911.

Davis, Joel. *Mapping the Code.* New York: Wiley, 1991.

Degler, Carl N. *In Search of Human Nature: The Decline and Revival of Darwinism in American Social Thought.* New York: Oxford University Press, 1991.

De Gobineau, Arthur. *The Inequality of Human Races.* Los Angeles: Noontide Press, 1966.

Derrida, Jacques. *Dissemination.* Trans. Barbara Johnson. Chicago: University of Chicago Press, 1981.

Ditzion, Sidney. *Marriage, Morals and Sex in America.* New York: Bookman Associates, 1953.

Divine, Robert. *American Immigration Policy, 1924–1952.* New Haven, Conn.: Yale University Press, 1951.

Duster, Troy. *Backdoor to Eugenics.* New York: Routledge, 1990.

Dyer, Thomas G. *Theodore Roosevelt and the Idea of Race.* Baton Rouge: Louisiana State University Press, 1980.

Engerman, Stanley L., and Eugene D. Genovese, eds. *Race and Slavery in the Western Hemisphere: Quantitative Studies.* Princeton, N.J.: Princeton University Press, 1975.

Englehardt, H. Tristram, Jr., and Arthur L. Caplan, eds. *Scientific Controversies: Case Studies in the Resolution and Closure of Disputes in Science and Technology.* Cambridge: Cambridge University Press, 1987.

Farrall, Lyndsay A. *The Origins and Growth of the English Eugenics Movement, 1865–1925.* New York: Garland, 1985.

Fausto-Sterling, Ann. *Myths of Gender: Biological Theories about Women and Men.* New York: Basic Books, 1985.

Fee, Elizabeth. "Women's Nature and Scientific Objectivity." In *Woman's Nature: Rationalizations of Inequity,* ed. Marian Lowe and Ruth Hubbard. New York: Pergamon Press, 1983.

Feyerabend, P. K. *Against Method.* London: New Left Books, 1975.

Fink, Arthur E. *Causes of Crime: Biological Theories in the United States, 1800–1915.* Philadelphia: University of Pennsylvania Press, 1938.

Finnegan, John P. *Against the Specter of a Dragon: The Campaign for American Military Preparedness, 1914–1917.* Westport, Conn.: Greenwood Press, 1974.

Fisher, Irving. *Prohibition At Its Worst.* New York: Macmillan, 1926.

Fisher, Walter R. *Human Communication as Narration: Toward a Philosophy of Reason, Value, and Action.* Columbia: University of South Carolina Press, 1989.

Foucault, Michel. *The Birth of the Clinic.* New York: Vintage Books, 1973.

————. *Discipline and Punish: The Birth of the Prison.* Trans. Alan Sheridan. New York: Vintage, 1979.

————. *Power/Knowledge: Selected Interviews and Other Writings, 1972–1977.* Ed. Colin Gordon. New York: Pantheon, 1980.

Frankenberg, Ruth. *White Women, Race Matters: The Social Construction of Whiteness.* Minneapolis: University of Minnesota Press, 1993.

Fraser, Nancy. "Struggle over Needs: Outline of a Socialist-Feminist Critical Theory of Late-Capitalist Political Culture." In *Women, the State, and Welfare,* ed. Linda Gordon. Madison: University of Wisconsin Press, 1990.

Fuller, Steve. *Philosophy, Rhetoric, and the End of Knowledge.* Madison: University of Wisconsin Press, 1993.

Glass, D. V. *Introduction to Malthus.* London: Watts and Company, 1953.

Godwin, William. *Enquiry Concerning Political Justice,* ed. K. Codell Carter. Oxford: Clarendon Press, 1971.

Golden, James L., Goodwin F. Berquist, and William E. Coleman, eds. *The Rhetoric of Western Thought.* Dubuque, Iowa: Kendall/Hunt, 1983.

Gordon, Linda. *Woman's Body, Woman's Right: A Social History of Birth Control in America.* New York: Grossman, 1976.

Gossett, Thomas F. *Race: The History of an Idea in America.* New York: Schocken, 1965.

Gould, Stephen J. *The Mismeasure of Man.* New York: W. W. Norton, 1981.

Graham, Loren. *Between Science and Values.* New York: Columbia University Press, 1981.

Grant, Madison. *The Passing of the Great Race.* New York: Scribner, 1918.

Green, Loren. *Between Science and Values.* New York: Columbia University Press, 1981.

Greer, Germaine. *Sex and Destiny: The Politics of Human Fertility.* New York: Harper and Row, 1984.

Gross, Alan G. *The Rhetoric of Science.* Cambridge, Mass.: Harvard University Press, 1990.

Gurevitch, Michael, et al., eds. *Culture, Society, and the Media.* London: Methuen, 1982.

Gusfield, Joseph R. *Symbolic Crusade: Status Politics and the American Temperance Movement.* Urbana: University of Illinois Press, 1986.

Haldane, J. B. S. *Human Biology and Politics.* London: British Science Guild, 1935.

————. *Inequality of Man and Other Essays.* London: Chatto, 1932.

Hall, Stuart. "The Rediscovery of 'Ideology': Return of the Repressed in Media Studies." In *Culture, Society, and the Media,* ed. Michael Gurevitch, et al., 56–90. London: Methuen, 1982.

Haller, J. S. *Outcasts from Evolution: Scientific Attitudes of Racial Inferiority, 1959–1900.* Urbana: University of Illinois Press, 1975.

Haller, Mark. *Eugenics: Hereditarian Attitudes in American Thought.* New Brunswick, N.J.: Rutgers University Press, 1963.

Harding, Sandra, ed. *The "Racial" Economy of Science: Toward a Democratic Future.* Bloomington: Indiana University Press, 1993.

Harwood, Jonathan. "Nature, Nurture and Politics: A Critique of the Conventional Wisdom." In *The Meritocratic Intellect,* ed. James V. Smith and David Hamilton, 115–209. Aberdeen: Aberdeen University Press, 1980.

Herrnstein, Richard, and Charles Murray. *The Bell Curve.* New York: Free Press, 1994.

Himmelfarb, Gertrude. *The Idea of Poverty: England in the Early Industrial Age.* New York: Alfred A. Knopf, 1984.

Hobhouse, Leonard T. *Social Evolution and Political Theory.* New York: Columbia University Press, 1928.

Hofstadter, Richard. *Social Darwinism in American Thought, 1860–1915.* Philadelphia: University of Pennsylvania Press, 1945.

Hogben, Lancelot. *Genetic Principles in Medicine and Social Science.* London: Williams, 1931.

——. *The Nature of Living Matter.* London: Kegan Paul, 1930.

——. *Science for the Citizen: A Self-Educator Based on the Social Background of Scientific Discovery.* London: Allen, 1938.

Holmes, Samuel J. *A Bibliography of Eugenics.* Berkeley: University of California Publications in Zoology, 1924.

——. *The Eugenic Predicament.* New York: Harcourt, Brace, 1933.

Holtsmark, Erling B. *Edgar Rice Burroughs.* Boston: Twayne Publishers, 1986.

——. *Tarzan and Tradition: Classical Myth in Popular Literature.* Westport, Conn.: Greenwood Press, 1981.

Holtzman, Neil A. *Proceed with Caution: Predicting Genetic Risks in the Recombinant DNA Era.* Baltimore, Md.: Johns Hopkins University Press, 1989.

Horton, R. F. *National Ideals and Race Regeneration.* London: Cassell, 1912.

Hubbard, Ruth, and Elijah Wald. *Exploding the Gene Myth.* Boston: Beacon Press, 1993.

James, Patricia. *Population Malthus: His Life and Times.* London: Routledge and Kegan Paul, 1979.

Jones, Gareth Stedman. *Outcast London.* Oxford: Clarendon Press, 1971.

Jones, Greta. *Social Darwinism and Biological Thought.* Sussex: Harvester Press, 1980.

——. *Social Hygiene in Twentieth Century Britain.* London: Croom Helm, 1986.

Jones, Kathleen. *The Making of Social Policy in Britain, 1830–1990.* London: Athlone, 1991.

Keller, Evelyn F. "Nature, Nurture, and the Human Genome Project." In *The Code of Codes,* ed. Daniel J. Kevles and Leroy Hood. Cambridge: Harvard University Press, 1992.

——. *Reflections on Gender and Science.* New Haven, Conn.: Yale University Press, 1985.

————. *Secrets of Life, Secrets of Death: Essays on Language, Gender and Science.* New York: Routledge, 1992.

Kellogg, C. F. *NAACP.* Baltimore, Md.: Johns Hopkins University Press, 1967.

Kevles, Daniel J., *In the Name of Eugenics: Genetics and the Uses of Human Heredity.* New York: Alfred A. Knopf, 1985.

————. "Out of Eugenics: The Historical Politics of the Human Genome." In *The Code of Codes,* ed. Daniel J. Kevles and Leroy Hood, 3–36. Cambridge, Mass.: Harvard University Press, 1992.

Kevles, Daniel J. and Leroy Hood, eds. *The Code of Codes.* Cambridge, Mass.: Harvard University Press, 1992.

King, Patricia A. "The Past as Prologue: Race, Class, and Gene Discrimination." In *Gene Mapping: Using Law and Ethics as Guides,* ed. George J. Annas and Sherman Elias, 94–111. New York: Oxford University Press, 1992.

Kinzer, Donald. *An Episode in Anti-Catholicism: The American Protective Association.* Seattle: University of Washington Press, 1964.

Kobler, John. *Ardent Spirits: The Rise and Fall of Prohibition.* New York: G. P. Putnam's Sons, 1973.

Kraut, Alan M. *Silent Travelers: Germs, Genes, and the "Immigrant Menace."* New York: HarperCollins, 1994.

Kuhn, Thomas. *The Structures of Scientific Revolutions.* Chicago: University of Chicago Press, 1970.

LaCapra, Dominick. *History and Criticism.* Ithaca, N.Y.: Cornell University Press, 1985.

Landman, J. H. *Human Sterilization.* New York: Macmillan, 1932.

Latour, Bruno. *Science in Action: How to Follow Scientists and Engineers through Society.* Cambridge, Mass.: Harvard University Press, 1987.

Ledbetter, Rosanna. *A History of the Malthusian League, 1877–1927.* Columbus: Ohio State University Press, 1976.

Lee, Thomas F. *The Human Genome Project.* New York: Plenum, 1991.

Levy, Harold P. *Building a Popular Movement: A Case Study of the Public Relations of the Boy Scouts of America.* New York: Russell Sage Foundation, 1944.

Lewontin, Richard C. *Biology as Ideology: The Doctrine of DNA.* New York: Harper-Perennial, 1993.

Lewontin, Richard C., Steven Rose, and Leon Kamin. *Not in Our Genes.* New York: Pantheon Books, 1984.

Lidbetter, E. J. *Heredity and the Social Problem Group.* London: E. Arnold and Company, 1933.

Lifton, Robert. *The Nazi Doctors: Medical Killing and the Psychology of Genocide.* New York: Basic Books, 1986.

Longino, Helen E. *Science As Social Knowledge: Values and Objectivity in Scientific Inquiry.* Princeton, N.J.: Princeton University Press, 1990.

Lowe, Marian, and Ruth Hubbard, eds. *Woman's Nature: Rationalizations of Inequity.* New York: Pergamon Press, 1983.

Lucaites, John L. "Burke's Speech on Conciliation as Oppositional Discourse." In *Texts in Context*, ed. Michael C. Leff and Fred J. Kauffeld. Davis, Calif.: Hermagoras Press, 1989.

Ludmerer, Kenneth. *Genetics and American Society: A Historical Appraisal*. Baltimore, Md.: Johns Hopkins University Press, 1972.

Lyne, John. "Arguing Genes: From *Jurassic Park* to Baby Jessica." In *Argument and the Postmodern Challenge: Proceedings of the Eighth SCA/AFA Conference on Argumentation*, ed. Raymie E. McKerrow, 437–42. Annandale, Va.: Speech Communication Association, 1993.

————. "Bio-rhetorics: Moralizing the Life Sciences." In *The Rhetorical Turn: Invention and Persuasion in the Conduct of Inquiry*, ed. H. W. Simons, 35–57. Chicago: University of Chicago Press, 1990.

MacKenzie, Donald A. *Statistics in Britain, 1865–1900: The Social Construction of Scientific Knowledge*. Edinburgh: Edinburgh University Press, 1981.

MacLeod, David I. *Building Character in the American Boy*. Madison: University of Wisconsin Press, 1983.

Malthus, Thomas R. *An Essay on the Principle of Population; or, A View of Its Past and Present Effects on Human Happiness*. 9th ed. London: Reeves and Turner, 1888.

————. "A Summary View of the Principle of Population." *On Population: Three Essays*. New York: Mentor Books, 1960.

Mandeville, Bernard. *The Fable of the Bees; or, Private Vices, Public Benefits*, ed. Douglas Garman. London: Wishart and Company, 1934.

Mayr, Ernst. *The Growth of Biological Thought*. Cambridge, Mass.: Harvard University Press, Belknap Press, 1982.

Mazumdar, Pauline M. H. *Eugenics, Human Genetics and Human Failings*. London: Routledge, 1992.

McDougall, William. *National Welfare and National Decay*. London: Methuen, 1921.

McGee, Michael Calvin. "The Ideographs as a Unit of Analysis in Political Argument." In *Proceedings of the Summer Conference on Argumentation*, ed. Jack Rhodes and Sara Newell, 68–87. Annandale, Va.: Speech Communication Association, 1980.

McLaren, Angus. *Birth Control in Nineteenth-Century England*. New York: Holmes and Meier, 1978.

————. *Our Own Master Race: Eugenics in Canada, 1885–1945*. Toronto: McClelland and Stewart, 1990.

Mill, John Stuart. *A System of Logic, Ratiocinative and Inductive*, ed. J. M. Robson. Toronto: University of Toronto Press, 1974.

Montagu, M. F. Ashley. *Man's Most Dangerous Myth: The Fallacy of Race*. New York: Harper and Brothers, 1952.

Muller, Herbert J. *Out of the Night*. New York: Vanguard Press, 1935.

————. *The Uses of the Past*. New York: Oxford University Press, 1952.

Müller-Hill, Benno. *Murderous Science*. Oxford: Oxford University Press, 1988.

Nelkin, Dorothy. "The Social Power of Genetic Information." In *The Code of Codes*, ed. Daniel J. Kevles and Leroy Hood. Cambridge, Mass.: Harvard University Press, 1992.

Nelkin, Dorothy, and Laurence Tancredi. *Dangerous Diagnostics: The Social Power of Genetic Information*. New York: Basic Books, 1989.

Nelson, John S., Allan Megill, and Donald M. McCloskey, eds. *Rhetoric of the Human Sciences: Language and Argument in Scholarship and Public Affairs*. Madison: University of Wisconsin Press, 1987.

Norman, Edward R. *Anti-Catholicism in Victorian England*. London: George Allen and Unwin, 1968.

Norris, Christopher. *Uncritical Theory: Postmodernism, Intellectuals and the Gulf War*. Amherst: University of Massachusetts Press, 1992.

Osborn, Henry Fairfield. *From the Greeks to Darwin*. New York: Macmillan, 1908.

Osborn, Michael. "Rhetorical Depiction." In *Form, Genre, and the Study of Political Discourse*, ed. Herbert W. Simmons and Aram A. Aghazarian. Columbia: University of South Carolina Press, 1986.

Osofsky, Gilbert. *Harlem: The Making of a Ghetto*. New York: Harper and Row, 1966.

Pastore, Nicholas. *The Nature-Nurture Controversy*. New York: King's Crown Press, 1949.

Paul, Eden, and Cedar Paul, eds. *Population and Birth Control: A Symposium*. New York: Critic and Guide, 1917.

Pearlman, Michael. *To Make Democracy Safe for America: Patricians and Preparedness in the Progressive Era*. Urbana: University of Illinois Press, 1984.

Pearson, Roger, ed. *Shockley on Eugenics and Race*. Washington: Scott-Townsend, 1992.

Pendleton, Hester. *The Parent's Guide: or, Human Development through Inherited Tendencies*. New York: S. R. Wells, 1871; rpt. New York: Garland, 1984.

Penrose, L. S. *Mental Defect*. London: Sidgwick and Jackson, 1933.

Perlmutter, Philip. *Divided We Fall: A History of Ethnic, Religious, and Racial Prejudice in America*. Ames: Iowa State University Press, 1992.

Pickens, Donald. *Eugenics and the Progressives*. Nashville, Tenn.: Vanderbilt University Press, 1968.

Popenoe, Paul. "A Roman Catholic View of Sterilization." *Collected Papers on Eugenics Sterilization in California*, 186–89. Pasadena, Calif.: Human Betterment Foundation, 1930.

Poynter, John R. *Society and Pauperism: English Ideas on Poor Relief, 1795–1834*. London: Routledge and Kegan Paul, 1969.

Prelli, Lawrence J. *A Rhetoric of Science: Inventing Scientific Discourse*. Columbia, S.C.: University of South Carolina Press, 1989.

Proctor, Robert N. "Eugenics among the Social Sciences: Hereditarian Thought in Germany and the United States." In *The Estate of Social Knowledge*, ed. JoAnne Brown and David K. Van Keuren. Baltimore, Md.: Johns Hopkins University Press, 1991.

———. "Genomics and Eugenics: How Fair Is the Comparison?" In *Gene Mapping: Using Law and Ethics as Guides*. New York: Oxford University Press, 1992.

————. *Racial Hygiene: Medicine under the Nazis.* Cambridge, Mass.: Harvard University Press, 1988.

————. *Value-Free Science: Purity and Power in Modern Knowledge.* Cambridge, Mass.: Harvard University Press, 1991.

Rafter, Nicole Hahn. *White Trash: The Eugenic Family Studies, 1877–1919.* Boston: Northeastern University Press, 1988.

Reilly, Philip R. *The Surgical Solution: A History of Involuntary Sterilization in the United States.* Baltimore, Md.: Johns Hopkins University Press, 1991.

Resek, Carl, ed. *The Progressives.* Indianapolis: Bobbs-Merrill, 1967.

Richardson, Norman E., and Ormond E. Loomis. *The Boy Scout Movement Applied by the Church.* New York: Charles Scribner's Sons, 1915.

Rosenberg, Charles E. *No Other Gods: On Science and American Social Thought.* Baltimore, Md.: Johns Hopkins University Press, 1976.

Rosenthal, Michael. *The Character Factory: Baden-Powell and the Origins of the Boy Scout Movement.* New York: Pantheon, 1986.

Russett, Cynthia Eagle. *Darwin in America: The Intellectual Response, 1865–1912.* San Francisco: W. H. Freeman, 1976.

Ryan, John A. *A Living Wage.* New York: Macmillan, 1906.

Ryan, John A., and Moorhouse F. X. Millar. *The State and the Church.* New York: Macmillan, 1930.

Saleeby, C. W. *The Methods of Race-Regeneration.* New York: Moffat, Yard, 1911.

————. *The Progress of Eugenics.* London: Cassell, 1914.

Sanger, Margaret. *Motherhood in Bondage.* New York: Brentano's, 1928.

Sapp, Jan. *Beyond the Gene: Cytoplasmic Inheritance and the Struggle for Authority in Genetics.* New York: Oxford University Press, 1987.

Schmiedeler, Edgar. *Sterilization in the United States.* Washington, D.C.: National Catholic Welfare Conference, 1943.

Schneider, William H. *Quality and Quantity: The Quest for Biological Regeneration in Twentieth-Century France.* Cambridge: Cambridge University Press, 1990.

Searle, G. R. *Eugenics and Politics in Britain, 1900–1914.* Leyden: Noordhoff International Publishing, 1976.

Secada, Walter G., ed. *Equity in Education.* New York: Falmer Press, 1989.

Selden, Steven. "The Use of Biology to Legitimate Inequality: The Eugenics Movement within the High School Biology Textbook, 1914–1949." In *Equity in Education,* ed. Walter G. Secada. New York: Falmer Press, 1989.

Simons, H. W., ed. *The Rhetorical Turn: Invention and Persuasion in the Conduct of Inquiry.* Chicago: University of Chicago Press, 1990.

————. *Rhetoric in the Human Sciences.* London: Sage, 1989.

Sinsheimer, Robert L. "The Prospect of Designed Genetic Change." In *Heredity and Society,* ed. Adela S. Baer, 436–43. New York: Macmillan, 1977.

Smith, J. David. *Minds Made Feeble: The Myth and Legacy of the Kallikaks.* Rockville, Md.: Aspen Publications, 1985.

Smith, J. David, and K. Ray Nelson. *The Sterilization of Carrie Buck.* Far Hills, N.J.: New Horizon Press, 1989.

Smith, James V., and David Hamilton, eds. *The Meritocratic Intellect.* Aberdeen: Aberdeen University Press, 1980.

Solomon, Barbara. *Ancestors and Immigrants: A Changing New England Tradition.* Chicago: University of Chicago Press, 1971.

Solomon, Martha. *Emma Goldman.* Boston: Twayne Publishers, 1987.

Soloway, Richard A. *Birth Control and the Population Question in England, 1877–1930.* Chapel Hill: University of North Carolina Press, 1982.

——. *Demography and Degeneration: Eugenics and the Declining Birth Rate in Twentieth-Century Britain.* Chapel Hill: University of North Carolina Press, 1990.

Steinberg, Stephen. *The Ethnic Myth: Race, Ethnicity, and Class in America.* New York: Atheneum, 1981.

Stepan, Nancy Leys. "Eugenics in Brazil, 1917–1940." In *The Wellborn Science,* ed. Mark B. Adams. New York: Oxford University Press, 1990.

——. *"The Hour of Eugenics": Race, Gender, and Nation in Latin America.* Ithaca, N.Y.: Cornell University Press, 1991.

——. *The Idea of Race in Science: Great Britain, 1860–1960.* Hamden, Conn.: Archon, 1982.

Stimson, Henry. *Issues of the War.* New York: National Security League, n.d.

Stoddard, Lothrop. *The Rising Tide of Color against White World Supremacy.* New York: Charles Scribner's Sons, 1921.

Sutch, Richard. "The Breeding of Slaves for Sale and the Westward Expansion of Slavery, 1850–1860." In *Race and Slavery in the Western Hemisphere: Quantitative Studies,* ed. Stanley L. Engerman and Eugene D. Genovese. Princeton, N.J.: Princeton University Press, 1975.

Sutherland, Halliday. *Control of Life.* London: Burns, Oates, and Washbourne, 1944.

Swazey, Judith. "Those Who Forget Their History: Lessons from the Recent Past for the Human Genome Quest." In *Gene Mapping: Using Law and Ethics as Guides,* ed. George J. Annas and Sherman Elias. New York: Oxford University Press, 1992.

Teitelman, Robert. *Gene Dreams: Wall Street, Academia, and the Rise of Biotechnology.* New York: Basic Books, 1989.

Timberlake, James H. *Prohibition and the Progressive Movement, 1900–1920.* Cambridge, Mass.: Harvard University Press, 1963.

Trombley, Stephen. *The Right to Reproduce.* London: Nicolson, 1988.

Unger, Roberto Mangabeira. *False Necessity: Anti-Necessitarian Social Theory in the Service of Radical Democracy.* Cambridge: Cambridge University Press, 1987.

Vose, Clement E. "The Eugenics Movement." *Constitutional Change: Amendment Politics and Supreme Court Litigation since 1900.* Lexington, Mass.: Lexington Books, 1972.

Walter, Herbert E. *Genetics: An Introduction to the Study of Heredity.* New York: Macmillan, 1928.

Watson, James D. "A Personal View of the Project." In *The Code of Codes,* ed. Daniel J. Kevles and Leroy Hood. Cambridge: Harvard University Press, 1992.

Webb, Beatrice. *The Case for the National Minimum.* London: National Committee for the Prevention of Destitution, 1913.

Weindling, Paul. *Health, Race, and German Politics between National Unification and Nazism, 1870–1945.* Cambridge: Cambridge University Press, 1989.

Weisbord, Robert G. *Genocide? Birth Control and the Black American.* Westport, Conn.: Greenwood Press, 1975.

Weiss, Sheila F. *Race Hygiene and National Efficiency: The Eugenics of Wilhelm Schallmayer.* Berkeley: University of California Press, 1987.

Werskey, Gary. *The Visible College: The Collective Biography of British Scientific Socialists of the 1930s.* New York: Holt, Rinehart and Winston, 1978.

Wexler, Alice. "The Oracle of DNA." In *Molecular Genetics in Diseases of Brain, Nerve, and Muscle,* ed. Lewis P. Rowland, et al. New York: Oxford University Press, 1989.

White, Andrew D. *A History of Warfare of Science and Theology in Christendom.* 2 vols., 1896. Reprint, New York: Dover, 1960.

Wills, Christopher. *Exxons, Introns, and Talking Genes: The Science behind the Human Genome Project.* New York: Basic Books, 1991.

Wingerson, Lois. *Mapping Our Genes.* New York: Dutton/Penguin, 1990.

Woloch, Nancy. *Women and the American Experience.* New York: Alfred A. Knopf, 1984.

Yee, Shirley J. *Black Women Abolitionists: A Study in Activism, 1828–1860.* Knoxville: University of Tennessee Press, 1992.

Government Publications

"Human Genome Initiative and the Future of Biotechnology." *Hearings before the Subcommittee on Science, Technology, and Space,* Committee on Commerce, Science and Transportation, U.S. Senate, 100th Congress, First Session, November 9, 1989, 1.

U.S. Congress, Office of Technology Assessment. *Mapping Our Genes.* Washington, D.C.: Government Printing Office, 1988.

Theses and Dissertations

Arness, Frank F. "The Evolution of the Virginia Antimiscegenation Laws." Master's thesis, Department of History, Old Dominion College, 1966.

Cowan, Ruth Schwartz. "Sir Francis Galton and the Study of Heredity in the Nineteenth Century." Ph.D. diss., University of Michigan, Ann Arbor, 1969.

Hassencahl, Frances. "Harry Hamilton Laughlin, Expert Eugenics Agent for the House

Committee on Immigration and Naturalization, 1921–31." Ph.D. diss., Case Western
Reserve University, 1970.

Kavounas, Margaret J. "Feeblemindedness and Prostitution: The Laboratory of Social
Hygiene's Influence on Progressive Era Prostitution Reform." Masters thesis, Sarah
Lawrence College, May 1992.

Lombardo, Paul A. "Eugenic Sterilization in Virginia: Aubrey Strode and the Case of
Buck v. Bell." Ph.D. diss., Department of Education, University of Virginia, May 1982.

Lucaites, John Louis. "Flexibility and Consistency in Eighteenth-Century Anglo-
Whiggism: A Case Study of the Rhetorical Dimensions of Legitimacy." Ph.D. diss.,
University of Iowa, 1984.

Mehler, Barry A. "A History of the American Eugenics Society, 1921–1940." Ph.D. diss.,
University of Illinois at Urbana, 1988.

Meier, August. "Negro Racial Thought in the Age of Booker T. Washington, circa 1880–
1915." Ph.D. diss., Columbia University, 1957.

Thomson, Brian William. "Racism and Racial Classification: A Case Study of the Virginia Racial Integrity Legislation." Ph.D. diss., University of California, Riverside,
August 1978.

Legal Cases

Buck v. Bell, 130 S.E. 516 (1925) 519.
Buck v. Bell, 274 U.S. 200 (1927).

Newspaper Articles

Breggin, Peter. "U.S. Hasn't Given Up Linking Genes to Crime." *New York Times* September 18, 1992: A34.

Burr, Chandler. "Genes and Hormones." *New York Times* August 2, 1993: A15.

Butterfield, Fox. "Dispute Threatens U.S. Plan on Violence." *New York Times* October 23, 1992: A12.

Carter, R. Brudenell. "The Feeble-Minded." *London Times* November 29, 1912: 6.

"Chromosome Cartography." *Wall Street Journal* March 16, 1989: 16.

"Civil Liberties Group to Sue over Virginia Sterilizations." *New York Times* April 7,
1980: 14.

"Coercive Philanthropy." *Manchester Guardian* July 31, 1913: 6.

"The Depopulation Spectre." *The Broad Axe* [Chicago] June 25, 1927: 3.

"Eugenics and Pauperism." *London Times* November 7, 1910: 13–14.

"Eugenics for the Layman." *New York Call* September 16, 1923: sec. 2, p. 9.

"The Fred Goodwin Case." *Washington Post* March 21, 1992: A22.

"Full Text of Pope Pius's Encyclical." *New York Times* January 9, 1931: 14–15.

Glassburg, John A. "Eugenics for the Layman by a Scholar and a Patriot." *New York Call* September 16, 1923: sec. 2, p. 9.

Hobson, J. A. "Race Regeneration." *Manchester Guardian* October 10, 1911: 6.

Hubbard, Ruth. "The Search for Sexual Identity: False Genetic Markers." *New York Times* August 2, 1993: A15.

Krisses, Joseph. "Eugenics and Euthenics." *New York Times* October 24, 1926: 16.

Lewontin, Richard C. "Women versus the Biologists." *New York Times Book Review* April 7, 1994: 31–35.

"The Mental Deficiency Bill." *Manchester Guardian* July 20, 1912: 8.

Miller, Kelly. "Is the Negro a Living or Dying Race." *Afro-American* September 10, 1927: 7.

"A New Class System." *New York Times* April 28, 1923: 12.

Olsen [Olson], Harry. "Check on Society's Defectives Seen as Urgent Need of Nation." *New York Times* September 2, 1923: sec. 7, p. 7.

"Preventing 'Inferior' People in China." *New York Times* December 27, 1993: A16.

"Proposed Legislation for the Feebleminded." *London Times* May 20, 1912: 9.

"Racial Integrity." *Richmond* (Virginia) *Times Dispatch* February 18, 1924: 6.

Rich, Spencer. "Federal Health Official Resigns, Citing Controversy over Remarks." *Washington Post* February 28, 1992: A4.

Schneider, Karen. "Study to Quell Violence is Racist, Critics Charge." *Detroit Free Press* November 2, 1992: A1, A11.

" 'Superior Classes' Urged to Procreate: Must Have More Numerous Progeny, Professor Tells Eugenists." *New York Call* July 27, 1912: 3.

"Unbleaching America." *Afro-American* [Baltimore] March 21, 1925: 10.

Webb, Sidney Webb. "Physical Degeneracy or Race Suicide?" *London Times* October 16, 1906: 7.

"Would Reform Society by Marriage Control." *New York Times* April 26, 1923: 31.

Index